Out of the Shadows

Out of the Shadows

Woman Abuse in Ethnic, Immigrant, and Aboriginal Communities

Edited by Josephine Fong

Women's Press

Toronto

Out of the Shadows: Woman Abuse in Ethnic, Immigrant, and
Aboriginal Communities
edited by Josephine Fong

First published in 2010 by
Women's Press, an imprint of Canadian Scholars' Press Inc.
425 Adelaide Street West, Suite 200
Toronto, Ontario M5V 3C1

www.womenspress.ca

Every reasonable effort has been made to identify copyright holders. Canadian Scholars' Press
Inc. would be pleased to have any errors or omissions brought to its attention.

Canadian Scholars' Press Inc./Women's Press gratefully acknowledges financial support
for our publishing activities from the Government of Canada through the Book Publishing
Industry Development Program (BPIDP) and the Government of Ontario through the
Ontario Book Publishing Tax Credit Program.

Library and Archives Canada Cataloguing in Publication

Out of the shadows : woman abuse in ethnic, immigrant, and aboriginal communities / edited
by Josephine Fong.
Includes bibliographical references.
ISBN 978-0-88961-467-3
1. Wife abuse—Canada—Cross-cultural studies.
2. Minority women—Abuse of—Canada. 3. Women
immigrants—Abuse of—Canada. 4. Native women—Abuse
of—Canada. I. Fong, Josephine, 1952–

HV6626.23.C3O98 2009   362.82'920971   C2009-906436-7

Cover design, text design, and typesetting by Aldo Fierro

Printed and bound in Canada

Canada

MIX
Paper from
responsible sources
FSC   FSC® C004071
www.fsc.org

Contents

Acknowledgements

I would like to thank every individual whose effort and support made the publication of this collection possible, especially Dr. Susan Silva-Wayne, Dr. June Yee, and Sabra Desai, who contributed many helpful comments in the process. Gratitude is also extended to activists, front-line workers, and survivors of woman abuse who participated in the various studies described in this book. These individuals took time and energy out of their hectic lives to educate all of us about woman abuse. Without the perspectives of such diverse communities and their significant contributions and openness, we would not be able to achieve such a level of understanding regarding woman abuse.

Introduction

Josephine Fong

Canada is a multicultural society whose composition has been shaped by the Aboriginal peoples of the country and by waves of immigrants and their descendants. Of the more than 13.4 million immigrants who arrived in the past century, the largest number was in the 1990s. Most immigrated to Canada from non-European countries. The minority groups and their ethno-specific cultures have indeed enriched the cultural mosaic of Canada; both long-established and recent immigrants are becoming the majority of Canadians. However, while it is true that the abuse of women has many forms and knows no boundaries, the majority of research studies, including conventional feminist inquiries, tend to simply examine woman abuse along the lines of class and gender, leaving the other identities of women unscrutinized. As most contributors to this book indicate openly in their chapters, while male violence against women is known to occur across different cultures, our society often overlooks how the other social locations to which ethnic women are assigned may affect the way they cope with their abuse. That is to say, when we investigate the long-established forms of abuse such as physical, sexual, emotional, economic, and psychological threats, we cannot ignore the structural and institutional violence that many ethnic, immigrant, and Aboriginal women and their communities experience. In order to understand the abuse of women in Canadian society, not only must we take into account the diversity of women, but we also need to address the experiences of those who have been historically excluded, thus placing them at the centre of study because of genuine interest rather than tokenism.

Out of the Shadows: Woman Abuse in Ethnic, Immigrant, and Aboriginal Communities gives priority to the situations of minority people who contribute to the diverse ethno-cultural composition of Canada, a cultural mosaic of which Canada is said to be proud. This book addresses the intersections and complexities of women's identities and experiences, particularly when they are challenged by male violence. It is aimed at providing readers with an essential understanding of woman abuse in different ethnic communities from different perspectives. To achieve these goals, its chapters are organized into three different sections for the coverage of theories, practice and policy, experiences of activists and helping professionals, as well as the lived realities of women from diverse communities. The uniqueness of this book is achieved by the diversity of contributors who are not only academic researchers, but also community activists and helping professionals who work directly with women on a regular basis. While the authors of this book critique the lack of culturally sensitive mainstream resources available to abused ethnic women, some of these authors also critically assess the shortcomings and/or traditionally sexist attitudes within their own ethnic communities. Collectively, the work of these diverse authors provides readers with a fuller understanding of woman abuse from culturally diverse perspectives. In other words, while each chapter has its own focus or addresses the situations of a particular group of women, the content and point of view of each complement other chapters in various ways.

Conventional anthropologists and social scientists have often assumed that there are inherent differences among races with respect to physical and genetic characteristics. Some have proposed that these differences are indicators of a racial population's intelligence, temperament, and personality, affecting both behaviour and relationships. While race and ethnicity cannot be used as reliable predictors of those qualities, the stereotypes may be used by those in the host country against those who are racialized. For example, in contrast to White Canadians, non-White people are labelled as "the minority," "subordinate races," "they," and "other." These socially constructed racial categories have implications for specific social relations between host and racialized groups, which then affect racialized people's lived reality. As Baskin and Chokshi, Desai, and Adamali point out in their chapters, it is the "otherness" that Aboriginal and visible minority groups are assigned that renders them as problematic populations while they are deprived of services that are appropriate to their cultural practices and needs.

Clearly, the Canadian government plays a crucial role in determining the social position of immigrant women through the Immigration Act. Under this act, women are coerced to become legal dependants of men, which results in civic and economic consequences for the women. Many authors in this book, such as Ngozi Nwosu, Sepali Guruge, Cyndy Baskin, Rita Chokshi et al., and Josephine Fong, who have examined women's life experiences, indicate that it is in part the government's politics and policies that perpetuate violence against Aboriginal women and women from racialized immigrant communities. Very often, it is this kind of systemic and institutional reinforcement of the traditional gender roles of patriarchal families that keeps women in their place and prevents them from combating and/or escaping male violence. In their chapters, not only do these authors show how ethnic and immigrant women's situations are complicated by the system, but also they remind community activists and helping professionals to keep an open mind in reflecting upon and re-evaluating the approaches they take to prevent, intervene against, and collaborate politically to address woman abuse.

One prominent point that arises from the chapters is that because of the intersectionality of their gender, race, ethnicity, class, faith practice, and social status in Canada, the women's responses are often based on the careful evaluation of the benefits and risks to themselves, their children, their abusers, other family members, and the reputation of their ethnic or cultural group. Individual authors understand that women's responses to abuse are socially, politically, and ethnically shaped, based on their beliefs about perceptions of abuse and the support and services available to help them manage their lives within their community and in the larger society. In addition, all of the chapters that refer to women's ambivalences in dealing with their abuse, especially in its beginning phase, indicate that women may sympathize with their abusers because they also understand the difficulties that their male counterparts experience as immigrants or visible minority group members in having to cope with downward mobility, under-/unemployment, deskilling, linguistic barriers, underachievement, racism, discrimination, and so on. Therefore, abused women often hesitate to report abuse or to take radical measures to stop the abuse in their relationships. Women usually put up with abuse for some time until it is finally beyond their endurance or until they are determined to break away. Many of the authors who interviewed women state that in the process of making the decision to end their abuse, the women must find the personal strength as well as the needed resources to help them do so.

In Nwosu's chapter, she openly criticizes the sexist practices in postcolonial Nigeria that make women more susceptible to male violence. She believes that it is the combination of Nigerian cultural values, Canadian immigration policy, the new economy in the host country, and structural discrimination that contribute to Nigerian-Canadian women's abuse. Hyman et al., who examine the risk factors that Ethiopian women face after immigrating to Canada, and Fong, who interviewed front-line workers, indicate that it is not culture that explains woman abuse in the Canadian context. Rather, it is the stressors associated with immigration—such as acculturation, a shift in gender roles, and the new power imbalance that emerges in immigrant families—that are increasing women's risk of being abused. However, during the process of acculturation and the related struggles between the couple, the new context that causes the conflict can also foster change, which may indeed bring out women's resilience and their desire for more personal autonomy. Although immigration means leaving behind a familiar environment and a solid support network, the resulting sense of social isolation and economic depletion often motivates these women to participate more actively in the labour force. This is a way for them to connect with the community while earning an income for their families, even though they still have to play a submissive role in the workforce as well as at home. In this way they regain or find new power to cope with male violence. Therefore, the above authors address the significance of enriching external resources to help women better cope with their abuse, and the positive changes that are observed in women's increased resilience, new bargaining power, and independence when they overcome their isolation and predicaments related to immigration. Our Canadian society needs to make sure that these women can have a fair share of community resources to support them in making positive changes and relevant decisions for themselves and their families.

In addressing women's agency within specific oppressive structures, such as in the example of Jewish divorce law, Lisa Rosenberg states that while abusive Jewish husbands try to control their wives by denying them a *get* (a dissolution of the marriage within the Jewish law), abused Jewish women often fight back by employing "creative" confrontational strategies. Some women cope individually while others act collectively to articulate their personal concerns or to advocate for others who remain trapped. Also, in examining women's experiences within another oppressive structure such as the Canadian criminal justice and judicial systems, Josephine Fong indicates that when abused women try to access systems to find some justice for themselves, they often discover that these systems are not really operating neutrally or objectively from the underlying power relationships in society. Patriarchal ideology and White supremacy do have a great impact, discouraging women from reporting and seeking outside assistance. Women need more support and to be taken more seriously when they gather the courage to report to an authority or seek professional help. As a society, we must support women who are trapped in abusive relationships, regardless of age, class, ethnicity, faith, race, or sexual orientation.

In conclusion, for the contributors to this book, women are subordinated to men because our society condones this in various ways. Men's abuse in relationships, in any ethnic or racial community, is often a result of sexism and racism embedded systematically and structurally in the society at large, rather than the result of being a particular ethnic group or minority culture. Many ethnic and/or immigrant women in Canada are undergoing assimilation continuously, and the culture that they develop is a mixture of both their ethnic origin and Canadian culture. Thus, instead of looking only for a cultural interpretation of the occurrence of woman abuse, each author in this book focuses on the systemic oppression of minority women or women of colour. The authors believe that if the government cares about these women's suffering and predicaments, it needs to do more to empower these women, shorten their long waiting periods for social assistance approval, and eliminate the unnecessary barriers that prevent them from coping with abuse effectively or ending abusive relationships quickly.

There are two perspectives in particular that are missing from this collection. First, the abuse of women perpetrated by same-sex partners is underreported, but it is known that abuse in lesbian relationships is commonplace. It is very difficult for abused lesbians to speak out and find help. Second, in understanding woman abuse perpetrated by men, it would be helpful to be aware of the experiences of male offenders and the perspectives of helping professionals who work with them. However, efforts to reach out to these communities through various connections were unsuccessful within the time frame of collecting articles for this book, even though it was extended a couple times. It is possible that because of homophobia and society's victim-focused approach, it is difficult for these respective groups to feel comfortable and confident enough to articulate their concerns and experiences. Future books on the topic of woman abuse should include the perspectives of lesbians, as well as the perspectives of male offenders and helping professionals who work with them. As Samantha Majic and Josephine Fong state in their chapters in Part I of this book, we must create opportunities to publicize the private, so that education about woman abuse may help to ensure the safety of women in the private realm and in all levels of public structures. If we cannot guarantee that we can create a violence-free environment, the least we can do is to provide women with a safe public space to address the issue.

Part I

Theories, Campaigns, Practice, and Policy

Chapter 1

Explaining the Abuse of Women: An Examination of Conventional and Dominant Theoretical Perspectives

Josephine Fong

Since the beginning of the 1970s, due to the efforts of community activists and feminists, woman abuse or male violence against women has been identified as a social problem, a crime committed in violation of a woman's personal rights, which also has been shown to have major implications for a woman's psychological and physical health. Woman abuse takes many forms and occurs in all cultures. However, while our society acknowledges that the abuse of women knows no borders, traditional research studies, including conventional feminist inquiries, continue to examine violence against women through the lenses of class and gender, thereby neglecting the other social locations to which ethnic women are relegated, and ignoring how ethnic identity and citizenship status affects the experience of abuse. Indeed, most literature and research on woman abuse focuses on the circumstances of the White populations, whether North American, European, or otherwise, so most contemporary theories of male violence against women do not address the specific issues faced by ethnic women, particularly those considered to be visible minorities.

This chapter provides a brief examination of dominant theories and counselling approaches that explain and help women to overcome the predicaments that result from having an abusive partner. Clearly, when trying to understand woman abuse, its possible causes and implications, we must ask: Why are more women than men subjected to violent treatment in intimate relationships? What has been done to address the issue of woman assault? How has the feminist movement changed our understanding of the issue, the women's situations, and the way society responds to the abuse of women? And how much do we know, from the various theories explaining woman abuse in the contexts of intimate relationships, about male violence experienced by women of different ethnicities? This chapter may not be able to answer all of the above questions directly, but I hope that by reviewing several major theories of woman assault in intimate relationships, including feminist responses to woman abuse, I will be able to provide readers with some frameworks through which to read the rest of the chapters.

In Canadian society, as well as in many others around the globe, the assault of women has a long history, but this issue was not taken very seriously before the women's movement rekindled it in the 1960s. While some people might believe that wife assault was a relatively new social problem resulting from the rise of industrialization, the modernization of a society, and/or the rise of feminism, closer scrutiny of historical research reveals that male violence against women and children is deeply rooted in Western culture and was evident long before the birth of the women's movement (Backhouse, 1991; Buckley, 1992; Chapman, 1985, 1988; Hammerton, 1992; Peterson, 1992).

Although contemporary society for the most part acknowledges the problem, the predominant perceptions, particularly those informed by misogynist attitudes, patriarchal beliefs, and some religious beliefs, view woman assault in intimate contexts as the result of women being provocative, dysfunctional communication patterns between couples, the economic stress of the family, childhood observation and experience of abuse, the influence of alcohol, stereotyped sex roles, and/or the personality problems of the batterers and battered women (Gelles, 1974; Martin, 1976; Roy, 1977). While these theories help to explain some behaviour patterns under certain circumstances, they generally have reduced the responsibility of batterers and/or increased that of battered women.

Three major theoretical perspectives explaining male violence against women are included in this chapter: the sociological, psychological, and feminist perspectives. Not only are these theoretical perspectives well established in various disciplines, but also the theories derived from each of these perspectives are widely accepted as sensible and "universal" explanations for the problem of the assault of women in society.

SOCIOLOGICAL PERSPECTIVES

Theories derived from a sociological perspective often focus on the characteristics of the family unit and/or the social environment in which the individual is raised, socialized, and influenced (Gelles, 1993). Three predominant theories informed by the sociological perspective are included in this discussion: (1) social learning theory, (2) systems theory, and (3) resources theory.

Social Learning Theory

Social learning theory is one of the most popular and widely accepted theories used by sociologists and social psychologists to explain marital violence. Basically, this theory states that people model the behaviour they had been exposed to as children (Miller & Dollard, 1941). In other words, violence, as a behaviour, is learned through imitation (Bandura, 1971). The direct or indirect observation of violent acts or interactions demonstrated by family members and role models in society helps to form an impression that violence can be used as a coping response to stress, or as a means to conflict resolution (Bandura, 1973; Gelles, 1993). Implicit in this theory is the assumption that people are violent because society is violent, and that society perpetuates violence through cultural and familial socialization and condones violent acts. For example, children experience violence in the family as a form of punishment, and we all learn from television programs and movies that violence is a part of life. Therefore, those who are more violent than others are indeed those who have been exposed more frequently to violence through childhood, media images, and messages, and they have thereby been positively reinforced in the use of violence.

Because the original social learning theory did not account for gender differences, some sociological researchers claim that violence not only occurs among all American families but also among all family members regardless of gender and age (Gelles, 1985; Gelles & Straus, 1988; Straus, Gelles & Steinmetz, 1980). They believe that spousal abuse between heterosexual couples is a two-way street and that men and women are "equally" violent in relationships because violence is a learned social behaviour. However, supported by statistical evidence, many other scholars, researchers, and community activists argue that in many abusive and violent situations, men are often the perpetrators while women are the victims (Dobash & Dobash, 1978, 1979; MacLeod, 1980). Such facts have led many researchers to revisit and/or expand on social learning theory.

Studies have shown that because men and women are socialized differently, they adopt different behaviour patterns; for example, men are often rewarded for aggression, but women are punished for it. Therefore, men learn to be aggressive and are likely to use violence to control a situation whereas women learn to be passive and are likely to endure violence (Pressman, Cameron & Rothery, 1989; Stanko, 1985). Indeed, some researchers argue that through social learning, especially in the context of male violence, not only are women's ordinary activities and personal development in various ways limited, but also they are kept in their place when other forms of social control have failed to do so (Dobash & Dobash, 1992; Mihalic & Elliott, 1997). In other words, these researchers maintain that through social learning, men see themselves as controllers of women, and because they are socialized in the use of violence, they are potential aggressors against women. This new extension of social learning theory helps to explain why men are more prone to use violence than women, even though both sexes are raised in the same society and influenced by relatively the same culture.

Systems Theory

Systems theory suggests an alternative structural explanation for woman abuse in relationships that incorporates social learning theory. According to Buckley (1967), a system is made up of sets of different parts with two things in common. First of all, these parts are interconnected and interdependent, so they mutually influence each other. Secondly, each part is connected to the other in a specific way over time. With systems theory, a family is viewed as an open system in which factors of individual personality traits, cultural norms supporting the use of violence against women and children (e.g., the marriage licence and the parenting licence are hitting licences), structural strains on the family such as unemployment, illness, and child-care responsibility, the amount of time family members spend together, and conflicting priorities and needs are all considered (Gelles, 1979; Giles-Sims, 1983; Hines & Malley, 2005).

A systems approach perceives violence to be a product of the family system, which assumes the family regulates itself through feedback. According to Margolin, Sibner, and Gleberman (1988), abusers who receive positive feedback or results from using violence (e.g., bringing a partner under control or maintaining authority over the wife) are likely to remain violent. Those who receive negative feedback or results (e.g., losing one's partner, encountering strong reactions from other family members, or being punished by the outside system) are likely to control themselves and refrain from further use of violence. While systems theory accounts for some individual, cultural, and structural factors that contribute to wife abuse, feminists have criticized it for its gender-blind assumptions and gender-neutral language, which, for the most, blame women for being masochistic or communicationally dysfunctional. Such gender-bias presumptions and terms often excuse abusive men's controlling and violent behaviour, ignoring the historical, social, economic, and political contexts in which women live and our society's tradition of patriarchy, which renders men more powerful than women (Bograd, 1984; Momsen, 2006; Myers-Avis, 1988).

Adopting a sociological perspective and looking into the family system within the greater legal and the wider social systems, many social historians argue that the problem of wife assault in human history is a result of "an autocratic patriarchal family structure" (Basch, 1982; Chapman, 1985, 1988; May, 1978; Perkin, 1989). These researchers find that the historic pattern of male-powered management of the family was often supported by the law, which deprived women of all their legal rights through marriage. It was society's prejudice in allocating fewer legal rights and a lower social status to women that encouraged wife assault. In other words, these researchers argue that when we try to understand how the family systems function, we also need to examine the other systems that circumscribe the family systems and influence their functioning. What feminists find problematic with the family systems approaches is how they interpret and intervene in wife abuse without taking into account the inequitable contract of marriage and the unequal treatment men and women have received historically. What is also problematic is that the family systems approaches are not synchronized with current theory and research in other disciplines concerning women, which indicate that even in today's society, women and men are prescribed uneven status and power. Therefore, by viewing the family out of context and failing to notice the relationships among historical, social, economic, and political contexts and family dysfunction, most feminists consider the systems theory explanation of woman abuse in intimate relationships very limiting and ineffectual (Bograd, 1984; Myers-Avis, 1988).

Resource Theory

The third sociological theory that is a widely accepted explanation for woman abuse is called resource theory. Basically, this theory presumes that individuals with more resources and power will dominate those with less resources and power (Bloode & Wolfe, 1960; Goode, 1971). It is supposed that within a family system there are four major resources (i.e., force, economic resources, prestige, and likability) by which a member can manipulate other members of the family to serve his or her ends. Traditionally, not only were men given more legal and social power over their wives, but they were also granted more material goods and wealth than women (Basch, 1982; Buckley, 1992; Perkin, 1989). Although laws that permitted the chastisement of wives have been lifted, certain cultural norms and practices continue to afford men greater status than women. As a result, men have retained power over their female partners as they usually have greater resources in income and social standing outside of the family (Allen & Straus, 1980).

According to resource theory, the more power and force an individual is able to demonstrate, the less likely she or he is to resort to violence in order to maintain control over others (Goode, 1971). However, in many wife abuse cases, we observe that even though a husband has power over his wife in general, he may still use violence to exert his control. This situation is interpreted, by the resource theory, as a husband's way of compensating for his depleting resources or maintaining his dominant position when he perceives a threat of the loss of his other resources (Allen & Straus, 1980; Bersani & Chen, 1988). For example, Finkelhor (1983) finds that when men suffer an actual or imagined loss of status and power, either through unemployment or a low-status occupation, they are likely to attempt to reinstate their status and power at home by using physical violence against their wives.

There are historical studies supporting the compensatory aspect of the resource theory. Examining the situations of working-class families in the 19th century and earlier, researchers claim that abusive working-class men were indeed provoked by their confusion about their own gender identity; when they were supposed to be "manly," because their class prescribed them a lower social status and a "submissive" role in the public sphere, they resorted to violence in the home to reinstate their manliness in the relationship (Hagg, 1991/92; Hammerton, 1992; Harvey, 1990, 1991). Also, some studies indicate that the dramatic changes of economic, social, and political structures, as well as the sexual division of labour within the family, often impose pressures and tensions on the relationship between husbands and wives; when men insist on women's compliance and do not understand their wives' burdens in the domestic sphere, and when the "old man" ideology clashed with the "new woman" ideology, marital conflicts were likely to turn into the assault of women (Hammerton, 1992; Finkelhor, 1983).

What is implied in resource theory is that whether or not men have more resources and power than women, they will continue to dominate and control women either through their "inherited" rights to a superior status and their greater material possessions or through the use of physical violence when their authority and dominance are challenged. In other words, the more women want to negotiate a new social and cultural definition of womanhood and demand gender equality, the greater the likelihood that male violence against women will be on the rise. However, while this theory paints a very bleak future in terms of the likelihood of ending male violence against women, it has been found that when women are provided with more social resources, their abilities to resist and stay safe in an abusive relationship will increase (Goodman, Dutton, Vankos & Weinfurt, 2005).

PSYCHOLOGICAL PERSPECTIVES

Within the psychological theoretical perspective, five major theories will be discussed: (1) psychopathological, (2) masochistic, (3) frustration-aggression, (4) situational, and (5) conditioning theory. By and large, theories derived from a psychological perspective focus more on the individual, dyadic, and/or triadic levels when explaining why the assault of women happens. Conventional psychological theories give little attention to the influence of external factors, but concentrate more on rectifying or modifying the wrongdoing or behaviour disorder of the person who is considered responsible for the abusive situation.

Psychopathological

Although cases of woman abuse have never been rare occurrences in our society, the batterers or abusers have been viewed as psychopathological individuals, especially by clinicians, psychologists, and psychiatrists prior to the 1960s before the problem was defined as a social issue (Pagelow, 1984). Psychopathological supposition assumes that traumatic childhood events and/or some personality characteristics or defects cause men to behave violently toward women. From time to time, convicted wife batterers are court-ordered into psychological or psychiatric examination because the judge or jury believes that the offenders' problems are psychopathological in nature (Snell, Rosenwald & Robey, 1964).

Thus, *psychopathological theory* hypothesizes that some people are predisposed to use force or other abusive means to inflict harm on other people because they are mentally or emotionally troubled (e.g., those with diagnoses of psychosis, neurosis, personality disorder, anti-social behaviour, and so on). Some studies have found that wife batterers tend to have low self-esteem and incongruent self-concepts (Dutton, 2007; Neidig, Friedman & Collins, 1986; Pagelow, 1984). Because of their drastic lack of confidence and emotional disturbance, they are likely to be pathologically jealous, passive, and/or dependent, which predisposes them to anti-social, sociopathic, or sadistic behaviour. However, although there are general characteristics found among some batterers who are considered mentally ill or pathological, Pagelow (1984), based on a review of many relevant studies, concludes that no matter how diligently clinicians tried to classify abusers into an abuser profile, the ones they studied did not clearly fall into one consistent category of psychosis or neurosis; the behaviour that pathological individuals demonstrated was no different from that of individuals randomly selected from a crowd on the street.

Masochistic

Parallel to the male-focused psychopathological theories in explaining woman assault is the psychoanalytic theory of *masochism*, which is used to explain the psychopathology of abused women. According to Cowan (1982), "masochism is a paradoxical, emotionally-laden, scientifically-named, and historically-conditioned psychic fantasy" (p. 6). In the broadest sense, a masochistic relationship is a "bondage-and-discipline" relationship in which the masochistic individual is constantly in pain, but insists on staying in the relationship for no apparent pleasure. This theory proposes that battered women are pursuers of suffering and are willing victims because they actually find pleasure in pain (Glick & Meyers, 1987). In other words, women who stay in an abusive relationship "enjoy" their physical and/or psychological abuse because of their masochistic tendencies.

According to the theory of masochism, women with masochistic tendencies demonstrate passivity, low self-esteem, submissiveness, feelings of inadequacy and helplessness, and chronic depression (Glick & Meyers, 1987). It is postulated that because these women experience sexual excitement in association with pain, their instinctual drives continue to motivate them to look for such pleasures or stimulation. What is implied in this theory is that women ask for abusive treatment, they escalate the situation, and provoke the abusers to use violence. If such interpretations are true, then there is no need to hold the abusers responsible for their violent behaviour and they do not need to go through counselling or any kind of treatment. Rather, it is the masochistic women who require help and clinical treatment. Some feminists argue that masochism is only a myth that is socially constructed to satisfy society's misogynist fantasy (Caplan, 1985; Russell, 1993). No matter whether masochism is a social construct or an enigmatic psychological complex or syndrome, it is clear that small samples drawn only from certain clinical settings and extreme cases cannot be generalized to describe battered women as if they are a homogeneous group.

Both the male-focused and the female-focused psychopathological approaches to understanding woman assault in relationships are limited in their narrow focus on the individual defects or deficits (in either the assailants or the assaulted) because they have failed to take into account the sociological factors that might contribute to people's behaviour and responses. Therefore, despite the early acceptance of the individual psychopathological model, more contemporary models tend to incorporate socio-cultural and situational factors (Bowker, 1993; Gelles, 1997).

Frustration-Aggression

The third theory in the psychological perspective is called *frustration-aggression theory*. This theory postulates that frustration leads to aggression. Psychologists who are interested in interactional factors look at couple relationships and external catalysts to explain men's aggression toward their spouses. Gelles and Straus (1988) point out that within marital relationships, because of intimate involvement in each other's lives, the couples possess much personal information about each other; they know their partners' weaknesses, and they know what they can say to hurt and/or irritate their partners. Anger and frustration have the potential to accumulate over time and to increase in intensity. The range and number of daily personal and family activities shared by a married couple provide them with plentiful opportunities to frustrate each other and hence to respond aggressively.

In addition, Shainess (1977) proposes that some abusers may possess an infantile personality, making them incapable of tolerating frustration. Some other studies indicate that when external stresses have accumulated during the day and/or over time, men who do not know how to handle their anger and frustration are likely to displace these on their wives when they come home (Gelles, 1974, 1985; Gelles & Straus, 1988; Straus, Gelles & Steinmetz, 1980). Aggressive responses are considered to increase in intensity and frequency in response to frustration. Hence, when conflict and frustration are commonplace in people's daily lives and when a couple often spend a great deal of time together, spousal abuse seems very difficult to eliminate. While the frustration-aggression theory may explain the cause of the aggression, it fails to explain the direction of the conjugal violence. We do not know why frustrated men often respond aggressively to their wives, but frustrated wives seldom respond violently to their husbands, given that both men and women experience stress and frustration daily in our society.

Situational

Situational theories seem to be developed in an attempt to respond to questions that are left unanswered by the frustration-aggression theory. These theories emphasize that unemployment, underemployment, low family income, and habituated situations such as drinking, gambling, and drug addiction are factors that precipitate men's assaults on women (Gelles & Straus, 1988; Hotaling & Sugarman, 1986; Jasinski, Asdigian & Kaufman-Kantor, 1997). Situational theories maintain that financial predicaments leading to excessive stress, frustration, and anxiety can escalate to violence, especially when the families have been exposed to violence and accept it as a legitimate coping response. Furthermore, when the individuals experiencing external stress are also regular drinkers, they are very likely to increase their alcohol consumption, which increases aggressive behaviour (Jasinski, Asdigian & Kaufman-Kantor, 1997).

While situational theories do contribute to our understanding of certain aspects of wife assault, we do not know whether the abusive husbands purposely get drunk so they can free themselves of the cultural inhibition against beating their wives or if they really "lose their minds" after drinking. We also do not know if abusive individuals use external stressors as an excuse to exert control over their female partners or whether they really do not have any other alternatives for dealing with stress but to resort to drinking and violence. Apparently, the explanations provided by situational theories may reflect the circumstances of some violent men and their families, but they fail to demonstrate why these men target women or abuse their wives and not others, and why violence is used only by some men or families while many others, who are equally exposed to various stresses in life, do not resort to violence. Alcohol abuse and external stressors are commonly identified by abusive husbands as the cause of their aggression. They say they do not intend to hurt their spouses, but somehow they "lose control" after drinking or when they are severely stressed. In fact, these excuses—blaming society, the economy, or other external factors for causing them to lose control—are only situational and do not explain abusive men's repetitive behaviour patterns of woman abuse.

Conditioning

Compared to the other psychological theories alluded to above, *conditioning theories* integrate the social, cultural, and psychological factors that contribute to a person's abusive, responsive, and coping behaviour. Some of these theories are expansions of the social learning theory. Donald Dutton and Lenore Walker are the two most prominent representatives of conditioning theorists in explaining the psychology of abusers and battered women. Adopting Bandura's (1973) social learning theory, conditioning theories maintain that positive reinforcement produces the most persistent behaviour patterns and negative reinforcement inhibits the most undesirable behaviour patterns. For example, compliant and submissive wives will positively reinforce the batterers' aggression, and resistant wives and social punishment will negatively reinforce the batterers' attempts to use violence (Dutton, 1995).

While some researchers suggest that men and women are equally violent in relationships because violence is a learned social behaviour (Gelles, 1974, 1985; Gelles & Straus, 1988; Straus, Gelles & Steinmetz, 1980), conditioning theorists do not think men and women are equally violent. They argue that generally men are more violent than women in many societies because male aggression is considered normal and rewarded whereas female compliance is expected, and aggression in women is often forbidden and punished (Dobash & Dobash, 1992; Dutton, 1995; Walker, 1984). Because men and women do not experience the same social conditions, they are socialized or conditioned to adopt different behaviour patterns. In an attempt to analyze why men are more violent than women, Dutton (1995) notes, "From a social learning point of view, males may be biologically predisposed to act aggressively, since they inherit greater musculature than do females. This musculature increases the probability that physically aggressive responses will produce their intended effects, thereby generating reward for the performer of the response" (p. 73).

Though Dutton is inclined to accept a biological predisposition for male violence, he also believes that violence is more or less a result of anger arousal. He asserts that not every observed behaviour will be practised, but the enactment of an acquired behaviour such as wife assault requires relevant stimuli, functional value, and reward (or punishment) for the performance. In a domestic dispute, a statement or action by the female partner would be a stimulus; the intended effect to regain control or resume authority would be the functional value; and the subordination of the woman would be the reward. "If violence resulted in reestablishing male dominance (at least temporarily), ending female verbal demands, and creating a feeling of male control, its use would be more likely in similar future situations" (Dutton, 1995, p. 81). With Dutton's theory, if violence resulted in punishment such as social intervention, losing one's female partner, or feeling guilty, the aggressor would cease his violent actions rapidly. What is puzzling in this equation is that very often when a woman threatens to leave her abusive partner, this increases the violence; the abuser becomes homicidal toward the woman. Perhaps the threat of losing one's spouse is not intensive enough or the enforcement of laws in our society is often inconsistent or the sentences are too lenient. When the punishment is not perceived as acute, the change of behaviour is not deemed necessary. Conditioning theorists believe that if abusive behaviour is learned, it can also be unlearned; the key is to teach abusive men to learn anger management techniques and to enforce stricter laws and harsher sentences (Dobash & Dobash, 1992; Dutton, 1995).

The conditioning theory proposed by Walker (1984) derives from Seligman's (1975) concept of "learned helplessness." Walker's theory attempts to explain why women seem to have difficulty leaving their abusive partners. Based on her study of 400 battered women in the Rocky Mountain region in Colorado, Walker described the so-called "battered woman syndrome," which explains battered women's behaviour in terms of learned helplessness and the cycle theory of violence. She asserts that because of repeated exposure to male violence, a battered woman may learn to react passively to this abuse, and be unable to take constructive action and leave the abusive relationship. Walker suggests that women living in abusive relationships often develop survival or coping strategies that keep them alive with minimal injuries. Occasionally, when the woman fears for her own survival due to the perpetrator's repeated death threats, she may suddenly become aggressive and eventually kill her batterer in a life-threatening situation.

Walker (1984) considers a batterer's violent behaviour as something socially learned and rewarded over a long period. She explains: "violence does not come from the interaction of the partners in the relationship, nor from provocation caused by possibly irritating personality traits of the battered women; but, rather, the violence comes from the batterers' learned behavioral responses" (p. 10). It is generally recognized that men who possess sexist attitudes, adhere to rigid traditional sex role stereotypes, feel insecure about the relationship, and/or have problems accepting a disparity in status between themselves and their wives are regarded as a high-risk battering group. In each of these cases, violence is used to reduce the perceived difference (e.g., traditional beliefs vs. observed reality) and anxiety.

Although Walker's (1984) "battered woman syndrome" has enhanced our understanding of some women's situations and helped some women to obtain acquittals in criminal trials for homicide, there are contradictions and gaps in her theory. First, she asserts that abused women have developed their own coping strategies to minimize their assault and injuries, so it appears that they are "active agents" rather than "passive victims" of wife abuse. Second, although Walker is not blaming the women for their fates by arguing that women have been socialized by society and conditioned by their abusers into believing they have no choice but to be "victims," she overlooks the fact that women's sense of having "no choice" or their "fear" for their own survival is because they have no marketable skills, are economically dependent, worry about how they can raise their children alone when living in poverty, and/or because they have been repeatedly threatened by their abusers. Third, the theory neglects to explain why, if prolonged exposure to violence, humiliation, degradation, and intimidation turns women into "helpless" victims, some women can ultimately overcome the abuse and end the abusive relationship. Fourth, when Walker claims that these women have developed "learned helplessness," she needs to provide some concrete, logical, and vivid accounts of how these passive, helpless women suddenly turn into dangerous aggressors who kill.

FEMINIST PERSPECTIVES

Along with sociological and psychological perspectives, feminist theories also enhance our understanding of woman abuse. Not only do feminist theories integrate the principles of several of the theories discussed previously but they also provide the historical and institutional context in which sex role learning and male status acquisition occur. Before discussing how feminist theories explain male violence and wife assault, it is imperative to note that it was grassroots feminist activists who first started working on the issue of wife assault and established shelters for battered women in the 1970s. Subsequently, feminist scholars responded by appropriating wife assault as a subject of serious study and by consolidating analyses of male violence into their critiques of family psychology and sociology (Walker, 1990). Indeed, focusing on women's social locations, their perceptions of the world, and their experiences, feminist theories condemn all forms of male violence against women as unacceptable.

Many feminists believe that "the social institutions of marriage and family are special contexts that may promote, maintain, and even support men's use of physical force against women" (Yllo & Bograd, 1988, p. 12); it is the culturally sustained ideology of heterosexual relationships that is structured in certain ways within the institution of marriage or partnership that creates the problem. Hence, feminist explanations of male violence against women utilize the social constructs of gender and power, regard the family as a socio-historical context for intensive analysis, and ground their theory in the lived experiences of women. Russell's (1990) study clearly outlines how society's ideology of family and marriage exploits women and minimizes their suffering at the hands of their husbands. She points out that although women may be raped by their husbands because they are "wives," this kind of sexual abuse has gone unnoticed for centuries. It seems that the social institution of marriage issues men a licence to sexually abuse women. When wife rape happens along with wife-battering, society tends to focus on the problem of the battering, leaving the matter of sexual abuse in marriage for women to handle on their own. Russell concludes that to deal with wife assault and wife rape is to deal with the unequal power in the relationship that is enshrined in the traditional concept of family. Wife abuse is not just the physical assault of women; there is a continuum of abuse that women have experienced that deserves society's attention.

MacKinnon (1990) maintains that power inequity and male dominance are the consistent conditions in every case and every form of male violence. She argues that society's patriarchal culture and capitalist practice endorses and sanctions male violence against women. Basically, many feminists, especially socialist feminists, believe that patriarchy and capitalism work hand in hand to exploit women by valuing and privileging men's skills over women's, and taking for granted women's unpaid labour in the family; hence, women are made to be economically dependent on men and trapped in their abusive situations (Gordon, 1988; Hartmann,

1981). MacKinnon (1990) argues that because patriarchy has been deeply embedded in the North American culture and women are exploited the most in capitalist societies, the oppression of women is the *fundamental* form of oppression. MacKinnon further asserts that because sexuality is gendered and gender is sexualized, women are sexually objectified and always live under the threat of sexual abuse. As such, to deal with male violence implies dealing with the oppression of women, balancing the power between men and women in society, and critiquing current notions of male sexuality.

However, because patriarchy is so very deeply rooted in Western culture, its effects, including male violence against women, are difficult to eradicate. Both historical and contemporary studies have shown that when society insists on the preservation of family and its privacy, social policies and the law continue to encourage women to deal with marital conflicts in private (MacKinnon, 1990). These studies have demonstrated that societal values and attitudes, as well as the criminal justice and legal system, have mutually influenced and shaped each other. In fact, many victims/survivors of wife assault and their advocates have often criticized the lack of protection afforded by the criminal justice system (Pagelow, 1981; Stanko, 1993). The police's traditional response is to tell the victims that there is nothing the police can do because they are not in the business of stopping domestic disputes or intervening in intimate relationships. For example, research studies conducted by Pagelow (1981) and Avakame (2001) found that the longer a woman remains in a violent relationship, the more likely she is to encounter unhelpful police intervention because the woman in the "problem family" is thought to be responsible for doing something to change her situation. Hence, the police officer is likely to maintain a detached, peacekeeping-only attitude. Fewer arrests are made and fewer charges are laid against men. On the contrary, systemic sexism often results in arresting women for self-defence (Miller, 2001; Rajah, Frye & Haviland, 2006).

Furthermore, feminists argue that the power imbalance between men and women in society has its ramifications in various authoritative social establishments. Because the ideology of family and marriage is so prevalent within the androcentric judicial system (which represents a male perspective of justice), when a case is brought to the court, it is very unlikely that the woman's suffering will be taken seriously (Chapman, 1988; Stanko, 1993). Because the status quo favours men and law enforcers are mostly male, they are more likely to support the male-defined notion of family than to sympathize with women's predicaments, so that claims of any kind of abuse are considered less important than preserving the abuser's rights to maintain his family. Stanko (1993) reports that an assault by a stranger is more likely to result in conviction and sentencing than assault or battering by a spouse. Most of these latter two types of cases resulted in dismissal and those that were prosecuted usually resulted in a light sentence.

Realizing that women's experiences were trivialized and they were often treated unfairly in the criminal justice and legal system in the past, many feminists, in the second wave of the women's movement, were convinced that new definitions and terms must be developed to reflect more accurately the diversity of women's experiences with male violence in intimate relationships. These feminists argued that as a result of male control over language and its meanings, conventional research on the assault of women often fails to take into account the complexity of how women define and understand their own experiences (Yllo & Bograd, 1988). They found that terms such as "family violence" or "wife-battering" do not adequately cover the whole range of violent situations that women experience. They suggested that new terms that reflect a wider spectrum of women's experiences with male violence would provide women with more public space or a stronger political platform to address their needs. Therefore, there was pressure among feminists and activists to find new definitions that would function as "conceptual coordinators for strategies" to convey a sense of interconnectedness between various types of struggles in dealing with male violence in different social contexts (Walker, 1990). That is to say, because women suffered not only within the context of family, the term "family" must be forsaken; also politically there was a need to make a connection between women's suffering, so that they were not held responsible or blamed for being abused. Wife abuse must be named as one kind of violence against women. The term "wife assault" (not wife abuse) was thought to provide "an organizing focus for women's anger, linking it to the 'violence against women' conceptual frame, which mobilized broad support among women for rape centres, 'Take Back the Night' marches, incest survivors' groups, and anti-harassment procedures" (Walker, 1990, pp. 48–49).

Though the change from "wife-*battering*" or "wife *abuse*" to "wife *assault*" helps women who suffered male violence in the home to identify with women who suffered it elsewhere, the new term has not been received without hesitation. On the one hand, the term "wife" excludes many women who are not wives; these women may cohabit with a man, consent to a steady intimate relationship with someone but not necessarily share a household space with him, or be in lesbian relationships. Although abuse within lesbian relationships is commonplace, people do not recognize its existence, thus making it harder for abused lesbians to seek help (Renzetti, 1992). Because lesbian couples are not allowed to legally marry or be recognized as common-law partners, when lesbians are assaulted by their "spouses," they do not know how to report it or bring it to the attention of social services. Also, they have no socially recognized status that enables them to take the case to court. The term "assault" often excludes threats and destruction of property as a means of exerting control, which is very common in abusive relationships, particularly in refugee and immigrant families (MacLeod & Shin, 1990). Many abusers in these families threaten to withdraw their sponsorship of the women, take custody of children after the women are deported, and withhold or destroy their passports. Therefore, to the non-wives and immigrant women who are assaulted by their partners, this change of label has no relevance to their situations and gives them little benefit.

In addition to redefining and theorizing male violence from a feminist perspective, there has been a struggle to press the state to reform the Criminal Code and judicial system. Because of the law's androcentric theory and practice, men's liberty and civil rights are protected whereas women's right to live free from male violence is jeopardized (Comack, 1993; Itzin, 2000; MacKinnon, 1990; Russell, 1993). In other words, existing laws and legal practice have put women at great risk of male violence and have left them with few options to confront the perpetrators and the law. One way of challenging the legal system is to get the police involved. Usually, the very first institution an abused woman may contact is either the hospital or the police. However, very often medical professionals and police officers are not trained to deal with issues of male violence against women. They tend to view wife assault as a "private matter." Hence, feminists have insisted that a more comprehensive procedure must be developed for medical professionals and police officers so that appropriate actions—such as filing a report, investigating the incident, and making an arrest—should be taken; all these responses can be used as evidence later in court (Itzin, 2000; MacKinnon, 1990; Russell, 1993). Some feminists also proposed that when police officers are called to the house, they should ensure the safety of the woman and take the abusive suspect to the station for further investigation.

After significant lobbying efforts, in the United States there is currently no jurisdiction that legally permits a husband to assault his wife, and attempts have been made to increase the frequency of arrests (Browne, 1987). Also, some states have established mandatory or presumptive arrest laws for violent partners (Buzawa & Buzawa, 1990). In Canada, at the end of the 1980s the definition of wife assault was broadened to include sexual assault, marital rape, emotional and psychological intimidation and degradation, and any physical violence inflicted by the male partner of a woman with whom she lives under the concept of marriage or common law (Walker, 1990). Such an expansion of the definition was made in an attempt to acknowledge women's different experiences with male violence and to lay a more solid ground for arrests and charges. Unfortunately, recent studies have shown that the increase in arrests does not prevent male batterers from abusing their wives or female partners again (Buzawa & Buzawa, 1990; Gelles, 1996; Schmidt & Sherman, 1996), so stricter laws and mandatory arrests have not proven effective in eliminating male violence.

Furthermore, some feminists who have engaged with the judicial system have begun to see some drawbacks in the strategy of using the "battered woman syndrome" to explain why women "passively" stay in the abusive relationships, but then "suddenly" fight back (Allard, 2005; Comack, 1993). They believe that the development of a rational explanation of a "reasonable survival strategy" may be much better than the reliance on a "syndrome" to interpret women's behaviour in coping with male violence. They are afraid that the persistent use of the "battered woman syndrome" as a defence will pathologize women's normal emotional state (e.g., anger could be a normal reaction to one's abuse), reinforcing an impression that battered women are "unreasonable" and mentally unstable (Comack, 1993). Also, they perceive that women who do not fit the characteristics of the "battered woman syndrome," yet hurt or kill their abusers out of reasonable fears, would not be able to benefit from such a defence. Snider (1991) believes that this kind of reform in the criminal justice system (i.e., accepting the "syndrome" as a defence) will invariably end up empowering the state rather than women themselves because it will leave the state with the power to determine who is more "worthy" of a fair trial and more "deserving" to be pardoned. Also, the use of the "syndrome" as a defence will ultimately shift women back to the victim status, denying their agency and forcing them to conform with the socially agreed upon psychological profile of battered women. The question is: Can the court accept the possibility that a reasonable woman may kill her abusive spouse in self-defence and/or as a very last resort to end her fears and long-term suffering?

In addition, feminists are concerned that the pathologization of women's situations and experiences will be used to support society's misogynist beliefs, which, in turn, blame women for their abuse (Allard, 2005; Caplan, 1985; Comack, 1993; Lamb, 1996). They find that society frequently blames abused women, who are blamed for "choosing" the wrong partner with whom to have an intimate relationship, for provoking male aggressiveness in "ordinary" domestic disputes, and for not taking "appropriate" actions to extricate themselves and their children from the dangerous relationship. No matter what they do, they are put in a no-win position. Unfortunately, while feminists insist that the analysis of the assault of woman should be concentrated on the context of women's position in society, dominant stereotypes of women often provide "the common sense information to divide women in two categories, those who are nurturers and caregivers, and those who are nagging, selfish, and in violation of women's expected role" (Stanko, 1985, p. 50). A number of historical studies have indicated that victim-blaming has existed in the social services sector (Armstrong, 1983; Gordon, 1988; Pleck, 1987). They find the misuse of psychological studies and child-protection procedures have encouraged women to minimize the external factors of abuse and to examine their own psyche to see if they need to change in order to protect themselves and their children. Armstrong, Gordon, and Pleck point out that victim-blaming only frees perpetrators from being held responsible for the harm they have inflicted. Gordon (1988) finds little difference between the responses of social workers to family violence and those of the legal system, and no evidence that abuse is successfully under control after the intervention of a social agency. All of these researchers plainly demonstrate their objections to the state's political agenda in preserving the family by manipulating women's behaviour, and criticize the state's ineffective social policy in controlling male violence against women and children.

No matter whether women leave or stay in the relationship, it is ludicrous to assume that they have never tried to protect themselves or to reduce the risk of their abuse or injury. Some feminists believe that women have a natural tendency to attempt to preserve life through their nurturing and co-operative habits; they are robust survivors even under extremely difficult circumstances (Gondolf & Fisher, 1988). Gondolf and Fisher describe women's survivor tendency as: "An inner strength, yearn for dignity, desire for good, or will to live appears despite one's previous conditioning and present circumstances. Even in the midst of severe psychological impairment, such as depression, many battered women seek help, adapt, and push on" (p. 20). They point out that even though women have this survivor tendency, we should not expect battered women to bounce back on their own without proper supports. By receiving the necessary assistance, women's inner strength can be realized and their resiliency demonstrated. In their study of White, Hispanic, and

Black women, Gondolf and Fisher find that many abused women make contacts with a variety of helping sources, and as the abuse becomes more severe and the abuser seemingly more dangerous and unmanageable, the diversity of the woman's contacts actually increases. Hence, they argue that although an abused woman may experience depression, guilt, and shame throughout her life, she should not be labelled as a victim characterized by learned helplessness.

To scrutinize the experiences of battered women, Hoff (1990) interviewed nine battered women and their 131 social network members to understand the complex relationships between these women, their social networks, and society at large. In theory, an abused woman can always find help either from her natural network (friends and family) or formal network (institutions of help) because it is the usual path women take to seek assistance. In reality, Hoff finds that as a result of factors such as the nuclear family, individual privacy, geographic isolation, and society's conception about couple relationships, an abused woman may not be able to obtain assistance from her natural network to deal with her abusive experience. Hoff reports that very often a battered woman's natural network is part of the problem rather than the solution. Abused women are damned if they leave and damned if they stay. For example, a battered woman is not supposed to be assertive when seeking help because assertiveness does not fit the stereotype of an abused woman; when there are signs of assertiveness, people may question her credibility or her story. There is also evidence that some members of battered women's formal networks have problems accepting battered women's decisions to stay in a relationship (Hoff, 1990). Some service providers believe that going on welfare to be "independent" is better than staying in the abusive relationship. They seem to lose sight of the kind of life battered women may live after they leave—a life of poverty, stigmatization, and ostracization from family. That is why Pressman, Cameron, and Rothery (1989) assert that social learning and the internalization of cultural norms in women predisposes them to remain in abusive relationships, yet they are made to feel responsible for the abuse perpetrated by their partners.

While most feminists agree that male domination and gender inequality are major factors contributing to the domestic assault of women, anti-racist feminists argue that in order to thoroughly understand family violence of any type, the issue of power should be at the core of the analysis (hooks, 1984). hooks asserts that although the assault of women in the context of family is an expression of male domination, violence is rooted in Western philosophical beliefs of hierarchical rule and thus is linked to all acts of violence that occur between the powerful and the powerless, and the dominant and the dominated. She believes that men are more likely to be perpetrators of violence because they generally have more power than women, and cites studies of violence in lesbian relationships to illustrate that "male domination" is not the only cause. According to hooks, to eradicate male violence against women in intimate relationships requires our attention and efforts to refuse any form of violence, including racism, that is traditionally overtly condoned and accepted, even celebrated in this culture. Other feminist advocates of anti-racist practice maintain that in helping women to confront male violence, there are a number of matters we must pay attention to. We must acknowledge the racist treatment that abused women of colour and abusive men of colour have received from medical settings and the criminal justice system, examine the power issue between dominant and minority groups, and discern the difficult position that racialized women face in determining what they should or can do about their abusive relationships (Greene, 1990; Skafran, 1990; Walker, 1995).

In summary, of the different conventional and dominant theoretical perspectives that explain the root causes of woman abuse, feminist theorists have made the best effort to integrate the principles of other theories and consider the social, historical, and institutional contexts in which women and men acquire their status in society. It is concluded that in the Western culture, men have been granted more privilege than women; they are taught and encouraged to maintain their power over women, thus male violence against women may be legitimately used as an authoritative means and justifiable excuse to keep their women in a subordinate position. Feminist theories have clearly shown that because the assault of women is a reflection of cultural norms, social attitudes, and economic reality, its eradication requires the co-operative efforts of all our social institutions; that is, the government, the criminal justice system, religious organizations, schools, the medical health community, and social services. More significantly, as indicated by anti-racist feminism, the issues of power and hierarchical rule that are entrenched in every structure in our society should be at the core of the analysis to thoroughly understand the abuse of women in any relationships.

Chapter 2

An Opportunity to Publicize the Private: Public Education Campaigns and Domestic Violence in Ontario

Samantha Majic

INTRODUCTION

Domestic violence is as old as recorded history and, in terms of the proportion of people victimized, it constitutes the most prevalent form of violence around the world (Klein, 1997). In Canada, the Centre for Research in Women's Health identified domestic violence as Canada's number one health issue (Duffy & Momirov, 1997). At the same time, the state has historically been reluctant to intervene in domestic violence disputes because it regards them as private issues that do not merit state attention (Mies, 1986). Ongoing funding cuts to services for abused women indicate that governments and the electorate still fail to understand the severely public nature of domestic violence. Therefore, this chapter will explore the role that public education campaigns can play in increasing awareness about domestic violence by framing it as a public issue that merits attention from both private individuals and the state. This chapter will also explore the role that these campaigns can play in challenging the societal conditions, such as poverty and sexism, that allow domestic violence to persist.

Before beginning this discussion, it is important to note that this chapter will operate from the theoretical premise that a liberal society is divided into private and public spheres. This division has long dominated liberal thought, resulting in the construction of women's roles and places in society as private and thus politically unimportant. This continued relegation of women to the private sphere has consequently resulted in the privatization of issues that predominantly affect women, such as domestic violence, shrouding these from public scrutiny and thus preventing them from receiving sufficient attention from the state.

Given this theoretical premise, this chapter will argue that, while not the only solution, public education campaigns that are developed and run collaboratively between the government and community groups that provide services for abused women can be an effective means of increasing public awareness of domestic violence. In turn, these collaborative public education efforts have the potential to both challenge the conditions that allow domestic violence to persist while also making this violence a salient public issue with the electorate and a dominant part of the law and policy agenda.

To illustrate this argument, focusing on the province of Ontario, this chapter will first briefly examine the battered women's movement's efforts to publicize domestic violence in Canada, and the federal and provincial governments' responses to the movement's efforts, in order to show that continued educative work is still needed to spur better law and policy action on the issue. Next, this chapter will explore the efficacy of public education campaigns by outlining their success regarding issues such as drunk driving as well as domestic violence, drawing from the examples of the Zero Tolerance Campaign in the United Kingdom, and the Domestic Violence Intervention and Education Program in New York City. Then this chapter will consider how public education campaigns can be especially useful for aiding and empowering women in racial and ethnic minority communities. Finally, this chapter will conclude by discussing how a domestic violence public education campaign can be modelled in Ontario, emphasizing the need for collaboration between women's groups and the government in developing such a campaign, and showing how this campaign can make domestic violence a salient public issue while challenging the conditions that allow it to persist.

MAKING DOMESTIC VIOLENCE A PUBLIC ISSUE

It is important to first briefly examine how the battered women's movement has publicized domestic violence in order to make it a salient issue with the electorate and legislators alike. This section will then focus on Canada and assess the state's response to this movement at the federal and provincial levels by examining the laws and policies passed that deal with domestic violence.

To begin, it is interesting to note that in light of the developments in family legislation and the consequent increase in legal intervention in the family, domestic violence was only recently discovered by law-makers and policy-makers alike (Mies, 1986; Moller Okin, 1989). In the Western world, the 1960s and 1970s were periods of flux when social movements sought to gain attention from the state. Social movements became engaged in tugs-of-war with the dominant social forces around the boundary marking the public-private divide; they worked to make so-called private matters subject to political negotiation and collective provision in order to expand the terrain of liberal-democratic citizenship (Brodie, 1997).

The battered women's movement (BWM), as it became known, was one such movement that directed specific attention to the plight of women in abusive relationships and pressured the state (particularly the criminal justice system) to act in the interests of these women (Jasinski, 2001; Minaker, 2001). The BWM was followed by similar movements against rape and molestation as women became increasingly vocal about the fact that human development and the attainment of success are impossible when living in a constant climate of fear (Mies, 1986). In short, the BWM's main aim was to transform domestic violence from a private issue to a public issue (Minaker, 2001).

A closer examination of the public versus private dichotomy with respect to domestic violence provides an explanation as to why such a movement was necessary. Historically, the state has refused to interfere in the private sphere of the home, where a man was the master of his home and thus had the right to chastise his wife. The state has continued to maintain that interfering in the domestic realm would be interfering with an individual's (the male's) right to act freely in his own interests; these interests have included the supposed right of an individual man to beat his wife in the private sanctuary of his home (Mies, 1986; Moller Okin, 1989; Schneider, 1994). Thereby, wife-beating by husbands has been omitted from definitions of criminal assault. By tolerating violence in families, the state has allowed power from the public realm to be brought into the home, thus supplementing the power that already existed in the family along gender and age lines. This power differential in families is one of the main reasons why so many women have historically been reluctant to report their violent partners to the police, not only due to fear of physical harm, but also because of the possibility of financial destitution and the loss of their children. Furthermore, many women who have appealed to the state to protect them from domestic violence have found their efforts to be futile.

In short, not only has the liberal concept of privacy long justified the state's refusal to intervene in domestic violence, it has also implicitly reinforced the notion that women are not sufficiently important to merit legal protection of their safety (Schneider, 1994). Thus, the law's failure to intervene in the private realm has led to the state's further failure to protect women from violence in the home (Morgan, 1995). Given the state's poor record in protecting women from domestic violence, the BWM and feminism had to teach that the norm of privacy, accompanied by the public denial that attended it, was keeping the social and psychological subordination of women from the reach of the law (Maslow Cohen, 1994). Furthermore, this movement had to challenge the unequal power relations in society, such as the financial disparities between men and women, which kept women from reporting and leaving their abusive spouses. The challenge was, and still continues to be, to change the discourse and social conditions regarding domestic violence.

THE BWM IN CANADA

Through the BWM, public silence gave way to statements of disapproval worldwide. What was once considered a hidden, private topic became a topic of public discussion. Negotiations between women and the state about this issue enforced the notion that the state could and *should* become part of the solution to men's violence against women in the home (Dobash & Dobash, 2000).

Between 1967 and 1970 the Royal Commission on the Status of Women (RCSW) was struck, and this was seen as a key event that brought attention to women and the distinct issues they face. The report covered many areas of life, such as the economy, family, taxation, immigration, education, child care, and the participation of women in public life. Although its profound silence about women's experience of violence is shocking from a modern perspective, the Royal Commission is still the formative event in the development of Canadian government laws and policies on women and it had an important influence on how domestic violence policy would develop (Levan, 1996).

In the first half of the 1970s, energies were directed to the creation of bureaucratic structures within the federal government to deal with the issues made visible by the Royal Commission. Some of the early examples of these structures were the placement of a coordinator on the Status of Women in the Privy Council Office, the appointment of a minister responsible for the Status of Women, and the establishment of the Women's Program to distribute funds and start programs for women, such as women's centres and rape crisis centres (Levan, 1996).

However, it was not until 1979 that the federal government began to pay attention to private issues such as rape and domestic violence, publishing *Towards Equality for Women*, the first federal government document to identify violence against women as a priority issue. While the report was criticized for not consulting the Canadian Advisory Council on the Status of Women (hereafter the Advisory Council), or other women's groups, and tended to ignore a number of issues such as daycare, abortion, and affirmative action, it did make some key recommendations with respect to domestic violence, including a promise to undertake a major study of the problem, establish a national clearing house of information, and review amendments to the Criminal Code related to the offence of rape (Levan, 1996).

In 1980, the Advisory Council published the report *Wife Battering: The Vicious Circle*, which played an important role in bringing public attention to the issue of domestic violence, setting the tone for the development of policy, and putting a strong emphasis on criminal justice solutions, including the reform of criminal proceedings in the law (Levan, 1996). Building on the success of this report, the Standing Committee on Health, Welfare, and Social Affairs (heretofore referred to as the Standing Committee) examined the issue of domestic violence, and in 1982 published a report that reflected the analysis that the problem of domestic violence was grounded in attitudes prevalent in society at large, and recommended that it be treated as a criminal activity (Levan, 1996).

However, when the Standing Committee presented the report in the House, the MPs laughed and showed gross disrespect for it, thus bringing attention to the deep misunderstanding of the severity of the issue. This response generated a high level of public concern about the issue and, as a result, in 1982, Parliament unanimously passed a motion to encourage the police to lay charges in cases of domestic violence, and the National Clearinghouse on Family Violence in the Department of Health and Welfare was established. In 1986, the federal, provincial, and territorial ministers responsible for the Status of Women reviewed the implementation strategies of the various governments; thus by the mid-1980s, the process of institutionalization was firmly established (Levan, 1996).

The responses to this institutionalization were mixed. In the 1987 the Advisory Council study *Battered But Not Beaten* was published, which examined the success of government intervention in the issue of domestic violence. This report demonstrated that on the one hand, government intervention had brought stable funding to women's organizations, increased the number of shelters, and enriched the professionalism of staff members. On the other hand, government intervention had also created hierarchies in women's organizations such as shelters, and had further diminished political activism around the issue and in many ways compromised the ideals of the women's movement. In short, government intervention continued to locate domestic violence within the family, not in a larger social system of gender relations, and instead of redistributing social power and reforming the institutions that dealt with domestic violence (such as the police), simply further institutionalized the issue (Levan, 1996).

By the end of the 1980s, policy around domestic violence seemed to have stagnated until the 1989 Montreal Massacre. This tragic event, in which 14 women were killed as a result of one man's attack on "feminists" at the Ecole Polytechnique engineering college, served as a serious wake-up call for law and policy-makers alike. The incident reinforced the notion that violence against women affected the well-being of all women, and demonstrated that this violence was tightly woven into the fabric of Canadian life, thus forcing a change in the policy direction regarding this issue (Levan, 1996). As a result, a public debate about the meaning, extent, and causes of domestic violence ensued, coinciding with the 20th anniversary of the RCSW. It was thus noted that the RCSW had failed to look at domestic violence and, as a result, the government received over 26,000 letters of support that a Royal Commission be struck to examine the issue (Levan, 1996). In 1991 the Canadian Panel on Violence against Women (hereafter the Panel) was struck to study the issue, and was comprised of women from a variety of backgrounds (Levan, 1996).

The Panel published its final report in 1992, making 494 recommendations that covered a variety of themes. However, these recommendations were not prioritized in any way, and its plan of action, which called for zero tolerance of domestic violence within seven years, seemed to most critics to be unworkable. As well, the report was feared to polarize rather than unite the different actors in the struggle against domestic violence. While some felt that it could be used to good purpose as a public education tool developed to generate public support and attention, it was a dismal failure (Levan, 1996).

Since 1993, family laws and laws about domestic violence have continued to evolve, but mainly in a piecemeal fashion that fails to make substantive changes to the overall situation of women. The province of Ontario's recent law and policy responses to the issue clearly illustrate this trend.

CURRENT ISSUES IN DOMESTIC VIOLENCE POLICY IN ONTARIO

In Ontario, public education and activism efforts with respect to domestic violence have generally been run by two different groups with similar yet competing interests: the government, and community groups that provide services for battered women.

Public education by the government in recent years has mainly demonstrated two thrusts: first, the education provided through the advertisement of resources and services for women who are in domestically violent situations, and second, the sponsorship of domestic violence training programs for those who work in fields where such violence may be detected, such as daycares. The government has educated the public about domestic violence through the media in an effort to publicize their action on the issue. Press releases and press conferences are commonly produced to do this, such as the example of the release cited above announcing the public education initiative. Another example of a government-led education initiative includes a guide for early childhood educators entitled *Understanding the Effects of Domestic Violence* (Baker, 2001), which is aimed at helping these educators become more aware about the prevalence and effects of domestic violence (Interview: L. Moyer, OWD, October 28, 2002).

Public education campaigns carried out by community groups in Ontario, such as women's shelters, have also provided public education materials about domestic violence in order to promote their services and to raise community awareness. These community groups have aimed to educate the public about domestic violence issues as well as the need for government recognition and support to combat the problem. For example, the Metropolitan Action Committee on Violence against Women and Children (METRAC), a non-profit organization that seeks to decrease and eventually eliminate violence against women and children (METRAC, 2002), has distributed, to places like shelters, numerous flyers and pamphlets that contain statistics about domestic violence, as well as handbooks for women who are being stalked, being sexually assaulted, or planning to enter into mediation proceedings with a spouse. However, groups like METRAC also act to ensure that the government is taking action to meet the special needs and interests of women who are in abusive relationships, and these groups further educate the public about government *inaction* on this issue. For example, METRAC has developed and maintained the Ontario Women's Justice Network (OWJN) website (www. owjn.org), which is a resource used by women in violent relationships as well as by equity-seeking groups that work on issues of justice for women (METRAC, 2002). This site also produces materials that are critical of government action on domestic violence and calls attention to the fact that many shelters are in need of funding, and that legislative responses to domestic violence have been highly inadequate (Cross, 2001, 2002a).

When one examines the educative efforts of the government and community groups, what becomes clear is that while their goals may seem similar, these two groups often act contrarily to each other. On the one hand, the government has a political imperative to show that it is taking action on the issue, and therefore is not likely to be self-critical; it is unlikely, for example, to admit that it is not providing enough money for shelters or welfare, and that women are being left fully dependent on abusive partners. On the other hand, groups that provide services for women, like the Ontario Association of Interval and Transitional Housing (OAITH), have such limited budgets that they cannot undertake large-scale public education efforts on their own, and must limit their educative efforts to promoting their services in their communities (Interview: E. Morrow, OAITH, November 6, 2002). Included in the efforts of groups like the OAITH and METRAC is raising public awareness of the need for government funding so that their services can be adequately provided.

In 2002, the Ontario government announced $5 million funding for a three-year public education campaign about domestic violence (Attorney General, 2002a). This funding announcement made up the largest part of a $21.4 million government commitment to fund a number of initiatives and services dealing with domestic violence, such as shelters, domestic violence courts, and the office of the chief coroner. According to the announcement, the goal of the public education campaign was to promote public education and prevention, and was to be developed by community leaders, agencies, and experts in the field. The campaign was to be a call for action to alert all Ontarians about the severity of the issue, and to actively engage them in prevention efforts (Ministry of Citizenship, 2002a, 2002b). Given that the government's and community groups' educative efforts often appear to be at cross-purposes, the question arises as to how the government came to announce that it would participate in a public education effort that involves collaboration with community groups like METRAC and the OAITH.

In June 2000, Gillian Hadley was shot to death in Pickering, Ontario, by her ex-partner, Ralph Hadley. Ralph Hadley had breached several court orders and was out on bail charges of assault, criminal harassment, and breaching orders (CSVAWSG, 2002b). This murder received high-profile coverage because it was one of the most public and gruesome murders that had occurred since the release of recommendations following the coroner's inquest into the death of Arlene May, who had died two years earlier at the hands of her partner; the latter recommendations were supposed to have been the starting point from which further intimate femicides would be prevented (CSVAWSG, 2002a, 2002b).

Clearly, the problem of domestic violence had not been prevented by the release of these recommendations. Led by METRAC, 160 women's and equity-seeking groups across Ontario came together to form the Cross-sectoral Violence against Women Strategy Group (herein referred to as the Strategy Group) to raise both public and government awareness about the issue of domestic violence. Together, this group created the Emergency Measures for Women and Children Document, which they aimed to have the government adopt in the Fall 2000 legislative session. These measures would cost $350 million and would fund community-based programs and services while also targeting the systemic inequalities that allow domestic violence to persist. These measures would include money for crisis lines, shelter funding for both staff supports and beds, second-stage housing programs, sexual assault and rape crisis centres, community outreach workers and counsellors, legal reforms (including legal aid funding and criminal and family law reforms), and economic survival and workplace safety through the funding of cost-of-living adjustments and pay equity for those working in women's agencies (CSVAWSG, 2002a).

While $350 million is a large sum of money, given the range of services covered by these measures, as well as the severity of the issue, the amount was relatively small. However, the Strategy Group was up against a government that had not had a generous record with respect to funding domestic violence initiatives (Interview: P. Cross, OWJN, October 17, 2002). The challenge therefore became how the Strategy Group could publicize the issue of domestic violence in order to ensure that the government would take action and adopt their Emergency Measures Proposal; adding to this challenge was the Strategy Group's limited budget, given its member groups' need to continue providing ongoing essential services to women.

The Strategy Group used a number of tactics, including a campaign encouraging individuals as well as women's and equity-seeking groups to fax a document, which included the Emergency Measures proposal and solicitations of government support, to their local MPPs, Minister of Women's Issues Helen Johns, and Premier Mike Harris. They also distributed flyers calling on people to become involved with a "Women's Clothesline," which was being staged on the lawn of Queen's Park on

September 20, 2000, the day that the Strategy Group was meeting with MPPs in order to obtain their signatures on a Declaration of Commitment to the implementation of the Emergency Measures.

On this day, the Strategy Group employed their strongest education and awareness tactic, a press conference at the Queen's Park media studio. Given the budgetary constraints of the Strategy Group, the massive reach of the media provided an inexpensive and efficient means of getting its message out (Ghez, 2001). At this conference, they distributed press kits that contained a press release outlining their demands, the Declaration of Commitment that they had wanted all three parties to sign, information about their group, and the Emergency Measures they were proposing. The high profile of the Hadley murder (and the fact that the May Inquest Recommendations were supposed to have prevented it) had already garnered the media's attention, and the efforts of the Strategy Group were covered extensively as a result of this momentum (Interview: E. Morrow, OAITH, November 16, 2002). The press conference they held was picked up by many of the major media outlets, such as the *Toronto Star* and *CBC Newsworld* (see Landsberg, 2000; Rebick, 2000).

Knowing that this press conference would be held at 10 o'clock that morning, the government hastily announced beforehand, that morning, that it would be allocating $5 million to create a domestic abuse child witness program, and $5 million in transitional support for abused women. While these allocations seemed to show rapid government action, they were simply re-announcements of funds that had been outlined in the spring budget (Cross, 2000). Both the Liberals and the New Democrats signed on to the Declaration of Commitment to the measures, but the Conservative government did not, citing that morning's announcement as suitable action on the issue (Cross, 2000).

However, the public attention drawn to the issue of domestic violence through the efforts of the Strategy Group sent a message to the government that they had not done enough, and a few days later, on September 27, 2000, the government responded by announcing a new piece of legislation entitled the Domestic Violence Protection Act (DVPA) (Attorney General, 2000). The government also went on to announce in October that it would be holding a coroner's inquest into the murder of Gillian Hadley (Attorney General, 2002b). These two announcements were simply reactive, and were indicative of the government's individualistic law-and-order agenda, and did little to prevent domestic violence.

The DVPA sought to protect victims of domestic violence by broadening the definition of domestic violence to include dating relationships and family members who reside together. It would also allow for victims of domestic violence to obtain an Emergency Intervention Order (EIO), which is similar to a restraining order, 24 hours a day, seven days a week. Breaches of an EIO would be enforced through the provisions of the Criminal Code, which would enable the use of stronger terms and conditions for the abuser. The DVPA also listed specific prohibited activities for the abuser, and allowed the seizure of weapons and removal of the abuser from the home (Domestic Violence Protection Act, 2000).

The introduction of this bill into the House received much media coverage in order to make the public aware of the government action. The announcement of the DVPA was broadcast on many of the major news channels and was also carried in every major Toronto and national daily, including the *Globe and Mail,* the *Toronto Star,* the *Toronto Sun,* and the *National Post* (see Artuso, 2000; Blackwell, 2000; Boyle, 2000; Mackie, 2000). While these articles outlined the provisions of the bill, they also pointed out the criticisms put forward by the Strategy Group, including its expense (EIOs would require justices of the peace to be hired and available 24 hours per day, and also would require the police to do more paperwork). Given the government's record on spending, there was great doubt as to whether the money would be spent (Cross, 2001). Further, while EIOs might be available all the time, they would not be beneficial for many, as it is estimated that only 10 percent of women call the police if they are experiencing violence (Mackie, 2000).

Following the announcement of the highly controversial DVPA, the government announced in October 2000 that it would conduct the inquest into the death of Gillian Hadley. The inquest began in October and took three months to complete. The Strategy Group had intervener status at the inquest and submitted their Emergency Measures Proposal. In February 2002 the inquest was completed and not only incorporated the suggestions from the Emergency Measures Proposal, but went beyond them to address the conditions that allow women's inequality to men to persist[1] (Interview: Eileen Morrow, OAITH, November 6, 2002).

Both the announcement of the DVPA and the completion of the Hadley inquest demonstrate how the government's educative response has been to announce new initiatives and laws to the public through the media, while community groups have educated the public and raised awareness about domestic violence in order to spur government action on the issue. However, these efforts, which are often in opposition, have done little to make domestic violence a consistently discussed public issue (like health care, tax cuts, and even the flu shot) and thus a dominant part of the law and policy agenda. Both the DVPA and the Hadley inquest are evidence of this. While the DVPA was passed in December 2000, it was never proclaimed into law. While government officials stated in 2003 that they were "still working out the details of the implementation" (Interview: Barbara Kane, Ministry of the Attorney General, November 5, 2002), representatives from the Strategy Group were doubtful that it would ever be proclaimed and worried that if it was, it would remain a highly insufficient and problematic piece of legislation (Cross, 2002b). The results of the Hadley inquest appear to be far more comprehensive and preventative in nature than actions like the DVPA, yet to this day they have not been fully implemented.

However, in 2003 the Liberals became the party in power in Ontario by a landslide, and on December 13, 2004 they announced a Domestic Violence Action Plan for Ontario (2004). While the plan included increased funding for community-based counselling, women's shelters, and workplace training for women, among a number of other programs, it also included the same (2002) announcement for a $5 million public education campaign. This announcement presents a key opportunity for the government and community groups to work together, not against each other, in order to make domestic violence a public issue. While these two groups have often seemed completely at odds, the current government's announcement provides an opportunity to look at how this collaboration could be effectively carried out.

MOVING FORWARD: THE POTENTIAL OF PUBLIC EDUCATION CAMPAIGNS

Given the evolution of family laws in Canada and the current political state of affairs in Ontario regarding the issue of domestic violence, the question arises as to what sort of public education campaign can be used to make domestic violence a more salient public issue. This section will first illustrate how public education campaigns have been effective regarding issues such as drunk driving. This section will then specifically examine the Zero Tolerance Campaign in the United Kingdom, and the Domestic Violence Intervention and Education Program (DVIEP) in New York City; both of these educative efforts demonstrate the potential to challenge the ideology of "the private," which keeps domestic violence from becoming a salient public issue with the electorate, and to simultaneously challenge unequal societal relations.

Domestic violence continues because the state and society have not articulated clear social norms that this is a serious public issue that merits attention; these norms must be articulated powerfully in order to get people involved in the issue (Ghez, 2001). It is hypothesized that domestic violence could be decreased by changing the public's attitudes about the issue and increasing societal involvement in the problem. Much of the attitudinal change would be a function of how salient the problem is perceived to be in people's personal lives. Domestic violence needs to be made as important an issue as drugs, pollution, health care, and taxes (Klein, 1997). People also must be educated to know that they can have a role in helping to solve the problem. Public education campaigns that employ effective communications strategies can play a key role in raising awareness and promoting changed attitudes and personal and community involvement (Klein, 1997).

The Don't Drink and Drive campaigns provide an excellent example of how such strategies can effectively change the way people think about and act on an issue (Klein, 1997; Interview: P. Cross, OWJN, October 17, 2002). Collaborative efforts among groups like Crime Stoppers, the police, schools, and the government launched a widely comprehensive campaign that led to the problem of drunk driving becoming nearly obsolete in a generation (Interview: P. Cross, OWJN, October 17, 2002). These campaigns not only made people talk about the issue and change their behaviour, but also generated such public interest in the issue that the government took policy action, including police road checks and laws that stated what one's alcohol level could be if tested with a Breathalyzer. In short, society now experiences far fewer incidences of drunk driving than it did a generation ago (Interview: P. Cross, OWJN, October 17, 2002).

Here the question arises as to whether similar action could be taken with respect to domestic violence. Drunk driving is in many ways a far simpler issue than domestic violence. It is a far more public issue as it involves an action in a public space that can diminish another's ability to experience freedom and safety in society. Campaigns against drinking and driving did not involve getting people to stop drinking altogether; they only controlled the action so that *one did not drive a car* while intoxicated and harm others. By contrast, domestic violence is a deeply complex issue that not only involves acts of violence, but also issues of women's financial dependence on their partners, their children's safety, where women can turn if they leave abusive situations, and stigmas related to domestic violence as a private issue. Furthermore, domestic violence is a highly *gendered* issue, and addressing it through the creation of laws and policies involves targeting men specifically, which is especially difficult to do in a legislative setting where most of the participants are men. While it is true that many male legislators are sensitive to the gendered nature of this issue, many are also likely to react by stating that labelling the issue in a gendered way is unfair as they themselves have never committed such violence.

However, while the two issues may not be exactly analogous, public education has played a role in raising awareness about drunk driving in order to get people to talk about the issues and to act on it, which is what is now needed to combat domestic violence. Domestic violence remains far too private an issue. Generating public discussion about domestic violence is key not only to changing public attitudes about it, but encouraging public action in terms of law and policy, including that which will confront the conditions that allow it to persist, such as poverty and misogyny. Fortunately, knowledge of how to create an effective campaign against domestic violence does not have to remain in the realm of theory and ideals. There have been some excellent examples of clear, cohesive, and comprehensive public education campaigns that can be used as models and drawn from for upcoming campaigns.

ZERO TOLERANCE

The Zero Tolerance Campaign was the first initiative in Britain to use public education through the mass media to directly challenge *male* violence against women and children (Gillan & Samson, 2000). What is especially interesting and relevant about this campaign is that it came to being in Britain, where neo-liberalism and neo-conservatism have grown to pervade the law and policy climate. In 1979 the right-wing Conservative Party was elected and governed on a platform that promoted the traditional nuclear family and a strong law-and-order agenda. By the late 1980s, these two agendas gave rise to the growth of Domestic Violence Police Units in police forces (Gillan & Samson, 2000).

At the same time, women's organizations, such as Women's Aid and Rape Crisis, were working with some success to make violence against women less invisible. However, these groups were also concerned with government interpretations of the problem of domestic violence that were prevalent at the time (Gillan, 1999). For example, the government conducted a survey asking women how safe they felt walking alone at night, and then contrasted their responses with the relatively lower rates of women disclosing incidents of crime (Gillan & Samson, 2000), thus allowing the government to redefine the problem of male violence against women as *women's irrational fear* of crime (Hester, 1996).

This reinterpretation of the problem led to the development of policy initiatives aimed at reducing women's fear of crime rather than men's perpetration of it (Hester, 1996). For example, the Home Office and the Scottish Office developed a policy initiative on violence against women called Positive Steps. This campaign took a law-and-order approach, producing leaflets and posters targeting women, and offering them advice to take actions like staying away from dark, unlit streets and keeping an "escape kit" on hand. As a result, domestic violence was redefined through a non-feminist discourse that promoted women's individual responsibility for their own personal safety (Gillan & Samson, 2000), thus maintaining the neo-liberal construction of domestic violence as a gender-neutral, private matter that is best dealt with individually.

By the mid-1980s, however, the Edinburgh district council, under Labour Party administration, established a Women's Unit with three Principle Office Posts, one of which was dedicated solely to campaigns and promotions. Women in Edinburgh were consulted regarding which issues were of concern to them, and safety emerged as one of the most prevalent. This concern, combined with the aforementioned shortcomings of the crime-prevention agenda, led to the development of a campaign to specifically address *male violence* against women (Gillan & Samson, 2000).

In order to convince the Edinburgh Council to put government money into such a campaign, more evidence was needed. As a result, a study was conducted in three secondary schools involving 300 young people aged 12–16. The study found that boys were more accepting than girls of violence against women; violence against women was more accepted when the perpetrator was married to the victim; and a significant number of boys thought they might use violence in future relationships (Gillan, 1999). The study also indicated that being exposed to information about domestic violence had an effect on reducing tolerance for domestic violence.

In light of this data, it was decided to run a high-profile mass-media campaign that would be informed by a feminist analysis of male violence stressing that this violence was about male power and control (Gillan & Samson, 2000). It is significant that this campaign was not generated and run solely by front-line women's organizations as these groups found themselves struggling with a lack of adequate funding, which required them to devote most of their resources to service provision for women. Thus, the Women's Unit, with its guaranteed government funding, was the group that focused solely on running this campaign, while consultation with the front-line women's groups was essential (Gillan & Samson, 2000).

Consultation with the front-line organizations ensured that the campaign development team recognized that public education was only one component of an overall strategy that also had to challenge the unequal power relations that allowed domestic violence to persist. This understanding led to the development of an underlying strategy called the Three Ps Approach: *prevention* of crimes of violence; *provision* of support services for women and children (in the form of both front-line services, as well as services to help diminish the poverty and dependence that prevent women from reporting and leaving their abusers); and *protection* under the law.

The clear strategic aim of this campaign was to move the issue of domestic violence up in the public and political agenda, and in doing so to inject gender specificity into the previously gender-neutral crime-prevention policy strategy (Gillan & Samson, 2000). Zero Tolerance wanted to make violence against women socially unacceptable, similar to drunk driving. The organizers noted that there had been huge efforts, backed up by legislation in many cases, to change public perceptions of drunk driving (Gillan, 1999). The goal was thus to create a space in which attitudes could and would be changed.

An important part of the campaign's development was the combination of skills that were used. Not only did the team have a clear theoretical perspective, it was also skilled in visual communications, public relations, media, and political lobbying. The creators of the campaign were clear from their perspectives as activists, front-line workers, and professionals working within the political structures that the only way to move the issue of domestic violence into the public and political agenda was to build broad-based support by publicizing the issue. It was hoped that this would make it easier for front-line service providers to lobby for increased resources in the long-term (Gillan & Samson, 2000).

Zero Tolerance used the principles of public relations theory to ensure that campaign had broad-based support weeks before the first poster appeared. All of the political parties in the council offered their support, and a number of high-profile representatives from the churches and local police force attended the launch of the campaign (Gillan & Samson, 2000). The campaign used posters, billboards, and bus and cinema advertising to challenge the norms and beliefs that give rise to male violence. Examples of these materials included straightforward black posters with white lettering, for example, which insisted that men have no excuse for carrying out acts of domestic violence, and that domestic violence would not be tolerated by society or law enforcement institutions (Elman, 2001). What was significant about these posters and other campaign materials was that the creative decisions behind them were all very much linked to the overall analysis. For example, according to one of the organizers, "this meant we would not, as a matter of principle, use any victim imagery. We would not show bruised and battered faces so beloved of advertising agencies who win huge accounts to put these campaigns together. We wanted the campaign to challenge men, but not at the expense of women. And that meant we would not use victim imagery" (Gillan, 1999, p. 23). Campaign materials aimed to challenge many of the myths that unfortunately prevail around the issue of domestic violence. One poster said, "She lives with a successful businessman, loving father and respected member of the community. Last week he hospitalized her."[2] Visually, this message challenged the myth that domestic violence is associated with social class (Gillan, 1999), while the poster also more subtly highlighted the issue that women often cannot leave a violent situation for fear of the social stigma attached to domestic violence, and because they could be left financially destitute.

Since the launch of Zero Tolerance in 1992, it has been taken up across the U.K. The campaign is run in areas where approximately 80 percent of the Scottish population lives (Gillan & Samson, 2000). Furthermore, the campaign has been promoted by the European Parliament and the Council of Europe, and member states have been called on to adopt and replicate the campaign (Gillan & Samson, 2000).

Yet while Zero Tolerance has now been used worldwide, the question of effectiveness must be addressed, specifically regarding the degree to which public education campaigns against domestic violence influence social norms about the problem (Ghez, 2001) and make it a public issue that merits significant and sustained law and policy attention over a broad range of areas, from front-line service provision to income supports that are needed so that women can leave abusive relationships. To date there have not been any comprehensive and sustained studies of the long-term effects that public education campaigns regarding domestic violence can have (Interview: L. Moyer, OWD, October 28, 2002), which is a function of the fact that campaigns like Zero Tolerance are still relatively new.

However, there have been a number of evaluations of the campaign by market researchers, universities, and individual researchers, and while the results have varied slightly from area to area, the reports have shown broadly similar findings: 80 percent of respondents believed that the public needs to know more about domestic violence; 80 percent believed that the Zero

Tolerance showed the council to be forward thinking and innovative; and the money spent on the campaign had been well spent (Gillan, 1999).

Further, the policy responses following the launch of the Zero Tolerance Campaign suggest that attitudes can be changed to a degree, and that law and policy action will follow as a result. At the same time, much of the initial action after the launch of the Zero Tolerance Campaign was in the form of reports and policy documents, for example, the government policy document entitled *Living without Fear*, which incorporated the Three Ps approach (although it does not acknowledge the source). While beneficial, such documents need to be backed up with policy implementation (Gillan & Samson, 2000).

Interestingly, following the high profile of the Zero Tolerance Campaign, the Scottish Office developed its own mass-media campaign without consulting Zero Tolerance. These ads actually perpetuated many of the myths that Zero Tolerance sought to challenge, such as the myth that violence against women was more highly associated with the lower class. But these ads run by the Scottish Office were heavily criticized by the public in this respect, a result that a qualitative evaluation confirmed was due to the successful myth busting accomplished by the Zero Tolerance Campaign (Gillan & Samson, 2000).

More effective and comprehensive policy responses were developed as the campaign went on, thus illustrating the need for such campaigns to be sustained and comprehensive. For example, it took five years of sustained campaigning for the Zero Tolerance effect to become apparent in other policy forums in Scotland (Gillan, 1999). By 1997, numerous policy reports about domestic violence were produced by different groups, including Her Majesty's Inspectorate of Constabulary, the Scottish Forum for Public Health Medicine, and the Convention of Scottish Local Authorities.

When the Scottish Parliament formed in 1998, it identified domestic violence as a key priority. The Scottish Executive has since acted concretely and released £3 million to establish a domestic abuse services development fund, with local authorities being asked to match funds, as well as another £2 million for expenditure on refuge provision (Gillan & Samson, 2000). Various initiatives have also been adopted by local health and policing authorities, such as the Spotlight Initiative, which was undertaken and developed by the Strathclyde Police Authority (the largest in Europe) to drive tolerance of domestic violence out of the police force (Gillan & Samson, 2000).

At the same time, it is important to note that the Zero Tolerance goal was to have government policy incorporate all three Ps into their responses to domestic violence. While the aforementioned initiatives are encouraging, they mainly seem to focus on violence after the fact. A case in point is illustrated by the Scottish Executive's Workplan, which identified domestic violence as a key priority. Out of the 92 items listed for action, fewer than a quarter deal with prevention, while the rest deal largely with the provision of services instead of the Zero Tolerance Campaign's more radical goals of challenging societal conceptions of acceptable male behaviour and changing women's social and economic position.

While service provision is certainly important, strategies also must be undertaken to prevent violence before it happens as opposed to simply dealing with its consequences (Gillan & Samson, 2000); failure to do this leaves male behaviour as underanalyzed and underproblematized (Gordon, 1988). This is not to advocate an individualistic behaviour modification approach that simply re-privatizes the issue of domestic violence as a matter best dealt with by the family and in the home. Instead, currently "acceptable" male behaviour needs to be problematized *publicly* so that attention is brought to the gendered nature of domestic violence, and socially accepted male behaviours and roles in society that keep domestic violence from being confronted as a serious public issue are called into question. Furthermore, the larger societal problems that allow domestic violence to persist, such as the feminization of poverty, need to be challenged as there is no impetus for men to change their behaviour if they know the women they are abusing have no other choice but to stay with them.

Examples like this illustrate that there are undoubtedly some concerns about the ways that politicians and policy-makers address the issue of domestic violence. Many of these concerns result from the fact that there are still few female legislators in governments worldwide, and so legislators have been slow to define domestic violence as a male issue. It is fair to say that domestic violence approached legislatively as a male issue is uncharted territory, as in Scotland, it is the first time a government has been elected on a platform that puts domestic violence as a high priority, a result not only of the efforts of Zero Tolerance, but also a long line of activist and scholarly work (Gillan & Samson, 2000).

The male specificity of domestic violence has been addressed to some degree by the Scottish Parliament. For example, a cross-party group has been established to address male violence against women and children, and to monitor the Executive's action on this issue. As well, the Home Office Crime Reduction Program is providing funding for development projects regarding male violence against women that were never previously available (even though it is only £6.3 million of the £250 million overall crime budget) (Gillan & Samson, 2000).

Clearly, actions such as these show that in its short operation, the Zero Tolerance Campaign has been relatively successful in increasing awareness about domestic violence and bringing law and policy attention to the issue. However, while the work of Zero Tolerance has mainly been done through public relations-style strategies (such as advertisements), there are other educative strategies that can not only educate the public at large, but can also more effectively bring law enforcement officials and community members together in the educative process.

THE DOMESTIC VIOLENCE INTERVENTION EDUCATION PROJECT

An example of such an educative strategy has been documented by Robert Davis and Bruce Taylor (1997) in New York City. This community policing initiative was called the Domestic Violence Intervention Education Project (herein referred to as the Project) and was undertaken in areas where there tended to be high rates of domestic violence, such as housing projects, and sought to transform the often antagonistic relationship between these communities and the police. In these areas the Project distributed flyers advertising services, and police officers and social workers attended community meetings to raise awareness about domestic violence and the need to report it. Key to the program was that a team consisting of a police officer and a social worker were dispatched to follow up on initial police responses to domestic violence calls. The results of the project were interesting: While there was no reduction in incidence of violence, households that had received public education materials, as well as those that had received follow-up visits, were more likely to report new violence to the police than those that did not receive any treatment. Moreover, the effect of the follow-up visit was most pronounced among households with more serious histories of violence.

The Project was certainly not perfect. It was far less comprehensive and preventative than the Zero Tolerance Campaign. It also targeted poorer communities with larger minority populations, which often had larger police presences to begin with; such targeting rested on the assumption that domestic violence was more likely among these communities than it was in wealthier and Whiter communities, a myth the Zero Tolerance campaign had rightly sought to dispel.

However, as problematic as aspects of the Project were, its results suggested that its interventions had increased citizens' confidence in the police's abilities to handle domestic violence situations (Davis & Taylor, 1997). Other projects similar to the Domestic Violence Intervention and Education Program, alongside Zero Tolerance-style campaigns, could provide especially effective means of engaging the police in initiatives and also for making a fundamental change in how policing is done (Davis & Taylor, 1997), away from a reactive, interventionist approach and toward one that is more community-focused.

IMMIGRANT AND VISIBLE MINORITY WOMEN AND DOMESTIC VIOLENCE

First, it is important to note that broad terms such as "immigrant women" or "visible minority women" tend to construct singularity out of diversity. Women who identify with these categories do not comprise a homogeneous entity, and while many might share similar experiences, their differences in terms of race, ethnicity, and citizenship status mean that many of these women are differently situated if they experience domestic violence (Pratt, 1995). Certainly it is true that immigrant and visible minority women share many of the same concerns as other women who have experienced domestic violence. Many feel fear and shame for their experience, hope their partners can be helped, want to protect their children, and are often not sure who to trust (CCSD, 2004).

Immigrant and visible minority women also often have unique vulnerabilities that need to be accounted for when discussing domestic violence in general, and when considering a campaign to help educate people and raise awareness about the issue more generally. Briefly, some of these vulnerabilities include: fear of the police and immigration officials, especially if the women have been sponsored by their husbands and are uncertain about their own citizenship status, therefore allowing the husbands to threaten the women with loss of status if they report violence; a lack of familiarity with the nation's official languages and laws, which can make actions like, for example, calling 911, very difficult; feelings of isolation due to the absence of family and support networks in the new country; coming from cultures where gender roles are rigidly stratified and the use of violence against women is seen as an appropriate way for a man to treat his wife; fear of poverty if they leave their husbands, especially if their employment credentials are not recognized in their new countries;

and a fear that speaking out against and reporting the violence they are experiencing will add to any negative stereotypes their racial/ethnic community might have in the larger community (CCSD, 2004; Jiwani et al., 2001; Pratt, 1995).

Any public education campaign that seeks to raise awareness about domestic violence among members of the general population must include materials and programming that address the unique needs of immigrant and visible minority women. Broadly speaking, a well-run campaign that accounts for these needs could have a number of aiding and empowering benefits for these women. For one, these campaigns could educate these women about their rights more generally, as well as where to turn for help regarding domestic violence. The campaigns could also educate these women that violence toward them in the home is not socially acceptable, and that they are not alone in experiencing such violence. By providing such information, these campaigns could empower immigrant and minority women, addressing many of their unique needs, many of which stem from a lack of awareness about basic rights and services available to them as residents of a new country.

MOVING FORWARD: AN ONTARIO CAMPAIGN

Ontario is clearly at a juncture where it can develop an effective public education campaign that can challenge the current ideology of the private that still surrounds the issue of domestic violence, and make this violence a salient issue with the electorate and legislators. While it is important to acknowledge that the challenges to doing this are numerous, this section will draw from the lessons learned from both the Zero Tolerance Campaign and the Domestic Violence Intervention and Education Project to outline what such a campaign could look like in Ontario. This section will discuss the need for the campaign to be collaborative, and will raise potential issues that could either impede or aid collaboration. This section will then specifically detail the elements of the actual campaign, and will discuss how it can be tailored to meet the needs of immigrant and visible minority women.

Co-operation between community groups and the government will be the key to the campaign's success. As noted above, the Ontario government has called for this collaborative effort. Community groups, such as the OWJN and the OAITH, provide essential services to women in violent situations and are also closely attuned to the needs of the communities in which they operate. For this reason, they can provide the government with important insights into how to best reach out to both their local communities, as well as the public at large, regarding the issues that women in violent situations face and the needs that they have.

However, as noted above, the events of the summer of 2000 in Ontario seemed to show that these two groups were constantly at odds, so that collaboration might prove very difficult. While the government has said that it would like to work with community groups to make this campaign as comprehensive and educative as possible (Ministry of Citizenship, 2002a), reality has proven differently in the past. For example, Pam Cross, of the OWJN, noted that while the Conservative government had expressed an interest in meeting with groups like hers to discuss planning the campaign, it had often given them only two days' notice for these meetings, which was insufficient time to adequately prepare with their membership (Interview: P. Cross, October 17, 2002).

However, with the Liberal government, it is quite possible that this collaboration experience could be different as a change in government often brings with it attendant changes in policy, strategy, and spending (Walker, 1990). In light of this, one could speculate that while a campaign under a Conservative government would reinforce the public-private divide by focusing on the family and criminalization, a public education campaign under a more left-of-centre Liberal government might aim to point to the systemic issues (such as "accepted" gender roles) that both reify the public-private divide and allow domestic violence to persist and negatively affect women's lives.

Assuming then that positive and reciprocal collaborative action could take place under the Liberal government, the question arises as to what methods and strategies such a campaign should employ.[3] Generally speaking, the campaign should be multifaceted and include a combination of strategies that challenge notions of domestic violence as an individual problem that is best dealt with within the private confines of the family (O'Brien, 2001). The campaign should therefore include the following three elements: (1) preventative education in schools beginning at a young age that looks critically at "accepted" gender roles; (2) a publicity strategy that not only provides society at large with information about services, but also about the severity and pervasiveness of the problem; and (3) educative programs that integrate the activities of law enforcement officials and the community at large.

Turning first to the issue of preventative education in schools, it is important to note that such programs have been going on to some degree in

Ontario since the early 1980s. For example, the Design for a New Tomorrow Program was started at that time by the Niagara District School Board to introduce the issue of violence against women and gender stereotyping into the local school curriculum, and other such initiatives have been supported by the Ontario Ministry of Education since the mid-1980s. By the 1990s, domestic violence had become a central issue that was entrenched in many schools' educational programs, starting with children as young as those in kindergarten (Duffy & Momirov, 1997).

Programs like this should therefore be continued and developed further, especially for older students. Drawing from the example of the Zero Tolerance Campaign, there are a number of ways this can be done. One is to establish programs similar to Zero Tolerance's Respect Initiative, which has been started in schools and allows young people to talk about relationships and challenge the constructions of male and female roles in society and the violence against women, which has been tolerated by the perpetration of these constructions (Gillan, 1999). While it is too early to tell how effective programs like this have been, it is important to remember that domestic violence is still a relatively new public issue. If one looks to the example of drunk driving, for instance, it took a generation for the "Don't drink and drive" message to become part of the national psyche to a large degree (Interview: P. Cross, October 17, 2002).

The public awareness campaign is needed so that the rest of the public, who have not had the benefit of such school-based programs, can be educated and made aware of this issue. The focus of campaign materials must *not* be on women and helping them protect themselves (thus privatizing the problem further), but on male violence against women and how it—and the conditions that allow it to persist—need to be spoken about publicly. A public education campaign could risk re-privatizing the issue of domestic violence through a focus on making it appear as if the government is taking action and being tough on crime, while also protecting families. If this campaign is to be effective in the long run, it cannot simply treat domestic violence as this year's fad, and must go beyond simply advocating increased legal sanctions; it is the subtle and pervasive acceptance of the problem of domestic violence, as well as the ignorance of the conditions of social inequality, that allow it to persist, and that must be eliminated (Klein, 1997; Rowland & Klein, 1990). Thus, an effective public education campaign needs to be *sustained over a long period of time* in order to bring the taboo subject of domestic violence to light, and to make what was once (and still often is) considered a private family issue an issue of community concern and public responsibility (Ghez, 2001).

A new set of truths about domestic violence must be created that will change and increase the profile of the debate around it. There is serious long-term work to be done here; the problem of domestic violence needs to be continually named publicly on an ongoing basis (Gillan, 1999). In doing this, it is important to keep in mind that attitudes *can* change and that this change can be lifesaving; campaigns against drunk driving have shown us that this is possible, but also that a long and sustained effort is needed (Ghez, 2001).

The methods and messaging used in the Zero Tolerance Campaign provide a good example of how a beneficial message can be promulgated. The materials used should include billboard-type posters in highly visible places in high-traffic areas, such as subways, bus stops, and transit stations. Similar to the materials used in the Zero Tolerance Campaign, these billboards should be simply presented, using black-and-white photos with clear lettering that makes it evident that domestic violence is a gendered issue transcending race and class lines in society. Furthermore, these posters should point out that such issues as poverty and child custody disputes make violent situations even more complex, and should also give numbers that people can call if they would like help or more information (for shelters, for example). Along with billboard-type publicity, it would also be effective for the campaign to develop television spots that are short, simple, and powerful, similar to those used in the drunk-driving and anti-smoking spots that have aired on Canadian television in recent years; the latter often involve black-and-white footage of an individual speaking personally about how smoking has impacted his or her life. Given the massive reach of television, this would be a highly effective way to educate the public about domestic violence and to spur demand for action on the issue. As well, it must be noted that when developing the messages for both billboards and television spots, it is imperative to consult with advertising and public relations firms; this was a key factor in the effectiveness of the Zero Tolerance Campaign.

Zero Tolerance was made practically feasible because it was begun in one city and expanded as its proof of success increased. Given the location of the provincial government in Toronto, the largest city in Ontario, the campaign could be started and closely monitored there, and then expanded later throughout the province. It must be noted that domestic violence campaigns run in large urban centres often increase calls to shelters and helplines. In San Francisco, for example, a domestic violence education campaign that was run around the time of the O.J. Simpson trial saw a 51 percent increase in the number of calls to domestic violence crisis lines (Klein, 1997). Examples like this show that the promotion of the message that domestic violence is a crime must be backed by services for women. Anti-domestic violence messages that are undermined by the authorities that provide redress to women can have severe consequences: placing faith in a system that provides inadequate protection can prove deadly for battered women (Elman, 2001).

One could conclude here that authorities like the police have never been on women's side when it comes to domestic violence, so they should not be expected to act any differently regarding the start of a public education campaign. However, Ontario is at an interesting juncture with respect to police relations and the public, and for this reason it is important to make this education campaign a joint venture between law enforcement officials and community groups. Recent media coverage has suggested a pattern of treatment by Toronto police in dealing with members of the Black community that could be consistent with racial profiling—targeting individuals of a certain race or ethnic background on the presumption that they are more likely to commit a crime (McCarten, 2002). As a result, the police have come under fire for their practices with respect to racialized minorities, which has consequently called into question their practices with other marginalized groups, including women.

Given this, a co-operative public education effort between law enforcement officials and the different communities they serve could be a good public relations opportunity for the police, allowing them to reach out to women and other marginalized groups. Drawing from the example of the Domestic Violence Intervention and Education Project in New York City, the Ontario campaign could also include a program in which police officers and social workers visit community centres and participate in meetings to discuss the issue of domestic violence and inform people of the need to contact the police if they are experiencing this violence. As well, similar to the Domestic Violence Intervention and Education Project, the police and social workers could make follow-up visits after violent incidents are reported.

This could be extremely valuable for racially marginalized women, who are often less likely to report domestic violence. An education campaign tailored to these women—for example, providing materials in languages other than English in communities with large non-English-speaking populations—would not only make these groups more aware of the problem and the need to report it, but would also allow them to work with the police and to help repair the often fractured relations between minority communities and the police.

While a public education campaign in Ontario must target the entire population, visible minorities are growing communities in Canada. The Canadian Council on Social Development (CCSD) (2004), noted that in 2001 these groups made up 13.4 percent of the Canadian population, and recognized that domestic violence must be addressed with specific consideration for this growing part of the population. At the same time, the campaign must be careful to not *target* marginalized groups as perpetrators, but rather to allow them the same access to information and resources. In order to form a public education campaign for immigrant and visible minority women that does not unfairly portray and target their racial/ethnic groups, but at the same time that meets their unique educative needs, it is clear that it will not be enough to simply translate the materials from the broader campaign into the languages of the various ethno-cultural communities. According to the CCSD (2004), the campaign needs to begin earlier and by making information about rights and the justice system available to immigrant women in their languages of comfort as soon as they arrive in Canada. As well, given that many immigrant/visible minority women are reluctant to report or speak out against violence due to fears of perpetuating cultural stereotypes about their communities, broader efforts need to continue to educate the general public about new immigrants to Canada, their important role in the country's development, and their ongoing contributions to the well-being of all Canadians (CCSD, 2004).

Furthermore, a campaign would need to be developed in conjunction with the members of the ethno-cultural communities in which many immigrant women reside. Where and when the broader campaign is run in ethno-cultural communities, it needs to reflect an awareness of the certain cultural roles and values that are specific to these communities and therefore tailor their messages to address these values. One instructive example of how to go about doing this appeared in the Cambodian community in Boston, where community leaders, formerly battered women, social work students, and other interested parties joined forces to create a video to educate members of the community about domestic violence. This video incorporated Cambodian religious, family, and community values to send the message that domestic violence destroys everyone (Klein, 1997).

Along with tailoring elements of the broader campaign to meet the needs and accommodate the values of the different ethno-cultural communities, education and information about domestic violence should be provided through smaller neighbourhood meetings and gatherings, where community leaders and/or special guests could inform community members about the issue of domestic violence and where to seek help for it in the broader context of discussions about new life in Canada (CCSD, 2004). Adopting such a strategy would make it much easier for those women whose husbands might not approve of them discussing such issues to join in and attend as the entire meeting would not be focused on the topic of domestic violence but around other issues they face in their community.

Clearly, regardless of the audience of the campaign in Ontario, an effective public education campaign that challenges the male abuse of power will be difficult to construct, especially given the state's historical reluctance to intervene in the family. At the same time, violence in the family affects all family members and their ability to function in the public realm. Therefore, if the government truly wants to protect the family and facilitate full participation by all its members in society and the economy, it will focus on the gendered nature of domestic violence and prevent perpetrators from endangering family members and limiting their access to the "public" realm.

CONCLUSION

Using public-private theory as the theoretical frame, this chapter has explored the feasibility of using public education campaigns to publicize domestic violence in Ontario in order to make it a dominant issue within the law and policy agenda. Though through the efforts of the BWM, domestic violence has become a far more salient and public issue now than it was 30 years ago, it remains a pervasive problem and receives sporadic legislative and political attention.

This chapter has shown that public education campaigns can publicize this private issue in order to make it a dominant part of the law and policy agenda if the education efforts are collaborations between the government and community groups that provide services to abused women. Such campaigns not only increase awareness of the issue but challenge the power relations that allow domestic violence to persist. In Ontario, while these two groups have traditionally operated at cross-purposes, the recent $5 million government commitment to fund a collaborative public education campaign provides an interesting opportunity.

Drawing from successful campaign models in other jurisdictions, such as the Zero Tolerance Campaign, a comprehensive campaign can be undertaken that brings the private issue of domestic violence into the public space, forcing the electorate to not only be aware of the problem and report it, but to demand that domestic violence receives law and policy attention from the state, which also challenges the unequal power relations that allow the violence to persist. Moreover, properly tailoring such a campaign to ethno-cultural communities has the potential to aid immigrant and visible minority women in their struggles with domestic violence by educating them about their rights and entitlements to safety and security in their homes and relationships.

While many feminists might argue that the state, as a patriarchal institution, has no interest in helping women and treating this issue as an important one, activism over the years, beginning with the BWM, has slowly drawn the issue into the light. Furthermore, women are a large voting group who are demanding attention to issues that impact them, thus leaving the government with a political imperative to pay attention. In light of this, this chapter has taken the stance that the $5 million funding announcement provides an opportunity not only for the government, but for the public as well, to begin to pay attention. Domestic violence is an issue that merits at least as much public attention as tax cuts and health care, and in order for substantive action to be taken, it needs to be an issue that is as salient as these other issues to the daily lives of the public. Public education campaigns should not be the only action; certainly there is inaction in other areas, such as policing, but public education campaigns are a starting point. Granted, we cannot expect results overnight; an issue like drunk driving took nearly a generation to virtually eradicate. Sadly, with domestic violence we are only at the stage where talk is beginning.

Chapter 3

Women Are Still Unsafe: Cracks in Best Practice and Mandatory Arrest Policies

Josephine Fong

Prior to the feminist movement of the 1970s, violence against women was not viewed as a social problem. This particularly affected women who were victimized in family and intimate relationships. Women's experiences were denied, disbelieved, or discounted for centuries. Due to the collaborative efforts of feminists and community advocates working in different institutions and social systems, pushing for change, the ownership of the problem of woman abuse has now broadened from the individual woman (who used to be labelled as a "bad wife" or a "rotten woman") to the family as a system, to the community of women in general, and finally to the society at large in which we all live and share responsibility. This move away from victim-centred treatment to a community-based view of the problem has provided us with a better understanding, thus allowing us to advocate, on behalf of all women, better practice in confronting woman abuse in intimate relationships.

When cases of male violence against women are made public, we can imagine that these women must have already gone through, or are about to go through, many experiences with the social service, health care, and criminal justice sectors, including the police force, which act as gatekeepers to receive and handle complaints from women before any charges can be laid. Both feminists and anti-racists working in the legal system would agree that the law, which we believe should serve and protect all citizens, regardless of class, gender, and race, does not operate neutrally or independently of the underlying power relationships in society. In light of anti-racist feminist theory, these "underlying power relationships" must be understood as having class, gender, and race connotations, which dictate women's experiences (hooks, 1984). Throughout history, ideas about the social locations of family, women, racial minority groups, and the relationships between them and society, have been effectively used to rationalize social inequality and inferior status. Patriarchal ideology and White supremacy have been quite successful in compelling racialized women to believe that their social, political, and economic subordination, including their psychological feelings of inferiority, are the consequence of natural forces rather than oppressive social relations. Even though the traditional ideologies of gender and racial relationships have changed somewhat over time, the tolerance of male and White supremacy has remained the same, more or less, overtly and covertly. This chapter discusses some controversial topics related to women's experiences with male violence in intimate relationships, and assesses whether women are better treated in our various social systems today after decades, if not centuries, of feminist efforts in making sure that women's appeal to live in a violence-free environment is to be taken seriously. The experiences of racialized minority women will be given special consideration throughout this chapter.

The problem of violence against women in intimate relationships is analyzed with respect to the context within which these incidents take place, and in the meaning of these events as experienced by the women involved. For instance, when wife abuse occurs in the family context, there is a distinct meaning for the victim and the perpetrator that is different from violence occurring in other social contexts. Many social historians point to the problem of wife assault in human history as being a result of "an autocratic patriarchal family structure" (Basch, 1982; Chapman, 1985, 1988; Perkin, 1989). Because men were granted higher social status than women, domestic assaults on women often reinforced their lesser status. This historic pattern of male-powered management of the family, often supported by the law, deprived women of all their legal rights in marriage. It was society's prejudice, in allocating fewer legal rights and a lower social status to women, that supported wife assault. History thus shows the way for our continued scrutiny of intimate partner violence. When we try to understand how family systems function today to oppress women, we also need to examine the other systems that have historically circumscribed family systems and influenced their functioning. If we study violence against women in intimate relationships without taking into account the contract of marriage and the unequal treatment men and women have received historically in the judicial realm, we will lose sight of the underlying power relationships between the sexes.

Although we have moved into the 21st century, we still witness today the unequal status and power prescribed to men and women. In Canada we find that women earn 30 percent less than men, even with post-secondary education (Morris, 2006). This implies that our society still regards men as more valuable in our production lines, workforce, and national economy.

Contemporary studies also show that because society supports the preservation of the family and its privacy, social policies and the law continue to encourage women to deal with marital conflicts in a private way (Pagelow, 1984; MacKinnon, 1990). These studies have demonstrated that societal values and attitudes, and the criminal justice and legal system, have mutually influenced and shaped each other, so the protection available for women is inadequate. For example, Pagelow found that the longer a woman remains in a violent relationship, the more likely she is to encounter unhelpful police intervention because the woman in the "problem family" is held responsible for doing something drastic or timely to change her situation. When the woman does not take these expected actions, the presumption is that the "violent episode" may not be as severe as reported because if it had been severe, the woman would have left the abuser a long time ago. Hence, the police officer who is called to the scene is likely to maintain a detached, peacekeeping-only attitude. As a result, fewer arrests are made and fewer charges are pressed.

There is a screening or filtering process involved in women's initial contacts with the law-enforcing sector. Police officers, as gatekeepers of the criminal justice system, often walk into a crime scene involving domestic violence against women with a personal set of values and beliefs about what comprises woman abuse by a male partner, as distinguished from a domestic dispute. Personal bias or "professional experience" can prevent 911 dispatchers, who pick up women's calls, from immediately forwarding women's cries for help to a nearby patrolling police officer for immediate action. Police officers who see "insufficient evidence" for a criminal trial may not take additional steps to bring the case forward to the court; in both circumstances, women are left to deal with their abuse alone. The only assurance that they secure is a verbal warning given to the abusive man before the police leave the scene. In other words, men who do not exhibit typical abuser stereotypes, or women who do not fit typical victim profiles, are screened out in "domestic dispute" scenarios. It is not uncommon to learn from news headlines about homicides of women whose families have been known by the police as having frequent "domestic disputes" prior to the tragedy.

Apparently, the power imbalance between men and women in society still has its ramifications in various authoritative social establishments.

When the ideologies of fixed gender differences and roles, family, and heterosexual marriage are so prevalent within an androcentric judicial system, if a case is brought to the court, it is very unlikely that the woman's suffering will be taken seriously (Chapman, 1988; Stanko, 1993). Because law enforcers are mostly male, they are more likely to support the male-defined notion of family than to sympathize with women's predicaments; thus claims of abuse of any form are considered less important than preserving the abuser's rights and autonomy in maintaining his family. Stanko reports that stranger assault is more likely to result in conviction and sentencing than intimate assault or battering. If abused women realize that the legal system may minimize, excuse, or accept a certain amount of violence in intimate relationships, they are likely to feel it is inappropriate or pointless to call the police when their intimate partners assault them. In fact, evidence shows that cases of wife assault are often dismissed or result in a lighter sentence (Comack, 1993; MacKinnon, 1990). It is observed that because of the androcentric legal system, men's liberty and civil rights are well protected whereas women's right to live free from male violence is jeopardized.

Over the past two decades we have witnessed a range of transformation in the response to intimate partner violence across all sectors of society, including the criminal justice and legal system, social service organizations, and health care institutions. The definition of intimate partner violence, particularly woman abuse, has been broadened to include not just physical assault but also psychological, economic, sexual, and verbal abuse inflicted by the partner of a woman with whom she lives under the concept of marriage, common-law union or live-in lovers (Mathes, 1991). This expansion of the definition illustrates an attempt to acknowledge women's different experiences of male violence and to lay a more solid foundation for arrests and charges. Learning from abused women's experiences, feminists and community advocates proposed that when police officers are called to houses where violence against women has taken place, they should ensure the women's safety by removing the abusive suspects for further investigation. This proposed practice attempts to address the protection that women need and the movement to prevent violence against women in the domestic sphere.

The provincial government of Ontario responded to women's quests by promoting a mandatory charge policy for domestic violence. However, this policy was not implemented widely and consistently until the launching of specialized domestic violence court in 1996 and 1997. The Ontario government invests $21 million annually through this Domestic Violence

Court Program (DVCP) to provide better support for victims of domestic violence and to hold offenders accountable for their violent behaviour. This province-wide court program aims at drawing police officers, Crown attorneys, probation officers, social workers, as well as those working with victims and offenders in the Victim/Witness Assistance Program and Partner Assault Response Program, to ensure the safety and other needs of domestic assault victims and their children.

In Toronto, there has been a coordinated community effort to address the issue of woman abuse (Woman Abuse Council of Toronto, 2002). The Metro Woman Abuse Council (MWAC) was established in 1991 to provide guiding force in creating a more integrated and coordinated community response to woman abuse, and to ensure better practice in service provision for assaulted women and their families. In 1999, MWAC incorporated itself as an independent non-profit organization and changed its name to Woman Abuse Council of Toronto (WACT). Instead of leaving it to the discretion of individual law enforcers, private practitioners, and service providers to respond to women's pleas for help, WACT takes a more proactive role in advocating for and with women, collaborating with all concerned sectors, and formulating Best Practice Guidelines for individual sectors involved to better improve their understanding of abused women's situations and to develop a more consistent response to ensure the quality of their services in meeting women's various needs.

Indeed, to respond to abused women's needs in a more effective and accountable way, some key principles and operational components are suggested to increase intra- and interagency consistency so that all helping professionals involved know how to handle woman abuse cases properly. According to WACT's Best Practice Guidelines (2002), first and foremost, every social institution or community agency must have some directive principles for its staff members to follow. There should be clearly stated policies and procedures made known to both the service providers and service users. To recognize the fact that no one organization can address fully the issue of woman abuse and meet all the needs required, it is recommended that a clearly articulated mechanism for interagency coordination and collaboration is identified. Because the responsibility of assisting abused women is shared within the community, all parties concerned are accountable for the women's safety and interests. Not only do individual organizations and helping professionals need to communicate with each other about the progress of the case, but also they need to assess their effectiveness as a team in providing services to the women. Independently and collaboratively, all organizations and individuals working with abused women are encouraged to advocate zero tolerance of woman abuse, and to educate the community at large to respond to the issue in an understanding and helpful way. Lastly, all policies, initiatives, and services are encouraged to monitor the development and evaluate the effectiveness of their individual work in meeting women's needs and holding their abusive partners accountable for their behaviour.

The concepts of providing Best Practice Guidelines for all concerned parties, and having specialized domestic violence court, are not unique in Canada as many states in America adopt a similar model to work with abused women in the context of family and intimate relationships (Buzawa & Buzawa, 1996; Syers & Edleson, 1992). This could be considered a North American approach, created as a more comprehensive response to intimate relationship violence. Theoretically, with the DVC program and the adoption of the Best Practice Guidelines by various service sectors of society, we should be able to see a decrease in domestic violence and hear women reporting a more positive experience within the criminal justice and health service systems. However, when we look into more recent statistics, we find that the provincial rates of spousal violence remain unchanged between 1999 and 2004, and that women continue to experience more severe violence than men within the family (Statistics Canada, 2005). Twenty-three percent of women reported that they were beaten, choked, or threatened with or had a gun or knife used against them by their intimate partner. In fact, recent studies showed that the increase in arrests does not necessarily prevent the recurrence of violence, and many women still do not feel they are safe or well protected (Buzawa & Buzawa, 1996; Dutton, 2003; Gelles, 1996; Schmidt & Sherman, 1996). Frequently, abusive men still opt for the use of physical force to exhibit their power and control over their female partners. In other words, while the Best Practice Guidelines may have shed light for some helping professionals to improve their professionalism in assisting abused women, there is still a gap between "the talk" and "the walk," and certainly stricter laws or mandatory arrest have not proven to be very effective either in eliminating male violence against women in intimate relationships.

As part of the DVC program, there are treatment groups for abusive men within the Partner Assault Response program (PAR) to address the issue of women's safety, and to increase men's accountability and responsibility for their violent temper and actions. The batterers' group program is a 16-week session in which participants are provided with an opportunity to scrutinize the beliefs and attitudes they use to rationalize their aggression, and to learn non-abusive approaches to handling conflict. Group participants are referred to, or mandated to join, the program as a part of their probation order, conditional sentence, or parole or as a requirement of bail prior to sentencing. The question is, "Do women who have a partner going through the PAR program feel safer and find some positive changes in their partners?" In their pilot study based on interviews with women of diverse backgrounds representing the Aboriginal, Southeast Asian, South Asian, Eastern and Southern European, and Anglophone communities, Pollack and Mackay (2003) reported that although there was a consensus among the women about the significance of the program, most of them felt stressed and tense, especially if they still lived with the abuser. The significance of the PAR program was that it provided the women with a sense of having a safety net to fall on in case violent threats occurred again during the time their partners were monitored by the program. However, the feeling of safety these women reported was transient, lasting only while their abuser was being watched. It is no wonder that all of the participants in the above cited study reported skepticism about whether their partners' behavioural change would last beyond the duration of the program.

If new protocols for mandatory arrests and batterers' programs do not work well enough to decrease male violence and increase women's safety in an authentic sense, how, then, could women protect themselves from male violence in intimate relationships or save themselves from life-threatening danger? A number of studies have indicated that more and more women are resorting to "an eye for an eye" responses to protect themselves or prevent their aggressive male partners from pinning them down (Busch & Rosenberg, 2004; DeLeon-Granados, Wells & Binsbacher, 2006; Henning & Feder, 2004; Martin, 1997; Miller, 2001). As a result, there has been a dramatic increase in the number of women being arrested and charged in domestic violence situations, both in the United States and Canada, when police assistance is called to the house. A study funded by the Status of Women Canada and conducted by the Woman Abuse Council of Toronto may shed some light for understanding this phenomenon of women's self-defence. It was found that 90 percent of the women who were charged in domestic violence circumstances were those who had experienced a history of physical, emotional, and sexual abuse by the same male partner. Ironically, in many cases it was the woman who, fearing for her life, called the police to her residence, thinking that she would acquire some protection from the authorities and have the police stop her male partner's abusive behaviour. To her dismay, at the end of an investigation, she was arrested because she fought back (Woman Abuse Council of Toronto, 2005). In Martin's study, mentioned above, she concluded that in cases of dual arrest there was a relatively large proportion of women who had been previously victimized in domestic violence episodes, and there was overenforcement of the mandatory arrest policy by some police departments.

While arresting and charging women with domestic violence may seem to be a fair response in some intimate partner violence situations, such an unintended consequence does increase women's risk of subsequent victimization by their partners, the criminal justice system, and society in general. Clearly, victim-blaming has become a frequent practice in our society's perception and treatment of abused women. Very often, women are blamed for "choosing" the wrong intimate partner, for provoking male aggressiveness in "ordinary" domestic disputes, and for not taking "appropriate" actions to extricate themselves and their children from dangerous relationships. Paradoxically, when women take "action" to protect themselves from immediate danger before the police can arrive at their house, or before any authority can issue a legally binding protection order, again they are blamed and punished for not responding "appropriately" to the circumstance. That is to say, no matter what they decide or how they act upon their decision, they are in a no-win situation and doomed. Women are obliged to choose between the two risks: accept the abuse and thus risk their lives, or fight back to protect themselves, at least temporarily, and thus risk being charged for responding with force. No wonder some feminists argue that although the analysis of the assault of women should be concentrated on the context of women's position in society, dominant stereotypes of women often provide "the common sense information to divide women in two categories, those who are nurturers and caregivers, and those who are nagging, selfish, and in violation of women's expected role" (Stanko, 1985, p. 50). When women are arrested and charged for self-defence, it is left to our judicial system to determine who is more "worthy" and who is more "deserving" to be pardoned or respectfully treated. In preserving society's traditional gender system and family structure, the judicial system codes women's behaviours negatively, thus blaming the victim once more, and freeing perpetrators from being held accountable for the harm they have inflicted.

Men and women arrested for domestic violence often represent different threats; further analysis of the circumstances of abuse is necessary. First of all, a number of studies have established that female defendants are significantly less likely to have a track record of violence that cautions for potential violence in the future (Busch & Rosenberg, 2004; Henning & Feder, 2004). Contrarily, many male defendants reveal a history of violent crimes committed inside and/or outside of the family, which poses a threat not just to the women and children with whom they live, but also to the general public. Secondly, women who act aggressively in domestic violence situations are those who have been victimized previously, thus they are more prone to responding violently in an attempt to defend themselves, especially when there is no help immediately available that they can count on (Martin, 1997; Stuart, Moore, Gordon, Hellmuth, Ramsey & Kahler, 2006). Thirdly, not only do women who use physical force in domestic disputes have a history of victimization in previous violence incidents, but quite a number of them indeed suffer from psychiatric disorders such as depression, anxiety disorder, post-traumatic stress disorder, drug dependence, and alcohol dependence (Tolman, 2001). In Busch and Rosenberg's study, substance abuse is frequently found in women who are arrested in domestic violence situations, so the cause of women's violent response is a complex one that calls for a deeper examination. Fourthly, it is reported in many studies that male offenders often minimize the severity of the damage that they have inflicted on their female partners whereas women offenders are more likely than men to testify that their aggression is primarily defensive in nature (Busch & Rosenberg, 2004; Henning, Jones & Holdford, 2005; Henning, Renauer & Holdford, 2006). When men do not see the harm they cause, they probably generate more fear and terror in their victims, whereas when women are in the defensive mode, and considering typical differences in physique, they are less likely to terrorize or dominate their male partners with threats of physical force.

The implication for women being charged for their "aggressive" response is multifaceted. First and foremost, the perpetrators may see it as an indirect way of controlling their female partners. On the one hand, knowing that when a woman is afraid of being arrested and charged, she is likely to tolerate his behaviour, the abuser may feel no need to control his own temper and aggression. On the other hand, believing that the police are going to press charges on any woman who resists with force, the abuser may lie about what happened by minimizing his violent behaviour, exaggerating his "injury," and ascribing all bruises or cuts to the woman's "violence." He can file a formal complaint and push the police to arrest the woman as well (Woman Abuse Council of Toronto, 2005). Rajah, Frye and Haviland (2006) pointed out that retaliatory arrests against women are common since the mandatory arrest policy has been implemented in all occurrences where police intervene in domestic violence situations.

In addition, the focus on an isolated episode that has occurred in the presence of the police, rather than on the continuum of violence and the power struggle between intimate partners in which the predominant aggressors are men only, indicates that the criminal justice system fails to utilize a gender analysis of women's use of force in domestic violence situations (Miller, 2001). Such an incomplete approach often benefits male perpetrators and disadvantages women. It was observed that in many domestic violence situations in which women were charged, the male abusers had criminal records that involved violent crimes, but the male violence was not brought up in court, thus resulting in the women being convicted of a violent offence (Woman Abuse Council of Toronto, 2005). What these cases show is that there is a crack in this gender-neutral mandatory charge policy when no context of the ongoing abusive relationship can be submitted for consideration when a woman is being charged for domestic violence. Moreover, when women are arrested and charged for their aggressive response to their abuse, they face a range of problems such as limited knowledge about their rights and court procedures, a language barrier (if their native tongue is not English or French), a loss of employment, imprisonment, a loss of child custody, and even deportation if they have not yet obtained their citizenship in Canada (Chesney-Lind, 2002; Gillis, Diamond, Jebely, Orekhovsky, Ostovich, Macisaac, Sagrati & Mandell, 2006). Hence, while the mandatory charge policy is originally developed out of a response to women's quest for protection, it turns out to work against their interests.

Furthermore, because of their social location, women of ethnic minority groups, immigrant women, and women of no official status are also negatively affected by this gender-neutral mandatory arrest policy. The Canadian Council on Social Development (2004) reported that abused immigrant and visible minority women often express concerns for systemic or structural oppression, such as concerns about their sponsorship arrangements if they decide to leave an abusive relationship, racial discrimination in the judicial system, the marginality of immigrant services, and a lack of access to legal information or support services. If these women are made to believe that despite their victimization, they will lose their status in Canada if they leave their abuser, and if they fight back and are arrested and charged, they may be deported, then of course they will feel trapped and immobilized. Realizing that they are economically poorer than the dominant White class, marginalized as second-class citizens, perceived as racially inferior, and with little knowledge about their new society and how its systems operate, these women are convinced to continue enduring their abuse in private.

If the mandatory arrest policy does not consider the whole range of social and gender factors that may affect visible minority or immigrant women, the policy's good intentions will be outweighed by its cost to victimized women. As we have learned from many previous studies, service providers, and personal testimonies, even when abused women are in great danger of personal harm, in order to avoid putting their male partners in jail (leading to a loss of substantial family income, disintegration of the family, deprivation of a father for their children, and the defamation of their entire family or ethnic group), many of them are reluctant to get the police involved. When their rights to defend themselves in violent circumstances lead to the judicial system's condemnation or reprimand, these women may well just put up with the abuse, risking death at the hands of an aggressive intimate partner. Does a gender-neutral mandatory arrest policy increase these women's vulnerability, further reducing their position in the social order?

Last but not least, while intimate partner violence is a problem affecting women of all races and ethnicities, socio-economic classes, and age groups, sexism, racism, classism, as well as ageism, will all work against the well-being and safety of racial minority women, younger women, and women possessing fewer means in our society (Avakame, 2001; Yoshioka, Dinoia & Ullah, 2001). In many visible minority groups, women are already assigned to a lower social status than men; they are encouraged to comply with their husbands' demands even if it means that they may suffer coercion and violence. If a woman resists by fighting back and subsequently is arrested by the police and prosecuted in the court, this practice and its entire process will definitely reinforce the traditional sexist attitudes and beliefs in their culture, labelling the woman who fights for her safety or for her life as an "aggressive bitch" who deserves imprisonment. And if the results of Avakame's study illustrate a general trend in which the police are more likely to arrest the offender and press charges if the victim is affluent, Caucasian, and older, then the chances for younger and poorer women of colour to find safety, to feel supported, and to secure legal protection are slimmer. Not only are women still at risk, but visible minority women are less safe.

In the past, society often blamed victims for staying in abusive relationships and not removing themselves and their children from physical and psychological danger. It was believed then that those who stay are willing and psychologically weak victims. As society progresses, we learn from different studies that because of a lack of information and financial resources, insufficient education and vocational training, continuous threats posed by the abusers, the stigma attached to single-parent families, and/or the constant fear of revenge, it is extremely difficult socially, economically, and psychologically for women to leave their abusive partners. In response to women's experiences and their quests for more resources and better protection, feminist advocates working in the community and in the judicial system have been successful in developing Best Practice Guidelines and pressing for a more protective policy to be implemented in the social services, health care, and criminal justice and legal sectors. As a result, the Canadian government has introduced new policies and mandates at the federal and provincial levels that acknowledge that woman abuse is a serious social problem deserving our attention and the investment of resources. However, as we have discussed here, more recent studies show that women continue to be victimized at the hands of their abusive partners and in the criminal justice system. They are still not safe and not well protected. Where do we go from here and what more can be done to remedy the unintended consequences of mandatory arrest policies?

There is a myth that abused women are generally good at estimating their own risk and taking appropriate action to protect themselves and their children. However, according to some current studies, only about half of the actual and attempted homicide women victims accurately determined their risk of fatality (Campbell et al., 2003; Nicolaidis et al., 2003). The findings of the above studies suggested that half the time women underestimate their risks because they are desensitized by the frequent violence in their lives. They are accustomed to witnessing their intimate partner's aggressive behaviour or being involved in domestic violence situations, so they cannot foresee the full force or the ultimate ramifications of this brutality, and they lose their lives. This is why it is not reasonable to expect abused women not to defend themselves with force when the circumstances require it. If we do not want to push women back to being passive victims, our practice and policies must allow a gender analysis of domestic violence situations. In the process of investigating what happens, the police and the judicial system need to consider the context of the relationship, and to identify the primary perpetrator of the violence before arresting or pressing charges against the woman. They also need to take into account the woman's psychological state to see if her behaviour is a manifestation of a long-standing abusive relationship or a psychiatric problem resulting from abuse. If either is the case, instead of pressing charges against the woman, the most helpful and effective treatment would be to send her for individual counselling, as opposed to the group socio-educational experience that is commonly ordered for male batterers.

As a matter of fact, the traditional DVPs oriented for male batterers are inappropriate for most female offenders in domestic violence cases.

Hamberger and Potente (1994) argued that unlike male batterers who are arrested for the harm they intentionally force on their intimate partners, women who are arrested are mostly real victims of male violence who happen to defend themselves during a violent attack by their spouse. As such, the appropriate treatment for these women should focus on deconstructing their feelings of victimization, the exploration of their resistance options, the formation of safety plans, and the effective regulation of emotions. With visible minority women and immigrant women who are not familiar with how the system operates in protecting their rights, and are concerned about systemic or structural oppression, treatment programs should also include helping them to build a more solid social network, get familiarized with the various services available in the community, cultivate a sense of trust and confidence, and connect themselves with some culturally appropriate programs. While we agree that "an eye for an eye" is not the way to confront male violence in the domestic sphere (or anywhere in the world), we also need to express our concern for gender inequality in intimate partner violence and the current flaws in the mandatory arrest policies.

Unfortunately, while our Canadian governments should commit more resources and efforts to promote gender equality in our society and help those who suffer male violence to confront the problem more effectively, there are only cutbacks. On April 1, 2006, the Conservative federal government announced that it would close 12 Status of Women offices across Canada to save $5 million in its budget. This action, no doubt, will ultimately affect all women's organizations across Canada, reducing the voices of women and limiting the development of many women's services. Obviously, there will be a rippling effect in this budget cut to diminish women's advocacy and grassroots organizations' ability to work for women's equality and welfare. When violence against women is still a huge social problem, the lack of a gender analysis in the context of domestic violence situations further complicates abused women's decision-making abilities in dealing with their abusive experiences. Abused women and their children are trapped in a no-win situation. If they stay in the relationships, they may end up dead. If they fight back, women are sent to court or put in irrelevant programs or, worse, lose their status in Canada and are deported from the country, their children losing their mothers, placed in foster care, and left with deep emotional scars for life. The Conservative government's arbitrary and inconsiderate move will keep abused Aboriginal women, women of colour, immigrant women, and non-status women in Canada, along with their children, disproportionately impoverished.

How will we change women's status if we do not have a national voice and equal access to law-making, in order to bring about equality and justice? How will we effectively advocate for abused women and their children if our feminist and grassroots organizations are further marginalized and struggling to survive in the face of the budget cuts? Given abused women's dreary realities and the many gaps we witness in the current systems and policies, the Conservative government should not be reducing resources for women, and thereby setting a bad example for the provincial and municipal governments. If billions of dollars can be spent on military training and defence attendant upon threats of "terrorism," why should our government not reallocate the money to help women cope with the nightmare of male violence in their lives? Victims and survivors of intimate partner violence do not need lip service or sympathy, nor should they expect incarceration. They need better understanding, supportive and tangible services, practical programs, justice, and, most of all, equality and safety in the real sense.

Part II

Experiences of Activists and Helping Professionals

Chapter 4

Challenges, Connections, and Creativity: Anti-violence Work with Racialized Women

Cyndy Baskin

INTRODUCTION

Scenario 1: A young Aboriginal woman is referred to a shelter with her three-month-old baby. Two weeks after she moves in, her boyfriend, the baby's father, assaults her during an argument. The police are called, he is charged, and a restraining order is placed on him to keep him from contacting her. Staff at the shelter support her through the process and refer her to a group for assaulted women. During the course of meeting with the group, she discloses that she still loves her boyfriend and that they have been seeing each other secretly. The group leader tells her that she is putting herself and her child in danger and that she must report this to the Children's Aid Society (CAS).

One week later, the young Aboriginal woman is visited by a CAS worker and told about the seriousness of returning to her boyfriend, a move that could place her baby in need of protection. She is encouraged to continue with the group and learn about herself, the cycle of abuse, and how to protect herself and her baby. The young woman returns to the group, but is mistrustful and careful about what she reveals. She continues to secretly meet her boyfriend and even though she is ambivalent about the relationship, she chooses not to talk about it with the group for fear of CAS intervention.

Scenario 2: A woman, her children, and her husband have come to Canada as refugees. The husband was abusive at home in East Africa and later in Tanzania, where they went after the civil war. He has applied for refugee status for the whole family, including his wife. In Canada, he continues to physically and verbally abuse his wife. She believes she cannot report because no one helped her in the past when she was abused. She is in a foreign country with a different language and culture. Her husband is the head of the household and every letter from immigration is directed to him. She has no one else to talk to, and her husband always reminds her that he can send her back to East Africa and keep the children with him. Sometimes he says, "I will fail the immigration and they will deport us back to East Africa or Tanzania; then I will kill you and marry another one who will look after the kids."

On the surface, it may appear as though the women in these two scenarios have little in common. One is Aboriginal, the other is East African. One lives in a shelter, the other with her family. One is a Canadian citizen, the other a refugee, yet they are both victims of domestic violence who have been silenced by Canadian systems—the first by child welfare and the second by immigration policies.

This chapter will explore similarities, differences, and connections among racialized women who are abused by their partners. It includes the voices of seven racialized women who work in the area of anti-violence as service providers, activists, and educators. It is set as an interview, with one woman (Cyndy Baskin) asking the others five questions about some of the issues regarding this form of violence and recording their responses along with references to the literature and an analysis. The format and the questions were decided upon through the consensus of us all. The women whose voices speak in these pages are connected through their involvement in many initiatives, such as Best Practices in Holistic Approaches to Safety within Families, which is coordinated through the Woman Abuse Council of Toronto. We wish to acknowledge and thank this organization for its leadership in anti-violence work and for presenting opportunities where the voices of racialized women are truly heard.

We seven are:

Habiba Adan (HA): Habiba has worked in the Violence against Women Program at the Family Service Association of Toronto for the past 10 years. She works with both Somali-speaking and non-Somali clients. Habiba has a master's degree in economics from Vanderbilt University (U.S.) and a BSW from York University.

Sharon Allen (SA): Sharon is a Muslim woman of African-Caribbean descent who has worked to address some of the issues that affect racialized, minoritized, and marginalized people living in Canada/North America. Her work and studies have centred on the intersecting experiences of oppression for women and children. She is an active director at the Islamic Social Services and Resources Association (ISSRA) and a front-line social worker at the Macaulay Child Development Centre. Sharon has an MSW from the University of Toronto.

Charlene Avalos (CA): Charlene has worked as a social worker for the last 25 years in both First Nations communities and at Native Child and Family Services of Toronto. She is dedicated to a holistic approach, which combines traditional Aboriginal models of healing with contemporary forms of intervention. Charlene has a master's of social work from the University of British Columbia and teaches as a sessional instructor in the School of Social Work at Ryerson University.

Cyndy Baskin (CB): Cyndy is of Mi'kmaq and Irish descent and currently teaches in the School of Social Work at Ryerson University. She has 20 years of experience as a social worker/helper with Aboriginal communities. Cyndy has a MSW from the University of Toronto and a PhD from the Ontario Institute for Studies in Education, University of Toronto.

Antoinette Clarke (AC): Antoinette is a Black woman of African-Caribbean descent who is an adjunct professor in the School of Social Work, Atkinson Faculty of Liberal and Professional Studies at York University. She has an MSW from Wilfred Laurier University, and teaches both in the School of Social Work at York University and in the Continuing Education program at McMaster University. Antoinette has over 25 years of experience working with abused women and marginalized populations. She is currently a co-facilitator for a workshop on Assessing for Power Imbalance and Domestic Violence in Mediation and the coordinator of the Peel Family Mediation and Parent Education Program.

Janet Kim (JK): Janet is a second-generation Korean-Canadian employed as the Domestic Violence Prevention Program coordinator at the Korean Canadian Women's Association (KCWA) Family and Social Services and as a pastor at the Korean Philadelphia Presbyterian Church. She holds a bachelor of arts degree in psychology and a master of divinity degree in counselling.

Angie Rupra (AR): Angie is a young South Asian woman who has completed her bachelor of social work at Ryerson University and master's of social work at York University. She is currently a community development worker with the Woman Abuse Council of Toronto and brings front-line experience in the violence against women sector to inform her work.

DEFINITIONS AND LITERATURE REVIEW

The seven women speaking to you from these pages and the many women they are referring to are from diverse communities. Together, we have chosen to refer to ourselves as "racialized women" because, despite our individuality, this is what all of us have in common vis-à-vis the dominant society. Racialized women face racism, are targeted by White supremacy, and are subjected to many forms of oppression based on their visible racial-ethnic identities. Thus, the primary objective of this chapter is to challenge the Canadian systems that are a result of colonialism, imperialism, racism, sexism, and classism, which cause and maintain violence against racialized women.

A review of the literature on racialized women who are victims of domestic violence indicates that they face a complicated challenge. For immigrant and visible minority women, the fact that they are abused is further compounded by factors such as immigration status, and the social, cultural, linguistic, racial, and legal environment in which they live. For Aboriginal women, the abuse directed at them is characterized by economic marginalization, racism, and sexism, making them the most marginalized population in the territory of their ancestors. Many reports on racialized women who are victims of domestic violence have been commissioned by Canadian governments and written by various community groups. In particular, those written by community groups have documented the gaps in services and emphasize the need for culturally appropriate and community-based agencies to fill the gaps (Agnew, 1998).

A common theme that arises from the literature is the need for more comprehensive research on the prevalence, nature, and characteristics of the abuse of racialized women along with the contributing factors (Baskin, 2005; Miedema, 2000; Province of Nova Scotia, 2000; Bruce, 1998; Tjaden & Thoennes, 1998; West, 1997; Macleod & Shin, 1990). Another is a call for support services in the voluntary sector and for personnel in the justice system to attain "cultural competency" in working with racialized women. According to Smith (2004), "this would ensure that immigrant and visible minority women who experience partner abuse can access services that are more appropriate to their needs, and that the patterns and determinants of violence in specific communities are better understood" (p. 2). Although I support future research on more appropriate services for racialized women to address their needs and examine the determinants of violence in our communities, I have two major concerns with much of the literature. The first is a lack of structural analysis when it comes to the abuse of racialized women with no mention of state violence. The second is a lack of support by many racialized women for the "cultural competency" approach. These concerns will be addressed throughout this chapter by the women who participated in it.

CHALLENGES IN ANTI-VIOLENCE WORK WITH RACIALIZED WOMEN

Cyndy Baskin (CB): Clearly, there are many challenges in anti-violence work with racialized women. However, what would you say are the most significant ones?

Charlene Avalos (CA): The most significant challenges in anti-violence work with First Nations women from a service providers' point of view is mistrust of the system and all it stands for. Over the last 10 years, numerous efforts have been made on the part of women mostly to draw attention to family violence and all its serious impacts on women and children. As a result, changes were recently made to child welfare legislation in respect to family violence and the duty to report. This has had serious repercussions. While the legislation can be heralded as very progressive for women in our fight for equality, it has caused problems in many communities.

In First Nations communities, violence cannot be dealt with in a piecemeal, linear, punitive way. It cannot be understood and approached from mainstream models of intervention. As a result of dealing with it in this way, much violence has gone underground in First Nations communities. Many women who try to get help around this issue learn very fast to keep it a secret for fear their children will be removed from them. This fear, which is all too real, both presently and historically, is the greatest fear Aboriginal women face. Many choose to live [with] and endure violence because of this.

Angie Rupra (AR): One of the biggest challenges in anti-violence work with racialized women is the abuse that stems from women's immigration status. I really believe an area of abuse that needs to be defined, in order to give it credibility, is immigration abuse. Another issue that the Women Abuse Council of Toronto has heard front-line workers say repeatedly is that often times when police are called to a home because of a domestic violence situation, interpreters are not called when a woman does not speak English. This is clearly discriminatory and unjust. It is an additional barrier that a woman who does not speak English often faces when in situations of abuse. If police are called on a domestic assault and they believe a woman does not have status, she may be reported to immigration.

Habiba Adan (HA): Women also may not understand that their children are affected when the mother is hit. They say, "He hits me, not the children." Being abused is a challenge. Some women don't see being hit as abuse. They may see being hit as part of marriage or there may not be any words in their languages for abuse. For example, in the Somali language, "beat up" and "kill" are the same word. Language barriers get in the way of needing to educate women of that in Canada. Obviously, some women only want to speak to another woman who speaks the same language and is from the same cultural background, so that she will be understood.

Janet Kim (JK): Another barrier related to language is mobility. Many women don't drive and their only access to transportation, including the Toronto Transit Commission (TTC), is in the company of their husbands. Since they don't know the language, they can't read signs and, consequently, they don't learn to access the transit system on their own. Their mobility is severely restricted for fear of getting lost and they would, almost always, have their kids in tow. Given the barriers, they think it's best to remain confined to their homes and the neighbouring areas.

AR: Sponsorship abuse is another issue that workers have repeatedly identified as a serious issue facing immigrant women. Abusive partners often tell women that they will be deported if they report the abuse, when in reality, this is not the case. A woman who is sponsored by her partner will not be deported just because sponsorship breakdown has occurred. Or a woman may feel trapped because her partner will tell her that he will be deported if she reports the abuse. If he is a Canadian citizen, he cannot be deported. However, if he is a permanent resident or a refugee and is found guilty of assault, he could be deported. This is a way in which the abuser may try to manipulate the woman to make her stay in the abusive relationship and not report the abuse.

HA: Yes, exactly. The woman believes him and stays silent out of fear. Also, if she comes forward and says she's abused by her partner, she may be labelled as a bad wife and woman by her cultural or religious community. She will be seen as the one who caused the marriage to break down. A divorce will be seen as her fault. There is often great shame in a woman living on her own and it is unlikely that anyone in the community will want to marry her. Then there's the issue of money. Chances are the man in the family is the breadwinner and controls the money. If he's gone, the money's gone. It's so hard for a racialized woman who does not speak English or French to raise her children on her own. She will inevitably live in poverty, be alone, and have to move from place to place. She will wonder if this life is better than what she had when she was with her husband. Then, of course, social assistance will make her go after the man for child support, which puts her in danger. Even so, most men don't follow through with support and, if they do, they dictate to the woman on how she can spend the money.

Sharon Allen (SA): It all comes down to systemic challenges. Is the system really intended to help women live violence free? Why are we not preparing young girls to know that violence in relationships is real and can occur to them? Why do we not teach girls to think about the potential of abuse? And why don't we train girls on what to do if or when it happens? The systems such as the courts, CAS, the police, social assistance, social housing, etc., are set up to make it as difficult as possible for women to live violence-free. The consequences are dire for women who try to get out of abusive situations. We end up playing a game because choices are so limited. Service providers are directing women as to what to do even though they don't have the same reality as their clients. We need to ask ourselves, "What are we helping?" and "Who are we helping?" Society is set up to actually keep women in violence. If we wanted women to live violence-free, then we would be working together to make it happen. Are we really working to end violence against women?

Antoinette Clark (AC): We give women a prescription of what to do rather than listen to what they want and need.

SA: Yes, whereas what we must do is let the women lead, rather than us service providers leading.

AC: Perhaps another challenge is how our cultures have been so tampered with that we have lost our supportive structures. In the Caribbean, for instance, there are both patriarchal and matriarchal structures. It's acceptable for a woman to leave a man who hurts her, but today colonial systems, such as religion and government, don't allow women to survive on their own here in Canada. It's no longer okay for women to be single moms perhaps, yet historically these women were accepted and there were ways of supporting them. These ways have been eroded over time by racist and sexist systems.

HA: In Somalia, a woman's family and community, especially her father and brothers, could take her out of an abusive relationship. Here in Canada, if a woman's brother hits a man who hit his sister, the police are called, and the woman's brother can be charged with assault.

Analysis

For racialized women who are immigrants, the first barrier they likely face is the lack of English or French language skills. This inability to communicate effectively keeps them powerless, isolated, and at the lowest political, social, and economic levels of Canadian society (Pinedo & Santinoli, 1991; Jawani, 2001; Miedema, 2000; Agnew, 1998; West, 1997). Thus, a language barrier affects their social relations and employment opportunities and limits their access to services and resources. However, the vast majority of Aboriginal women in Canada speak English, and yet they are the most marginalized population in the country. Clearly, there is much more to this than a language barrier.

I would emphasize that one of the contributing factors to domestic violence for many racialized women—both Aboriginal and immigrant women—is the loss of support networks. By migrating from a reserve community to an urban centre or immigrating from a home country to Canada, women may face vulnerability through being isolated by geography, culture, friends, and family. In their reserve communities and countries of origin, women may have been able to go to their extended families for help. Respected elders and spiritual leaders could assist in resolving problems, supporting women, and holding abusive men accountable for their behaviour. However, when these traditional methods of dealing with problems are no longer available to women, they must approach strangers in social service agencies for help. This Westernized concept of going to a stranger who gets paid to help is a foreign one to many racialized women and culturally inappropriate. In addition, as the women participating in this chapter have pointed out, racialized women fear that services intended to help may report them to immigration or CAS. These are not irrational fears. We all know situations where this is exactly what happened.

Racialized women who immigrate to Canada are in a terrible bind referred to as the "sponsorship effect" (Smith, 2004). Most of them come here as family members, so their immigration status is dependent on the status of their husbands. A woman who has been sponsored by her spouse is indebted to him. She feels gratitude and a sense that she has no control over her life. Add to this a situation where a man deliberately keeps the woman unaware of her rights, telling her she has none since he sponsored her into Canada. There is no doubt that an abused woman will believe she will be deported and lose her children. Social service agencies, medical services, and schools ask about one's status and then base their responses on it while often reporting the answers to immigration. Plus, women cannot get landed status if they are not self-supporting or are on social assistance, which they likely will be if they leave their abusive husbands.

Men's "brainwashing" and women's fear, however, are not the whole story here. Abused racialized women are, in fact, discriminated against by certain laws. The police have a directive to contact immigration if a woman calls them for help. This means they have no right to safety or protection as they cannot go to the police. Aboriginal women know only too well what it is like to not be able to go to the authorities for assistance. Consider Oka, 1990, when the Canadian military were called against Canadian citizens for the first time in history—citizens who were Aboriginal women and children. Consider Ipperwash, 1995, when the Ontario Provincial Police (OPP) did the same. Consider all of the missing and murdered Aboriginal women over the past 20 years, particularly in Western Canada.

Then there is the justified fear of what will happen to racialized men if the police and other forms of the criminal justice system become involved. It may be that some of the racialized men who come to Canada are from countries where they have been jailed and tortured, and they fear that this, too, could happen here. It may also be past experiences in Canada for Aboriginal peoples, who are overrepresented in jails and prisons and receive longer sentences than White men. It may also be that racial profiling is a grim reality in cities such as Toronto, especially for Black youth and Muslim men at the present time.

PROMOTING EMPOWERMENT AND SAFETY

CB: Anti-violence work focuses on facilitating empowerment processes with women while doing everything we can to ensure their safety and that of their children. How do you promote both women's empowerment and their safety?

AR: The traditional understanding of safety and how it is often used in violence against women's services is a very mainstream concept. It is often interpreted to mean women's physical safety. While this is an important element that cannot be ignored when working with women who are experiencing violence, it cannot be the only component assessed.

For example, the sense of community may differ from a newcomer woman and a woman whose identity has been shaped by Western norms. Many qualitative research studies have described a newcomer woman's identity as being strongly linked to the identity of her community. Service delivery issues often arise as many violence against women services are individualistic in nature. Women are often seen one-to-one with the counsellor and issues relating to her family cannot be adequately met because of limited organizational mandates. This has often been the case when a woman seeks support for herself and her partner. Very few social service agencies in Toronto are able to meet this need, although it is a service [that] many front-line workers say has been requested by women. True, issues have arisen around keeping women safe while they are engaged in couples therapy with an abusive partner; the woman's safety must, of course, be taken into consideration. However, that doesn't mean we should ignore what women are asking from us. Given the financial and resource constraints of agencies, organizations have not been able to give this issue as much attention as it deserves. It is a form of service delivery that challenges mainstream notions of working with women experiencing violence. Fortunately, there are a few communities in Toronto that are beginning to explore this issue further. A few, such as the Punjabi Community Health Centre and the Family Group conferencing model at the George Hull Centre in Toronto, are doing so.

AC: When it comes to safety in mediation approaches, screening for violence and the severity of it, along with the kind of approach that will be taken, is crucial. There must be a safety plan in place throughout the process. A standard set of questions ought to be asked of the man and of the woman to avoid her of being accused by the man for providing information about his behaviour. If, however, the woman wants to proceed with mediation, there are different ways of doing so. For example, the couple can be in separate rooms whereby the mediator goes back and forth between them, which we call "the shuttle." They can arrive and leave at different times. Options are available to women and they can make decisions. This is different from court, where a woman is told by a lawyer what to do. There are always individual sessions before a couple ever meets together. Some of these are educational sessions, where women learn about the systems in place so they understand what may or may not happen and the consequences of this. It's important to remember, though, that the structures and plans put in place are only as good as each individual mediator.

CA: I believe that in First Nations communities women's empowerment, as well as their safety, can be promoted by attacking the issue of family violence holistically and in a framework of community development using Aboriginal-specific models and interventions. The present legislation must be examined and changed to create more opportunities for culturally based approaches. This work needs to be multidimensional and include education, prevention, intervention, treatment, and healing.

On an individual basis, women need to feel secure enough with service providers that they can work through their many ambivalent feelings and still make their own choices. Many want their abusive partners to receive help and they do not want to leave them. Women need to know that workers will be helpful and supportive, giving them alternatives and room to make decisions. It is through this relationship that women feel supported enough to make difficult choices. Safety and empowerment also refers to men who are abusive. Abusers need to be given an opportunity to heal. Many abusive men are very hurt and traumatized individuals who never learned how to deal with their own pain constructively. Many were abused growing up and/or witnessed abuse themselves. They must be given the opportunity to do the work they need to do to make changes.

AR: Safety and empowerment should not be viewed as two sides of one coin; there is not a clear dichotomy between these two terms. Some agencies have been able to effectively use family-based methods in situations of woman abuse by meeting women's needs while still promoting their safety.

Granted, we need to be cautious of what we mean by "effective." This is an area where our service sector needs to become active and we need to begin documenting what we mean by effective. Documentation is power and if we are to push the mainstream service sector to widen its scope and mandate, we will need to be able to show them how women's safety can still be promoted in these approaches.

If we revisit what the definition of empowerment means, then our services are in dire need of change. What I mean by this is that many newcomer women are telling us that traditional and mainstream services need to change to meet their needs! How "empowering" can our services be when they are ignoring the needs women are expressing? This is not to discount the work that the woman abuse sector has done. What currently exists needs to continue to exist as it does meet some of the women's needs. What I'm saying is that we need to look at service delivery along a continuum, and on a continuum of servicing needs, we are falling short. Therefore, in addition to what we are already offering, we need to be offering other options for women whose needs are not being fully met by what currently exists. For instance, while traditional mainstream-type services focus on addressing women and children's physical safety, they may not address the danger women will feel when their community finds out they have disclosed abuse. Just as much weight needs to be placed by social services on emotional safety, financial safety, and spiritual safety.

SA: Rather than empower women, we need to remind them that they have power. In some Muslim communities, the Qur'an has been used to disempower women. This is not its purpose. Men and women need to be aware of this. Thus, ISSRA [Islamic Social Services and Resources Association] has created a document [*Conflict Prevention: The Islamic Perspective*], which provides evidence from the Qur'an that women have God-given rights and power. This document frames and conceptualizes what the Qur'an says about relationships between men and women without a patriarchal slant, which is where interpretations that disempower women come from. This is why ISSRA was created—to remind men and women in Toronto about the systemic interpretations that is man- or woman-made.

Analysis

Empowerment and safety are about social risks that are the external conditions, pressures, norms, and practices that contribute to the dangers of an abused woman (Jaaber & Dasgupta, 2003). Outsiders to a particular community may not be aware that certain social risks—which can be personal, institutional, or cultural—exist. Nevertheless, they are only too real for women on the inside. These risks are not individual to a particular woman nor are they based on isolated incidents. Rather, they are the current results of history, policies, and practices that may have been created to protect society, but which, in reality, further marginalize abused racialized women. If I am a homeless, Aboriginal woman who has been drinking alcohol with my boyfriend who assaults me, how likely is it that I will contact the police for assistance? I know that the focus will be on the fact that I am a "homeless, drunk Indian" rather than an assaulted woman. If I am a Muslim immigrant woman from Iraq who speaks no English and knows no one other than my husband's family, how likely is it that I will leave my abusive husband? I know that I will be socially ostracized by both my husband's family and my community, and by Canadian society as a whole based on what they think I am. As we saw in the previous section, the systems—family and criminal courts, child welfare, social services—are social risks for most abused racialized women as well.

In terms of assessing a woman's safety while reminding her of the power she holds inside, service providers need to look at a woman's situation from all imaginable angles. This must include looking at her survival skills, strengths, and gifts and how she has used these thus far. How has she coped with and resisted both the abuse she has endured and the discrimination she faces?

For Aboriginal women, the reminders of their power need to include cultural empowerment. Aboriginal women traditionally played a central role within the family, community, government, and in spiritual ceremonies. Women need to hear the traditional teachings that were passed on through the oral histories of Aboriginal peoples from generation to generation, which focus on men and women as being equal in power and having autonomy within their personal lives. In this way, they will come to understand that they were never considered inferior in Aboriginal communities until European economic and cultural expansion undermined their value as equal partners in these communities. I believe a major key to putting an end to female mistreatment in Aboriginal communities is the return of women to their traditional roles. A restoration of women's traditional responsibilities and positions of equality in the family and community is one of the ways of eliminating family violence, perhaps not only for Aboriginal women, but for all racialized women.

I will finish this section with a quote from Andrea Gunraj (2005), the outreach manager at the Metropolitan Action Committee on Violence against Women and Children (METRAC) in Toronto: "True safety doesn't come from individuals. I can buy security gadgets and learn how to defend myself, but it won't do anything to make the world a safer place. And it definitely won't benefit those who are most vulnerable to experiencing violence. True safety comes from community, from diverse people creating an inclusive vision for safety and working together to make a difference" (p. 8).

POWER IMBALANCES

CB: The vast majority of service providers and activists in anti-violence work are women as are the victims of domestic violence. There exists the potential for power imbalance between these two groups of women, which is, of course, a huge issue in relationships between women and the men who abuse them. So how do you address these power imbalances between women who are service users and those who are service providers?

JK: Addressing the power imbalance requires a sensitivity and mindfulness of the women we serve as service providers. The tension that exists between service providers and service users is not simply between the provider of help and the recipient of help. It is also a woman's vulnerable self being exposed and known by another, seemingly more "together" woman. Service users frequently feel inferior to service providers and the feeling is triggered by something as basic as how we dress. Hence, we need to be cautious about dressing like a "professional" or an "expert" and refrain from presenting ourselves as financially better off than the women we serve.

We also need to be conscious of how our own personal relationship status affects service users. At our agency, a co-worker never wore her wedding rings out of sensitivity for the women who were divorced from their husbands or in the process of escaping from them. Service users will notice the engagement ring or the wedding band on your left hand and may experience heightened vulnerability as they reflect on their own painful marriages and their abusive husbands.

The women come from marriages where the husband did everything, so in this new relationship, albeit a professional relationship, they may transfer that same responsibility and expectation to the service provider. They may ask the service provider for everything. There needs to be a balance so service providers assist the women, but also facilitate their ability to do things independently.

SA: I agree. It may be that the service user needs the service provider to take the place of the husband by telling her what to do. The provider needs to deconstruct this form of interaction with the service user. For some women, there has never been a time when they were not subservient to someone. Today, it's a husband, before it was a father. Today it's an employer or social assistance, before it was a brother. Sometimes women need to ask an *imam* (religious leader), who is seen as an authority, "What should I do if he hits me?" and hear from the *imam*, "You leave him." This is challenging for us at ISSRA and for many service providers, who can inadvertently take on the abusive husband's role by telling a woman what she must do. The aim is to assist the woman in developing a critical understanding of why she makes the choices or accepts the decisions that she does. Is the woman doing something because someone else tells her to do so or because she has made the decision that this is what she will do? These are some of the questions we must ask ourselves. We must also keep them in mind in our work with abused, racialized women.

Analysis

As service providers, activists, and educators, ultimately our role is to facilitate the reclaiming of power that is denied to abused, racialized women. Power takes on many forms and it exists in the relationships between "professionals" and "clients." Abused, racialized women who reach out for help and get out of violent relationships are strong survivors. Once they learn about the dynamics of domestic violence and begin to heal, they need some economic power that comes from training, education, and opportunity. However, what tends to happen is that we "professionals" refer them to training that will lead them into low-paid, dead-end jobs. Why is this the case when, for example, racialized women who are survivors of domestic violence could instead be in an empowering place of reaching out to women currently facing abuse in their communities? Would this not be a way in which women could be agents of social change, thereby truly empowering themselves? One of the reasons why they are not in these positions is because the field of social services is professionalized, requiring providers to have academic qualifications and professional work experience. Pinedo and Santinoli (1991) support this analysis:

> Professionalism mitigates against our values of diversity and of giving former battered women leadership in the movement. There are growing numbers of formally battered women in the ranks of professionals today. But their number is still small. Racism and disproportionate poverty among visible minorities in this country continue to limit the number of women who can complete the lengthy and expensive training required for professional certification. (p. 7)

Such power imbalances also reveal themselves in the fact that racialized women are predominantly in jobs that serve the privileges of dominant women, such as child care and housecleaning. Furthermore, racialized women are a part of the reserve labour force, which means that those who are working at home without pay can be used by the labour market as cheap labour at any time. This, in turn, gives a great deal of power to employers, who can keep all women's salaries low (Pinedo & Santinoli, 1991).

In many ways, non-status immigrants are the backbone of Canada in terms of the work they do, work that no one else will do, such as kitchen work in restaurants, toilet cleaning in hotels, and driving taxis. Immigration allows people into Canada, but when it does not grant status, it is because this best serves the economy since these are the workers who can most easily be exploited.

Another area in which power imbalances occur between social service agencies and service providers and the women they serve is funding. According to Smith (2004):

> ... there is a cycle that occurs that supports the further oppression of immigrant refugee women. The government recognizes the communities as special interest groups, so a pot of money is given to that community for specific services.... The service exists for two or three years ... but it's a band aid effect. If it doesn't work well enough for what the government wants, then those are the first programs to go when there are funding cutbacks. (pp. 26–27)

This is exactly the same situation that happens with Aboriginal social service agencies that are mandated to assist abused women and their children. Furthermore, for agencies that service Aboriginal and other racialized women, there is a disproportionate allocation of funding even though the demands are rising. Again, according to Smith (2004), "there has to be some recognition of changing needs. Money has to be matched with the demographic shifts. We are the marginalized groups, so we end up in the very strange situations of being forced to compete with each other for scarce funds" (p. 29). Thus, service providers end up experiencing power imbalances among themselves depending on which of their agencies receive funding and how much. They also experience further power imbalances with the women they service because they become the reluctant, but inevitable, gatekeepers of who is eligible for services and what can be provided.

CONNECTION TO STATE VIOLENCE

CB: Often when we engage in anti-violence work, we focus only on domestic violence—violence perpetrated upon women by their male partners predominantly, yet racialized women particularly experience violence by the state—from the police, immigration, the mental health system, racist policies, systemic barriers that cause poverty, etc. An excellent example of this is that the state did not investigate the disappearance of over 500 Aboriginal women over the past 20 years until a White woman went missing in the same area. Only then did this come to the country's attention. What do you think is the connection between state violence and domestic violence for racialized women?

CA: There is a huge connection between state violence in First Nations communities and domestic violence. The history of First Nations peoples must be seen through an examination of colonization when dominance, power, and control were used as a means to assimilate and deal with the "Indian problem." The legislation through the Indian Act created huge disparities, and First Nations peoples have endured years of blatant racism, discrimination, and multiple abuses. Racism and systemic oppression have resulted in culture loss, high levels of poverty, unemployment, and incarceration, as well as low levels of education and poor health. Many families are suffering from traumas experienced firsthand and/or intergenerationally as a result of the residential school system, the child welfare system, addictions, and so on.

Residential schools are but one example where physical, emotional, psychological, and sexual abuse were rampant. It is no wonder that today family violence is a huge issue in First Nations families and communities. Violence begets violence; it has invaded whole communities over the last 500 years and cannot be considered a problem of a particular couple or individual household.

Despite what people like to think, violence is still fostered and sustained by a racist social environment that continues to perpetuate stereotypes of

First Nations peoples while present-day legislation continues to be Euro-centric in every way.

SA: There are many intersecting oppressions that are connected to state violence. We live in a world of post-slavery, colonialism, racism, globalization, sexism, and discrimination based on sexual orientation. At the macro level, the capitalist state allows exploitation such as violence. Violence then filters down to the micro level, which is our communities and families. An example of this is evident in some men of African descent in Canada who are unable to provide adequately for their families. Many engage in various activities to prove their masculinity or to assert some level of control or power. These men do not strike out at the actual source of their frustration. Instead, they internalize the oppression and women often become the victims of it through violence.

Analysis

All racialized women are facing structural or systemic oppression, which I believe is state violence. As Smith (2004) asks and then answers: "At what point does an immigrant cease to be considered an immigrant and start to be recognized as a citizen? Even after immigrants become naturalized citizens, their citizenship can exist only on paper; they are visible minorities, so they remain forever immigrants in the society" (p. 28).

This becomes especially serious when we know that three of four immigrants to Canada are members of visible minority groups, which makes them and their communities vulnerable to racism (Smith, 2004). Racism and other forms of oppression—or state violence—can keep racialized women from talking about abuse because they do not want mainstream society to know about it as there is already discrimination toward them. As Smith (2004) states: "People may not want to talk about it because there is already a lot of discrimination against their community. There is domestic violence in our community, but we don't talk about it because we don't want to reinforce the prejudice. It can feed into stereotypes. People already think you come from a violent place ..." (p. 4).

State violence also occurs at the economic level. Many immigrants face a rejection of the credentials they earned in their countries of origin and discrimination in the labour market. Why are the qualifications and work experience that got an immigrant into the country not recognized by Canadian professional bodies and employers? How many immigrants can afford the time and money to re-qualify to work in their profession? Why is it acceptable for me to see a Nigerian doctor trained in Nigeria when I am there, but not acceptable to have her as my doctor when she immigrates to Canada?

Historical events of systemic or state violence toward Aboriginal peoples abound and include:

- the brutality perpetuated upon Aboriginal peoples by the French and English in securing pelts during the fur trade
- abuse against Aboriginal peoples during the period of their slavery (early 1600s to 1833) in New France
- the use of women for the purpose of breeding as the direct result of a rule passed in 1770 that sought to address the shortage of English and Scottish labourers
- the extermination of the entire Beothuck nation on the East Coast
- the wars waged against the original peoples of the Plains as a result of the British government's desire to settle the West
- the hanging of seven Aboriginal men, including Louis Riel, in 1885 in Western Canada
- the banning of political activity in Aboriginal communities from the 1800s to the 1960s, which eliminated any challenges to colonial rule (Adams, 1999)

The Indian Act (1867) was the vehicle by which the goal of assimilating Aboriginal peoples was to be implemented and it governed every facet of Aboriginal life. This act, along with the creation of the reserve system, imposed a White, capitalist, patriarchal governance structure on Aboriginal communities. Through the Indian Act, the Canadian government sought to make Aboriginal peoples into imitation Europeans, to eradicate Aboriginal values through education and religion, and to establish new economic and political systems and new concepts of property. This all led to the disempowerment and devaluation of Aboriginal women and their roles within families and communities.

Specific practices of assimilation were the outlawing of traditional Aboriginal ceremonies, the enforced training of men to become farmers and women to become domestics, and a systemic indoctrination of Christian theory and practice through the residential school system. The establishment of residential schools was rationalized by the belief that these institutions would make Aboriginal children competitive with Whites, moral, industrious, and self-supporting. These schools equated Euro-Canadian socio-economic standards and materialism with success, progress, and civilization. They taught Aboriginal children to aspire to be like Euro-Canadians rather than who they were.

Residential schooling is a direct cause of family violence in Aboriginal communities because, in addition to the widespread abuse of the children who attended these institutions, it led to the decline of parenting skills as children were denied their appropriate parental role models. This removal of Aboriginal children from their parents, extended families, and communities continued with the child welfare system, which consistently placed children in non-Aboriginal families and communities. Hence, generations of Aboriginal children did not learn about the central role of family in their culture.

An oppressive, bureaucratic system of government has been imposed upon Aboriginal peoples at the cost of many of our traditional governing practices and spiritual beliefs. Such government promoted hierarchical, male-dominated, political, economic, and social structures that led to the disintegration of the tribal structures, which were clan-oriented and based on the concepts of the extended family collectivity. This, in turn, has created great social confusion within Aboriginal communities. Canadian-Aboriginal relations have provided the environment from which the profound social and economic problems, such as family violence, have taken root. The issue of family violence cannot be separated from the larger issues in Aboriginal-Canadian relations because it has arisen from, and in response to, these larger issues.

From an Aboriginal analysis, family violence in our communities is the result of, and a reaction to, a system of domination, disrespect, and bureaucratic control. It stems from the consequences and devastation of forced White colonial policies of assimilation and cultural genocide over the past several centuries. Aboriginal peoples have internalized this oppression and thus the impact is felt in the family. The treatment of women and children within the family is a reflection of the treatment of Aboriginal peoples in a broader context.

One of the most blatant forms of state violence toward Aboriginal women is the disregard that Canadian forms of justice and society as a whole have for our women who have disappeared or been murdered. As I write this, the example that stands out in my mind was triggered by the release of Karla Homolka in the summer of 2005. At the same time as Homolka and Paul Bernardo were all over the media for the murder of two innocent girls in Southern Ontario, a man by the name of John Crawford in Saskatoon, Saskatchewan, was hardly given a glance. Crawford did not go after White, middle-class girls. He preyed on Aboriginal women. In

1981, at the young age of 19, Crawford pleaded guilty to manslaughter for the killing of Mary Jane Sirloin, who was from the Peigan First Nation near Lethbridge, Alberta. He was released from prison in 1989. Then, in Saskatoon, he murdered three Aboriginal women and is also considered as a suspect by the RCMP in the murder of at least three other Aboriginal women (Cuthand 2005). However, Crawford's trial was overshadowed by the Homolka-Bernardo trial.

According to Cuthand (2005), the racism in Crawford's case was horrific. The public pretty much ignored the fact that these Aboriginal women had been murdered. While on a stakeout, the police sat and watched Crawford beat and rape an Aboriginal woman as they did not want to blow their cover. As Cuthand asks, "Would they have had a different response if the woman had been white?" (p. A13).

Today there are over 500 missing Aboriginal women in Western Canada, but Canadian society does not care. Cuthand (2005) points out: "For years people warned the Vancouver police that a serial killer was loose in the city. Finally they uncovered the pig farm in Port Coquitlam. [Furthermore], after years of suspecting it, Edmonton police finally admitted that they may have a serial killer in their city" (p. A13).

As in the past, through genocide, residential schools, child welfare, and environmental poisoning, the state views Aboriginal women as people with no value to mainstream society who can simply be thrown away. It is highly unlikely that domestic violence will ever be eradicated in Aboriginal communities when the Canadian state continues to allow this to take place.

CREATIVITY AND INNOVATION

> CB: All of you are doing some amazingly innovative work in the area of anti-violence with racialized women. Of importance is the fact that we are all connected through the Woman Abuse Council of Toronto, which brings us together to develop Best Practices that are relevant to work with racialized women. Can you tell me about some of the innovative responses you're working on in connection to Best Practices?

> JK: Our agency is developing partnerships with the Korean religious community, which is predominantly Protestant. Client reports and our own experience with the religious community have shown that churches tend not to help women experiencing abuse, yet the church is a powerful and

integral force in their lives, so we need to educate the religious community, especially its leaders, in the prevention of woman abuse. I've put together an information and resource manual for religious leaders and provided training on the definitions and signs of abuse, relevant Canadian laws, and the role they can take in helping families experiencing violence. I am even asking them to examine the theologies and the practices that perpetuate violence and keep women in abusive situations. I challenge them with questions such as "What are you teaching your congregation when you keep silent about abuse?" and "How are you providing health for families?" I've found that many first-generation Korean-speaking pastors are resistant to taking on the responsibility of addressing woman abuse, whereas the second-generation English-speaking Korean pastors are more open and it's probably because they grew up in a society that identifies woman abuse as a crime. Nevertheless, both generations of pastors need to figure out how to help abused women, so I'm helping them to identify abuse and encouraging them to speak publicly against it. I'm also trying to inspire ways in which each church can be mobilized to directly support these families, rather than simply passing them off to various services around Toronto. The Korean religious community and service providers must all work together in the efforts to hold a man accountable, assist a woman and any children, and restore them all to health and well-being.

AC: My work is currently focusing more on outreach to promote the notion of communities helping themselves. We are offering teaching and training in mediation that includes more than risk assessment regarding abuse. We're looking to assisting members of diverse communities, who have an under-standing of abuse, to become mediators. Then we can be more culturally specific to diverse communities.

HA: I am helping women develop safety plans that are specific to their cul-tural communities, so they'll have a better chance of being effective.

AR: Services for women in Toronto have evolved based on women-centred approaches that typically separate women from their abusers as a means of protecting women's safety. However, ethno-specific and Aboriginal com-munities, as well as women survivors, have identified that separation is not necessarily the most appropriate or useful form of intervention. They have identified the need to explore additional modalities of programming that protect women's safety within a community-based intervention model based on their needs, values, and experiences. In addition, this need to integrate current approaches of servicing women with programming that is relevant to diverse contexts affecting women's lives was formally identified by presenters and participants of the Woman Abuse Council of Toronto's (WACT) 2003 conference, Woman Abuse: Differences Matter.

We at WACT acknowledge that bridging approaches can be a challenging process, but view this as having the potential for important partnerships and collaborations that can create more appropriate services for those affected by woman abuse. Thus, we are presently involved in a one-year project called Best Practices: Reflecting and Integrating Diversity. The purpose of the project is to explore existing alternative and holistic intervention approaches that serve the diverse communities in Toronto. This is being achieved by consulting with women and men service users who have utilized alternative intervention approaches in ethno-specific and Aboriginal agencies as well as with service providers. The project has three goals, which are to:

- increase the capacity of those working with abused women by expanding WACT's Best Practices Guidelines to integrate Toronto's diversity

- identify key safety principles that can be incorporated into the existing WACT Best Practices Guidelines

- develop policy guidelines that will help practitioners utilize holistic, culturally relevant programming within a family and community context that can effectively protect the safety of women and hold abusers accountable

Several Toronto organizations have been involved in the project, including the ones represented by the women in this chapter, plus Punjabi Community Health Centre, South Asian Women's Centre, and Vasantham, Tamil Seniors Wellness Centre.

Analysis

In addition to the initiative on best practices as discussed above, major other innovative approaches come from the WACT, which aims to achieve a comprehensive and coordinated response to the abuse of women. WACT brings together social service agencies, survivors of woman abuse, and representatives of systems such as the police, courts, and immigration law to challenge the structural barriers and work toward positive change. It calls on all levels of government—municipal, provincial, and federal—to collaborate on a multisystem response.

A grassroots group made up of radical, feminist, racialized women, which originated in the United States, called INCITE!, has recently made its way to Toronto, which is the first Canadian city to organize. INCITE! is implementing creative ways to advance their movement to end violence against women and their communities through critical dialogue, direct action, and nurturing the health and well-being of racialized communities.

Abuse prevention and the education of the younger generation is another innovative practice taken by some community-based agencies. Thus, agencies such as Native Child and Family Services of Toronto are working with children on a culturally appropriate anti-violence program adapted from the Changing Ways Child Assault Prevention Program, which helps children to identify abuse and who to go to for assistance.

The South Asian Women's Centre has a program for female youth to educate them on abuse prevention. The young women then do speaking engagements at high schools and community centres to pass on what they have learned to their peers. The Violence Intervention Program (VIP) at East Metro Youth Services works with youth in conflict with the law in terms of their individual education and training, and in taking on leadership roles to raise awareness about abuse to other youth and the police.

A further innovation currently in the works by several agencies in Toronto is the Don't Ask, Don't Tell Campaign. Toronto residents without full legal status as citizens or permanent residents face serious barriers to accessing necessary services, such as emergency medical care, food banks, education, social housing, and health care. A Don't Ask, Don't Tell policy would make services available to everyone without discrimination on the basis of immigration status. Services would no longer need immigration status-related information, and service providers would not be allowed to ask about or share such information with Citizenship and Immigration Canada or other government agencies or authorities. There are currently over two dozen cities in the U.S. that have adopted this policy. The campaign in Toronto is urging the city's mayor to set a precedent for cities across Canada by being the first city to adopt this policy.

Some of us are also working on innovative approaches in terms of servicing diverse cultural groups. We take issue with how the idea of cultural competency has become the catchphrase for human services in the hugely diverse city of Toronto. Cultural competency involves learning about the shared characteristics of a particular group of people and using this information to better understand how to work with people from that particular group. However, since culture is individually and socially constructed and ever changing over time and context, how can we become competent at understanding it? As an example, if we consider having Aboriginal women as clients and working from a culturally competent perspective, what might this look like? Which of the 614 bands across Canada would we be considering culturally? When we think about culture, what comes to mind? Images from centuries past as though Aboriginal peoples are frozen in time? Movie images such as *Dances with Wolves, Pocahontas,* and *Peter Pan*? A homogeneous culture that all Aboriginal peoples follow? How could it be possible that my Mi'kmaq culture, connected to the Atlantic coast of what is now Canada, would be the same as that of my Innu sister in the far North?

Authors such as Laird (1998) and Dean (2001) suggest that what service providers need to do is become aware of their own "cultural baggage" and keep it in mind at all times in order to limit its impact on their work with those who are from cultures not their own. As Dean (2001) asks, "What if we shift the focus so that we are as concerned with increasing self-knowledge as with increased understanding of the other?" (p. 625). However, this self-knowledge needs to be viewed within a socio-political framework on oppression and social justice. As Green (1998) suggests, issues of "minority group oppression" are often confused with "minority group differentness" (p. 99). Thus, as a Mi'kmaq woman, I have a cultural identity based on traditional teachings and practices of Mi'kmaq culture and an identity that comes from how Aboriginal peoples are treated by the dominant culture. As Green (1998) writes, "cultural, racial, and sexual orientation differences are not problems in and of themselves. Prejudices, discrimination, and other forms of aggressive intercultural conflict based on these differences are problems" (p. 100).

It is the racism and sexism toward racialized women that service providers, activists, and educators need to learn about and challenge, not the details of the many cultures that these women are a part of. Rather than studying the cultures of racialized women, we must "study our society to reveal the ways that forms of oppression create problems out of difference" (Dean, 2001, p. 629).

CONCLUSION: WHERE TO FROM HERE?

Literature (Smith, 2004) tells us that we need further research on women's victimization, especially through conducting surveys and focus groups in languages other than English or French. I would say that even though this may be so, what we really need is action. The voices in this chapter have clearly articulated what the problems and barriers are for racialized women to live free of abuse. They have also demonstrated how they are chipping away at these barriers and how they are working with communities to take responsibility and make positive changes. What troubles me is that a small group of racialized peoples seem to be the only ones involved in these changes. Where is the social and political will to make further changes?

Canada needs ongoing public education beginning with young children in school about the history of colonization, how it has impacted upon Aboriginal peoples, and how society as a whole has benefited from this. Public education must also focus on the importance of immigrants to Canadian society.

The literature (Smith, 2004) also makes several recommendations, such as training for police, access to independent cultural interpreters, greater access to legal aid, the recruitment of racialized peoples into the justice system, and equal opportunities for training and education for them. Again, I agree, but stress that these micro suggestions are not enough. Rather, I would suggest that we need to immediately take a look at immigration policies through a critical gender analysis. There needs to be amnesty for abused racialized women without status. We need to eliminate sponsorship altogether. There must be a critically conscious mass of women working within immigration who support these practices and know about the issues surrounding violence against women.

For Aboriginal women specifically, the larger picture centres on self-determination and sovereignty. This is the inherent right of Aboriginal peoples, and social ills that plague us will never be adequately dealt with until there is sovereignty for us all. However, what needs to happen now is the political inclusion of critically conscious Aboriginal women in leadership roles in the negotiating process of sovereignty. This will be the only way in which Aboriginal women will have representation in issues of violence against them.

When racialized women come together at conferences and other gatherings, we speak about solidarity—there is no doubt that we will only initiate true change if we work together in large numbers. Organizations such as WACT and grassroots groups such as INCITE! exist to do exactly this, but our talks must lead to action. Let us begin to plan, for it is now time to act.

Chapter 5

Beyond Cultural Stereotypes: Chinese-Canadian Helping Professionals' Perspectives on Woman Abuse within the Chinese-Canadian Community in Toronto

Josephine Fong

Violence against women is pervasive and takes many forms. While all women are vulnerable in the presence of male violence, first-generation immigrant women, especially those who belong to visible minority communities, are more susceptible to it in the face of racism, classism (including immigration-class categorization, which often lumps women in the family class), institutional or systemic obstruction, as well as other oppressions in our Canadian society.

While all abused women have hurdles to leap before they can deal with their abusive experiences publicly or reach out for help, immigrant women and women from visible minority groups usually find it more difficult to come forward because of additional barriers. This is why many feminist advocates and community activists from diverse cultures often emphasize the significance of providing culturally sensitive and ethnically appropriate services to battered women. The assumption is that service providers coming from the same culture as the abused women could naturally do a better job in handling the women's experiences, compared to those who do not share cultural beliefs and values with the women. Many studies indicate that the presence of cultural bias is very persistent among helping professionals in North America (Leong & Lau, 2001; Leong & Ponterotto, 2003; Pedersen, 2003). The core problem is that because many psychotherapy and counselling programs are primarily based on a White, middle-class, theoretical framework, as a result, those who are trained within such a framework are unable to provide culturally sensitive services to their culturally different clients. Limited by their biases and intervention approaches, these helping professionals are incapable of empowering their clients for change.

Learning how "cultural insiders" understand woman abuse in intimate relationships, and what barriers they encounter in the process of helping, can become practical information for those who assist women in coping with abuse, yet are unfamiliar with a particular ethnic population. The discussion on woman abuse in this chapter is based on a qualitative study in which 11 Chinese helping professionals were interviewed to share an insider's perspective on woman abuse in intimate relationships. Hundreds of pages of information were generated from the interviews, in which the participants spoke about their experiences working with Chinese immigrant women in Toronto. Primarily, the interviews were focused on their observations of how Chinese immigrant women experience wife assault, these women's general reactions and/or coping strategies, their needs for support and community resources, and the impact of culture and immigration on the women's experiences. Consequently, the data were organized into seven major themes pertaining to the situations of abused Chinese immigrant women as reported by the front-line workers: predominant types of abuse, strategies employed, observed causes, major barriers, experiences with help, proposed remedies, and limitations of service.

As indicated by Glasser (1992) and Patton (1990), data analysis in qualitative research rises both from the data and the perspectives the researcher holds; when coding this set of data, I chose to pay attention to participants' input about themes and categories. For example, some helping professionals explicitly said that in order to avoid unnecessary racial stereotyping, they did not want to hold culture responsible for the occurrence of woman abuse in intimate relationships; rather, they viewed traditional values and beliefs as one of the barriers to women's prompt responses to their abuse. Hence, in accordance with, and with respect for their views, culture was coded under "major barriers."

1. PREDOMINANT TYPES OF ABUSE

Many helping professionals in this study reported that woman abuse in intimate relationships within the Chinese immigrant community did not conform to a single or unitary form of abuse. Much of their clients' experience involved not only physical abuse but also psychological, sexual, economic, and/or in-law abuse. However, these abused women were unaware of the legal definitions of wife assault; they thought that their situations could be considered only as marital conflict, and that only severe beating by their husbands could be considered wife assault. As a result, when they presented their situations to others, including social workers and counsellors, they tended to downplay the seriousness of the abuse until they were told that they were deemed to be in an abusive relationship. These helping professionals concurred that although woman abuse has been an issue in Chinese families, it is not particularly serious in the local Chinese community as compared to other ethnic communities in the greater Metro Toronto area.

In terms of the *physical assault* of a wife, the helping professionals observed that there was a wide range from mild to severe physical attacks, although some of them believed that physical violence is less prevalent than non-physical abuses in the Chinese community. The mild forms involved pushing, slapping, and pinching. The severe ones involved punching, kicking, stomping, and the use of weapons. These helping professionals had witnessed bruises, swollen faces, black eyes, cuts, stab wounds, and broken joints, ribs, or legs of their clients. It was indicated that most abuse cases began in the country of origin; for those who came to Canada as overseas brides, their abuse took place only in Canada.

According to these helping professionals, *psychological abuse* happened in every wife abuse situation. A health counsellor said: "When there's physical abuse, there's emotional abuse. Verbal abuse exists in every abusive case." Because of the slippery nature of psychological abuse, it was not something the abused could easily recognize or use to take their husbands to court; however, its ramifications in these women's lives were more complicated than one might think. One counsellor maintained: "In my experience, psychological abuse and the posing of threats are more serious than other abuses. I have come into contact with more of these cases. You know, to put the other person down and to make threats are commonplace in the Chinese community.... I think these forms of abuse make it more difficult for the woman to reach out to others for help because the definition of abuse is not so clear to them."

Concerning *sexual assault*, the helping professionals disclosed that while sexual abuse was not infrequent among their clients, the reporting rate in this regard was relatively low because Chinese immigrant women do not talk about sex openly. Indeed, it was pointed out that because their clients embraced formal marriage more than common-law relationships, when they were forced to have sex against their will, they perceived it as part of the marriage package. Many of the helping professionals expressed a sense of sadness; they lamented how their clients were socialized to believe that there was no such thing as "unwanted sex" in marriage. Many of their clients reported that they did not want to have sex with their husbands, especially when they were forced to do so; however, their husbands often took them for granted. Because these husbands were so good at manipulating these women's lives and forcing them to comply with their sexual appetites, they made these women feel that as wives, it was their responsibility and obligation to co-operate and satisfy their spouses. As such, the women would not complain until matters became quite extreme. Many of the helping professionals found it very hard to help their clients understand that they were indeed abused sexually and that they did not have to comply any more.

Financial abuse or economic exploitation was another common type of wife abuse in the local Chinese community. It was pointed out that due to a lack of a paying job, or because of immigration status, some women had to stay home to look after their children when there was no extended family around to lend a helping hand, and their husbands would exert financial control over them to ensure that they would do what they were told. Sometimes financial control was exercised to prevent the wives from advancing themselves by learning English, getting in touch with society, accessing information, socializing with others, and participating in community programs. Other times, it was used to prevent the women and their children from obtaining their basic needs.

In addition to the more prominent types of abuse alluded to above, some helping professionals also observed the occurrence of *abuse perpetrated by in-laws* (especially parents in-law). It was reported that if in-laws embraced traditional beliefs about women's roles and duties in the family, not only would they not help the abused wife to confront her abuser, but they would also exert stricter control over her and ostracize her if she did not comply. A social worker described a woman's situation:

> This family immigrated to Canada many years ago. They sent their son back [to China] to find a wife. They perceived the roles of a wife in a very old-fashioned way. They think that a wife must be responsible for all the household chores. When the expectation of the new wife is high, very often the woman is not only suppressed by her husband but by his entire family.... Very often, the in-laws play an important role in creating a lot of conflict between the couple.

2. STRATEGIES EMPLOYED

Generally, the helping professionals in this study observed that most women would try to tolerate the abuse initially and would not report it to the authorities; however, after they had been abused repeatedly, they would generate their own strategies to cope, and protect their own safety and that of their children. The eight coping strategies identified by the helping professionals as the most common ones employed by their clients included tolerance, pleasing, avoidance, fighting back, telling others, making a community connection, calling the police, and finding a job. While these strategies did not result in total resolution, it was said that the abused women were becoming more determined to confront their abusers and extricate themselves from the abusive relationships as they coped along.

Tolerance was considered the strategy when the women demonstrated no active search for external intervention, but indirectly poked around for information relating to divorce. In doing so, these women were taking time to examine relationship issues and to contemplate some culturally appropriate responses to the problem. Participants of this study pointed out that while many women did it more consciously, others might still be in a denial stage, making up excuses for what happened, or rationalizing their situations. In either case, women responded slowly and conservatively to the abuse. Weighing the consequences of individual responses and alternatives, although some women might have a hard time resolving their passionate feelings for their husbands, their concerns were more about their financial losses and their children's welfare if they were to leave. Quotes from two different helping professionals explained these points well: "These women asked many questions about divorce.... Because they don't know the financial implications if they file for divorce, they just let the relationship drag on and endure the abuse." "Many women feel that when the children are still young, they should tolerate their husbands' behaviour for the sake of keeping the children's father in the family.... They think that having a father is better than having no father at all."

Pleasing was used when the abused women realized that brutality was part of their husbands' personality and their daily experiences; in order to reduce further conflict and abuse in the relationships, they would try to satisfy their husbands so that these men would not be irritated. One health promotion worker stated: "They need to survive and so they will think that they should try everything not to provoke their husband's anger but to please them. They will do things according to their husbands' liking."

When pleasing was not working well, or when the abused women were tired of agreeing with their husbands, *avoidance* was used to simply reduce the interaction time with their husbands. This strategy was considered a great way to avoid uncalled-for rebuke. A social service worker claimed:

> I heard from many women that they would have dinner together as a family, but other times they would just do things on their own. It's like "You go your own way and I go mine." ... So, there's no communication between the couple and it doesn't really function as a family. There's no intimacy between the couple.....Although living in the same house, they avoid each other. They feel that since they can't accept each other, they should each live in their own social circle. For these couples, they just want to keep the family together superficially for their children.

It was reported that some women would go to their parents' or friends' houses to stay for a couple of days, trying to avoid their angry husbands. If they had grown children, they would stay in the same room with their husbands only when their children were physically there with them.

Some abused women told the helping professionals that *fighting back* was a self-defence they used to confront their husbands' violence. Although some women fought back to protect themselves from serious injury, it was not something many women could feel proud of when talking about it because it is not considered appropriate or "womanly" in their culture. While the helping professionals deemed fighting back a "natural response" of these women to protect themselves, it often made them lose their credibility when trying to hold their husbands responsible for the incident. In addition, because it was not recognized as a proper strategy, some women would not admit that they did it.

The fifth strategy that the helping professionals identified was *telling others*. It was said that after their initial attempts failed, many abused women would find ways to tell others about their predicaments. Frequently, the very first group of people told was the women's families. The abused women might not tell the details of the abuse, but they would reveal enough information to invite intervention. When their family members or close relatives were sensitive and understanding, they would lend their support to the women, but if they were not very sympathetic, they might encourage the women to endure the "conflict" and reconcile with their husbands. Those who did not have families or close relatives around might tell their friends, co-workers, ESL teachers, doctors, church ministers, or use phone inquiries to ventilate their feelings. No matter what source of support was available to them, and to whom they disclosed the abuse, it was observed that these women's informing others was purposeful, and that they had to trust the person before they could tell him or her about their situations. A social worker summarized: "They would see who could make the greater impact on their husbands to determine to whom they would tell. The ultimate goal is to have someone tell their husbands that what they did was wrong."

Making a community connection with agencies or organizations was a strategy that was usually used in the later stage of women's abusive experience, especially when the women were more ready to learn about their rights and options. It was often through these channels that they began to receive counselling, or were referred to other services relevant to their needs. According to the helping professionals in this study, by connecting themselves with social service agencies, the abused women were hoping to achieve more goals in addition to obtaining pertinent information and resources. They wanted to let their husbands know that they were connected (rather than isolated), and to get the husbands involved in receiving help. One participant remarked: "Although they are staying in the relationship, I feel that they are becoming stronger; stronger in a sense that they will not put up with the abuse anymore.… They will tell their husbands that they are seeing a counsellor. Then their husbands learn that these women are not isolated and helpless anymore. These husbands will … try to control their own behaviour."

It was observed that sometimes these women would not present their abuse up front when they first approached professional help. Some were too embarrassed to say it, while others may have wanted to test the trustworthiness of the professional helper. One helping professional explained:

> They would not present the abuse issue first.… They would say that they had problems with child care. They would first present something that was more practical and essential to family life.… Once they established a relationship with the worker or had a chance to get to know the worker better, when the worker asked them why they needed this information, they would gradually reveal the core problem in their marriage. I had a woman who came to me to talk about the procedure of applying for welfare assistance.… It was after about a month that she started to tell me [about] her abusive experience.

Some helping professionals reported that some women had to find a way to connect themselves with the community resources. For example, they might have to lie about where they were going. A counsellor said: "Some women's husbands only permit them to take English courses. They aren't allowed to do something else.... Some community centres also run women's groups along with English classes so that sometimes these women would have an opportunity to participate in a women's group too, but their husbands wouldn't know." Women who were either afraid of being identified, or who shied away from making the initial contact, would ask their friends to represent them, calling an agency or a particular counsellor to request information. No matter what they did initially, if the helping professionals were sensitive to women's attempts to approach external help, in the end many of them were able to make the direct connection.

Making the direct connection with community resources was not just about getting some emotional support to confront their husbands; most women needed very specific and detailed answers to help them make decisions. This decision-making process was usually long, but very essential for the women in their struggle. A wife assault counsellor explained:

> Obviously, with Chinese women, they want to know some very practical information.... They usually come to us with very specific legal questions because there are many things they need to deal with themselves.... I told many women I worked with before that knowledge is power. Even if they decide that they don't want to come to see us anymore, we will still give them as much information as possible to help them in the future. Once they have the information, perhaps sometime someday when they are ready to take any action, perhaps the information we have given them would play a role in their decision-making process.

Calling the police was the seventh strategy related by the helping professionals as something abused women would try, but many women were not very impressed with the outcome. One helping professional recounted:

> Many women told me that they were not very satisfied with the result.... Of course, the typical case was that only the husband could speak English and the wife couldn't.... Of course, the wife is in a disadvantaged position.... When neither the father nor mother could speak English, the children were asked to translate for their parents.... Very often, when a woman calls the police, she only wants to be protected. She doesn't want to ... put her husband in jail. She's afraid that once she puts him in jail, when he gets out, he will take revenge or beat her even more severely.... Secondly, if the man is taken to jail ... he will not be able to go to work and his extended family or relatives would blame her for what happens.... Many of them called the police once and after that, they would never do it again.

The last strategy observed was *finding a job*. It was pointed out that if the abused woman did not have a paid job, and was relying on her husband financially when she was thinking seriously about leaving him, very likely she would try her best to look for a job to ensure that she could support herself and her children. She would not want to depend on her ex-husband financially. Many of these women might not have a marketable skill, but would try every possible way to test their marketability. For example, some women would babysit for others, or provide domestic and/or senior care services for others. They did not mind working in factories and doing manual jobs for long hours, as long as they could earn enough to support themselves. One counsellor stated that some women would take a part-time job without telling their husbands because they wanted to save some money for "a rainy day." They often worked very hard to be somewhat financially independent.

3. OBSERVED CAUSES

The front-line workers interviewed identified seven possible contributing factors to spousal abuse against women in the Chinese community, which were directly or indirectly linked to the aggressiveness of the abusers and to the responses of the abused women. These factors included power imbalance, extramarital affairs, trust, immigration, financial hardship, anger displacement, and mental illness.

With regard to *power imbalance* within couples, the participants pointed out that as a result of having fewer resources and marketable skills, inadequate English skills, and being the dependants in the immigration system, many immigrant women were under their husbands' control and given a lower social status. When abusive husbands realized that they were in a better position socially and economically, or when they were afraid that they might lose that position, they took advantage of their greater power and became violent toward their wives. The report of one of the helping professionals summarized this:

> I will say that there's still inequality between men and women. Men still have a higher social status than women in our Chinese community. I think this is a fundamental problem. The other thing is, it is always true that the one who brings a paycheque home has more power.... I conducted a study some years ago; the result showed that it's more than just having a job; it's about the women's English ability. When they had no English skills, they lost their self-confidence

and felt more powerless.... When they had better English skills, not only would they gain more power in the relationship, they were also more likely to leave their husbands when they were abused.

Another factor identified as contributing to wife abuse was *infidelity*. It was indicated that when a third party became involved in the established marital relationship, more conflicts would arise and domestic disputes could evolve into violence. This issue could be very complicated, especially when one spouse immigrated first and the other came to Canada later to find out that her husband had another partner. Some participants reported that they had witnessed more of these situations with families who came from mainland China.

Lack of trust was another observed cause of wife abuse, especially for those whose marriages were arranged (i.e., overseas brides). In this situation, because the couple did not know each other well in advance, the husband was often afraid that his wife might have someone else from when she was still in China, or because the wife was much younger and pretty, he was afraid that she would meet someone else in the new country and leave him. In both cases, more control was exerted over the wife, and when she resisted, violence would be used to affirm his authority. There was a vicious cycle. Sometimes the demonstrated distrust and control might cause the overseas bride to resent her husband even more; when she happened to run into a man with whom she had a better rapport, the husband's jealousy might escalate to violence.

Immigration was perceived as one of the causes of wife abuse because the process of acculturation often generates much stress on men, which in turn creates more conflicts between couples. Due to men's inadequate coping behaviours, they sometimes turned their frustration into aggressive behaviour toward their wives. A worker explained:

> In the process of acculturation, there's a greater impact on men's self-image. I find that men have more difficulties adjusting to the new environment. They are less flexible than women.... I find that women are tougher and they can tolerate.... They are more willing to take up lower-status jobs.... I mean men's coping skills affect their behaviour and turn them into wife abusers.... They felt that they had a better control in their country of origin, but ... here, they feel that they have lost it, so they become violent. You know what makes men stronger than women? It's only their physical strength, so they resort to this aspect of power.

Also, because Chinese immigrant women were more adaptable and accommodating than their husbands, even though they were not satisfied with the new environment and menial jobs, they were more willing to make the best of a bad situation. However, when their flexibility threatened their male counterparts' sense of adequacy, a power struggle began. Another worker said:

> I think the process of immigration may have played a role in making many already shaky relationships worse. I think the shift of power is something needed to be looked at too. Perhaps back to the old days, the man was the only breadwinner and the wife the housekeeper … but after immigration, perhaps the wife was the first one to have found a job before the husband because his qualification couldn't guarantee him a higher position, yet he couldn't accept other low-status jobs, so he felt that there was a shift of power between them, so he felt that he had to assert some more power. I think in many situations like that, the problems between the couple become intensified after immigration.

Moreover, it was pointed out that immigration created a relatively greater amount of time for a couple to pick on each other. In their country of origin, many couples were busy with work, extended families, and established friends, but after immigration, without a prospective full-time job, a closely knitted social network, and an active social life, they were forced to turn inward and focus on their partner. When there were so many accumulated bitter feelings and the focus was on finding fault, the relationship could easily become negative. One helping professional claimed: "When you don't have to spend so much time together, there are a lot of things you do not need to know or deal with. But now, since you have to spend so much time together, there will be more conflicts between the couple about each other's habits. Such conflicts may be intensified." It was further indicated that because many immigrant women were so dedicated to establishing their new lives in Canada, they often forgot or neglected the signs of abuse, attributing their husbands' abusive behaviour to frustration associated with acculturation, so they were more likely to tolerate it. A community educator explained: "They might think that although he put me down sometimes in the past, at least he was a responsible man. So, when physical abuse happened after immigration, they might conclude that perhaps it was the pressure he was under which turned him into another person.... They thought that if their husband could overcome the difficulties of acculturation, they would be the same old person ["Mr. Responsible"] again."

Closely related to the factor of immigration was *financial hardship*. Some participants pointed out that very often when the couple was trying to establish themselves in Canada, yet had difficulties finding jobs, they experienced some financial hardship. They often had different ideas of how money should be spent and what the priorities were in reducing family expenses. Also, having no job often increased the husband's financial anxiety. A participant explained: "Chinese men, no matter whether they come from the northern part of China or from Hong Kong, feel that they are responsible to provide for the family; when they can't handle the financial burden, they are likely to take their frustration out on others. I have seen it in many new immigrant families."

The next two contributing causes, *anger displacement* and *mental illness*, were closely related to immigrant men's adaptation to the new environment and their problematic coping strategies. A social worker stated: "Many emotional abuse cases I observed involved anger displacement. This is to say that while the man was angry with something, instead of directing his anger at the person or the event that provoked him, he displaced it to the woman, to someone close to him. He might be aware that it was not the fault of his wife and he might say sorry to her afterwards, but it has become a vicious cycle." In terms of linking *mental illness* to wife abuse, some participants believed that when the difficulties and stresses associated with immigration become unbearable, it costs some immigrant men their mental health. In such cases, because of the illness, the man may become easily agitated and soon aggressive. Some participants in this study described several severe cases that involved psychological maladjustment and mental illness. Although these helping professionals tried to persuade the women to put their own safety and that of their children first, sometimes they still chose to stay until their lives were threatened. One participant said: "We have a woman whose husband is seriously ill and he often scolds her.... I asked her why she still wants to stay in the relationship.... She said, 'Because he's ill so I think I should be more patient with him.' I have another woman whose husband became insane all of a sudden. He stabbed her and her two children. He is now in jail and she's recovering from her own injury. She's been very supportive [of her husband]."

4. MAJOR BARRIERS

In their daily contacts with abused women, the helping professionals identified a whole range of barriers that these women faced, which affected their responses to their abuse. These barriers prevented them from disclosing their situations right away and/or from dealing with the abuse in a more timely and effective way. These recognized barriers included the lack of official language skills, traditional values, soft-heartedness, isolation, children, lack of financial security, and immigration status.

Lack of Official Language Skills

It was remarked that lacking the *official language skills* was very detrimental to abused Chinese immigrant women in obtaining information and accessing services that are available for Canadian women who can speak the official languages. Also, being unable to communicate in English, regardless of their educational and vocational backgrounds, affected their self-esteem. A counsellor said: "To new immigrants, language barrier is an issue. Because they don't know the language, they feel so inadequate to be on their own." Even if some women were able to overcome the initial language barrier and reach out for help, they still had to face the language issues in the process of dealing with the system. Although some community organizations have tried to provide interpretation services for women, because of funding and staffing limitations, this kind of service was not always available. A woman abuse counsellor lamented:

> It's so difficult for Chinese women to find a Chinese lawyer! Of course we have a list of lawyers, but only two or three are Chinese. However, they don't always take legal aid cases, so very often the women have no other choice but to see an English-speaking lawyer.... Similarly, when a woman goes to a shelter ... the staff there wants to help the woman, but she doesn't understand what the staff is saying. How could she even understand the house rules?

Traditional Values

The second barrier the helping professionals referred to was the *traditional values* of the abused women and their families. These traditional cultural values regarding gender, family, marriage, saving face, and problem solving often prevented women from formulating or choosing certain strategies to deal with the abuse.

In a collectivist community, the individual women's welfare is deemed insignificant; the integrity of the family always comes first. As a result, women are led to sacrifice themselves for the greater cause (i.e., the family):

> Living in a society that embraced the traditional values, we don't weigh the self so importantly.... Many Chinese women, even though when they are forced to do certain things against their will, once they get used to the idea of collectivism, they would just accept things that are imposed on them.... Many women still want to keep their family intact. If the family as a whole is all right, even though this woman is not happy, she still thinks that ... her suffering is insignificant.

Although Chinese women were not taught formally (i.e., in school) to sacrifice the "small self" for the "greater self," they followed the traditions of preceding generations. They were trapped in an "apprenticeship" model, trying to be virtuous women by observing or learning from their mothers. One helping professional claimed:

> Women of our preceding generations are so unbelievable.... I think it is not about what they said, but about what they did to show us this is the way to be [a woman]. I have seen many women who didn't say a word no matter how demanding or problematic their husbands are.... I think it is deeply rooted in our Confucian thinking about women's three obedience and four virtues.... I don't know if we can isolate ourselves from the experiences of our previous generations, but I am very sure that Confucian beliefs—the three obedience and four virtues for women—do play an important role in the way we present and behave ourselves.

In addition to the "apprenticeship" model, women also learned their gender roles from the mass media. Movies and soap operas often portray women earning love and respect through endurance. A health counsellor asserted:

> Looking at Pak Yin's and Chan Po Chu's movies [in the early 1960s and 1970s], we can trace how our Chinese traditions portray a woman's role in the family. In *Family, Spring and Autumn*, if a woman is humble and modest in the relationship, no matter how hard life has been for her, at the end she would be praised.... Indeed, classical Chinese movies do reflect the cultural values at the time.... You know, those old movies reflected the woman's image as one that endures bitterness and abuse. My clients who are older, about 40-something to 50-something, really think that those are their idols.

No matter whether through informal socialization or the influence of popular culture, many Chinese women learned that they had to be loyal to their husbands and families. These values of family obligation, loyalty, and women's virtues put women in a position more vulnerable to wife assault, making them reluctant to confront their husbands in a radical way as these women's personal success or failure is tied to their marriage.

Moreover, traditional values consider men more important and respectable. They have been the heads of the family because of their higher social position in society. Some women might even believe that the inequality between the sexes is intrinsic and it is women's destiny to be secondary, so they would not challenge inequality openly, although they might feel unfairly treated. A wife assault counsellor asserted that: "The first belief is that 'Men are more respectable than women,' especially in the minds of older Chinese people. Of course we can see this in the White culture as well, but in the older generation of Chinese, many older Chinese women have been enduring their husbands' verbal and physical violence. The reason they stay in the relationship is because they think this is their fate."

The other issue related to traditional values is that Chinese people are very concerned about how other people view them. To save face means to avoid being looked down upon or shamed by others. If certain actions would cause them to lose face or feel ashamed, they would rather remain passive or try to conceal the truth. A participant said: "In the view of Chinese people, divorce, separation, or having marital discord is something to feel shame about.... Many Canadians who are divorced pay no attention to how other people view them, but with Chinese, divorce is a taboo and shameful.... If you are divorced or remarried, it's like there's a label ... on your forehead." For many women, one way to preserve their personal pride and self-esteem was to conceal their abuse, especially in the beginning. One helping professional claimed that:

> I have come into contact with some abused women who are [university] grads in China or teachers, but they do have those traditional values.... They dare not to seek help from the outside. They feel that seeking help from outsiders is a way to shame themselves and their families.... They feel that if other people know that highly educated women like themselves would still be abused, it's a personal shame, so they will not tell others or seek help in order to save face.

Sometimes, even if a woman was willing to reveal her abusive experience, cultural beliefs about family harmony might prevent others from intervening. When they realize that no third-party intervention is forthcoming, the abused woman will be even more hesitant to disclose the abuse because doing so will only mean "showing one's dirty laundry to others," which, in turn, will shame the woman and/or her family.

According to the participants of this study, Chinese people usually rely on a private family network for problem solving; they seldom speak to strangers about their issues. One participant maintained: "Chinese don't believe in professional help.... If you are my friend, I will enlist you in my source of support and help ... but if you are only my social worker, I will feel that I am only a subject of your work. In that case, the social worker will know less than a friend. Those who are more educated would feel that they are not a subject of study to the worker, so they may not feel comfortable seeing a social worker and disclosing their issues." Furthermore, counselling and social services are a Western concept of social benevolence that is unfamiliar to many Chinese immigrant women. Therefore, these women are either unaware of the existence of such services or are not used to looking for and using them. Even if they later learn that there are such services, they often feel it would be inappropriate to seek the help of counsellors or social workers if they don't understand that they are paid professionals. Therefore, they bring fewer issues to the helping professionals and talk to them only when their lives are threatened. A counsellor said: "Sometimes they feel that social workers are so busy, they have so much work to do, and they may not have time to talk to them about their issues. They think they can save the social workers some time. In this way, they put their issues aside instead of dealing with them promptly."

While all of the participants considered Chinese traditional beliefs a barrier to the abused women's ability to cope effectively and seek help, some of them argued that these beliefs were problematic only because men, especially the abusive ones, misuse them to benefit themselves and keep women in line. One helping professional explained it clearly in great detail:

> I think there are a lot of good things about Chinese culture, such as forgive and forget. Those Confucian teachings are very good for people to live a harmonious life. However, I think it is not right for an abusive person to take advantage of these teachings and expect his wife to tolerate him even though he beats her.... Confucian teachings would not tell men to beat their wives and ask the women to bear such behaviour. Confucian thinking asks us to be kind with each other and forgive one another's faults. I don't think it means that one person can have unlimited power to exert control or use violence and the other party has to take it and bear with him all the time. The thing is Chinese are very modest and receptive.... I really think that tolerance is part of our cultural beliefs. We do

think that without tolerance, there will be no family harmony. Tolerance is a virtue applying to both men and women in all families. There is no implication that women must tolerate everything.

Soft-Heartedness

Some helping professionals attested that very often women's *soft-heartedness* made them hesitate to seek external help because they did not want to "ruin" their husbands' prospects. Many women would forgive their husbands when they showed remorse or they would drop their charges when their husbands said they would change. Consequently, the women's soft-heartedness only prolonged their personal suffering. Here are excerpts from two interviews with helping professionals:

> [T]heir cultural background makes them so considerate of their husbands' future as well. A client sometimes told me that she sympathized with her husband and understood what he was going through, so she felt ambivalent. When she was beaten, pushed, and insulted by him, she was very angry, but when she was calm, she showed sympathy and protected his dignity.

> You know, once you lay [a] charge, there's a possibility that the abuser will be jailed, so they didn't want to ruin their husbands' future. I often heard them say, "After all, we are husband and wife. I don't want to make his life too miserable." … Very often women are too soft-hearted and too considerate, so they often accept men's excuses and forgive them over and over again.

Isolation

The fourth barrier indicated by the helping professionals was *isolation*. Having no or few friends or relatives in Canada, lacking English skills, and being unfamiliar with the community often confined many abused Chinese women to the home. The only people they interacted with daily were their husbands and children. Their husbands were the only adults and close kin they could rely on socially, emotionally, and economically. As a result, not only did they feel inferior in the relationships, but they also felt useless, especially when their husbands kept telling them so. Therefore, their isolation became a major barrier to their effective coping with their abusive situations. A wife abuse counsellor affirmed:

Many of them are new immigrants; they don't know where to locate community resources and where to take public transportation. They don't have the money to [take] buses or get other things. They have so many obstacles.... They aren't aware of their rights, they have no friends, they don't know their way around.... It gives their husbands the opportunity to exert control over them.... You know, things like that will make the women powerless and men powerful.

Children

According to the helping professionals, *children* became the abused women's liability when coping with wife abuse because they did not want their children to live in a fatherless family. As such, although they wanted the abuse to end, many of them ruled out the possibility of leaving. In fact, social pressure and stigmatization play a role in women's decisions to stay in abusive relationships because, in both mainstream and Chinese communities, single-parent families are considered burdensome for society. To avoid being labelled a burden, many women would rather cope without external intervention from the social service sector. Also, because Chinese people are generally very concerned about the continuity of children's education, many abused women try not to interrupt their children's schooling. Hence, they would neither want to go to a shelter nor move away from the neighbourhood to escape their husbands, even though their safety might be at risk. They do not want their children's schooling to be interrupted. While it might be safer for them to move to another neighbourhood, this would require that their children switch schools and adjust to a new learning environment; their family problems would be disclosed, and their children would be labelled in school. Women were having a hard time making a sound decision because of all of these children-related considerations.

Lack of Financial Security

As one helping professional indicated, job and financial issues were the biggest hurdles many abused Chinese immigrant women faced. Since they were not trained in Canada, even if they had above-average qualifications, they would have a hard time finding a job that paid a decent salary to support themselves and their children. Very often, they would have to rely on welfare after the divorce, but doing so would hurt the women's self-esteem, so some women chose not to end their relationships unless it was necessary to save lives. According to some helping professionals, when their abused clients had no money for themselves and could not find a job, when they tried to flee from a life-threatening situation (before the intervention of the social worker), they spent the night(s) on the street. However, when their safety on the street became threatened, they would quickly return to their abusive homes. In addition, the lack of a regular job often pushed some women to move from one abusive relationship to another because they had to rely financially on men. A health counsellor affirmed:

> Why did the woman I mentioned still stay with her husband although he beats her so hard? It was because she had no job and depended on him financially. In Canada, she doesn't know a word of English. She doesn't have a marketable skill ... so the only thing she could do was to take his fists or slapping a few times a day. She just wanted to keep her children in the family.... She just thought that as long as they had something to eat and put on, that's fine because their basic needs were met.

Immigration Status

The last barrier identified by the helping professionals had to do with the *immigration status* of the abused women and their understanding of immigration policy. It was reported that when the abused were misled to believe that they could be denied the right to stay in Canada or when they did not have a firm refugee or immigrant status, they almost had no choice but to endure the abuse in despair. For example, a helping professional reported:

> A client of mine obtained a visitor's visa to come here. She then married [her husband] here; in theory, of course, she could have stayed here legally, but the thing was her husband didn't submit an application for her! ... He lied to her because she didn't know a word of English! ... She was so unfortunate and had been abused for almost 10 years just because she didn't have a status to stay in Canada and no financial resource to be independent.... She couldn't apply for welfare because she had no [legal] status. She was truly a tragedy, a very sad story.... I received many phone calls of this nature in which the woman wanted to find out more information about the kind of alternatives they may have.

5. EXPERIENCES WITH HELP

In their daily contact with abused women, the helping professionals interviewed in this research learned what their clients had experienced with
various other external assistance and services. In general, these helping
professionals could comment on their clients' experiences with the justice
system, shelters, the health sector, and the welfare system.

With regard to the *justice system* (i.e., police officers, legal workers, attorneys, and judges), many helping professionals were very disappointed with
both process and outcome as it often caused more stress for their clients, yet
the abusers were allowed to walk away free. Most clients thought the police
officer(s) who came to the scene of domestic violence had not been very fair
with them. First, the police officer(s) often talked and listened to the one
who could speak English, which was usually the husband. In most cases,
the police officer(s) would tell the husband to calm down, advise him not
to use any force but to talk things out. Although it made sense in a general
way, it did not help the woman who had been abused in the relationship to
feel safer after the police officer(s) left. It was pointed out that even though
sometimes the police officer(s) might take the situation more seriously when
they saw bruises on the woman, they usually just removed the woman from
the home and sent her to a shelter, thinking that the woman would be able
to get some help from the shelter. Essentially, the woman was viewed as a
problem to be passed on to someone else to handle. The helping professionals felt good about the new police protocol, which grants the police
more authority to lay charges against the abusers, but they observed that
some immigrant women did not realize that their complaints would result
in the arrest of their husbands or of themselves. One participant claimed:
"[M]any women were shocked because when they reported to the police,
they thought they were only doing something to frighten their husbands,
but they didn't know that ... the police officer would take away their husbands or keep them in custody and put them on bail.... Also, sometimes the
husbands would press counter-charges to accuse them of something ... so
they would be very confused and felt lost." Of the 11 helping professionals
interviewed in this study, only one of them stated that she had a client who
received some support from the community police, who went the extra mile
to check upon her and her children after the abuser was removed.

With reference to the legal system procedures, many helping professionals believed that not only was it not a user-friendly process, but it
was also victim-blaming, favouring the offenders' rights over those of the
abused. A counsellor asserted:

The court is not very supportive of women because it needs so much proof and it requires a statement from you and your husband. Very often, because these women are in fear and when they are asked to repeat the incidents many times, they may get confused; thus, they may be inconsistent in their statement. As a result, their credibility is compromised. So far, I have never seen a case successfully charged.... I had a few cases in which they had to go to the justice of the peace to lay charges.... You know, the women might have fought back, so when they lay charge against their husbands, they might lay a countercharge against their wives. When you had two charges laid, the police often hope that you could resolve the matter outside the court.

Some helping professionals commented that even when a case was successfully brought to court, because of case overload, ambivalent feelings, and misunderstandings, both the attorney and the abused might not be well prepared for a court appearance. As a result, sometimes cases were dismissed easily. A participant said: "Sometimes I found the prosecutor didn't do a very good job in preparing women for the court procedure.... When they didn't know what was going to happen, they would just minimize the abuse to lessen their husbands' troubles.... The prosecutor would blame the victim for not presenting the case clearly or concealing some facts to protect the abuser.... Ultimately, the victim was revictimized in this process." Also, abused women were hurt the most by budget cuts in legal aid services. Many matters that used to be handled by legal aid lawyers were no longer covered. Many women were screened out from the program and their interests were not represented.

All of the helping professionals in this study concurred that when their clients were living in shelters, they all had some negative experiences to report. Often their clients would not go to a shelter if there was another alternative, but when there was no other choice and they were in a life-threatening situation, a shelter was a temporary option. Their clients said that their lives were miserable in the shelters. The kind of problems most abused Chinese immigrant women faced in shelters were related to difficulties in communication, food, living arrangements, and racial discrimination.

At the time of this study, the helping professionals observed that out of all the shelters in Greater Metro Toronto and its adjacent areas, only one part-time staff was able to speak a Chinese language. Most often, they could not refer their clients to this particular shelter. One participant said: "[I]t really depends on which one has a vacancy for our women. At the critical moment, you often feel lucky that there's a vacancy somewhere for your client. I was just happy to locate a space for my client and I never had the luxury of choosing a shelter for my client.... You have to take the space immediately before anyone else takes it." So with the communication barrier in the shelter, their clients felt anxious, isolated, and stressed out.

Most shelters provided meals for their residents, but the food was foreign to the women because they were accustomed to Chinese diets in which hot steamed rice and cooked vegetables are the standard items in their daily meals. The toughest was when their children refused to eat, so usually these women would try to leave the shelter as soon as they could. Often returning home was a better option for many.

In terms of the living arrangements in the shelters, clients told many helping professionals that the ideology of communal living in a shelter did not work for them. It is understandable that living with people with whom they did not share the same language, culture, customs, diets, and lifestyle was very difficult, especially when everyone was traumatized and under a lot of stress. Most women panicked when they were given the responsibility to cook for other residents in the shelter because they did not know how to prepare Western-style meals. In theory, they could have made Chinese meals when they were on duty, but in practice they either were not given the right means and supplies to do so, or were afraid that other women would not like Chinese meals. A participant explained that instead of getting emotional support and comfort in the shelters, their clients often felt oppressed by other women with whom they could not communicate. She said:

> First of all, I think Chinese women are too shy and modest. They don't know how to fight for their rights. In shelters, you do have to fight for things. They felt that they were abused in shelters. For example, if there are clothes to distribute to them, the good ones will be grasped by the other women, leaving them what no one wanted.... They said their lives in there were so miserable! They didn't feel comfortable living in there at all. You know, everyone there was not in a good mood. Everyone was so emotional, so it is quite likely that they can be abusive to each other.

One of the negative experiences with shelters reported by clients was racial discrimination. Indeed, this was a very touchy subject, but these helping professionals felt that they should understand it from their clients' point of view. When their clients were badgered or discriminated against by the residents of other races, they could not find any support from the staff in the shelter. One social worker claimed:

[M]y clients often reported that they encountered racism in the shelter from the people around them; sometimes it even came from the staff of the shelter. They felt that the staff were not sympathetic with them.... Therefore, after they stayed there for a night or two, they would rather go home. At least the home is a familiar environment.... Of course, some women felt that they were well supported by the staff and others in the shelter, but it seems to me that there are more negatives than positives.

In terms of the clients' experiences with the *health sector*, again, the biggest problem was the lack of translation services in hospitals when they went for a physical examination after being battered. It was also suggested that the medical professionals were not sensitive to issues of wife abuse, although they usually were the first people to have contact with abused women. A counsellor complained: "In hospitals, it's the same old problem that there's no interpreter available. When the abuser is with the woman, it is obvious that they would not be able to say anything, but the hospital staff are not so sensitive to this issue … so many abused women don't find the staff there very helpful.... Some family doctors don't want to take these patients because they don't want to write reports or go to court."

Because financial security was crucial to the abused women's decision to stay or leave, many helping professionals in this study found that the tight nature of the *welfare system* often made it more difficult for their clients to leave the abusers. One participant remarked: "For women who are not used to living in poverty, it's very threatening to them to leave their husbands. In the welfare system, there's no leeway for them to have a sense of financial security because it expects them to use up their last penny before they could obtain welfare assistance.... When there's a delay of service and once these women get frustrated, they would rather return to their abusers." In addition, it was believed that recent welfare policy has made it more difficult for abused women to obtain a welfare cheque, which they need the most. One counsellor explained the problem in detail:

Okay, this woman has been in Canada for about two years before she applies for welfare. The welfare officer asks her if she has a sponsor because she's supposed to be taken care [of] by him. This officer asks the woman to show a proof that her sponsor no longer takes care of her. The problem is, this is an abused woman. How can she show a proof that she's no longer taken care by the abuser? Can she ask the abuser to go to the welfare office in person and say that he no longer takes care of her? … There are situations in which the woman has no prior contact with any agency; where can she go to get some proof? …

> You know, some women don't go to the police; they just sneak out from the house to escape their husbands. To these women, this becomes an obstacle.... Also, some women work for employers who don't report everything to Revenue Canada.... [I had] this woman who had to go to the Human Resources Centre, the UI department, to obtain a form to apply for UI. She had to go back to the officer to report the reason she couldn't obtain an employment record from her employer. Then, in the Human Resources, no one speaks Chinese at all. She had the form, but she didn't know how to fill it.... This is a woman who has to spend three hours travelling each time she comes to see me. She asked me to help her with the form and then she had to take the form back there. The officer asked her so many questions yet she didn't understand a word! After the questioning, the officer gave her another two sets of forms [laugh] ... so you can imagine how difficult it is for the women to deal with all [this red tape].

It was also pointed out that the geographic differences between a woman's original residence, the shelter she goes to, and the social assistance office she deals with when planning for separation may create more stress for her. Very often because of safety and/or vacancy issues, a woman has to go across the city to be admitted into a shelter. Once she is taken in by a shelter, all her needs would be provided. However, she still has to deal with the court on her own. Also, when she leaves the shelter to start a new life, complications may arise depending on her choice of a new residence. One wife abuse counsellor provided an example:

> A woman who lived in York region was referred to a shelter in Scarborough.... Though she lives in Scarborough ... court proceedings follow where her matrimonial home is, so she has to go back to the Newmarket courthouse, so transportation is a big issue for her. Also, you can't always take your kids with you when you go to court, but no one can look after her kids for her! ... She needs to apply for social assistance; she has to go to the Scarborough office because she's now living in Scarborough.... If she finds an apartment in York region, the social welfare office [in Scarborough] will not cover for her. It becomes a big problem! ... The service sector needs to do something to fill such a gap.

6. PROPOSED REMEDIES

The helping professionals in this study made some suggestions to prevent woman assault in the local Chinese community and improve the existing services. The different domains these participants covered include education, ethnic-specific approaches/new initiatives, individual and group counselling, and programs and services for men.

Education

It was pointed out that because knowledge can empower women and restrain men, the education of Chinese immigrant women and men is crucial in preventing male violence against intimate partners in the local Chinese community. Women need to be made aware of their rights, realizing that regardless of their legal status in Canada, wife abuse is a crime; they do not have to tolerate any violence. Also, women need to learn the negative impacts of spousal abuse on children. They must recognize that while they may think that they must tolerate the abuse in order to maintain an intact family for their children, they may actually jeopardize their children's healthy personality development and well-being. One counsellor stated:

> Women have to learn that they need to seek help. It is not a shameful thing to do. They are not disclosing a family secret; they are indeed saving lives. The cost of their tolerance can be very high. Recently, two small children in a Vietnamese family have to stay with the Children's Aid because their mother was killed by their father.... Tolerance can lead to a very tragic consequence, so education is very important for women to learn their rights and learn how to seek help.

While immigrant women could learn about their rights and the available community resources, immigrant men could be made more aware of the consequence of their aggression. A wife abuse counsellor commented: "Men need to know that they are committing a crime when they beat their wives.... I have some clients whose husbands ended up telling them that 'Now I know I can't beat you. Some friends of mine told me that I can't do it.' ... I think more publicizing does serve the purpose of inhibiting or regulating men's violent behaviour."

Some helping professionals believed that public education about wife assault could also focus on couple relationships. They indicated that because of some traditional practices, many traditional Chinese couples do not openly express their passionate feelings, and often keep their daily communication mostly on a functional level, focusing on how to raise children or how to help the older generation. As a result, their relationships become tense, leading to the possibility of family violence. Therefore, public education could emphasize communication skills between couples and emotional intimacy. It was proposed that the means to educate women and the public on issues of wife abuse could be multifaceted. The formal education system, ESL curricula, mass media—such as TV, radio, movies, newspapers, and magazines—could all be used to reach out to people. Those who are not affected by woman abuse directly could also benefit because they could help pass on the message to people who need it.

Education should also be extended to any helping professionals who work directly with Chinese immigrant women in the social service sector, health sector, or criminal justice system. If people are not sensitive enough to detect whether or not their orientations, assumptions, and practices fit their clients' frames of reference and/or needs, they will not be able to provide effective intervention. Some participants stated: "I think cultural sensitivity training will be very helpful for workers in the field of social services. You know, very often the kind of theory or framework we use in working with abused women is very Western.... I think we need to get people engaged in self-reflection to examine their own experiences." "I think we need to advocate more and educate family doctors and medical professionals in hospitals. Many people working in Emergency are not very responsible. I have seen some situations ... you know, they saw the bruises and wounds, but they never questioned the situation."

Ethnic-Specific Approaches and New Initiatives

Helping professionals interviewed indicated that new initiatives are necessary to ensure that ethnic-specific needs will be met. They felt the urgency to hire more Chinese-speaking staff in mainstream agencies, to allot more resources to establish more innovative, ethnic-specific organizations to accommodate culturally specific needs, and to promote cultural sensitivity among front-line workers through on-the-job training. A Chinese hotline for family violence was thought to be urgently required because "Women should be given an opportunity to talk about their emotions and feelings in their own language when they feel that their psychological health is being jeopardized and they are emotionally distressed." It was also noted that new community initiatives could provide a better political platform for concerned Chinese-Canadian citizens to articulate their concerns and advocate for women. Also, the establishment of more ethnic-specific agencies could provide Chinese immigrant women with a safer and more comfortable space in which to interact with others, become familiar with community resources, and seek practical assistance. When the language and cultural barriers are removed, these women will be able to develop a sense of belonging more readily, so they will be more able to reach out for help. Having a shelter just for Chinese women was considered the ideal scenario because, as one participant put it, "When you live in a shelter for Chinese, you can start building a support network around you right there.... When these women get together, they can empower themselves to do something.... They can help themselves to rebuild their lives."

In addition, when providing ethnic-specific services, helping professionals could take note of Chinese values and beliefs, showing respect and understanding when the client is working on a strategy or decision. Two participants noted:

> To many Chinese women, this is where their ambivalence is. They have great difficulties answering the question 'What are you going to do? Stay or leave?' ... They need time to struggle before they allow themselves to even think about the question of leaving. So, if you ask the question too early in counselling, you will be pushing her out of your door.... She would think 'This counsellor wants me to leave him.' Then she will never come back to you.

> Family is an important value to the Chinese. It is very difficult if you want to change that value. You can't say to a woman that there's nothing wrong to view the self as the centre of life. This is a challenge to her cultural beliefs. However, if you want to sell her the concept of self or ask her to look beyond the cultural baggage about family ... you need to reframe it as a health issue.... In that way, we can say to her that she must take care of her own health and emotional state first so that she will be able to do other things. If we know her culture and reframe the issue this way, it would be easier to sell the concept [of self].

Helping professionals considered *individual and group counselling* to be equally important and effective. For example, a wife assault counsellor stated: "One-to-one emotional support is sometimes more desirable than group support because they often feel uneasy about sharing their personal feelings with a group of people. Some women may have a greater need for group support.... Some women who are very isolated may want to make more friends in a group setting.... These women may need more support from a group of friends, so group work will be more useful to them." In terms of individual counselling, they believed that through this in-depth contact with the women, counsellors would be able to help the women to reflect, analyze their situations, and make informed decisions about their relationships. One participant remarked: "There was a woman whom I referred to Chinese Family Life for counselling. She found the social worker there very helpful to her, so gradually she accepted the idea of going to a shelter and then she was empowered to initiate a divorce." In terms of group work, when they first reached out, many abused women did not think that meeting with other women in the same situation would be helpful due to fear of being labelled, but once they realized the advantage of participating in a group, they benefited greatly from it. Some helping professionals reported: "[G]roup work is a very good approach to help women break their isolation. They can feel that they are not alone.... Also ... they can continue to call each other and be the support for each other.... In the beginning, many people [are] afraid that they may be talked about or be identified.... However, once I get a group started, I found that they could really stick together and use the group process for personal healing." "Women's groups provide a very important source of support too.... You know, a worker can't follow a woman 24 hours a day to protect her or encourage her. She needs a social network she can rely on."

Programs and Services for Men

Besides counselling and group work, some helping professionals referred to the significance of developing programs and services for men in order to deal effectively with male violence against women in intimate relationships. Basically, they felt that the education of men is necessary because men need to unlearn their destructive aggressiveness toward their spouses, and learn a more healthy way to handle their anger. Some participants argued that having these services would prevent women from further suffering:

> I don't think the only way to deal with wife abuse is to remove the client from the abusive relationship. We can help both men and women cope with their situations. You know, practically we don't have enough resources to help so many women who are out of the relationships. Many women struggle to survive after they are removed from the relationship. They are miserable and lonely out there. They feel lost and [are] still in a process of grieving their loss. We need programs for men so that the problem could be prevented or would not deteriorate that quickly.

> Some of my clients aren't the first wife of their husband's, and he had abused his first wife before. That means he has been abusive in all his intimate relationships with women. He hasn't changed a bit, so we need to do more work with men. I

think we need to reinforce court-ordered counselling. It is not enough to just provide counselling for women. We need to do some work with men too. Among all the cases I have, none of the abusers has been ordered to receive counselling.

7. LIMITATIONS ENCOUNTERED

The helping professionals recruited in this study were very dedicated individuals who had been working with Chinese immigrant women for many years in the community, yet they sometimes found it not very fulfilling because of the limitations they encountered in helping those in great distress. They believed that many of these restrictions could be removed if our society was willing to acknowledge the predicaments their clients experienced, and accommodate their needs. The limitations that were articulated by the helping professionals included limited resources, timely access to a group, and issues of professional objectivity.

Limited Resources

It was pointed out that although some mainstream agencies have hired a Chinese-speaking front-line worker, often this appointment was motivated by political reasons (e.g., it was funding driven or plain tokenism). Often, this person was hired part-time, so she was unable to meet the needs of many clients and had to prioritize her responsibilities. Because ethnic-specific agencies were mostly new, small, and had very limited resources, even though they knew the needs were great, they did not have the resources to do as much. As these participants indicated, there were insufficient resources for Chinese immigrant women; no matter how willing front-line workers were to help their clients, their hands were tied and they experienced frustration similar to that which their clients felt.

Timely Access to a Group

Although participants rated group work highly, women who wanted to participate in a treatment or support group often had to wait for a long time because of limited resources. As a result, some women who showed an initial interest lost their motivation, or their schedules changed over time, preventing them from participating. Consequently, the commence-

ment of a group might have to be further delayed until enough participants were recruited. This became a vicious circle because at a later time,
women who were very ready to join a group would again have lost their
interest in the second round of recruitment.

Issue of Professional Objectivity

The third limitation some participants mentioned was related to the
subtlety of professional objectivity and the dynamic between the worker
and her client. It was reported that as helping professionals worked closely
with abused women, occasionally their own emotions might have been
too evident in the counselling sessions. They believed that some workers
might be more sensitive and skilful than others in not influencing their
clients' decisions, or avoided being judgmental when they did not concur
with the decision their clients made. On the one hand, when the woman
perceived that she might have "failed" the worker, she might feel ashamed
and withdraw from the relationship. On the other hand, in order to show
genuine support, yet restricted by her own professional boundaries, the
helping professional had a very tough time handling her own emotions.
Burnout was a possible consequence. One participant described this dynamic vividly:

> Some of the clients rely very heavily on the worker to get [them] support and
> the kind of services they need. When they are under the circumstance that they
> have to change their mind to return to their husbands, they feel that … they
> have betrayed their workers. They feel that they have let the worker down after
> she has done so much to help them be independent. … I feel that in many situa-
> tions, it is not easy for the worker as well. When you support totally the woman's
> decision to leave her husband and could see that returning to her husband is
> not a workable alternative, yet if the woman wants to return, you have to let her.
> It is very difficult for the worker emotionally and I don't know if somehow the
> worker may have communicated subtly to the client that she's disappointed.…
> It is very common that the woman would leave and return to her husband many
> times. … When you work with women in these situations, it's rather fatal to the
> worker because you are afraid that the woman is going to get hurt again. … Yes,
> you want to support the woman's decision in all cases, but in some situations,
> you feel bad about her decision. … Say if the woman had been very emotionally
> dependent on the worker, when she was not dependent on the husband, she
> depended on the worker, so she might be afraid that her decision would disap-

point the worker. That's why I said as a social worker, we try to be very objective and open to all kinds of decisions. However, we are only human and we may somehow communicate our feelings in our interactions with the clients.... I just feel that things like that really consumed my energy and worried me so much as a worker.

DISCUSSION

The findings of this study indicated that the issue of woman assault in intimate relationships in the local Chinese community is a complicated one, which has implications for our general understanding of woman abuse, service delivery models, and professional development for front-line workers, especially regarding issues of cultural stereotypes and cultural sensitivity. Generally, according to the participants of this study, although individuals' experiences with wife abuse are unique, there are similar patterns of coping that could be traced in the course of their struggles.

Because of their professional experiences with abused Chinese immigrant women, the participants' accounts, to a certain degree, resonated with the self-reported experiences of the abused reported in a later chapter. While the women sometimes sympathized with the abusers and persuaded themselves to stay in their relationships, hoping that someday their partners might change, they did take action to protect themselves, signal their crises, and seek advice. Though leaving their husbands was often deemed a last resort, Chinese immigrant women, with appropriate assistance from helping professionals, gathered their courage and asserted their independence to take action as the situation required or when they were ready. Although most abused Chinese immigrant women were socialized into believing in the traditional ideologies of women's virtues and family, when they realized that keeping the relationship would no longer benefit them or their children, most of them ended the relationship.

In the following, I will discuss the findings of this research in light of other related studies. Anderson (1992), Gallin (1992), and Goodwin and Tang (1996) have pointed out that because of the patriarchal beliefs and values of their culture, Chinese women are often expected to be submissive, and are thus placed in more vulnerable positions. However, participants of this study also noted that because the Confucian ideas that have heavily influenced Chinese culture disapprove of aggression and emphasize harmony among people, there should not be cultural stereotypes that conclude that woman assault or wife abuse is a result of Chinese culture.

When we note that it is the position of immigrant women that makes them susceptible or vulnerable to male violence, we need to examine both the women's social position in their country of origin and their cultural and social positions in Canada. As indicated by the participants in this study, because of immigration and acculturation, Chinese immigrant men and women are given a lower social status across the board; Chinese men's frustration and coping style, when exacerbated by inadequate anger management and male chauvinism, sometimes can give them the excuse to abuse women. The problem is about how men in general, no matter whether they are Asians or Caucasians, grant themselves a higher social and political status and exert power over women to their advantage in various public domains.

The participants of this study reported observed aspects of their clients' abusers that correspond to the propositions that men who abuse their wives are likely to possess personality problems, experience structural strains, and lack effective coping skills for handling frustration (Gelles & Straus, 1988; Shainess, 1977; Dutton, 2007). In addition, some participants in this study agreed with the explanation given by Chambon (1989) and Berry (2001) that a combination of circumstances resulting from negative experiences during acculturation can increase immigrant men's violent tendencies and escalate wife-beating.

The helping professionals in this study observed that when the abusers learned that by law they could not inflict physical harm on their wives, and that their wives had been made aware of the new standards in Canada concerning wife abuse, they either reduced their physical aggression toward their wives or stopped it completely. This corresponds to Dutton's (1995) conditioning theory, which proposed that intensive punishment would help to stop male violence. In addition, the helping professionals' reports on women's reluctance to leave relationships in order to avoid the dissolution of family and undesirable social labelling seem to support arguments by Yllo and Bograd (1988), MacKinnon (1990), and Russell (1990, 2000) that the social institutions of marriage and family are the sites of many women's struggles against male violence. Citing the influence of women in the older generations and the popular culture's portrayal of women, the helping professionals clearly revealed that it was the culturally sustained ideologies of women's virtues, marriage, and family that trapped women in their abusive relationships, preventing them from exploring or accepting other alternatives. As a result, the women had to struggle for a long time before they felt sufficiently justified to confront their husbands or end their relationships.

Furthermore, feminist historians such as Gordon (1988) and Hartmann (1981) have argued that it is society's patriarchal culture and capitalist practices that endorse male violence against women, make women economically dependent, and provide women with few options to leave abusive relationships. The helping professionals of this study seemed to agree with this position. They observed that the patriarchal assumptions embedded in the immigration policy and the capitalist structure of the Canadian society force women to rely on their husbands financially and emotionally. Also, the lack of affordable child-care facilities, the highly competitive Canadian job market, and the women-unfriendly social welfare system have created major barriers for abused Chinese immigrant women to leave abusive relationships, while at the same time their lack of information and English skills also prevents them from doing so.

According to the helping professionals in this study, in order to more effectively help abused Chinese immigrant women to cope with their situations, there should be short-term goals to empower women and bridge the language gap in the existing systems. They strongly recommended that the ESL curriculum include Canadian law and issues of human rights and family violence. They believed that more resources should be given to enhance current services, especially for the translation of existing written materials on woman abuse and interpretation assistance. Long-term goals would entail lobbying for a Chinese women's shelter and a Chinese helpline. In-depth, culturally sensitive, and ethnically specific counselling, as well as continuous public education for both men and women, were also considered necessary to meet people's needs.

Concurring with the findings of Pederson (2003) and Leong and Ponterotto (2003), the Chinese helping professionals in this study raised concerns about cultural biases and cultural ignorance among their non-Chinese colleagues and other health professionals who assist abused Chinese immigrant women in dealing with their situations. The most pivotal point made by these professionals, who work directly with abused Chinese immigrant women on a daily basis, was that in order to help women organize, it is necessary to provide them with the right platform and support, and empower them on their own terms so that they can build their own support network to make a new life for themselves after they have survived abuse.

Chapter 6

Experiences of Front-line Shelter Workers in Providing Services to Immigrant Women Impacted by Family Violence

Angie Rupra

PURPOSE AND RATIONALE OF STUDY

The purpose of this research study was to explore how front-line work-ers in shelters for abused women and children provide support to im-migrant women impacted by family violence. The idea for the study emerged from situations I encountered while working at two shelters for abused women and children. In conversations with colleagues, front-line shelter workers expressed difficulties in providing support to immigrant women. Working with immigrant women whose cultures, religions, and languages were different from theirs was viewed as a chal-lenge by the workers, who were supposed to provide effective support for the women. Given that the issue of service provision to immigrant women has been addressed in the literature, I became interested in exploring the challenges that workers continue to experience in their professional practice.

RESEARCH ISSUES AND QUESTIONS

In order to better understand shelter service provision to immigrant women, this research study's overarching question was: How do front-line shelter workers experience providing services to immigrant women who have been impacted by family violence? This research study set out to examine three key issues:

1. the training of front-line shelter workers
2. the experiences these workers encounter in providing services to immigrant women
3. workers' recommendations for how shelter service provision could be improved to better support immigrant women

The three sub-questions that followed were:

1. What training have front-line shelter workers received in working with immigrant women impacted by family violence, and do they perceive the training they have received to be effective?
2. What factors make providing services to immigrant women impacted by family violence challenging for front-line shelter workers?
3. What changes need to occur in order for front-line shelter workers to better support immigrant women impacted by family violence?

LITERATURE REVIEW

Historical Context

During the 1960s and 1970s, family violence shifted from being viewed as a private matter to a public issue (Loseke, 1992; O'Keefe, 1994; Yick, 2001). The emergence of shelters for abused women and children coincided with the rise of the feminist movement's focus on politicizing the issue of violence against women (Donnelly et al., 1999; Epstein et al., 1988; Srinivasan & Davis, 1991; Supriya, 2002). As awareness of the issue has grown, so too has the number of shelters (Donnelly et al., 1999). Thus, the 1970s saw the emergence of family violence as a social issue and shelters as a public response.

Shelters now serve as one of the primary resources available for women and children escaping situations of violence (Davis, 1988). The efforts of local women's groups, many of whom were of Western European heritage and high economic status, have often been credited with the establishment of the first North American shelters (Donnelly et al., 1999). This historical development is important in understanding shelter service provision as it applies to immigrant women.

Norms based on the experiences of White middle-class women have become inherent in the structure of shelters for abused women and children (Bonilla-Santiago, 1996; Donnelly et al., 1999; Klein et al., 1997; MacLeod & Shin, 1993; Supriya, 2002). This has resulted in the assumption that all women residing in shelters share the same needs. Normalizing practices based on North American food, language, dress, and child-rearing practices have created a "typical" type of shelter user (Supriya, 2002), constructing the immigrant woman as an example of an "other" type of resident (Campbell et al., 1997; Donnelly et al., 1999; Supriya, 2002). Women responsible for the formation of the shelter movement were trained in feminist approaches to provide services for women, which have implications for the way services have been delivered to immigrant women (Supriya, 2002). I will discuss this point later in this chapter.

CHALLENGES AND BARRIERS UTILIZING SHELTER SERVICES

It is now widely reported in the literature that immigrant women who have been abused experience difficulties utilizing community and social services (Bonilla-Santiago, 1996; Huisman, 1996; MacLeod & Shin, 1990, 1993; Paredes, 1992; Preisser, 1999; Rafiq, 1991; Raj & Silverman, 2002; Sharma, 2001; Supriya, 2002). The majority of the literature that emerged during the 1990s specifically explored social service provision to immigrant women impacted by family violence. This literature clearly illustrated that immigrant women who used social services did not receive support that reflected their needs, values, and world views.

Although several attempts have been made to research immigrant women's experiences in accessing and utilizing community services, shelters for abused women and children have not been the focus of these studies. However, critiques of services by immigrant women who had utilized shelters still emerged through various studies assessing social service provision to immigrant women. The existing literature has demonstrated that the operation of shelters does pose specific challenges for immigrant women.

Many immigrant women are unfamiliar with the structure and services of shelters because such facilities may not have existed or been discussed publicly in their countries of origin (Acevedo, 2000; Lee, 2000; Rafiq, 1991). Even if immigrant women are familiar with the existence of shelters, many may view them as culturally inappropriate or unacceptable (Raj & Silverman, 2002). This is partly because of the stigma many immigrant women may face when they attempt to leave their abusive relationships. They will be offered no support from their families and communities if they do so.

Shelters provide a safe haven for women to begin living independently from their abusers. This aspect of shelters is empowering to women and children who have been impacted by family violence (Loseke, 1992). Feminist ideology places importance on women's safety and individual needs (Sharma, 2001), which is reflected in the focus of many shelters that encourage women to live independently from their abusers. This model of empowerment rests on feminist perspectives about social service delivery (Yick, 2001). Leaving the abuser is a mainstream conceptualization of intervention that may not necessarily be empowering for many abused women (Lee, 2000).

Although it is one important form of service delivery, the individualistic focus of shelters that encourage women to live independently from their abusers may not be congruent with the needs of many immigrant women (Lee, 2000; MacLeod & Shin, 1993; Rafiq, 1991). Many immigrant women may link their personal identities and happiness to their families and communities. A lack of family-based support in shelters is viewed as a critical gap for women who may use the services; it reflects that the familial system is often ignored in woman abuse services (MacLeod & Shin, 1993). For example, existing literature states that family counselling may be one useful way of responding to family violence among families of various cultures (Lee, 2000; MacLeod & Shin, 1993; Paredes, 1992; Rafiq, 1991; Wiebe, 1985). However, feminist principles assert that before this can occur, individual interventions must take place to ensure that family interventions are safe for the women and children involved (Lee, 2000; Rafiq, 1991).

Racism continues to exist in shelters for abused women and children (MacLeod & Shin, 1990; Sharma, 2001). Through informal interviews with service providers, MacLeod and Shin (1990) found that some residents in women's shelters have no tolerance for immigrant women cooking their ethnic food or practising their religious customs in the shelters. Cultural insensitivity is another barrier inherent in shelter services to women (Raj & Silverman, 2002). The shelter staff, meals, and facilities often do not reflect the diversity of cultures and the realities of many women living in our society.

Current literature has identified a significant need for professional development among shelter staff. One key area identified is for shelters to build better working relationships with cultural and ethno-specific agencies (Paredes, 1992; Lee, 2000; Raj & Silverman, 2002). Better relationships between shelters and ethnic-specific agencies would facilitate ongoing networking and sharing of information and resources. Training on immigration policies has also been identified as another important area that would help front-line workers provide more effective services to immigrant women (Access Alliance Multicultural Community Health Centre, 2003; Legault, 1996).

Gaps in the Literature

Despite their growing number, few shelters across North America have been evaluated (Davis, 1988; Epstein et al., 1988; Tutty et al., 1999). Research has tended to focus on prevalence rates of abuse, severity of abuse, and characteristics of women using shelter services (O'Keefe, 1994; Tutty et al., 1999). Most research has looked at the experiences of White middle-class women, neglecting issues pertinent to immigrant women, which represents a racial bias in the research (Huisman, 1996). With this gap, mainstream social services, including shelters, do not have research to inform changes in the model of their service delivery. Little research has been done to explore the effectiveness of services provided by shelters. Although exploring the effectiveness of service delivery to immigrant women is a relatively new area of focus (Rafiq, 1991), current literature clearly states that shelters are one of the problematic areas of service delivery. Given the critiques of shelters that have surfaced, it is important to explore how shelters provide services to immigrant women impacted by family violence. This would then allow for a meaningful exploration into better provision of services (O'Keefe, 1994; Raj & Silverman, 2002).

METHODOLOGY

A combination of evaluation, action research, and feminist methodologies was used to conduct this research study. Qualitative interviewing methods were used for data collection with front-line shelter workers. As one of the important stakeholders in the field of service delivery, front-line shelter workers were given the opportunity to become actively involved in the research process by providing information and identifying their needs and opinions.

Four front-line workers participated in this study, each employed by different shelters across Southern Ontario. Three of the four participants self-identified as immigrant women. Two participants were visible women of colour. Participants held varying degrees of educational and professional experience. The range of their shelter working experience varied from one to 13 years.

Both the executive director of each shelter as well as each participant signed letters of consent indicating their participation in the study. All personal identities were kept anonymous for confidentiality. I made my role as a shelter worker known to all participating shelter directors and participants. This shared characteristic indeed helped me build a rapport with the participants more quickly. I benefited from understanding the organizational structure and power dynamics inherent within shelters, which allowed me to work more effectively within the system to further the research process. However, there were differences between the participants of this study and me, which included our racial and ethnic identities, immigration statuses, religions, ages, educational experiences, and professional experiences.

It is important to note that findings from this research study cannot be generalized to the experiences of other front-line shelter workers. The qualitative nature of this study captured participants' experiences; however, because attempts were not made to obtain a representative sample, the findings cannot be applied to all shelter workers in Southern Ontario. Furthermore, the experiences of other social service providers, such as settlement workers and ethno-specific practitioners, were not captured. Workers in women's centres and community agencies may also have valuable contributions regarding how shelters can better support immigrant women impacted by family violence. The voices of immigrant women who utilize shelter services were not included in this research study. The absence of these critical voices was due to my lack of resources, including time and access to interpreters. As a result, immigrant women's perceptions of difficulties in the working relationship with front-line shelter workers were not accounted for, nor were their ideas included regarding what changes are needed in shelters. While these are important areas to be pursued as they have not been given enough attention in the existing literature, because of the limitations of this study, I leave them for further studies in the future.

FINDINGS AND DATA ANALYSIS

Prior to analyzing the data, three categories for analysis were determined based on the purposes of this study: (1) participants' training; (2) challenges experienced by participants in providing services to immigrant women; and (3) changes identified by participants that would allow immigrant women to be better supported.

1. Training

Participants were asked introductory questions related to their professional experiences. Their experiences working in shelters ranged from one to 13 years. In terms of specific training they received to work with immigrant women impacted by family violence, none of the four women reported that she had received training from shelters focused specifically on the issues relating to immigrant women and family violence. In addition to not receiving training from shelters, three of the four women stated that they never received any educational, workshop, or seminar training related to the issue. In other words, only one participant identified having received training relevant to the issues of immigrant women. The shelter at which she was employed at the time of this study had arranged for some training from an outside agency on a few occasions that was led by women of colour and immigrant women. These training sessions focused on issues of discrimination experienced by diverse groups, including immigrant women and women of colour. The participant who received this minimal training stated that the training did not address the issues that immigrant women experience when abuse occurs. It also did not focus on how shelter service could be delivered in a way that would better support immigrant women. Therefore, although she identified having received some training regarding immigrant women, it did not make any linkages to issues of woman abuse.

Another participant said she received anti-racism training from the shelter, but she assessed it as being heavily influenced by "Western" perspectives. She stated that although the anti-racism education had raised her awareness of the issues of racism, it did not address any concrete skill-building in serving immigrant women. Furthermore, the anti-racism courses did not specifically address issues pertaining to immigrant women dealing with family violence. Therefore, the data of this study suggest that anti-racist responses have not been adequate in directly helping the participants—the front-line workers—to support immigrant women who were abused by their partners.

2. Challenges

All four participants indicated that in their jobs they provided support services to immigrant women on a regular basis. These supports included providing informal counselling, crisis counselling, child care, and advocacy. The latter advocacy consisted of assisting women in applying for welfare; acquiring housing and financial support; finding employment; and dealing with educational, legal, and immigration issues. In describing the challenges that they experienced when providing support to immigrant women in shelters, language was raised as one area with which they had great difficulties, especially in the translation process.

In the following comment, one participant pointed out how cultural expression could be lost when an interpreter was used: "A lot is lost in translations when you use an interpreter. You're looking at body language, which is cultural. You're looking at intonation.... Um, all sorts of non-verbal communication is lost when you use an interpreter. And as a counsellor, a lot of what I use is non-verbal, right?" (lines 164–169). Another example was given in which a front-line shelter co-worker misinterpreted a woman's tone of voice to be angry when she was speaking to her child because she was speaking loudly. The study participant had to explain to her co-worker that just because the woman's tone of voice was louder than other women in the house did not necessarily mean she was angry. Both examples revealed the complexity involved with language barriers, which often caused misunderstandings.

A bonding between workers and the women who speak the same language was identified by the participants. One worker identified that she felt supported by her manager because her judgment in translation was trusted. That is to say, when a woman came to the shelter and spoke the same language as the worker, the management expressed trust in the worker's ability to support the woman because of the common language they shared. She said: "When we have someone who is the front-line worker at the shelter, and who comes from an immigrant background, I would say automatically there is a link between the woman who comes to the shelter, [and] speaks the same language ... it doesn't matter what department you do—the children, the women, the outreach—there is the link. The woman wants to talk" (lines 374–379). As a front-line worker fluent in a language other than English, she stated: "We, the people from certain communities, would see more" (lines 402–403). Therefore, the participant regarded the ability to speak a specific language that was familiar to the women coming to the shelter as encompassing more than just an understanding of words. It also implied an understanding of one's expression in a cultural context.

Some previous studies have indicated that children are commonly used as interpreters for immigrant women utilizing social services. Participants of this study confirmed that this practice continues to occur, which can be problematic. Because of a lack of availability of interpreters, one participant stated she witnessed on a few occasions that children were used to act as translators between their mothers and the staff of the shelter: "The resources are not there. We recently had a woman who spoke Chinese and whose English was really—it was really hard to understand her. And communication was practically non-existent. So we relied on the children to translate for household things and things like that" (lines 96–101). This participant described feeling extremely frustrated by having to use children as translators. She felt that she was unable to provide the woman with the same level of support that she provided to other women who spoke English.

Other participants stated that using children as interpreters was particularly problematic because these children had already witnessed or experienced abuse at home and should not be put in such a compromising situation to fill the gap. The translating process may cause these children to relive certain traumatic experiences or may bring up experiences of which they had no prior knowledge.

In addition, participants reported that they felt very upset and frustrated about the language barrier that keeps women who cannot speak English isolated from other women in the shelter. As a result of the language barrier, there was a division between immigrant women and Canadian-born women in the shelter. One participant reported: "She'll be more isolated and also it's more likely that the other, uh, immigrant women will uh, bond with her than women who have been Canadian. They'll tend to bond together, but not with the immigrant women" (lines 130–133).

Participants also identified the fact that they experienced cultural barriers when working with immigrant women impacted by family violence. Not being able to understand the cultural traditions or customs of a woman was stated as a barrier to providing effective support. One participant reported: "We act strictly based on our Canadian society's expectations of what counselling should be and expect them to act according to what we think is appropriate" (lines 172–175). This idea was also raised as a key barrier to effective service delivery with immigrant women in the literature reviewed earlier. It identified that the White, middle-class norms inherent in shelters have affected the way services are delivered to immigrant women.

The comment that women are expected to adapt to Canadian counselling norms highlights this issue. The participants in this study explained that workers often expect women to understand how the counselling process works without considering the woman's level of understanding of the social service sector. This could result in the worker and woman entering the counselling relationship with different expectations.

3. Changes

Each participant was asked about what changes need to occur so that front-line workers can better support immigrant women in shelters. All four women identified and described a wide range of changes that would improve service delivery to immigrant women.

Systemic changes were identified as needed in order to better support immigrant women impacted by family violence. All women stated that there is a need to diversify shelter staff. They identified the need for a greater range of racial, educational, and experiential representation among the shelter staff. Hiring more immigrant women was described as important because it would lead service users to perceive the shelter as more approachable. The atmosphere of the shelter would be more welcoming, and women using the shelter services would be able to understand and relate to some staff members.

It was believed that a culturally mixed environment would provide immigrant women with a sense of comfort and peace of mind that they are not "singled out." However, one participant was careful to note that the hiring of an immigrant woman as a shelter worker does not necessarily mean that this worker will understand an abused woman's circumstance and experience. That is to say, training such front-line shelter workers to be culturally competent and understanding of issues of woman assault is just as significant as hiring more visible minority women in the shelter. Among the participants of this study, there was an assumption that immigrant status and cultural competence are critically linked.

Two participants of this study agreed that knowing another language would also help staff members to have a better understanding of immigrant women's cultural context. More importantly, since women using the shelter services are able to fully express themselves in their own language, having staff members who can understand the language would be a major benefit. Part of the reason that the participants expressed the need to diversify shelter staff was because of their concerns about whether other front-line shelter workers might have experienced some challenges in supporting immigrant women. They stated: "I've heard co-workers say that they find it too stressful talking to them because they don't understand what they're saying, which I take issue with" (lines 126–128). "I'm not saying that people are not working well with others, but I am saying little small insensitivities" (lines 298–299). These insensitivities included not taking the time necessary to explore issues affecting immigrant women. Rather than attempting to go beyond the language barrier, this participant observed that some workers spent less time with immigrant women who were not fluent in English than with women fluent in English. She interpreted this lack of sufficient support to be an insensitivity in working with immigrant women.

It was also identified that workers often do not see the cross-cultural differences that may affect women. A woman from China may indeed speak Vietnamese, but workers will tend to make assumptions based on the country she came from rather than asking her about her mother tongue or her needs. One participant observed that shelter workers tend to make assumptions based on the women's heritages, which may result in service delivery gaps. Rather than asking women which language they would like to receive services in, or which type of agencies they would like to be referred to, workers tend to make these decisions on their own without consulting the women. The participant described such a practice as disempowering women and devaluing their input.

All four participants raised the issue of training as a critical area in which change was definitely needed. Ideas for training that would help front-line shelter workers better support immigrant women included topics of immigration laws, legal issues, medical and health issues, impacts of family violence on immigrant women, and cross-cultural training in working with women from diverse cultures.

The need for on-the-job training about the immigration system was raised as a very concrete recommendation that should be adopted by shelters to better equip their front-line staff. It was also stated that workshops on topics of immigration policies and laws would be helpful for women residing in the shelters. One participant said that while much attention has been placed on reminding women of their family law rights, immigration policies relating to family violence are often neglected. She noted that issues affecting women are often interconnected, and a solid knowledge base in these areas is necessary to advance service provision for women.

Three participants identified the fact that issues pertaining to immigrant women are not often discussed among front-line workers at the shelters in which they work. If information about women is presented in a sensitive and informed manner, staff could use these opportunities on an ongoing basis to gain more awareness of barriers that abused immigrant women may have experienced. One participant expressed the need for immigrant women to share their experiences in staff training workshops so that front-line workers can learn from their lived reality. These findings demonstrated that despite critiques of cultural awareness and competency approaches, the participants identified the need for shelter workers to gain culturally specific knowledge.

Another idea suggested for systemic change within shelters that would allow for more effective support for immigrant women was to create spaces in the shelter for personal learning and growth. Shelters could set up in-house libraries that consist of a variety of educational materials for their service users. It would be appropriate to make computers available for women's use so that they could have better access to more information and community resources.

One participant suggested hiring a worker to deal specifically with im-migration issues. She stated that the role of the immigration worker could include working with immigrant women on legal and medical matters. The worker would be familiar with appropriate community resources and would be responsible for making referrals. Another participant recom-mended that an immigration worker would also be responsible for provid-ing training and seminars on immigration-related issues to both women residing in the shelter and to the staff. "So you made a phone call to 911. Hey, I want to flee this abusive relationship. It's hard to maintain this sort of mind. There are so many pressures: financial, emotional, you know. So … education, education" (lines 614–617).

Participants discussed ways that women could be better supported in exercising their religious and/or spiritual practices. One of the participants stated that a room in the shelter should be devoted to this purpose: "I think that if we have just … a room, saying it's a prayer room, if somebody wants to go there for meditation or prayer or whatever they want to do. A special room, no noise there, always clean, it will be nice. Because they are coming from abuse, you know, they need some peace of mind" (lines 435–440). It was identified that such a space would promote women's inner strength. "We are very good to provide them housing and legal information. We are very [emphasis on the word "very"] good at doing this sort of work, but I think we need to focus on their inner peace" (lines 685–688). Similarly, another participant suggested the idea for a "quiet room," which could serve as a prayer or meditation room. It could also be used for counselling and receiving visits from outside workers or professionals. It would therefore be a multipurpose room addressing women's religious and spiritual identities.

Participants raised examples in which their shelters have tried to support women's spiritual and religious well-being. "One woman requested wake-ups. She didn't want to use an alarm clock to wake up her roommates so she requested the overnight staff to wake her up so she could pray" (lines 249–252). "I have asked some women to try and keep the noise down because the other women were praying. I understand they were on leisure time, but uh, there's nothing wrong with being a little bit considerate to what others are doing" (lines 214–217).

When speaking along the lines of making necessary changes, participants of this study raised concerns about identity challenges that immigrant women often face, which warrant broadening the scope of counselling for women. "For many people there is a crisis of identity. There is the regular counselling for everyone, there is the counselling for abused women, for survivors, a lot of counselling" (lines 692–695). One participant described the immigration process as one that alters people's self-identity, which can make people feel lost in a new country. As such, the participant stated that counselling on identity is needed as it will address this issue and help newcomer women to build self-esteem by instilling more confidence in them. Although these women's primary needs may be shelter and food when fleeing abuse, issues related to their identities as visible minority immigrant women living in a predominantly White country may surface later, which require attention as well. The same participant further stated that acculturation can lead to loneliness, cultural isolation, and social alienation, especially with elderly immigrant women. She also pointed out that the lack of language-specific counselling often puts immigrant women, elderly immigrant women in particular, at further risk of isolation.

Because of the many perceived gaps existing in women's shelter work with immigrant women, approximately half of the interview time with each participant was spent discussing recommendations and remedies. Participants spent more time talking about what changes needed to happen based on their tremendous knowledge gained from working in shelters. In presenting their recommendations, participants also identified barriers that may prevent these changes from happening in shelters. For example, one participant noted that in order to implement her recommendation of hiring an immigrant worker, more funding would be required. Another participant expressed her frustration about not seeing recommendations implemented because of limited vision. She said: "The unfortunate thing is that, with this shelter in particular, we can have all the creative ideas that we want to and nothing's gonna happen because we have an obtuse mind, that's just so pathetic, running the place" (lines 830–833). Such a comment clearly illustrated participants' cynicism in the shelters' abilities to adopt changes presented in this study. Participants also identified the issue of organizational structures that could prevent changes from occurring. For example, when talking about anti-racism training, one woman responded: "A lot of it, though, is just for the full-time team" (line 430). "And part-time and relief are not included, so there is a split on the team" (lines 435–436).

CONCLUSION

This research study served three purposes: (1) to explore the training of front-line shelter workers; (2) to explore workers' experiences in providing support to immigrant women; and (3) to elicit their recommendations for how shelter service delivery to immigrant women could be improved. While these areas were discussed separately, the data collected from interviews with four front-line shelter workers in Southern Ontario revealed that these three areas are interconnected. Gaps in training and the experiences in providing support clearly informed the participants' recommendations.

The findings of this research study raise issues about creating social services for a multicultural population. They illustrate that there is a need for women's shelters to make changes so that their services can be made more accessible and appropriate for immigrant women. Participants did not identify the need to create separate shelters specifically for immigrant women and children, but rather recommended that shelters should take responsibility to ensure culturally appropriate support for immigrant women. Clearly, service delivery issues may continue to exist as shelters try to support abused immigrant women and their children. It is important to see continuing efforts in identifying ways to improve service delivery for them.

While this study has not attempted to explore the organizational structures of shelters, the findings show that organizational structures may impede the implementation of recommendations. Future research studies could explore organizational structures to assess whether shelters are being operated in a way that facilitates change to better support women. Implementing change can be difficult when resources are limited and organizational structures are not conducive to change. However, given that many of the recommendations could potentially benefit both immigrant and non-immigrant women, implementing changes would be of great benefit to women using shelter services. The current study should be viewed as one step in the process of implementing changes in shelter services to immigrant women.

Chapter 7

Overview of Domestic Violence in the South Asian Community in Canada: Prevalence, Issues, and Some Recommendations

Ritu Chokshi, Sabra Desai, and Andalee Adamali

I didn't really want to understand domestic violence. I'd heard about it happening to other Asian women but I did not want anyone to know it was happening to me. I was ashamed to be called a battered woman.... You are expected to suffer in silence. You just keep it hidden behind closed doors and hope that it will go away. Getting the police involved is not really the done thing around here. You just get through it yourself.... (Rashpal) (Gill, 2004, pp. 474, 479)

It's a question of maintaining an honourable appearance and saying to people that the marriage is good. But really I knew it was bad but was too scared to say. (Kamal) (Gill, 2004, p. 474)

"B.C. Shooting Victim Speaks out against Domestic Violence" was another headline in recent news featuring domestic violence within the South Asian community ("B.C. Shooting Victim Speaks out against Domestic Violence," 2007). The victim, Gurjeet Kaur Ghuman, speaks out against what she calls "an epidemic of domestic violence in the Indo-Canadian community," and urges the community to recognize its presence, and women to take charge of the situation. This story features one of five recent cases of reported domestic violence incidents (with brutal violence and death as results) within the Indo-Canadian community in British Columbia, marking an alarming number of incidents within this particular community. Media coverage like this signals a concern about an issue that is perceived as community-specific. It is not clear if the portrayal implies that the South Asian community is facing a crisis of domestic violence, being stereotyped and considered as "other," or is being made to be responsible for finding solutions within its own process. From an immigration, settlement, and integration viewpoint, it becomes important to look at this community and address individual, institutional, and structural issues about domestic violence. In this chapter, we explore: (1) the prevalence of domestic violence in the South Asian community; (2) theoretical frameworks to enhance the understanding of intersecting issues pertaining to violence and South Asian women; (3) a community-based organization's attempt to address the issue in a culturally appropriate way; and finally (4) some recommendations for furthering work in this sector.

South Asian, immigrant, and woman—South Asian women's experiences of abuse can be understood within these three identifications and their intersections with one another. Being South Asian implies belonging to a culture and its set of norms; it also indicates an ethno-racial construct, of being a visible minority. Being an immigrant in Canada has its own implications in terms of social, economic, class, and racialized location. Being a woman also dictates participation in the construct of gender, gender roles, and negotiations with patriarchal power structures. When these identity constructs intersect with one another, another set of implications arises. Each of these social locations has a direct relation to how abuse is manifested, experienced, and understood, and what resources are available for these women. While these intersections and complexities are apparent in the lived reality of racialized immigrant women, the traditional feminist "violence against women" movement continues to emphasize a unidimensional, gender-based understanding of violence, ignoring the other forms of institutional and structural violence facing these women and their communities.

The current mainstream discourse and media portrayal of abused South Asian women are built largely around the depiction of a pathological community, thus placing the blame for domestic violence within the South Asian community as if it is an inherent result of South Asian culture ("B.C. Shooting Victim Speaks out against Domestic Violence," 2007). This further isolates the community and absolves the larger Canadian society from responsibility for examining the intersecting issues and finding solutions that mitigate them. The ongoing depiction of South Asian men as being inherently violent and South Asian women as being submissive feeds stereotypes and further marginalizes the community. Mainstream constructs of domestic violence intervention focus on an Anglocentric approach. This approach is based on an inter-personal violence model with emphasis on providing post-crisis services in the form of shelters, and ensuring the safety of women. This model is an important part of the domestic violence service provision process, but it fails to take into account certain unique needs of its South Asian clients. Inaccessible institutions, culture-blaming discourse, community stigmatization, and ongoing stereotyping of the South Asian community constitute a gravely inadequate response to meeting the needs of abused South Asian women.

The institutional and systemic barriers in accessing services that meet the needs of South Asian women need to be addressed in Canada, es-pecially in a major immigrant-receiving centre like Toronto. The South Asian community is the fastest-growing ethno-racial immigrant commun-ity in Canada. Statistics Canada has predicted a presence of more than 1 million South Asians in the city of Toronto by 2017, of which 70 percent will be first-generation immigrants (Belanger & Malenfant, 2005). This growing diverse community has unique needs that ought to be under-stood, and services that are responsive to the growing diversity in Canada have to be incorporated. Race, class, and gender oppressions within Can-adian society and their impact on abused South Asian women's access to services need to be acknowledged. What does it mean to be an abused South Asian woman in Canada? This chapter is presented within this context, which looks at abused South Asian women as part of a racialized immigrant community, avoiding a simplistic culturist or gender-based understanding of woman abuse.

The United Nations Declaration on the Elimination of Violence against Women (1993) defines violence against women as: "any act of gender-based violence that results in, or is likely to result in physical, sexual, or psychological harm or suffering ... including threats of such acts, coercion, or arbitrary deprivation of liberty whether occurring in private or public life." Domestic violence occurs when a family member, partner, or ex-partner attempts to physically or psychologically domin-ate or harm another. It takes many forms, including physical violence, sexual abuse, emotional abuse, intimidation, economic deprivation, or threats of violence. Domestic violence occurs in all cultures; people of all races, ethnicities, religions, and classes can be perpetrators of domestic violence (WHO, 2005). It is important to note that culture is not the cause of domestic violence; rather, it mediates and shapes the manifestation of violence in the family. Media portrayal, the exotification of minority women's experiences, the Anglocentric framework of analysis, the prevalence of pre-existing stereotypes about ethno-cultural groups, and the "imperialist gaze" all factor into the problematization of domestic violence as a cultural issue within the mainstream discourse (Burman, Smailes & Chantler, 2004; Liao, 2006; Das Dasgupta, 2000; George & Ramkissoon, 1998; Gill, 2004; Jiwani, 2005).

South Asians form the second largest visible minority group in Canada, and it is one of the fastest-growing visible minority groups in Canada (Tran, Kaddatz & Allard, 2005). South Asian ethnic identity is a social construct. It homogenizes diverse populations from distinct ethnic, religious, and linguistic groups with varying ancestries, immigration histories, and personal experiences. South Asians consist of immigrants from India, Sri Lanka, Pakistan, Bangladesh, Nepal, and twice-migrants from Guyana, Fiji, Tanzania, Kenya, Trinidad & Tobago, the United Kingdom, and Uganda. (Twice-migrants are people who have been living in other countries for multiple generations but they trace their original ancestry to the Indian subcontinent.) Despite all these differences, Tran, Kaddatz, and Allard (2005) believe that "the South Asian community is one of the most unified when it comes to the value they attach to family interaction, the maintenance of social networks within their cultural group, and the preservation of ethnic customs, traditions and languages" (p. 20). For convenience of discussion, South Asians are presented as a unified group, but it is important to remember that they do come from diverse subcommunities with distinct regional, religious, ethnic, and cultural identifications. Moreover, George and Ramkissoon (1998) state that South Asian women's experiences can be read through the broader constructed lenses of "immigrant women" and "women of colour"; this is clarified further by their quote of Ralston (1988), which situates South Asian women's identity in Canada as "fundamentally a social matter, not an individual matter," constructing their experiences as outside their own agency, which removes the self and situates entities like communities and society as central to their experiences (p. 104).

PREVALENCE OF DOMESTIC VIOLENCE WITHIN THE SOUTH ASIAN COMMUNITY

Empirical data on the prevalence of domestic violence within the South Asian community is scarce. Anecdotal evidence from focus groups, women's organizations, and media coverage of abuse-related deaths are the only sources available as insight into the empirical rate of incidence within this community. Statistics Canada's General Social Survey assessment of the victimization of women, especially that of women in minority communities and marginalized backgrounds, has been noted by academics as critically lacking (DeKeseredy & Schwartz, 2003). No large-scale studies looking into the rates of domestic violence within immigrant communities have been conducted in Canada, yet most media coverage focuses on immigrant and marginalized communities as sites in which domestic violence is prominent. This marginalization of the problem of domestic violence as a "community problem" and the Canadian government's reluctance to take a proactive stance in understanding and preventing the perpetration of domestic violence in marginalized communities poses a "double victimization" of South Asian women (like women from other visible minority and ethno-cultural groups). South Asian women are thus "doubly victimized": first by the violence perpetrated against them, and then by Canadian society, which often not only fails to provide the appropriate support and interventions that would empower these women, but also perpetuates the formation of stereotypes and racialization of immigrant cultures as inferior and traditionalist, which is causative of violence (Gill, 2004).

Ahmad, Riaz, Barata, and Stewart (2004) look at patriarchy as an ideological construct that impacts the perceptions of abuse within the South Asian community in Toronto. They have found that women agreeing with patriarchal social norms are less likely to identify subtler forms of spousal abuse. As a result, these women tend to be more tolerant of patriarchal constructs of traditional roles of wives and daughter-in-laws, and to reject the rights of women within their community. Of the women screened, 67.4 percent experienced tension in an intimate relationship and had difficulty in working out arguments. Of these, 24 percent experienced physical abuse perpetrated by their partners during the past five years, a statistic that is three times higher than Statistics Canada's General Social Survey 1999, which indicated that 8 percent of women in the Canadian general population experienced physical violence by their partners during the past five years. The above study is the first one of its type, not only in its empirical approach regarding violence prevalence, but also in its focus on the South Asian community in Canada. However, certain shortcomings of the study should be kept in mind. First, the response rate was low at 28.1 percent within a sample size of 47 participants. Second, questions of abuse were screened only after the participants admitted that there were tensions within the intimate relationship, which may have automatically screened out women without asking them about abuse outside the marital relationship (family, etc.). Third, the method of collecting information (20-minute telephone interviews) might not have been conducive to gaining reliable information on such a sensitive issue. Fourth, geographic limitation (only Greater Toronto Area participants) makes generalization of experiences to other South Asian communities in Canada impossible.

Another existing literature on South Asian community that we tracked was a community-based, empirical research study conducted in Boston with 160 South Asian immigrant women. Looking specifically at the rates of domestic violence, Raj and Silverman (2002) found that 40.8 percent of the women had been physically and/or sexually abused in some way at the hands of their current partners; 36.9 percent reported having been victimized in the past year; such rates were much higher than in the general population. Only 11 percent of the women reporting domestic violence indicated that they had used counselling services regarding their abuse. Another alarming statistic was the underusage of legal and police assistance. Only 3.1 percent of the abused South Asian women in the study had ever obtained a restraining order against an abusive partner, a rate substantially lower than that reported for all women in Massachusetts, which is over 33 percent in the past five years. These statistics show that domestic abuse within the South Asian community is underreported and there is a significant underusage of support services despite high rates of incidents. A larger study, covering more geographic areas, with an in-depth look at who these women are and what risk factors might be associated with intimate partner violence, would have enabled a more holistic view of the domestic violence situation in the South Asian community.

Richardson, Coid, Petruchevitch, Chung, Moorey, and Feder's (2002) cross-sectional study on domestic violence found that the prevalence of physical abuse for South Asian women in London, England, within the past year was 14 percent, with an overall lifetime rate of 41 percent—a rate that is significantly higher than the national average.

The prevalence of physical abuse for South Asian women, while established statistically, is still lacking more exhaustive study. This is especially true in the case of Canada, where the above cited study's small sample size, limited geographical analysis, and lack of understanding of common risk factors make it especially important to fill research gaps in order to better understand the phenomenon. The lack of analysis of ethnicities within the South Asian diaspora may further give a homogeneous expression to a South Asian identity that is socially constructed. While researching each community might be hard to accomplish, an acknowledgement of the possibility of differential needs and prevalence rates would be helpful in targeting communities that have a more acute need for interventions.

DOMESTIC VIOLENCE AND THE SOUTH ASIAN COMMUNITY: THEORETICAL FRAMEWORKS

George and Ramkissoon (1998) state that integrative anti-racism is a suitable framework for understanding the post-immigration experiences of South Asian women in Canada. The integrative anti-racism approach, a form of systemic analysis of experiences of racialized immigrant groups, was created by Calliste, Dei, and Belkhir (1995). It posits that "race could provide a point of entry through which other forms of oppression (including gender, sexual orientation, and disability) could be investigated" (George & Ramkissoon, 1998, p. 104). This approach enables us to look at incidences of domestic violence for South Asian-Canadian women through an analysis of their experiences from a systemic intersection view where gender, race, and class all come into play. Immigration category (e.g., family class or independent), length of stay in Canada, and linguistic abilities also play a role in the integration experiences of South Asian women. Multiple oppressions of race, class, and gender need to be considered when evaluating the status of South Asian women in Canada. Gill and Rehman (2004) included an evaluation of the status of abused South Asian women in London, England, through the framework of "dual oppressions," which took the status of racism that South Asian women face, and the levels of sexism within the South Asian community and the host society, as indicators of their vulnerability to domestic violence. This framework moves away from a simplistic "culture-blame" ideology and looks at various systemic barriers that immigrant women and women of colour face in host societies.

Jiwani (2005) challenges the notion of a "culturalist" interpretation of domestic violence within immigrant communities. Not only does a cultural explanation of occurrence of violence subsume the importance of structural and systemic issues related to domestic violence within immigrant communities, it also creates an essentialist discourse of "culture-blame." When immigrant communities and their culture are claimed as causal factors for social issues, racialization of culture occurs, creating an environment of denoting certain cultures as inferior, thereby further racializing the people represented in the cultural group. Certain cultural practices may lead to perpetuation of violence within the community, but this does not mean that the culture is the reason for the occurrence of domestic violence. It is important to look at factors affecting the prevalence rate and how these can be addressed.

Socio-historical processes, according to Burman, Smailes, and Chantler (2004), lead to "minoritization" of certain groups and communities. This approach challenges the ahistorical notions and construction of "minority ethnic groups"; it permits identification and analysis of continuities and differences of positions between women from different minoritized groups, thereby opening up the inquiry into how specific forms of racism and gender oppression intersect. It is important to be critical of how discourses of culture appear to marginalize and further exclude women from services. Burman et al. (2004) noted that "explicitly cultural or racialized explanations for domestic violence warranted in overlooking violence in favour of problematizing culture" (p. 340). These processes also lead to complacency in service provision, developing a form of institutional racism in which the needs of South Asian women are overlooked because of their ethnic identity rather than addressing their needs as members of Canadian society.

Patriarchal structure within the South Asian community is noted as one of the most crucial factors in assessing the risk of domestic violence within a family. Patriarchy is a universal ideology embodying a set of ideas and beliefs that justify male domination over women. This social ranking is an important determinant of gender relations as it creates and reinforces differential power between genders (MacKinnon, 1983, as quoted in Ahmad, Riaz, Barata, and Stewart (2004)). Severe manifestations of patriarchy within the South Asian community can be detected in instances of honour killings and dowry deaths. Intersection of gender, ethnicity, culture, and immigration status increases the risk of experiencing adverse manifestations of patriarchy, particularly conflicts in spousal relations. Ahmad, Riaz, Barata, and Stewart's (2004) study reviewed above established the influence of patriarchal beliefs in South Asian women's perception of abuse.

Das Dasgupta and Warrier (1996) studied how ideologies and conditions form the realities of the lives of Asian Indian immigrant battered women in the United States. They found that childhood indoctrination into the ideals of "good" wife and mother that suggest sacrifice of personal freedom and autonomy was one of the most significant influences in these women's lives. The women studied also felt that the reputation of their families in India, the preservation of traditions, and the presentation of an "unblemished" South Asian image to the U.S. mainstream were also their duties as women, leading to their refusal to expose the abuse they experienced. Therefore, understanding domestic violence in South Asian immigrant women needs to include investigating the impact of the pre-scribed role of women within the community and noting the immigration status and resettlement factors that add to the silencing of a community's issues in a racist host society.

Current research and literature on South Asian-Canadian immigrant women and their experiences of domestic violence is largely invisible, especially in Canada. Research on South Asian women and issues of domestic violence within that community have been neglected by the feminists and activists working in the field of gender rights and issues, furthering marginalizing the experiences of women of colour, and creat-ing implications for how violence within the community is perceived and the Eurocentric advocacy related to this perception. It therefore becomes important to challenge the impact of imperialist concepts of Western feminism and institutional racism on the delivery of appropriate and ef-fective services to South Asian women.

ISSUES RELATED TO DOMESTIC VIOLENCE IN SOUTH ASIAN COMMUNITY

South Asian immigrant women affected by domestic violence can be studied through two main influences in their lived reality as immigrants in Canada. First is the influence of their culture of origin—the value sys-tems, prescribed gender roles, customs, social structures, and other socio-cultural factors that create a cultural script for identity formation and play an important role in how certain issues are perceived and handled by the individuals and the South Asian community. The other strong influence is the living condition in the host culture, including the group's reception, adaptation, processes of acculturation, and levels of available support ser-vices, all of which play an important role in the lives of immigrant women in Canada. The compounding of these factors results in how abuse can be understood from the perspective of South Asian women's experiences and community. The following is an attempt to capture the complexities of multiple interactions at multiple levels noted in current literature.

In the case of the South Asian diaspora, patriarchy stands out as an overarching influence in prescriptions of gender roles within the com-munity, both within academic and community groups' research reports and experiences. Patriarchy as a theoretical concept was explored earlier and its implications for abuse perceptions are clearly demonstrated in Ahmad et al. (2004). A report submitted by the South Asian Family Services to the Canadian Panel on Violence against Women (1992), quoted in Agnew (1996), clearly shows the role of the existing levels and structure of patriarchy within the South Asian community as an important issue in understanding how violence against women is perpetuated. It states:

> We believe that the crucial variable in the explanation of violence against women is patriarchal power and resulting social inequality between men and women. Capitalism has encouraged possession of material property and women are also considered property to be possessed and dispensed with. Gender social-ization has always emphasized that man is the "head of the household," "the bread winner" and "the lord and master of all." Women are to be submissive, quiet, and obedient. Assertiveness is equated with selfishness.... [South Asian women] spend most of their lives under strict supervision of the family, in order to acquire appropriate "gender specific" behaviour. (p. 197)

Strong patriarchal beliefs lead to perpetuation of the view that domes-tic violence should be dealt with "inside the family." The public and the private space are again guarded by patriarchal norms. Rafiq (1991) states that there is a great deal of resistance to disclosing violence due to these norms, as well as a resistance to creating an adverse image of the com-munity within mainstream perceptions. Family structure and the role of women in South Asian families adds another dimension of cultural differ-ence from mainstream society (Abraham, 2000, 2005). Choudhry (2001) states that "family and kinship provide the basis of the individual's identity as well as facilitating continuity of culture and religion" (p. 378), which is to say that family needs are perceived to supersede those of the individual, and the individual is responsible for being an active actor in maintaining the continuity of cultural and religious norms of the family—women be-ing the main "culture bearers" of the community.

The role of women is also prescribed within the socio-cultural norms and socialization of girls, resulting in specific gender role behaviours and expectations. It is important to remember that gender roles and socio-cultural norms are varying and non-static. Choudhry (2001) states that "the role of women varies with generational, socio-economic and edu-cational levels. It can be patriarchal or egalitarian. Nevertheless, women are socialized to a prescribed role encompassing dutiful wife, obedient daughter-in-law, and loving mother. Marriage is for life, and happiness or sorrow is fated" (p. 380).

Migration increases women's vulnerability to experiencing detrimental expressions of patriarchy. Immigrants encounter economic, systemic, informational, cultural, and linguistic barriers to accessing support and services. The magnitude of these barriers is often higher for women due to their multiple caregiving responsibilities (Ahmad et al., 2004). Women face "double workloads," both salaried and domestic, adding to the pressures of adapting to a new environment, and making them more vulnerable and disadvantaged when other stressors (like marital conflicts) are added.

Arranged marriages and unions where women migrated under the family reunification class were found to be more prone to incidents of domestic violence. Liao (2006) found significant evidence of susceptibility for this group, with rates of acculturation as another marker of differential rate and form of domestic violence. Issues of acculturation often result in various mental health problems. In studying both first- and second-generation South Asian immigrants in Canada, Abouguendia and Noels (2001) found them to be vulnerable in coping with acculturation. Higher acculturative stress is compounded with in-group hassles and "everyday racism" (Ahmad et al., 2004).

The presence and influence of extended family networks, the role of mothers-in-law in condoning and perpetuating violence within a family, the concept of dowry, the lack of a social network in Canada, the lack of information about available services, unfamiliarity with and lack of faith in the institutional system and services, language incompetence, fear of ostracization from the community, low employability skills, lack of ethno-specific shelters, a lack of faith in the police and the Canadian justice system, immigration status and vulnerability of sponsorship status, the pro-charge and pro-prosecution legal system, etc., are factors that determine instances of domestic violence in the South Asian community. All these uniquely shaped culture of origin influences interact with migration status to create a huge challenge for the mainstream professional community in addressing the issue of domestic violence within the South Asian community in a socio-culturally sensitive manner. There is a need to be aware of the pre-migration culture, and its impacts on their clients' world views, and then to compute the complexities of what it is like to be immigrants in Canada when searching for approaches relevant to their clients. All of this is further compounded by data from Reitz's (1995) study, which found that these communities had a significantly low rate of utilizing many important social and health services despite the evidence of significant need in Canada, the U.S., Britain, and Australia.

Das Dasgupta (2000), academic and founder of Manavi (1985), a grass-roots organization fighting for social justice for South Asian immigrant women in the U.S., outlines the historical waves of immigration from India to the U.S., the shifts in the structure of the South Asian community, the denial of abuse and infractions within the community, and subsequent measures taken from within the community (mainly by feminist academics) to provide a voice for women. Her work recognizes the need to provide culture and ethno-specific services as mainstream services are often unable to understand the complexities of an immigrant woman of colour's needs.

Current services available for abused South Asian women are not designed to meet their unique needs. Kim (2002) identified the key service provision responses available through mainstream organizations as defining domestic violence within a limited interpersonal realm, with the primary goal of intervention being for the survivor to leave the relationship. Survivors are assisted through the shelter system, and the abuser is prosecuted through the criminal legal system. Immigrant women often come from countries where they are not used to having these kinds of services; they might resent such an approach. Response to violence against women has been institutionalized, with rigid professional boundaries, stringent rules, and regulations. Interventions have been standardized to fit a homogeneous survivor profile, disregarding race, ethnicity, class, sexual orientation, and immigrant status.

Shriwadkar (2004) assesses the state of services available to Indo-Canadian women in Canada, and presents a critical view of the policies and programs within Canada that act as a barrier in outreach, provision of services, and access to culturally sensitive solutions in this community. She notes that the pressures of cultural, social, and family ties prevent abused women from getting the necessary help to fight their abuse, while Canada's pro-prosecution, gendered immigration policies, and lack of awareness to accommodate differential needs create a precarious situation in which women cannot access the help they need.

Agnew's (1998) is another critical article addressing the status of services provided to South Asian women and discussing how service provision, even within ethno-specific organizations, is limited to short-term goals of providing access to social services. These services fail to advocate for change that will support women's rights, challenge patriarchal structures, and expose systemic power relations embedded within the larger community. They do not address the structural issues that perpetuate violence against women. Also, limited government funding is reported as a major obstacle for ethno-specific agencies to expand their programs beyond immediate settlement needs. Feminist agendas often take a back seat in addressing the needs of ethno-specific communities and issues of accessibility. In other words, both mainstream and ethno-specific settlement agencies fail to provide appropriate services. According to Agnew (1997), ethno-specific agencies, while making language-specific programs available, fail to go beyond incorporating language and cultural awareness within their programs. The basic structure and model of intervention retains mainstream conceptualization and interventions against violence. Shelters also recreate the hostile host environment against which marginalized women already struggle. They are bound by rules and regulations, lack cultural awareness of immigrant communities, are only a temporary reprieve, and are generally reported as alienating for South Asian and other immigrant women of colour (Agnew, 1998; Preyra, 1998).

It is only more recently that academic as well as community initiatives have started focusing on community-specific approaches to meeting the needs of ethno-racial immigrant communities. Models that advocate incorporating culture as the main context of designing interventions (Almeida & Lockard, 2005), awareness about specific needs of South Asian women (Agnew, 1998; Liao, 2006; Reavey, Ahmed & Majumdar, 2006), and needs analysis and evaluation of available services (Merchant, 2000) are some steps taken to create a body of literature that is specific to meeting the needs of South Asian women. While steps are taken to identify community-specific needs, with academic studies and community reports recommending that culturally appropriate solutions should be incorporated, none of them has been able to outline what this solution would look like for the South Asian community.

EXPLORING A NEW APPROACH TO DOMESTIC VIOLENCE IN SOUTH ASIAN COMMUNITY

In observing such gaps in literature and research studies, we chose a community-based organization's intervention strategies and programming to illustrate how domestic violence can be addressed in a culturally appropriate way. The following is a case study of the Punjabi Community Health Centre's (PCHC) domestic violence program and intervention strategies, looking at an approach understood as alternative programming that is more appropriate in meeting the needs of South Asian culture. We hope to present PCHC's approach as a reference for current service delivery practice so that more innovative ideas can be launched. Each community has unique needs, and this case example presents only a community-based organization's own experience of how it has created and implemented programs to meet its clients' needs. It should also be noted that the efficacy of PCHC's programs has not been evaluated. However, this innovative approach to meeting the challenges and needs related to domestic violence within the community is worthy of examination as an alternative to mainstream services. PCHC's model could as such be adapted by various communities facing similar challenges regarding institutional, personal, and structural dimensions of domestic violence.

The data collection process drew on multiple sources of information, such as key informant interviews and organization documents. Primary sources were interview transcripts and secondary sources were research reports, community presentations, and agency statistics. Key informant interviews, with open-ended questions, were conducted to gain information from the executive director (ED)/founder of the organization and one support group facilitator (SGF) for the domestic violence programs. The interviews with the ED and SGF enabled us to gain an organizational profile of the agency and an in-depth understanding of the mandate, history, current services, and statistics of service provision for the target group. Questions were also aimed at understanding the conceptualization of these services, the context of service provision, and the processes involved in engaging the community. Inquiry about program highlights, indicators of success, replication, and how such family-based interventions can be promoted within the service provision realm was also included.

Punjabi Community Health Centre (PCHC) has been serving the South Asian community around issues of health promotion, domestic violence, and addictions for 17 years. Its mandate includes serving the Peel community through community development and providing culturally appropriate services in meeting the needs of the South Asian community, especially Punjabi- and Hindi-speaking members. Due to South Asians' dissatisfaction with the mainstream services that are available to community members dealing with domestic violence, community efforts led to the formation of PCHC's culturally appropriate domestic violence programs.

Noting that the mainstream/traditional domestic violence intervention approach often serves men and women separately in cases of domestic violence and ignores the need to involve both partners and the extended family in mobilizing change, PCHC decided not to use a "blame-based" approach to engage South Asian men in ending violence as it does not seem to be culturally appropriate. Violence-related programming is often limited to the interpersonal level, not going beyond this to look at other contributing factors. Also, the institutional response of offering counselling and shelters for women often does not fully meet the needs of the South Asian community. For South Asian women, leaving the relationship often means leaving the community, which is a source of identity, familiarity, and resources.

PCHC noted that domestic violence interventions are governed by rules and regulations. Organizational mandates, rigidly structured intake, and professional emotionally distant counselling processes often alienate South Asian clients. Linguistic accommodations and having representatives from within the community might mitigate some of this sense of alienation, but the structure of these programs and professional mores attached to them continue to have a greater impact of isolating clients from ethno-racial immigrant communities. Also, the current domestic violence service provision sector is organized around post-crisis interventions. There are no systems in place to prevent violence. Post-crisis interventions are also severe in their form (involving law enforcement), making them the last resource that victims access; victims fight the battle alone until it goes beyond their capacity to handle. PCHC recognizes that there is a definite need for creating spaces that are secure and safe, where relationship issues can be discussed in a supportive environment.

PCHC understands violence against women as something that goes beyond patriarchal gender structures. They posit that within the South Asian community, utilizing a broader understanding of violence is essential in addressing the needs of the community. Violence against women by women, committed by members of women's extended families or natal families, is real and is almost always present to varying degrees in most cases. PCHC treats violence against women within the South Asian community context as something that is complex and has multiple intersections of causes. Moreover, within the context of immigration, the South Asian community is relatively new; this has implications for the community in terms of dealing with multiple stressors of acculturation, socio-economic struggles, racialization, marginalization, adaptation to a different lifestyle, and a myriad of other issues. According to PCHC, the marginalized status of immigrant families in the host country needs to be added as a layer of understanding the lived reality of both partners. This not only affects their ability to cope with issues and conflict, but also has severe implications for their access to post-crisis resources. Domestic violence service providers need to adopt a realistic perspective in understanding what cultural and larger systemic risks are involved in the lives of racialized immigrants.

Alcohol abuse is noted by PCHC as a compounding factor in more than 90 percent of the abuse cases that have been referred to them. This is a very high statistic and needs to be addressed while planning interventions that aim at stopping violence. Higher rates of alcohol consumption may be related to acculturation stressors. (These statistics were derived from a research study conducted by PCHC, assessing rates of consumption within the Punjabi community.)

PCHC places violence against women within the realm of patriarchy, acculturation stressors, addictions, differential cultural norms, and many other such complex intersecting issues specific to the South Asian community. PCHC focuses on enhancing the skills of the couple, as well as their family, in being able to have effective resources to resolve conflicts and lead violence-free lives. Creating healthy families and thereby creating a strong healthy community is an underlying goal of all PCHC activities.

PRINCIPLES THAT GUIDE PCHC'S DOMESTIC VIOLENCE INTERVENTION PROGRAMS

Working with the Punjabi community, PCHC has established certain key principles that guide their approach to addressing community needs. These principles are:

Community development: "Community development to me means that we have to ultimately rely on the strengths of the community [… and a] variety of ways to engage the community into the healing processes of the community itself" (ED of PCHC). PCHC centres itself within the community. It accesses community resources in the form of volunteers, donations, and advocates, and channels them into engaging the community in adapting to Canadian society and healing issues like domestic violence within families. Networks are created with other agencies and places of worship, increasing the outreach and scope of engaging the larger South Asian community. PCHC advocates using a strengths-based approach, in which community strengths are energized to meet community needs.

Client-centred: "If the client wants us to talk to the husband, we will talk to the husband. If the client wants us to engage them in couples' counselling, we will engage them in couples' counselling. It's whatever the client wants us to do, we will do. We will not say that, okay, we are stuck with this particular therapy and we are only going to apply the therapy, whether it works on the couple or not.… That's not how we work, so we work from a point of view of whatever the need of the client is, and we tailor that to make the services based on that" (SGF). PCHC's client-centred approach moves beyond just accommodating the client's needs to centring the need and creating programs that will meet them. Clients determine what will benefit them, what will assist them in coping with their issues, and how they would like to be involved in the process of healing.

Culturally appropriate: "It means that we need to have a sound understanding of a culture and create interventions based on that understanding" (ED). PCHC aims at creating programs that are culturally appropriate. They centre their knowledge about the Punjabi culture and create programs that will incorporate the culture. Supporting clients in the evening and weekends, organizing programs through *Gurudwaras*, making home visits and engaging the extended family, working with men, and creating a non-threatening safe space for clients and their families were all noted as different ways in which knowledge about the strengths and challenges within the Punjabi community informs PCHC's program planning.

Empowering women: The longer the woman is in an abusive situation, the more traumatic the effects. Reduced decision-making ability was noted as the single most disturbing factor for workers working with abused South Asian women. A women's group supports creation of a safe space in which they can share their experiences, draw strength from collective sharing, find comfort in being part of a "sisterhood," and eventually become empowered to make decisions that are best suited to their needs.

A healing approach to stopping violence: Programs are based on a healing approach in which finding fault is not the key objective; rather, clients are encouraged to determine their own behavioural deficits, and a skills-based approach aimed at mitigating these deficits is taught through the program. This minimizes the stigma attached to participating in these groups, making it possible to engage the community in a sensitive issue that is usually suppressed.

Family-centred: While the abusive man is the primary client, services are structured to facilitate inclusion of his partner and the extended family is also encouraged to get involved in the healing process. PCHC defines violence against women as "family violence" and its programs are structured, keeping in mind the family structure and gender roles within South Asian families and their part in the risk assessment for abused women. Violence committed by extended family members (such as a mother-in-law, sister-in-law, natal family, etc.) is part of understanding as well as minimizing the risk for abuse.

Strengthen the family: PCHC posits that with immigration, there are changes in the gender roles, partners' expectations, and the structure of the family. Many immigrant families in Canada are unable to shift roles to adapt to a different lifestyle, culture, and economy. PCHC works with clients to "realign and re-adjust the basic belief system of the family or the couple" (ED), which means helping them understand their perceptions about gender roles, marriage, and partners' expectations, and reorganizing them to reduce conflict and increasing their strength as a family.

PCHC'S INTERVENTION STRATEGIES

In achieving the goals of meeting the unique needs of the Punjabi community in coping with domestic violence, PCHC adopts the following strategies:

Parallel healing: PCHC believes that is important to involve both men and women in their domestic violence programs. All their programs are structured in a similar way, creating a separate yet parallel space in which both partners follow the self-knowledge and skill-building processes. PCHC believes that it is the perpetrator, not the victim, whose actions need to be primarily modified. The underlying objective in working with women is, firstly, to use them as experts on the relationship and to take guidance from them in terms of assessing their partners' progress. Secondly, there are issues within the relationship that also need to be addressed, which requires women's participation and commitment to change.

Leveraging children's welfare: While there might be conflict between the husband and wife (or partners), often both parties are equally concerned about their children. PCHC believes that children can be used as leverage to get a dysfunctional couple to seek professional help. The option of attending a parenting program creates a non-stigmatized space in which men and women are introduced to topics of abuse and conflict within relationships and encouraged to build healthier relationships. While effects of abuse on children are emphasized in the parenting program, facilitators also actively encourage participants to consider joining a men's or women's program if spousal abuse is identified.

Flexibility: Organizational mandate, outreach programs, etc., are not restricted in PCHC's organizational structure, which enables it to quickly assess community needs and to create programs to meet them. Peer-mentoring and youth programs have recently been established to engage Punjabi youth, enabling them to participate in programs that respond to their issues about identity and gender roles. Relevant to the domestic violence programs, the counsellors and group facilitators are given flexibility to meet the client wherever they are, be it at the local Tim Horton's, the client's doctor's office, or the grocery store.

Identifying and addressing intersecting issues for men: PCHC's study of alcohol consumption and abuse revealed that 90 percent of the Punjabi men who abuse women are also addicted to alcohol. Based on these findings, the men's program is structured to address alcohol abuse and anger management. PCHC also recognizes that many men from the Punjabi community are from low socio-economic backgrounds and have lower levels of literacy, so such factors are considered when addressing domestic violence issues.

REFLECTIONS ON PCHC'S MODEL OF DOMESTIC VIOLENCE INTERVENTION

Through its innovative programs and grounded perspective on the needs of the South Asian community, particularly the Punjabi community, PCHC tries to meet many of the intersecting, complex needs of its service users. Programs are designed with the community's attitudes, cultural values, barriers, and social norms in mind. Community strengths are developed and utilized in the process of service provision, a key aspect that has not been tapped into by conventional programs. Knowledge of the stigma and shame about domestic violence and the emphasis on maintaining families is intrinsic to South Asian culture, so strategies to overcome the barriers and facilitate the goal of maintaining families are factored into the program initiatives. Earning the community's trust about such a delicate, taboo issue is commendable and essential in furthering the dialogue about violence. Moreover, working with clients' family belief systems about gender roles and facilitating a more egalitarian relationship are positive steps in mitigating the strong influence of patriarchy in South Asian family structures.

PCHC's attempts to meet the needs of its South Asian clients by viewing them in the context of their culture, immigration status, and socio-economic background has provided a good example for mainstream organizations to work with racialized clients. PCHC's South Asian clients are not treated as members of a bounded cultural identity, but as people who are struggling at various marginal positions. Program initiatives that take into consideration the various social locations of their clients, especially the intersecting oppressions they face, are necessary in addressing their needs. This approach moves away from stigmatizing the community and places issues faced by abused South Asian women within the challenge of fighting cultural, institutional, and structural barriers. PCHC provides an environment that lessens the impact of institutional and cultural barriers that most abused South Asian women face.

While PCHC's programs do not overthrow the status quo, they definitely go beyond simplistic analysis of violence and challenge many of the rigid cultural norms that inhibit South Asian women's self-determination. In engaging the community in the discussion of domestic violence, PCHC succeeds beyond what is usually observed in most other institutional settings. However, in challenging patriarchy, its attempt might have fallen short. Shifting cultural mores is perhaps the most difficult task faced by each successive generation of a culture or a community. It takes a lot of shifts in belief systems to make it happen. With PCHC's credibility in the community, it has opened up avenues for it to challenge patriarchal norms, to influence consensus, and to mobilize the Punjabi community into creating a healthier community.

PCHC's model can be replicated, keeping in mind that each community has unique needs, its own unique "strings," that will assist an organization in weaving together and engaging in critical issues. In moving away from conventional interventions and centring the needs of the community by creating culturally appropriate programs, communities can take the lead in challenging norms and showing alternatives that work if created with a more grounded perspective. PCHC's executive director suggested building coalitions among similar communities, using a community development approach, and making clients the force behind their own healing process. These values are salient across communities and open a new pathway in a more egalitarian power relationship between institutions and the communities they serve. Will feminist ideology that addresses women's independence from men be an acceptable solution for all abused women, especially when domestic violence occurs? Can we afford not to engage men from marginalized communities in confronting patriarchy and gender inequality?

When not overlooked, intersections of race, gender, class, culture, and immigration status will invite alternative thinking and programming. When evidence of service gaps exists and when alternative programs are gaining recognition in meeting the needs of diverse communities, it is time to call upon a shift in mainstream service provision. Engaging different ethno-specific communities in dialogues about meeting their needs and developing culturally appropriate approaches in working with immigrant women of colour is very crucial as it provides a safe space and the critical support required for these communities in stopping domestic violence. It is important to recognize and mobilize community strength in these immigrant communities.

Within these immigrant communities' stigmatized cultures lie untapped resources. It is time that community and academic efforts are channelled toward unearthing these innate strengths and supporting these communities in meeting challenges and facilitating healing. Those ethnic groups that comprise the host societies have structures and institutions in place that have eased their path in their time of need; it is now time for our society to provide the space for new immigrant groups to gain their credibility and support to meet their needs.

CONCLUSIONS AND SOME RECOMMENDATIONS AT MULTIPLE LEVELS

Awareness of the inequalities in the lives of immigrant women in the interlocking systems of race and class, and underpinned by religion, gender, and location, needs to be raised not only in academia, but also within the community and mainstream discourse on understanding domestic violence. Such awareness needs to be raised in academic pursuits regarding the issue of woman abuse, with an emphasis on finding solutions that take into consideration systemic barriers and a culturally sensitive approach to services. Gill and Rehman (2004) discuss the 1980s women's rights movement in Britain where successful alliances between women activists of all colours and academics were formed to lead mass protests in campaigns against rape, immigration laws, and forced marriages, and for the rights of women who had been imprisoned for killing their abusers. These campaigns also led to protests against institutionalized racism and religious fundamentalism. As inspired by such precedent, there is hope for collaboration among all the different sectors in addressing existing gaps in the system, and in the area of service provision, so that the rights of cultural groups and their issues will not be silenced and made invisible.

Primary-level interventions should be advocated, such as strengthening the demand for a woman's right to control her own life and body; community education and discussion in general, especially about patriarchy; challenging cultural norms that marginalize women; and promoting gender equality and emphasis on healthier communities. It is important for activists both within the mainstream and in the community to challenge the notions of "cultural privacy" and address their "race anxiety," making sure that women are at the centre of their concern, rather than tiptoeing around cultural sensitivities (Burman et al., 2004). Very often, human rights trump cultural rights and freedoms, leaving the perpetuation of women and class oppressions within a culture unchecked. These problems need to be addressed as well.

Extensive training programs should be developed to empower women through increased access to and control over resources, using activities such as language skills development, vocational training, career counselling, and employment opportunities through strategic partnerships with local employers. It is important that funding for these programs be secure and prioritized. South Asian women have low labour market access and mobility, a situation that needs to be amended through these programs, so that the women can become independent and break away from abusive relationships.

Women from ethnic and racial communities confront cultural, social, and racial barriers that obstruct their access to services from mainstream agencies, but community-based organizations can provide "culturally sensitive and linguistically appropriate" services to women from these groups (Agnew, 1996). State agencies' allocation of inadequate funds to these agencies, the necessity of extending their programs, and existence of racial bias in mainstream service need to be addressed. Where there are no community-based organizations, service providers need to be trained to be culturally sensitive and, where possible, advocacy teams should represent the groups that they serve. Language interpreters should be readily accessible and women should be made to feel comfortable about the confidentiality and the support they can access from these agencies. Culturally sensitive mental health interventions should be introduced when clients need and accept these interventions. Service providers should be mindful of the "newness" of these institutional approaches in addressing something that South Asian women consider to be a private and a family matter. They should also be mindful that when a South Asian woman leaves an abusive situation, her kinship network might turn against her, and she may feel more vulnerable if outside advocates "march in" to "assist" her.

Legal information, especially about immigration rights and laws, should be made readily available so that the "sponsor abuse" situation is mitigated. Burman et al. (2004) recognized that immigration legislation is an "extraordinary" barrier and demands urgent attention. Gendered immigration laws need to be amended as they play a role in perpetuating women's dependence on men in entering Canada. Information to reduce anxiety about child welfare services should be made available. In turn, social services like the Children's Aid Society should be sensitized about varying cultural practices as well as be more cognizant of parenting norms within diverse families.

In Agnew's (1996) evaluation of information from shelters in languages other than English or French, she found that most shelters did not have enough resources to produce translated information. This is further compounded by case studies in which South Asian women (and other women of colour) have faced incidents of discrimination and racism in shelters. Alternative housing and/or shelters that are diverse and inclusive increasingly need to be established. Small housing co-operatives could be explored as a potential resource to mitigate this need.

Support groups for abused women should be promoted within the community in an accessible manner, so that outreach results in formation of community development and in support for South Asian women in precarious family conflict situations. The risk factor of isolation is reduced by the provision of unbiased support. Recognition of South Asian women's agency in the discourse and promotion of the strengths that they hold should also be voiced. "Some of the qualities like sense of responsibility, patience, and belief in fate, that led them to accept their abusive situation, now help them to come to terms with their new life" (Cloutier, 1989, p. 15, as quoted in Agnew, 1996, p. 204).

One of the recommendations that Shriwadkar (2004) makes is inclusion of a binational (for example, India and Canada) research approach in grounding the services provided and advocating policies and programs that are relevant and able to address the diverse needs of ethno-cultural groups. There is a large amount of research and advocacy information available in the source countries of immigrants, which needs to be accessed so that certain services and modes of effecting change that are relevant to immigrants' experiences can be utilized.

Reforms on many levels are necessary so that South Asian women will be able to ensure their own safety within Canadian communities in the future. Experiences of our diverse communities suggest that we need to address our current approaches and instigate changes that overhaul both the invisible and often visible biases against culturally diverse communities. Our roles as researchers, activists, policy-makers, community workers, etc., need to include the vision of making Canada a truly inclusive country.

Domestic violence emerges as something that can be overlooked or even excused for "cultural reasons," as a "homogenized absence," or, alternatively, as "pathologized presence," producing heightened scrutiny of minoritized women both within and outside their communities (Burman et al., 2004, p. 332). The media must stop "pathologizing" immigrant communities and instead promote a more realistic view of domestic violence within immigrant communities while advocating on behalf of these communities to address the systemic and structural barriers facing them in Canadian society.

The South Asian community faces the challenge of addressing the presence of domestic violence within the community while empowering women to take charge of their own abuse-free lives, and fighting for their rights as a community with needs that are not being met and perceptions that are distorted. Canadian society also needs to acknowledge its own cultural barriers that marginalize immigrant communities. Everyone has a role to play in creating a more harmonious and safe society, and it is about time that we, as individuals and as members of the human community, take the steps to do so.

Part III

The Lived Experiences of Women

Chapter 8

Changes in Gender Relations as a Risk Factor for Marital Conflict and Intimate Partner Violence: A Study of Ethiopian Immigrant Couples in Canada[1]

Ilene Hyman, Robin Mason, Sepali Guruge, Girma Mekonnen, Noreen Stuckless, Taryn Tang, and Hiwot Teffera

INTRODUCTION

Violence against women is present in every society and culture (Locke & Richman, 1999). Some studies have suggested that post-migration changes in gender relations affect the power dynamics between men and women, thereby increasing the risk of marital conflict and intimate partner violence (IPV) in newcomer couples (Bui & Morash, 1999; Morash, Bui & Santiago, 2000; Morrison, Guruge & Snarr, 1999; Narayan, 1995; Oxman-Martinez, Abdool & Loiselle-Leonard, 2000; Raj & Silverman, 2002; Tang & Oatley, 2002; West, 1998). It is also well established that marital conflict is in itself a major risk factor for IPV (Jewkes, 2002; Jewkes, Levin & Penn-Kekana, 2002).

In 2001 a partnership was formed between the Ethiopian Association in Toronto (EAT) and academic researchers to address community concerns about increasing levels of marital conflict and IPV. The main objective of this community-based study was to better understand risk factors associated with intimate partner violence and inform the development of violence-prevention strategies. Our specific objectives were to understand the ways in which gender relations change in couples after they migrate to Canada, and to identify patterns of change and factors associated with change.

We present a brief overview of the literature, followed by a description of the background, design, and results of the study. The implications of our findings for the development of theory on the etiology of IPV in newcomer communities and violence-prevention strategies are discussed.

LITERATURE REVIEW

Different etiological theories have been proposed to explain the causes of violence against women. At sociological and structural levels, feminist theories and status inconsistency theories predominate.

According to the feminist perspective, gender inequality and male domination underlie violence against women (Dobash & Dobash, 1979). It is hypothesized that violence stems from women's traditionally devalued and inferior role in the family and wider society. Research suggests that IPV is more common in patriarchal societies in which cultural values, including social mores and religious beliefs, dictate male dominance in gender relationships, condone violence against women, and create separate codes of conduct for men and women (Sugarman & Frankel, 1996; Yick & Agbayani-Siewert, 1997).

According to theories of status inconsistency, the family is a power system with different members having more and fewer resources. Those who are threatened by their lack of resources, or perceive their status to be inconsistent with social norms, may use violence as a strategy to compensate for lack of power (Campbell, 1992; Goode, 1971; Yick, 2001). Status inconsistency frequently occurs after migration as post-migration stressors such as poverty, underemployment, minority status, discrimination, isolation, and role reversals affect the power dynamics between men and women (Bui & Morash, 1999; Narayan, 1995; West, 1998; Yick, 2001). Previous work further suggests that post-migration changes in gender relations may be associated with IPV in immigrant and refugee populations. Changing gender roles have been cited as a significant contributor to increasing levels of conflict, divorce, and IPV among Southeast Asian refugees (Kulig, 1994). Morash et al. (2000) found that physical abuse was reported in 37 percent of Mexican immigrant families when one of the partners changed gender role expectations. Data from pilot interviews with Chinese immigrant women and service providers show that when a husband's role as breadwinner is threatened, he may reassert his power and control through physical and psychological forms of abuse (Tang & Oatley, 2002). Raj and Silverman (2002) suggest that changes in gender relations not only serve as a justification for IPV, but also increase women's vulnerability to abuse.

Predominant theories may not capture the realities of IPV in newcomer couples. For example, some structural approaches fail to consider what happens to marital relationships when couples are confronted with change, as is the case with migration from a predominantly patriarchal non-European society to North American society. It is well established that immigration to and settlement in a new country entail significant stress and a period of adjustment, particularly in social relations (Canadian Council on Multicultural Health, 1989; Canadian Task Force on Mental Health Issues Affecting Immigrants and Refugees, 1988). At the same time, immigration offers some people the opportunity to recreate, reinvent, and negotiate established gender relations (Bui & Morash, 1999; Canadian Council on Multicultural Health, 1989; Canadian Task Force on Mental Health Issues Affecting Immigrants and Refugees, 1988; Morash et al., 2000; Morrison et al., 1999; Sorenson, 1996). Theories of status inconsistency consider change, but only in negative terms, i.e., losses of power. Some research suggests that immigration offers the possibility of change in traditional gender relations that otherwise would be difficult to negotiate and may offer women previously unavailable or suppressed employment opportunities (Krulfeld, 1994).

THE ETHIOPIAN COMMUNITY IN TORONTO

As a result of civil war, since the mid-1970s, an estimated 1.25 million Ethiopians have fled to neighbouring countries such as Sudan, Kenya, Djibouti, and Yemen, while a smaller proportion have immigrated to Europe and North America (McSpadden & Moussa, 1993). As in the home country, the Ethiopian community in Toronto is characterized by tremendous diversity in ethnicity and religion. According to the EAT, the current Ethiopian population of Toronto is 35,000 (B. Menkir, executive director, Ethiopian Association in Toronto, personal communication, December 20, 2002).

In 2001, the EAT identified prevention of marital conflict and IPV as a priority concern. Post-migration stresses such as poverty, underemployment, minority status, and discrimination, which increase women's vulnerability to partner abuse, have been noted in the literature (Bui & Morash, 1999; Morash et al., 2000; Morrison et al., 1999; Narayan, 1995; Tang & Oatley, 2002; West, 1998). However, these were factors that the

EAT believed it could not address. Although empirical data were unavailable, the EAT staff and board members and the research team decided to focus this study on exploring the ways in which gender relations changed after migration to Canada, the patterns of change, and the factors associated with change. The findings would be used primarily to inform the development of community-based violence-prevention strategies.

METHODS

In this community-based pilot study, all phases of the research, development of objectives, recruitment, development of research/interview questions, and analysis were determined together with the EAT staff. Since relatively little was known about the issue in question and since this was an exploratory study, qualitative methodology was chosen. Participants were recruited via newspaper advertisements, flyers distributed at EAT headquarters, and word of mouth.

Ethics approval for the study was obtained from the Sunnybrook and Women's College Ethics Board. In order for a couple to be eligible, both partners had to be immigrants, both partners had to agree to participate, the couple had to have been married or living together prior to migration, and both partners had to be of Ethiopian origin. After having all the risks and benefits of participation explained to them, the participants provided written informed consent and were offered an honorarium for their contribution to the study. Data were collected by two (one male and one female) Ethiopian (Amharic-speaking) research assistants (RAs) trained in interview and focus group techniques.

The interview schedule consisted of two sections: (1) a short questionnaire on socio-demographics and migration history, and (2) a set of open-ended questions on gender roles in Ethiopia and Canada, relationship changes, and types and sources of support. Eight Ethiopian couples living in Toronto participated in the in-depth individual interviews. The couples were interviewed separately to ensure that the presence of a partner would not influence responses. During pretesting it was determined that participants did not have a gender preference regarding the interviewer, so the same person interviewed both partners in each couple. The interviews took between 1.5 and 2.5 hours to complete. After completion of the in-depth interviews and preliminary data analysis, two focus groups (one for men and one for women) were formed. Each focus group consisted of five participants, and lasted between two and three hours. Six participants who had been interviewed were unable to attend the focus group discussion due to family or work commitments. The two RAs facilitated the focus group discussions, the purpose of which was to confirm the themes that emerged during the initial data analysis and to generate data for ongoing analysis. All interviews and focus group discussions were audiotaped, transcribed, and translated into English (with the exception of two interviews conducted in English).

DATA ANALYSIS

The two RAs cross-checked and validated all interview data. Data from the interviews and focus group discussions were organized using QSR N6 software. Concepts noted in the literature served as an initial guide for the development of a coding scheme. Additional codes were developed as the first interviews were coded and significant codes were grouped as subthemes. The coding scheme initially consisted of more than 120 codes, which were later reduced to 11 subthemes. Subthemes were then collapsed and condensed into themes. The findings reported here are those pertaining to three themes: (1) main areas of change, (2) patterns of change, and (3) factors associated with change. Regular team meetings of all the investigators and the two RAs were held in order to discuss and reach consensus on the codes, subthemes, and themes, and on the terminology to be used in describing them.

RESULTS

Characteristics of Sample

The participants varied with respect to age, the number of years married, and the number of years in Canada. Less heterogeneity was observed with respect to educational and religious background. Most participants were well educated, though men were more so than women. The majority of participants were members of the Ethiopian Orthodox Church. All of the women and most of the men were employed. The sample was fairly homogeneous with respect to socio-economic status in Ethiopia, and was indicative of the Canadian immigration selection process—that is, it reflected those who had the means to immigrate. Thus, for example, all of the couples had pre-immigration "instrumental support," which was not the case once they arrived in Canada. Table 8.1 summarizes the main characteristics of the participants.

Table 8.1: Characteristics of Sample

Age: 27–71 years (mean = 47 years)
Education: High school graduate to doctorate
Religion: Ethiopian Orthodox (15) and Protestant (1)
Number of years married: 3–42 (mean = 21)
Number of years in Canada: 3–20 (mean = 13)

In the interviews, the participants were asked to describe their roles and responsibilities as a wife or husband in Ethiopia. The findings indicate that the women were primarily responsible for taking care of the household and children, or inside matters, while the men were primarily responsible for supporting the family financially, or outside matters. The majority of men did not share household tasks, and those who did so performed tasks such as gardening or household repairs. According to both male and female participants, in Ethiopia there were no expectations that men would or should share in household tasks. One of the male participants pointed out that as a child, he had been reprimanded if he "smelled of smoke," the result of wandering into the kitchen. During the focus group discussion the women said that as young girls they had been encouraged to acquire domestic skills, but that boys had not been.

The majority of female participants (80 percent) had been employed in Ethiopia and had fulfilled a double role, responsible for both contributing financial support and running the household. Both male and female participants acknowledged that the reliance on instrumental support in Ethiopia was an important contributor to the smooth functioning of the household. This instrumental support was provided by both hired help and extended family. Both male and female participants reported that the man had been considered the primary breadwinner, with the woman's income being regarded as supplementary.

MAIN AREAS OF CHANGE

Three main areas of change in gender relations in Canada were identified: (1) household (inside) responsibilities, (2) work (outside) responsibilities, and (3) marital interactions.

Household (inside) responsibilities: The findings suggest that men share in more household tasks in Canada, but overall responsibility remains with women. One female participant said: "Seventy percent of the work is mine.... In Canada we both are working, but I still take on most of the responsibilities." Most of the men indicated that they helped with shopping, cleaning, and child care.

Work (outside) responsibilities: While the majority of the women had been employed in Ethiopia, all were employed in Canada, a significant difference being that in Canada, unlike in Ethiopia, the woman's contribution to the household income was considered essential and as important as the man's. The focus group data show that the men believed that women should be employed, for the well-being of both the women themselves and their families, and that most of the men considered their wives' incomes necessary to make ends meet. The majority of female participants reported that they worked both out of financial necessity and because it gave them more autonomy. Both male and female participants observed that many women derived other benefits from employment besides the additional and necessary income, such as reduced isolation and increased adaptation.

> When somebody stays home, you know, the condition of this country … you can't have the kind of socialization we have had in our culture. Therefore, she won't be comfortable if she is not working. She can't share ideas with anybody unless she is working. If she always stays home while I am working and coming home, it will create for her some sort of stress. It is because to work and come home and staying home do have big difference. Besides, it also brings some additional income if she works. [40-year-old man]

Marital interactions: The marital relationship was a major area of change, both positive and negative, for the majority of couples. One of the positive changes was described as an increase in joint decision making. Although in Ethiopia there had been some shared decision making on major financial issues, most male participants indicated that they had much more decision-making power in Ethiopia than their wives. A 60-year-old female participant stated: "We always discuss whenever we want to do something, like I may say, 'What if we give this much for this wedding?' We also discuss the money that we give for the church. We discuss everything. I don't hide anything from him and he doesn't hide anything from me."

Another positive change in some relationships was that husbands and wives were spending more time together and growing closer. The same

60-year-old woman stated: "There are a lot of changes, like usually we spend the evenings together, my husband and I. He doesn't say, 'Now I am going with my friends.' ... He is always with me and I am always with him. We go for a walk together and even sometimes we go to bars together. It very much brought us together."

On the negative side, some couples faced new stresses and experienced conflict as a result of their different work schedules, long working hours, and fatigue, as described by a 39-year-old female participant: "Of course you would be happy if you could spend some time with your husband and if you could talk and chat with your husband, whatever the topic. But when you can't do that because of shortage of time, you may say, 'Until when?' ... You may spend [time] alone most of the time and you may tend to say, 'What is the difference if I live alone or with him?'"

PATTERNS OF CHANGE

The men and women adapted to their new roles and responsibilities in Canada in different ways. The different patterns were most apparent with respect to household tasks and were clearly important in the couples' lives. Both concordant and discordant patterns of change were observed.

Concordant patterns included acceptance of the old ways, and negotiation of new ways. Acceptance of the old ways: Both partners were comfortable with or at least accepted the traditional division of responsibilities and tasks. This allowed for a relatively harmonious relationship with minimal stress: "Regarding activities in the house, I am telling you frankly, as far as the woman can do the job it is not necessary to impose on him. This is our culture; we get used to it since childhood. If they are willing to learn and help, that would be great, but it is not necessary to lose your long-term relationship because he is not doing it now" [39-year-old woman]. Negotiation of new ways: According to this pattern, couples negotiated tasks and responsibilities in Canada using criteria such as: Who does it better? Who has more time? Who enjoys doing the task? A 41-year-old male participant explained: "If your wife is a good cook and you are a lousy cook, it should be your wife that is doing the cooking. But if she is a lousy cook and you are better, then you should do it."

Discordant patterns of change included one partner resisting change, making sacrifices, and/or tolerating the old ways. Resisting change: This pattern was most evident among male participants, with some of the men frequently expressing an unwillingness to take up certain responsibilities and tasks, particularly those they felt belonged to women. For example, one man stated that he did not mind making coffee using a percolator, but that it was a woman's job to make it the Ethiopian way, accompanied by the traditional coffee ceremony. An example provided by a 71-year-old participant concerned the traditional bread, *enjerra*, an Ethiopian staple: "The reason why I am not baking *enjerra* is that first of all, my body doesn't even accept it; it is a matter of acceptance. But if I [am] compelled to do so and if I am in a situation where I feel that somebody could be in danger if I don't do that, then I may consider doing that, but I don't know because that hasn't happened yet."

Making sacrifice: Some female participants expressed a willingness to take on the double burden of inside and outside work in order to maintain household harmony. They accepted the idea that their primary mission in life was to do whatever was necessary to raise their children and provide them with a good education: "He used to say to me … 'You work at night and come back home, you have to get some sleep, and you have to take care of the kids, and you have to come fetch me; this is not good.' At one point I was not even able to open my eyes, but I did not want to show it to him … so I never said I was tired. I worked and I took good care of my kids" [48-year-old woman].

Tolerance: This pattern was observed when female participants spoke about wanting change, but believed that, in order to avoid conflict, women must be patient and not make demands on their husbands:

> So we hold on to the idea of not going for divorce. So, to avoid such mishap, I tolerated. I believe that it was patience that prevented me from taking that kind of major decision—my silence, my working without complaining. He then started saying, "What?" So we were able to get to this stage. It wasn't because my husband was nice to me around the time we came here or that he had changed automatically. It was because I tolerated.… [53-year-old woman]

It was evident from the interviews and focus-group discussions that the patterns of change were not fixed; couples adopted different patterns at different points during the process of settling in a new country. Indeed many couples themselves recognized that this process was dynamic.

Analysis revealed three distinct stages of change, not necessarily corresponding to the number of years in Canada. The first stage consisted of maintaining the division of tasks as it was in Ethiopia as a way of maintaining links with the culture. The participants reported that during this stage, most men did not help with household tasks, expecting their wives to run the house on their own. However, adherence to traditional roles and patterns of behaviour required agreement by both parties. During the first stage, the women had no expectations that their husbands would or should help with housework. As described by one of the male participants: "If you see couples who just came here for the first time, soon after they came the women don't even allow you to get into the kitchen." The female participants also found it difficult to ask their husbands to help because "it is a little difficult to break that barrier and say to men, 'Do this.' They might think, 'She is giving me an order,'" which would not have occurred in Ethiopia. A number of participants noted that cultural adaptation is a gradual process.

During the second stage, mutual discussion and joint decision making emerged as indicators of change in the relationship. As one of the male participants pointed out, "things are decided together." Interestingly, the participants also indicated a growing recognition that, in light of the absence of instrumental help, husbands now had to help their wives. One 53-year-old female participant recounted how her husband had changed over time: "I think he watched me through the window going far pushing the cart. He felt it and started saying, 'Does she have to do all this by herself?'"

During the third stage, tasks were described as having become routine or "carried out simply by habit," resulting in a decrease in the gendered division of labour. As a 42-year-old male participant put it: "For example, if the man does ironing clothes one or two times, first she will say, 'Please do also these ones,' but later it will specifically be his task and continue doing that."

FACTORS ASSOCIATED WITH CHANGE

Data analysis revealed several factors associated with patterns of change. Age and length of marriage were perhaps the strongest influences on change. The older women tended to be more patient, tolerant, less demanding, and more accepting of the traditional gender division of tasks. Both men and women who had been married a long time stressed the importance of mutual understanding and were much more comfortable with the traditional division of labour than those who had not been married for very long. The older women did not expect their husbands to help out at home, while the younger women did. The former were reluctant to ask for help, citing their partner's age and/or consideration for his social status back in Ethiopia. Older participants were much more vocal on this point than their younger counterparts, and were critical of the younger women's views.

Experience in a third country also played a part in couples' adaptation to their new roles in Canada. Those who had lived in a Western country before coming to Canada adapted more quickly and smoothly to their new roles because of their exposure to different lifestyles. Even those who had lived in another non-Western country observed that the process of migration facilitated change. For example, when the participants were asked how the traditional division of tasks had changed for them in Canada, one woman responded: "We have come through a different country. Since both of us did housework, we were hired by families to do housework. When we come here, it is not a big deal for my husband to do housework. All of us started working right away—equally."

Finally, it was apparent that gender socialization influenced patterns of change among the couples. Most of the female participants accepted the fact that they had more responsibilities because this was part of woman's "nature." They maintained they had more household responsibilities than their husbands because they had taken it upon themselves to do more. Many male participants also expressed a belief in a "natural" division of labour and, regardless of their age or educational background, showed a resistance to change.

DISCUSSION

The aim of this community-based pilot study was to better understand risk factors associated with intimate partner violence (IPV) by exploring changes in gender relations, patterns of change, and factors associated with change in a sample of Ethiopian couples living in Toronto. The findings provide strong evidence of change in gender relations following migration, particularly in the areas of housework, paid work, and marital interactions. In Ethiopia, the men had been the principal breadwinners and were accorded more authority in relationships as a result of education, income, and cultural influences, while the women had fulfilled the dual role of wage earner and household manager, though usually with the support of hired help and family members. In Canada, there was strong evidence of change in the gendered assignment of household tasks, though change was frequently described in terms of sharing specific tasks rather than sharing overall responsibility.

For most couples the marital relationship was a significant source of change, with participants reporting both positive and negative changes. Concordant and discordant patterns emerged with regard to changes in the couples' relations. Concordant patterns of change were those in which both partners either accepted the old ways or negotiated new ways, while discordant patterns were those in which one partner resisted change, made sacrifices, and/or tolerated the old ways. Although discordant patterns might be considered less adaptive, it must be stressed that all eight couples interviewed were in intact marriages, indicating that the couples had developed effective strategies for resolving their differences.

The findings also indicate that the process of change was dynamic and that one partner or both may have gone through several different stages of change during the resettlement period. According to Berry (1995), individuals relinquish the behaviours and values of their traditional culture and acquire and retain those of the new culture to which they are adjusting. Thus, newcomer couples are continually striving to balance and combine the heritage and host cultures, creating diverse patterns of change, some of which may invoke risk, while others may offer security. According to Dobash and Dobash (1997), without fundamental changes in gender relations, we may continue to experience a legacy of violence. The effects of different patterns of change on outcomes such as marital conflict or partner abuse were not assessed in the present study. However, new analyses of the 1999 General Social Survey have found that recent immigrant women (less than 10 years in Canada) experienced significantly lower rates of intimate partner violence than their Canadian-born counterparts (Hyman et al., 2004).

Some limitations must be noted. Because our sample was restricted to couples who had been married in Ethiopia prior to migrating to Canada, we were unable to examine other types of marital relationships within the Ethiopian community. For example, the data may not reflect the challenges that Ethiopian couples who were newly married in Canada face. The interviews carried out as part of the present study and informal discussions with members of the Ethiopian community suggest that individuals who were newly married in Canada may experience more marital conflict than couples who were married in Ethiopia. In addition, the majority of the sample had lived in another country prior to coming to Canada. The experiences of migrating together and facing common challenges in Canada appear to have strengthened the couples' relationships and marital resiliency. Finally, the sample did not include individuals who had separated or divorced post-migration; therefore, we could not ascertain the extent to which changing gender relations contribute to divorce or separation.

IMPLICATIONS

Research findings have implications for the development of theory on the etiology of IPV in newcomer communities, and violence prevention strategies. Feminist theory largely focuses on factors that underlie the occurrence of violence, namely, gender inequality and male domination, but does not consider what happens when these structures are challenged, for example, following migration. Couples who migrate from non-European societies where patriarchal ideologies prevail may find themselves forced to confront more egalitarian notions of male-female relations. For couples who embrace more liberal ideologies, the result is likely a shift in gender roles (and responsibilities) and associated power relations that may disrupt established patterns of relating and communicating with one another.

Theories of status inconsistency take change into consideration, but focus only on the negative aspects of change in the power dynamics between men and women, not on positive changes such as increased resiliency. The couples in our research study found that positive changes—such as increased intimacy and communication, female autonomy and independence, and flexibility in accepting formerly gendered responsibilities— buffered the impact of migration-related stress on their relationship. These too should be taken into consideration when applying theory to the occurrence of IPV in immigrant communities.

Recognizing post-migration changes in gender relations can inform the practices of settlement organizations and the development of violence prevention strategies for newcomer communities. Acknowledging the changes in levels of instrumental and personal support, enhancing communication between the spouses, encouraging more sharing of household responsibilities, and identifying positive outcomes associated with increased female autonomy may also assist newcomer couples in their positive adaptation.

Further research is needed to address questions about the mediating factors identified in this study (i.e., age, previous experience in a third country, and gender socialization) and to determine whether concordant and discordant patterns of change are associated with different outcomes. Research is also necessary to extend these findings to other types of marital relationships within the Ethiopian community, including the relationships of those who marry in Canada. Finally, similar research should be conducted with couples from other immigrant communities to determine whether the patterns identified have meaning beyond one particular community.

In conclusion, this study represents a first step in addressing information gaps related to risk factors for IPV in newcomer communities. The findings are currently being used by the EAT to inform the development of culturally appropriate and gender-sensitive violence prevention strategies, to increase community awareness of the changes in gender relations following migration, and awareness of the both positive and negative impacts of migration on marital relationships.

Chapter 9

Chinese Immigrant Women Confronting Male Violence in Their Lives

Josephine Fong

OVERVIEW

In examining the existing literature that relates to the issue of wife assault and woman abuse, I have found that little attention has been paid to
non-White immigrant women, and that the focus on Chinese immigrant
women is marginal. Chinese women are often portrayed as inadequate,
passive, naive, or submissive individuals who are prone to be abused in
relationships. Such a portrayal contradicts my personal and professional
contact with these women. In my experience, many abused Chinese wom-
en actively seek ways to minimize the risk of being abused. Very seldom,
if ever, would they willingly remain defenceless, even though they do not
always acknowledge their defensive responses as "strategies." They simply
do, within their ability, what their culture and circumstances permit them
to do at the time. Sometimes their responses are perceived by their community as radical action to combat male violence because they do indeed
resent and resist the abuse rather than accepting it as part of their culture
or as a way of life. This chapter is about recognizing Chinese immigrant
women's strength in coping with spousal abuse, and putting their voices
in the centre. The examination of these women's long-standing struggle
against abuse will provide helping professionals and academics with a
thorough understanding of their reality, thus enabling them to develop a
better approach and more effective policy to help combat the problem.

By examining women's experiences in their authentic form, we are able
to look at women's issues and needs beyond the lens of the status quo,

and to disengage from the perspectives of professionals, so that women's experiences are not appropriated or interpreted by therapists, doctors, counsellors, or social workers. It is through this kind of phenomenological research that we learn the specific details of women's despair, isolation, lack of support, and daily struggle with abuse and battering. This chapter shows what Chinese immigrant women's abusive experiences are, how these women have exercised their agency of change, and what specific strategies they have used to resist or confront male violence. We will learn how these women seek help and whether they find it effective, what barriers they have encountered in the process of help-seeking, and how their culture may have impacted their responses. In addition, this chapter confronts problems of racial stereotypes and generalizations, calls attention to recognize women's strengths and needs, delineates a local theory to explain the phenomenon of spousal abuse against women in the Chinese-Canadian community, and provides some recommendations for working with this population.

DEFINITIONS

Spousal abuse against women is prevalent in many Canadian families, and consists of a wide spectrum of violence. Statistics indicate that in heterosexual relationships, 89 percent of spousal abuse is perpetuated by men, and the majority of victims are female (Statistics Canada, 1998). Recent statistics also indicate that women are more vulnerable to spousal abuse and spousal homicide during pregnancy and marital separation. Therefore, in this chapter wife assault is defined as the abuse of a female partner by her common-law or legally married husband. It is also understood that violence against women (VAW) is not necessarily limited to hitting, pushing, pulling out hair, slapping, punching, or kicking. While these extreme forms of violence can leave severe physical and emotional scars, other less corporeal forms of violence such as continuous threats, scolding, belittling, and bodily confinement can also leave abused women with serious psychological damage and long-term mental disturbances. The abuse described in this chapter represents a continuum of VAW in relationships. I thus treat the terms "wife assault" and "wife abuse" as synonymous. Moreover, because marriage is still prevalent among heterosexual couples in Chinese communities, the terms "wife assault" and "spousal abuse against women" are used interchangeably in this chapter to describe these women's experiences.

DISCUSSION OF RELEVANT LITERATURE

Recognizing that a discussion of conventional theories of male violence against women is provided in an earlier chapter, the literature review in this chapter will focus on aspects of Chinese culture that are relevant to this study. While attempting to provide an account of Chinese culture, I have no intention of essentializing Chinese or suggest that all Chinese are the same. To some scholars, the terms "Chinese" or "culture" are extremely complex constructs requiring years of study to understand their meanings. It is understood that because of China's vast population, and the dispersion of Chinese descendants all over the world, there are many diverse Chinese cultures, each with its own local characteristics. However, regardless of the diversity of Chinese culture, there are shared traditional values and ethics that can be identified, which can influence people's value systems, line of thoughts, and behaviour patterns.

According to James (1989) and Liang (1994), culture provides a blueprint for people's lives. As a result of living in the same society and being influenced by the same history, people come to embrace a set of similar social, political, and economic concepts; they adopt and express similar customs, lifestyles, and socially approved behaviours. Usually, those who dare to be different or refuse to comply with the social norms may be considered outcasts and may be isolated. Generally, the basis of the Chinese culture consists of values and beliefs that derive from the traditions of Confucianism, Taoism, and Buddhism. Of these three, Confucian thinking has the greatest and deepest influence on Chinese culture.

Several critical cultural doctrines are worth reviewing here. First of all, in Chinese culture, no individual is completely independent from others. As stated in King (1993), according to the Confucian definition, every person is situated in a web of human relationships (mainly among men!); the five fundamental ethics of human relationships are the blood relation between father and son, the loyalty between the sovereign and his chancellors, the role differences between husband and wife, the order between elder and younger brothers, and the trust between friends. Within each relationship, everyone is assigned certain responsibilities and obligations. Every individual is obliged to uphold and perform well his or her given role.

According to Confucianism, the perfect personality of a complete person should possess the four basic human virtues, namely *Chung* (loyalty), *Hau* (filial piety), *Yun* (genuine empathy and compassion), and *Yee* (dedication and allegiance) (King, 1993). When Chinese people are properly socialized and acculturated, they should perform their jobs faithfully and be trusted by their employers; should show respect for, and comply with, their parents; should be considerate, compassionate, and caring; should take responsibility for watching over friends, relatives, and co-workers; and should keep their word.

Although this set of virtues is prescribed for every Chinese person, Confucian teaching has prescribed an additional or modified set of virtues for women. Traditionally, because Chinese women were not usually engaged in public service outside the home, they were supposed to be socialized and acculturated to develop other gender-appropriate traits. According to Confucius, a good woman must demonstrate the three obediences and four virtues (Ho, 1990): she must obey her father in his house, obey her husband after marriage, and obey her son in old age; in addition, a good woman's virtues include complying with traditional ethical codes, speaking less, maintaining an appearance that is pleasing to the male sex, and doing all of the family household chores (Lee Yao, 1983; King, 1993). Undoubtedly, all of the above could be contested by new feminist thought in China today. However, in the old China, a wife was expected to serve her husband as a chancellor serves his sovereign; also, the parents-in-law were the undisputed heads of the family and they had unquestionable authority over their sons and daughters-in-law (Lee Yao, 1983). Thus, a good woman was to serve her husband and her parents-in-law without a word of complaint so that "harmony" could be maintained.

In typical Chinese society, family plays a very important role in everyone's life. Chinese people find their identity and social position within the familial atmosphere and environment (King, 1993). In each stage of life, people are expected to observe closely the five fundamental ethics of human relationships, and to perform the attributed duties that are inherently associated with each of these relationships. In the process of becoming a desirable and respectable member of society, one must adhere to the social norms and act accordingly to maintain a harmonious relationship with everyone in all dimensions. As such, individuality and personal rights are ranked secondary. One's purpose of existence is not to discover and actualize one's personal abilities to the fullest extent, as emphasized in Western culture, but rather to relate to others in different relationship orders, and fulfill the expectations of society within those orders, so that social harmony can be sustained.

Both King (1993) and Liang (1994) point out that *Yun Ching* (being sympathetic, understanding, and thoughtful) is the most important quality all Chinese people must possess and apply to all human issues and interpersonal relationships. The concept of *Yun Ching* can be concretely observed in people's daily interactions with others as a way to assess their personal maturity. The cultivation of *Yun Ching* prepares Chinese people to become considerate, put themselves in other people's shoes, understand others' situations, forgive others, be sensitive to other people's needs, know how to make sensible decisions, and know how to respond properly to other people's requests or appeals. Because Chinese women traditionally did not participate in the public arena as much as men did, they were considered even more relationship-oriented than men. Thus, women are expected to demonstrate a greater sense of *Yun Ching* in their day-to-day interactions with people around them.

Parallel to the concept of *Yun Ching* is the concept of "face." An old Chinese saying, "A man needs his face as a tree needs its bark," really reflects the importance of "face-saving" in Chinese culture. Bond and Lee (1981) define this kind of culture as subjective culture. There are two kinds of "face." The first one, *mien-tzu*, is derived from personal success and achievement, which is socially recognized. The second one, *lien*, represents society's confidence in the integrity of one's moral character; the loss of it will make it impossible for the person to keep his or her head up in front of others and function properly within the community. For example, when people live in a community that disapproves of premarital sex or extramarital intimacy, engaging in such relationships will make them feel guilty because they know that they will have no face (*lien*) to associate with others. While the former face (*mien-tzu*) requires an audience, the latter (*lien*) does not because it is internalized as a sense of immorality or guilt.

Cheung (1986) points out that Chinese people are likely to be shame- and guilt-oriented as a result of Confucian teaching, which emphasizes personal virtues, obedience, self-discipline, and social norms. Thus, as Chinese culture places great emphasis on harmonious interpersonal relationships within the community, especially among family members, any failure in this regard is likely to induce feelings of shame and guilt. In other words, as family and marriage are still highly valued by contemporary Chinese people, shame and guilt are significant constructs in the understanding of family dynamics among Chinese families, and women's responses to marital conflicts and/or family breakdown (Lee Yao, 1983).

Within Chinese communities, when there is conflict between people or among family members, mediation is the most widely used and acceptable way of resolving the conflict. Leung (1991) indicates that even in contemporary China, mediation is still considered important in resolving any kind of dispute, be it interpersonal or organizational. He points out that of the four major forms of mediation in China—namely, mediation by court, people's mediation, administrative mediation, and mediation through lawyers—people's mediation is the most frequently used tool to resolve interpersonal conflicts, especially family conflicts. People's mediation operates at the level of neighbourhood and work unit production group. It is practised by indigenous and non-professional helpers; mediators are often local residents living in proximity, or colleagues working in the same work unit. Usually the most respected individuals are invited to perform the mediation. Thus, instead of going to a professional (e.g., a social worker or trained mediator) to seek advice, assistance, or service, Chinese people rely more on others within their informal networks to help them resolve personal, family, and/or marital conflicts.

Regardless of various social, economic, and political changes over the decades, and different social reformations to facilitate a more egalitarian gender system, social and familial structures in contemporary China are still quite hierarchical. Traditional beliefs and values still grant men more power than women. Youths are expected to obey their elders, especially when the elders are male. Therefore, younger women in traditional Chinese families are relatively vulnerable to male domination and abuse; they are raised to assume that their designated positions and duties within the family are those that involve nurturing. Under the governance of Mao and Deng Xia Ping, communist China has gradually recognized the talents and competencies of women, especially those who are educated, and women have been encouraged to take paid jobs and other prominent roles in various public domains (Chang, 1992). Therefore, in recent decades, urban women have become highly educated and very much career-oriented. However, rural and village women have not enjoyed the same status change as their urban sisters. They are generally deprived of the opportunity for education, and are still inclined to comply with traditional Chinese beliefs and values (Croll, 1983). Those who escape rural destitution and migrate to the cities in search of a new life work long hours for low wages to support themselves and their families back in the villages (Lee Yao, 1983). Women left behind continue to work in the fields: sowing, cultivating, and harvesting grain, rain or shine; or they work in small rural factories. Chinese women who resent living in China often look for the opportunity to leave the country; marrying overseas is one of the options.

Hong Kong was originally a part of China, but as a result of imperialism and war, it was a British colony for about 150 years until July 1997. As a result of this political history, Hong Kong has been greatly influenced by the British system and Western culture. However, Hong Kong is a unique city where the majority of residents are of Chinese origin, so many Chinese customs have been preserved. In addition, because of the continuing influx of immigrants from mainland China, the adopted Western beliefs and practices are constantly tested by the long-established and deeply rooted Chinese culture. On the surface, Chinese women's social position in Hong Kong seems to be well established, especially when one looks at the government bureaus, corporate structures, and the political arena. However, the abilities, talents, and successes of these elite women do not guarantee gender equality for the average Chinese woman in Hong Kong. Generally, as with many women in the West, although most women in Hong Kong participate in the labour force, they are still expected to take care of the home and meet the physical and emotional needs of all family members. Nevertheless, Wong (1981) finds that married women's paid employment has provided them with status relatively more equal to that of their husbands, and has enabled them to participate in decision making and bargain for a reduced domestic workload, although women are still held responsible for nurturing, and are judged by their performance as good wives and mothers.

Both in China and Hong Kong, although women do not always talk about their abuse publicly, it is not unusual to hear stories from friends or relatives about wife abuse, or to read in newspaper accounts that women are abused physically, sexually, and psychologically in their families. Gilmartin (1990) reports that since the early 1980s, there has been a growing number of reports of violence against women in China. According to the Embassy of the United States (March 6, 2007), a 2004 survey by the All-China Women's Federation (ACWF) indicated that 30 percent of families had experienced domestic violence and 16 percent of husbands had beaten their wives. The ACWF reported that it received some 300,000 letters per year complaining about family problems, mostly domestic violence. The actual incidence of woman abuse is believed to be higher because spousal abuse went largely unreported. The use of violence against women often maintains the status quo and discourages any challenges to the traditional norms of authority (Milwertz, 2003). Abused women in China are often described not only as failing to please their husbands, but also as failures for many other reasons, such as suspected affairs, failing to give birth to a son, refusing to comply, and so on.

Although living relatively farther away from mainland China, Chinese women in Taiwan and other Southeast Asian countries do not necessarily enjoy a better social status than their remote counterparts in China and

Hong Kong. Indeed, it is believed that the further away from China a Chinese community is, the more conservative it will be because of the desire to maintain a balance between the local culture and the original culture, and also because of the aspirations of community elders to preserve the hierarchy within the Chinese culture (Ong, 1995). Also, the specific time of emigration determines the nature and strength of the cultural values that are carried by the family to the new country. The earlier the arrival of Chinese immigrant families in another country, the older the cultural values that might be preserved in those families, regardless of the longer period of exposure to the new culture and environment. Of course, other internal and external factors may also come into play regarding culture, transforming the family's value system and behavioural patterns in the new country and creating interpersonal conflict in the family. Whatever the case, it is conceivable that women living within the boundaries of Chinese cultures would be governed to some extent by their inherited values and beliefs.

The history of Chinese immigrants in North America can be dated back to the 18th century (Dawson, 1991). Forming a great diaspora starting from the 1840s to 1930, early Chinese immigrants were mostly of rural origin, coming to British Columbia to help build railways and engage in mining businesses (Li, 1988; Wright, 1988). Despite their valuable contributions to Canadian society, Chinese immigrants were discriminated against and oppressed. They were excluded from various trades, businesses, and labour markets. Ultimately, they retreated into the ethnic business sector, working in laundries and restaurants to avoid racial discrimination by, and competition with, White employers and workers (Woon, 1998). In addition, early Canadian immigration legislation was loaded with racial practices. Immigration policies were selective in that they gave race-based preferential entrance to Canada by way of people's country of origin: The preferred countries were Anglo-Saxon (Wright, 1988). Although Chinese men were able to enter Canada to do the arduous work that Canadian residents found too menial and physically demanding, Chinese women were excluded systemically. Expensive head taxes for entry were imposed on Chinese immigrants between 1885 and 1904, and from 1923 to 1947 there was an Immigration (Exclusion) Act prohibiting Chinese-Canadians from bringing their families over (The Women's Book Committee, Chinese Canadian National Council, 1992; Woon, 1998). Hence, many Chinese couples were forced to separate until after the Chinese Exclusion Act was repealed.

In 1967, a universal point system was adopted, and since then more Chinese immigrants have been able to come to Canada as independents or as nominated relatives sponsored by Canadian citizens or permanent residents (Li, 1988). The Canadian census of 2006 indicated that about 1,216,570 people reported Chinese ancestry; of these, 486,330 resided in the Greater Toronto Area. Many were recent arrivals in Canada, and came mainly from China, Hong Kong, and Taiwan, as well as from Malaysia, Singapore, and the Caribbean. The Chinese ethnic group was numerically the top-ranked visible minority group in Canada for many years until the most recent census (Citizenship and Immigration Canada, 1998; *Sing Tao Daily*, 2008). Approximately one out of four Chinese immigrants to Canada are married women whose first language is either Cantonese or Mandarin. While some women are able to integrate successfully into the new environment with minimal assistance, many face significant challenges and substantial barriers.

Although the size of the Chinese community is considered enormous in a White-dominated society, and the Chinese business sector is growing, Chinese-based social service organizations are still underdeveloped. The conventional approach adopted by the mainstream social service agencies is quite reactive in their response to the needs of ethnic communities. Usually, after noticing a demographic change in their catchment areas (e.g., more racialized residents moving in), they might apply for extra funding to hire an ethnic worker to provide services for a specific group. Unfortunately, this extra funding is often piecemeal, only good for a part-time staff worker and limited services. Therefore, the demand and supply are usually not balanced. Also, while Chinese families are spreading across the GTA, most of the community services and Chinese organizations are clustered in downtown Toronto and the old Chinatowns. Only in the past few years have some Chinese community organizations, which provide direct community and social services to Chinese people, started moving to the Toronto city border and the city outskirts (i.e., York region and Mississauga).

Like families from many other immigrant groups, Chinese immigrant families generally come from economically or politically unstable territories. They leave their country of origin and hope to find new opportunity and/or excitement in the new country. Although nowadays many new Chinese immigrants are professionals, skilled workers, or merchants, upon arriving in Canada, they must face acculturation and may find themselves feeling lost and powerless in the process. If these new immigrants continue to experience stress in the new environment without adequate support from their significant family members, and without adequate assistance from the new country, their mental health may be jeopardized. Jiwani (2002) points out that the problems of racialization, racism, impact of migration, bicultural existence that induces "role overload," social isolation, and structural barriers to community services all contribute to the high risk of wife assault in immigrant families.

Though both immigrant men and women are subject to similar process-es of acculturation, women's experiences, especially those who are abused, can be distinguished from men's (Dion & Dion, 2001). In immigrant families, marital conflicts often arise as a result of a combination of home-sickness, resettlement adjustment, the husband's unstable employment, the wife's employment outside the home, and difficulties in interpersonal communication between the couple, especially since the relationship is being tested in a new and relatively risky environment. Chambon (1989) cites cases in which husbands found themselves "losing their control" over their wives after these women entered the North American labour force and/or were influenced by their North American friends with respect to concepts of marital satisfaction. It is reported that this circumstance was perceived as stressful, and the husbands often reacted with violence. Les-lie (1993) indicates that prior exposure to war-related violence increases people's likelihood of acquiring paranoiac ideation and anxiety. Although the circumstance that involves the wife and/or the family as a whole may not be as bad as the husband may think, because of his paranoiac anxiety, he may overreact to it by losing his temper and beating his wife.

Immigrant women who have experienced abuse or language barriers in the host country can develop low self-esteem, which not only slows down their adaptation to the new environment, but also increases their risks of further subjection to male violence, and decreases their ability to deal with abusive relationships appropriately. Pilowsky (1993) finds that low self-esteem and lack of self-confidence often immobilize these women; she explains that "immobilization is conceptualized as a state of temporary paralysis wherein [immigrant] women do not perceive themselves as either empowered or morally fit to leave an abusive relationship" (p. 151). Studies have identified several major barriers that increase immigrant women's vulnerability to male violence. Immigrants are often subject to racism and discrimination because they are viewed as a source of competition in the labour market, as well as their lack of official language skills and local job experience (Ca-nadian Mental Health Association, 1989; Naidoo, 1990). A lack of English or French language skills prevents them from accessing information and resources in the new environment (Crichlow, 1993; Edwards, 1989). This is particularly problematic for women who are assaulted by their partners in a strange land where they know no one but their partners.

Second, because of sexism and racism, immigrant women who have no language or marketable job skills are forced to depend socially and economically on their male partners, or on welfare. Some women may be fortunate to find a job that closely matches their skills or even one that pays them minimum wage, but many women find themselves stuck at home, with no job and no income. Ng (1996) argues that although there are subsidized programs and services to help immigrant women deal with their day-to-day problems, these services often fail to meet the needs of these women. They are expected to survive with minimal English that they learn from a subsidized ESL course, and settle in a low-paying job and/or stay home while their husbands work. Ng concludes that the social structure of Canada is organized so as to assign the class locations of immigrant women and make them reliant. Being in the lower social class also means being poor and deprived of many potential sources of social support. For instance, a woman has to have enough money to go to a service agency or attend regular ESL classes. Thus, the only perceived option for many immigrant women who are poor and suffering abuse is to endure it.

Third, the lack of social networks to combat feelings of loneliness, isolation, and helplessness often leaves many immigrant women in dismay, struggling to survive their predicaments alone. MacLeod and Shin (1990) maintain that immigrant women are not born with the sense of helplessness. Being away from significant family members and friends, having no connection with one's own ethnic/racial group, and knowing no one in the new community make them more susceptible to social isolation, and hence vulnerable to male violence in the home. Menjivar (2002) echoes the above study, pointing out that the host country should establish more programs and assistance to help newcomers, especially women, overcome their isolation and sense of helplessness so that they can deal with their abuse more effectively.

Fourth, cultural values and beliefs shared within an ethnic group have a very strong influence in immigrants' lives and affect their coping strategies. Evidence shows that most immigrant families are very proud of their cultural value of the family, and its integrity and cohesiveness. They put so much emphasis on "family harmony" and on the role of the collectivity in overcoming adversity that sometimes the welfare of one family member (e.g., the woman who is abused) may be deemed secondary (Gallin, 1992; Goodwin & Tang, 1996). The point is that women who agree with patriarchal beliefs and values are less likely to see subtle forms of domestic violence as wife abuse; those who accept patriarchal norms are more likely to delay active coping and help-seeking (Ahmed, Riaz, Barata & Stewart, 2004), and if the roles of husband and wife are considered complementary rather than adversarial, the idea of rescuing oneself by sending the abusive husband to jail may inhibit immigrant women's motivation to reveal or report their abusive experiences (Coutinho, 1991; Valiante, 1993).

Adopting a feminist framework of analysis, some researchers assert that violence against immigrant women is not only a result of systemic control and power exerted by men over women, but is also perpetuated by the immigration policies and categorization devised by Canadian society (Community Legal Education Ontario, 1994; Thakur, 1992). Clearly, the use of a points system to decide whether people can become permanent residents of Canada is a systemic discrimination against the female gender. For instance, the kinds of vocations and professions that merit more points are usually male-dominated ones, from services to technical and professional positions such as kitchen chefs, machinists, and engineers. In order to earn more points, the applicants must also have recognized credentials and uninterrupted years of service in the desirable job categories. These requirements are not in favour of women's situations. Further, priorities in determining services for new immigrants are often set to prepare the "head" of the family to be employable in the labour market, and recommended programs or training for immigrant women are usually superficial and inadequate (Ng, 1996). Thus, not only are the immigration policies sexist to begin with in determining who are eligible to become permanent residents, but what happens after immigrants have entered the new country also perpetuates male dominance by keeping women in a disadvantaged position socially, linguistically, and economically.

Some cultural studies have found that the major cause of the assault of women in immigrant families is rooted in the unequal resources and power divisions between immigrant men and women (Jang, Lee & Morello-Frosch, 1990/91; Williams & Rouette, 1993). It is evident that immigrant women are completely marginalized and isolated because they are unable to communicate with other people besides their spouses and children, they have no knowledge of community resources, and are unaware of what is going on in their community. In this situation, power and control over the woman automatically falls into the hands of the husband whose second language skill is superior, who has more resources and information as a result of his engagement in the public domain, and who is the one being recognized as the "head" of the family. Williams and Rouette (1993) indicate that the ideology of women being subordinate to men prevails in many cultures, including Canada. Some countries are more subtle about the ideology, whereas in others it is cast in stone. Unfortunately, in many countries where immigrant families come from, women's social status is relatively lower than that of women in Canada, and the woman's role is usually confined to the private domain. The Canadian government's immigration policies and practices, which assume the subordination of women and their dependence on men, indeed may be welcomed by many immigrant men. When there is a perceived discrepancy between cultural norms and beliefs in the country of origin and the new country, immigrant men may use violence to keep their spouses in the traditional subservient role (Nah, 1993; Frye & D'Avanzo, 1994).

U.S. and Canadian studies have found that traditional values have a tremendous impact on the lives of Chinese immigrant families, and thus could give rise to woman abuse in intimate relationships (Ho, 1990; Ong, 1995; Yip, 1995). Because these values are more geared toward the family and the group rather than the individual, the needs of the family as a whole are more important than the needs of its individual members. The relationships within the family are organized in a hierarchical order from elder to younger and from male to female. In this way, women are given fewer privileges and viewed as less important. Because of the power differential between the sexes, the man in the house has more control over the woman and sometimes violence is used to maintain such control.

In studying the lives of women who emigrated from China and Hong Kong to the U.S., Ong (1995) indicates that Chinese immigrant women are often "expected to be the preservers of home traditions as well as the vehicles for family emigration and continuity in the West" (p. 357). However, because conflicts arise between personal desires and cultural norms, and between the interests of the husband's family and those of the wife's family, some women find themselves experiencing abuse and social isolation after emigration. Ong observes that when immigrant families are detached from the larger home society, and also relatively isolated from the host society, their desires to maintain cultural ideologies and domestic regulations may become stronger in an attempt to accentuate their ethnic identity. Sometimes, when such desires are blocked, violence against women may occur. Having been exposed to Western philosophies concerning individual rights and personal happiness, women living in unhappy relationships may desire more personal rights and freedom when the old social rules are no longer enforced outside the family. Divorce, which was once out of the question, may become a possibility for Chinese immigrant women who have experienced male violence, especially when there is a supporting social network available for them.

In Chin's (1994) study of "overseas brides" in the U.S., she reports that since 1986 the U.S. government has been granting women entering the states to marry only "Conditional Permanent Resident" status for the first two years following their arrival. At the expiration of this status, if the couple has divorced or the original petitioner does not file another application for regular permanent status, the woman could face deportation or lose her legal status to stay in the country. This policy puts many Chinese women who enter the country to marry at high risk of enduring abuse at the hands of their "husbands." That is, if abusive men know their social and legal power over their wives, they may see themselves as the "masters" of their wives, and the women may feel obligated to please their "masters" in order to maintain their legal status and stay in the states. Chin's data show that as a result of arranged marriages, misunderstanding and mistrust often occur in the couples' marital relationships. Consequently, these out-of-town brides often find themselves subjected to verbal and psychological abuse. In some extreme cases, these women are also sexually and physically abused by their husbands.

In Canada, we gradually learn more about how Chinese-Canadian women cope with the issue of male violence. This kind of understanding comes from research projects within Chinese communities in which there are researchers who investigate women's situations, and there are women who voluntarily reveal their own experiences. For example, 130 interviews with Chinese-Canadian women were conducted by the Women's Book Committee of the Chinese Canadian National Council (1992). This council represents the concerns of Chinese-Canadians and is funded by the federal government. In individual interviews, when women were asked to talk about their lived experiences as immigrants, some of them disclosed that they were survivors of wife abuse. This demonstrates that at least some Chinese-Canadian women are no longer silent about their abuse experiences.

In studying the experiences of 54 assaulted women in Toronto between May 1986 and March 1989, Chan (1989) reports that not only is wife assault an issue in the local Chinese-Canadian community, but there are also increasing demands for counselling. Although there is evidence that much violence took place before migration, Chan argues that the stress associated with migration may be responsible for the escalation of the problem. Also, many women in her study reported that going to a shelter is not an option for them because living in a shelter increases feelings of homelessness and helplessness for them. Other studies have shown that while Chinese women may not have sought external help as actively as White women, they often reported experiencing psychological distress, insomnia, fatigue, depression, forgetfulness, loss of interest in sex, and emotional confusion (Health and Family Services Sub-committee, 1994;

Zhang, Snowden & Stanley, 1998). Instead of identifying the source of their health issues as abuse, many Chinese immigrant women in the above studies only insinuated that there were "marital conflicts" that troubled them. Based on other evidence and observations of the Chinese community, it is not unrealistic to suspect that many of these women are indeed victims/survivors of male violence in their homes.

Another Canadian study assessing Chinese immigrant women's needs in the process of settling in Canada shows that many women who emigrated from China as "overseas brides," or to reunite with their husbands, were abused physically, sexually, and psychologically (Fong, 1999). Although these women gradually learned of the community resources available to help them advance themselves in different ways, and were informed of their individual rights to fight wife abuse, most of them had a very tough time disengaging themselves from their husbands' control and finally leaving relationships. These women reported that traditional values, beliefs, concepts of family obligation and responsibility, as well as lack of support in the new environment, were the major obstacles of their long-term struggles.

METHODOLOGY

This study is based heavily on feminist standpoint theory, which has proven to be pertinent for studying women's experiences. Not only is it based on the everyday lived experiences of women, but it is also focused on the specific experiences within a particular group of women. As such, this theory is perceived to be an exploration rather than a progression toward a destination. Additionally, through the efforts of race-conscious feminist theorists, feminist standpoint theory has gradually evolved into one that is pluralistic rather than singular, which encourages diversity and self-definition among women. The research approach this study has taken is qualitative and participatory, which allows a greater opportunity for interactions between the researcher and the researched community. Autonomous organizational action within the local Chinese community and collective efforts among participants have emerged from the research process. This study is based on individual interviews with 14 abused Chinese immigrant women in the local Greater Toronto Area Chinese community. All interviews were conducted in the participants' native language (Cantonese or Mandarin) and then transcribed for analyses.

DISCUSSION OF FINDINGS

Six major themes focusing on abused Chinese immigrant women's lived experiences emerged from the data; these included: (1) cultural traps, (2) coping patterns and strategies, (3) utilization of support network, (4) feelings associated with abuse, (5) issues of immigration, and (6) life focus and goals.

Under *cultural traps*, these women reported that they were constantly living with *male chauvinism*. Because their abusive husbands possessed a male chauvinistic view of a spousal relationship, these women were not allowed to do things against their husbands' wishes. To the abusers, "a husband should always have the upper hand over his wife" (p. A13). What was interesting in the women's reports was that although they complained about male chauvinism, they actually internalized sexism and perpetuated it. For example, they accepted women's traditional role of sacrificing themselves to maintain family harmony. A woman explained: "As a woman you should bend yourself for the totality of the family" (p. A01). Such beliefs also influenced the overseas brides in this study to think that they should feel grateful to their abusive husbands for sponsoring them to come to Canada instead of confronting them about their abuse. They thought it was only appropriate that they "tolerated" some of their husbands' behaviour. Indeed, they were not aware of their own role in supporting male chauvinism by tolerating it in the beginning. A woman said: "I was neither pretty or smart; if there was someone willing to take me as a wife ... I was indeed very grateful" (p. A11). It was because of such a mindset that some women thought they should just "tolerate" the situation and work around the problem. Another woman said: "Chinese women don't expect too much from marriage. We think that perhaps every marriage is troublesome and you have to overcome all the difficulties" (p. A06).

Another subtheme of cultural traps was these women's strong belief in *fate*. Many of these women thought that being abused by their husbands was an unavoidable suffering predetermined in their destiny, so they had to withstand it at some point in life: "I don't know if it was predestinated [*sic*] like it was because I owed him something before this life so that I must pay him back in this life" (p. A04). Other women who accepted their abuse as fate tried to look at it from a somewhat hopeful angle: "We think that once you overcome the worse situation, good fortune will follow" (p. A06).

Regardless of their perspective, 12 out of the 14 women ended up divorcing on the grounds of abandonment or abuse. As a result of cultural emphasis on *family unity and harmony*, all these women suffered a great deal before the divorce was finalized. They all thought that keeping the family together was more important than their personal happiness. According to them, it was not a good idea to reveal that the family was falling apart because of "marital conflict" as it would shame the family as a whole. To avoid being shamed required them to conceal everything, which would help to save everybody's *face*—their own face, the abuser's face, their children's face, and the face of their parents back home. All of these cultural values had trapped them for quite some time, living in pain, before they could leave this part of their "destiny."

The second emergent theme was the women's *coping patterns and strategies*. There was a succession of coping methods observed. All these women began with a *self-reliant* tactic. They endured the abuse quietly, although not without instantaneous physical or verbal resistance. Some women coped by confronting the abuser with reasons, by distancing themselves emotionally and/or physically from their husbands, or by gratifying their husbands' needs to prevent further abuse.

As they realized that their self-reliance strategies were not working effectively to their benefit, they then resorted to getting some help from their *informal support network* within the family system, asking their parents, siblings, parents in-law, or other relatives to intervene, even though many of them could only do this through telephone contacts or mail correspondence. For example, they would ask a member in their extended family to talk some sense into their husbands. Although some women were able to solicit certain assistance in this way, such amateurish aid was proven ineffective in many cases.

When this initial support network strategy failed, the women then turned to *external resources*, ranging from checking out information over the telephone with someone (e.g., a neighbour) or through a community centre, to inquiring in person about community resources or personal counselling available for abused women. After they had taken this step, they came up with a tentative or more concrete plan for leaving the abuser. During this preparatory stage, they wanted to secure a paid job and some financial means to ensure that they could be on their own for at least a short while. Thirteen out of the 14 women had left their abusive husbands at some point; during the course of this study, only two women ended up staying. Four women left of their own free will, six women were divorced not completely by choice, and two women's husbands went missing after the abuse was reported to the authorities.

Related to the above was the third emergent theme of these women's *utilization of a support network*. The women reported that there were always people in their community who were approachable and who were willing to provide a helping hand; their experiences with their informal supporting network were generally positive. Many women who had an *extended family* to rely on would turn to it for emotional and practical support. However, they did not always tell them the whole truth in the beginning. Usually confessing the abuse to other family members was done in the anticipation that things might get out of control, so they needed these family members to ask the husbands to refrain from their abusive behaviour. Those who had no extended family around would sometimes turn to *new acquaintances* for support. Again, they would minimize the problem or reveal only part of it to gain "just enough" empathy or emotional support. Once these women learned from their new acquaintances about other community resources that they could access, they would go directly to those resources such as the 911 service, legal aid clinics, doctors' offices, hospitals, women's shelters, community organizations, and welfare offices.

Calling 911 was usually regarded as one of the very last resorts for these women unless they were in immediate danger. Only half of the women interviewed had used this service. However, they said that knowing that this option was available gave them a sense of power as if they were armed. A woman explained: "One of the biggest helps was knowing that I could call 911. It's like I have something I can refer to. It has provided me with a sense of security, knowing that he couldn't threaten me or point a knife at me or beat me" (p. A09). On the other hand, some of the women who reported to the authorities did not know clearly what might be involved in their action, and thus often had mixed feelings about the unexpected outcome. The two biggest concerns were whether or not their husbands would be put in jail, and whether their long-term status in Canada would be affected. They wanted their husbands to be warned officially by the authorities, but they did not really want their husbands to be criminalized or to lose their citizenship. Nevertheless, none of these women really felt guilty about calling the police. A woman recounted her fortunate encounter with the police:

> When I reported to the police, a [Chinese] police officer was quite nice to me. I told him once that I wanted to die. He told me that my children need me.... After that, sometimes this officer would drop in to visit us.... He asked me if I had ever thought of dying again.... Sometimes he dropped in and sometimes he called to see if we were doing fine. He would counsel me sometimes. I was so depressed and disturbed around that time. I had no one else to talk to. So, he was there for us. Although he didn't provide us with any tangible assistance but emotionally he was there to support us and make us feel better. (p. A10)

Of the 14 women, eight reported having contacts with *legal/paralegal workers and lawyers*. Generally, they found the staff in community legal clinics quite helpful. These individuals often advised the women to do things that benefited their cases. They frequently acted as a bridge between these women and their lawyers, and they connected the women to other relevant community resources. The women believed that their lawyers worked to protect their interests, but some mentioned that their communication with their lawyers was hampered because there was no interpreter provided. As a result of poor communication, these women felt that they might not get the full benefit of having a lawyer. This finding reflected the disadvantaged position these women were in when fighting for their rights.

Medical health professionals often came into contact with abused women, and their responses to woman abuse were significant to these women's experiences. An unethical medical health professional would worsen a woman's situation. Nevertheless, a helpful and conscientious one would help not only to identify abuse cases but would also help abusive women to alleviate their emotional trauma. A typical example was a woman who sought medical advice after being raped by her husband's friend. In retrospect, she suspected that it was a plot. Right after the rape, she was extremely disturbed psychologically. She recalled her experience with the first doctor and said: "I sat home all day crying. I couldn't sleep. I told him about the rape. He said I shouldn't report the incident to the police because the guy was my husband's best friend. He blamed me for what happened. I was so angry about it" (p. A10). However, with the second doctor, she recollected: "I still had a problem sleeping and by referral I went to see Dr. W.… He told me that I should have reported to the police and have the guy nailed.… He asked me if I would like him to call the police on my behalf. He said he could interpret for me.… Very soon they arrested the guy.… I felt a burden had just lifted from me and there was some justice for me in this society" (p. A10).

Social service and community workers were considered part of these abused women's support network. In the course of their struggles, 13 women had come into contact with a social service or community worker at some point. Some women received long-term counselling, whereas others had only a brief informational encounter with a professional helper in person or over the phone. In either case, most of the women expressed gratitude toward their helpers, and took their professional advice seriously. All of the helping professionals mentioned spoke the same language as these women. When these women were in great distress, they needed to work on their emotions and find some practical solutions for their situations. They all reflected that had they not gone through their ordeal with a helping professional on their side, they would not have been able to survive it and be the people they were at the time of the interview. More importantly, their contacts with a social service or community agency provided them with an opportunity to learn more about their rights and options. A woman testified: "My counselor really showed me the right direction and encouraged me to deal with things one by one. Had I not called this agency, I wouldn't have known my rights to call the police. Then, I would have been beaten to death" (p. A06). Another woman echoed by saying: "When I think back I really appreciated D's help. If she was not there to help me, I don't know if I knew what to do. Women need to know their basic human rights and how they are protected by the Canadian law" (p. A07).

Of the 14 women who participated in this study, only three reported that they had been to the *women's shelter*. A few other women mentioned that they could have used the shelter service, but chose not to because there were better options such as staying with a friend, or they had the financial support to rent a place temporarily. Two of the three women who used shelters did not find them to be particularly welcoming or warm environments, especially when there were no staff people who spoke their language. They found themselves being isolated by the residents and misunderstood by the staff. Hence, they described their lives in the shelter as more stressful and disoriented. The only woman who was pleased with her stay admitted that she was lucky to have a shelter worker who spoke her language and who took good care of her whenever she was on duty. She described that her life in the shelter was better than life with her abusive husband at home.

The fourth major theme that emerged from the interview data was the women's *feelings associated with abuse*, which were negative.

Similar to findings reported by numerous other studies, these abused women often felt *helpless* in the beginning of their battle because they did not think they could change their situations much, and could not find anyone to help them. Sometimes it was the thought of being trapped or stuck that made them feel helpless, especially when they felt that they had no one but themselves to blame for their situations. Seeing no way out, or in some cases being pregnant, reduced their motivation and mobility to take a more radical step in ending the abuse, so they just tolerated it.

Some women said they felt very *confused* in the process because they felt they had done what they could to change the situations, yet the abuse remained the same, if not even worse. They truly did not know what else they could do, when leaving the abuser was considered the very last resort.

For all of these women, the feeling of *distress* was a constant. During this period, they were unable to sleep well, and some even lost their appetite. The thought of "wanting to die" often came to mind, although there were no concrete plans to end their lives. They left their husbands either temporarily or permanently when this distress was intensified, and after they had found some viable options.

Disappointment was also one of the common feelings. When these women found that their commitment to maintain the integrity of the family and efforts to save the relationship were unrecognized or taken for granted, they became very discouraged and frustrated. Such disappointment in a way helped some of them to make up their minds to leave the abusers.

Although these women were not passive victims of wife assault, when they were under the control of their husbands, they often felt very *nervous and fearful*. They were afraid that there would be further or more vicious violence in store. Such fears were so strong that they were reactive rather than proactive. A woman claimed that:

> Starting from that night, I always lived in fear when I was with him. When I was with him, I didn't feel I was a wife. I didn't know who I was. From dawn to dusk, 24 hours a day, I lived in fear. Sometimes when he made a move, I reacted involuntarily. For example, when I heard him come home opening the door, my body would start shaking. I always feared that he might kill me. I can say that when I was with him, I felt so ... so frightened. I was manipulated by him. In those days, living with him, I was not his wife but something else. (p. A01)

Fear still followed some women even after they left their husbands. They feared that they might run into their ex-husbands or be targeted for revenge. Those who chose to stay in their relationships had their fears too. They reported that after they returned from a shelter, the physical abuse stopped, but the emotional abuse was still a daily routine, and the threat of revenge still haunted them.

Anger was another negative emotion these abused women experienced daily while trapped in the relationship. This anger was often directed toward the abusers, but sometimes it was directed toward themselves too. Anger directed toward the abusers was often accompanied by frustration as they were let down many times by their husbands' repetitive aggression. However, such emotion often motivated them to either come up with new ideas to change their situations or confront their husbands more radically. When they found that there was nothing more they could do to improve the situation, or when their husbands finally filed for divorce, their anger often helped them come to terms with dissolving the marriage for good. Three women admitted openly that they regretted not making a more timely decision to get out of their situations or to terminate the relationships.

The majority of the women said that they were happier without a husband. Interestingly, although they found some peace and happiness through leaving their abusive husbands, many participants also reported *a sense of loss* after they left. The women all dealt with their feelings of loss differently, whether as a result of their long-term psychological trauma, their residual feelings for their husbands, or their high regard for family life. While some often wished that there was someone to help them decide whether they should take the abuser to court, or just let him go to give themselves some peace, or have someone to help guide them in building a new independent life, others coped by hoping that one day their husbands would change and reunite with the family. For the former, the sense of loss was about missing a life direction, but for the latter, the sense of loss was linked directly to the loss of a life partner.

The overseas brides reported the feeling of *victimization*, which was twofold. First of all, as a group they shared similar reasons for marrying; they said they did it to gratify their parents' wish for emigration or a new life in the West, so they had sacrificed their personal happiness in romantic love for the welfare of their families. Then when they found out that they were actually married to a violent man in a strange land, where they had minimal means, skills, and mobility to leave, they were victimized once more. A couple of the women who were not overseas brides also felt victimized because of their abusive experiences and their dissatisfaction with the justice system in the process.

Immigration issues were a fifth major theme that emerged from the data. All of the women, except one, talked in great detail about how the dream of emigrating overseas created some problems for them and trapped them in abusive relationships because they had lowered their standards in choosing a spouse in exchange for an immigrant status, or because they were isolated from their family of origin, relatives, friends, and colleagues. However, four out of the 13 women revealed that their abuse had actually begun when they were living in their country of origin. They disclosed issues associated with immigration that made these women vulnerable to wife assault; this vulnerability applied not only to overseas brides but also to other women who came with, or came to reunite with, their spouses.

First of all, *immigration brought changes*. One of the changes was in the area of law. According to these women, the laws that were available to protect the interests and personal safety of women in their country of origin were relatively loose when compared to laws in Canada. Such a difference directly and indirectly affected how they were treated by their husbands. Very often it was not that the "old rules" condoned wife abuse, but that people generally were more tolerant and prioritized family harmony over divorce. Under such circumstances, an abused woman might feel that she had to tolerate it longer before she could tell anyone. Nevertheless, in the new country, where more people disapproved of male violence, it was easier for abused women to gain moral and substantial support. This opened their eyes to alternative family structures. A woman said: "Why didn't I do anything in the past two years? It was because I didn't know about Canadian law and didn't understand what this community believes.... Now at least I knew that there is such a law to protect me" (p. A09). What she meant in the full context was that she could get substantial support to start a new life in Canada.

Secondly, *immigration paralyzed survival skills*. Living in a completely new environment where people speak a foreign language seemed to paralyze the normal functioning of these women. One woman's comments demonstrated this point very well. She explained:

> If I were still in China, I would have my family around and they would have been able to help me. I would not have lived a miserable life like this. Perhaps I would not have [been] married to him in the first place or would have divorced him even sooner. You know, I would have known about the resources in my environment because everything would have been in Chinese. I would have known what department to go to and where to seek help. I didn't know where to go for help in here. The greatest barrier was my isolation! (p. A02)

Indeed, many of the women came to Canada without their extended family. They did not have a safety net to fall back on when they needed it. Also some women who came from a village had never lived in a city. Toronto was an isolated, unfamiliar land to them. They had great difficulties finding their way around, not to mention the different lifestyle and language barrier. Going out and getting home often became a major adventure for them. Hence, it was clear that their limitations inhibited their mobility and access to information and services. However, once they learned more about their environment and knew their way around, this helplessness and anxiety diminished considerably, especially after they were divorced or separated.

The other issue associated with immigration that put women in a vulnerable position to wife assault was *the transformation of their social and employment status*. This was especially so for those who immigrated with their husbands. It was reported that in their country of origin, when both the husband and wife worked, the wife would have a relatively equal status in the family. However, immigration usually left women without a paying job, leaving them with no choice but to rely on their husbands financially. In return, they gained less respect in the relationship. One woman stated:

> He treated me much better then because back then I had my own status. I was the chief editor in the publishing department; he worked for the Social Science department, nothing particularly significant. Indeed, his social and economic status was lower than mine, therefore … he had never beaten me before and I think we seldom quarrelled…. [Here,] his financial status provides him the freedom to do whatever he wishes. There is a gap between us…. In China, if the financial status between the couple is not the same, the husband could ill treat his wife. My situation here is like that also. He felt that I was his subordinate…. He doesn't respect women at all…. [In Canada,] I have to take care of my child and I feel stuck…. She's too little. But men don't have to care about all these, they go out and work aggressively outside the home. So, it is easier for them to get engaged with society…. This becomes a gap between us…. There has been some changes in … our social status. In his case, he felt that he had been very successful, other people thought that he had been doing quite well, so he felt that he's a successful man who deserved a better woman. (p. A12)

So after immigration there were no close relatives to help take care of children, no affordable child-care facilities available, no recognition of women's qualifications to work in the new country, and no language skills to find a job that matched their credentials. Thus, the social and economic status between the husband and wife would be completely off balance, giving rise to male chauvinism and woman assault.

Life focus and goals was the final theme that surfaced from the interview data. Clearly, every woman who participated in this study had a very tough life battling woman abuse. Some managed to leave their relationships or live without a partner, while only a couple of them were still trying to fix the relationships and give them another opportunity. Whatever their decision, the majority of them said that they had something on which to focus and look forward to. Paying more attention to *personal development* was one of their major goals. These women realized that they needed to upgrade their skills in order to live independently. The very first priority was to strengthen their language abilities. The next goal was to find a job to support themselves and their children. Regardless of whether the women were by themselves or were still with their husbands, all of them mentioned that they considered their *children's well-being* their top priority. Not only did they want their children to receive a proper education and be raised in a loving environment, but also they wanted to build a better relationship with them. One of the mothers' words confirmed this goal and focus:

> My two daughters are the most precious things in my life now. I care so much about their health and their learning progress. Whenever they get sick, I feel so worried and I couldn't sleep well. Right now, I don't have anything but my daughters. I wish them a life different from mine. I want them to do well and have a brighter future.... I don't know what I can do in the future but I think it's very important to make sure that my daughters get [a] good education. (p. A02)

In terms of improving their *chances of getting a job,* the women wanted to get more relevant training so that they could be better equipped for the labour market. Living with the minimal assistance provided by the welfare system could not satisfy their desire to excel and be completely independent. They wanted real jobs that could support their families. Those who anticipated being hampered by child-rearing duties and thus unable to work full-time talked about their plans for volunteer work. They found that helping others provided them with a sense of self-fulfillment. Some even talked about using their experiences to help other women in the same boat. They felt that because they had come a long way to overcome their difficulties socially and psychologically, they could better understand what many abused women have to face, which would put them in a very good position to provide support for those who are still struggling. In fact, a couple of women in this study ended up working with the researcher voluntarily in another community project, advocating for abused immigrant women and educating community members to prevent male violence against women.

CONCLUSION

Generally, the findings of this study showed that many participants who were affected by wife abuse shared similar experiences in the course of their struggles. These women took action to protect themselves and confront their partners in their own ways. While they were often influenced by their cultural values and bound by their limitations as immigrant women and by their sympathies with the abusers, so as to persuade themselves to stay in the relationships, they tried to regain control over their situations and took every opportunity to seek help. After they realized that keeping the relationships would no longer do themselves and their children any good, they let go. Once they were free from violence, they took every measure to better equip themselves for single-parenthood and focused on the welfare of their children. Clearly, the experiences reported by these women in the local context cannot be universalized to imply that all abused Chinese immigrant women's situations are the same. However, it is significant that we examine these women's experiences in the context of the intersection of cultural traditions, sexism, racism, and anti-immigrant discrimination, which may create barriers for them in their pursuit of lives free from violence and abuse.

Echoing studies referred to in this chapter, women in this study did suffer from spousal abuse of various forms. Their coping behaviours were no doubt greatly affected by their internalization of Confucian thinking, which is important to their culture, especially the expectations to be a loyal family member, be considerate, tolerant, and to demonstrate a sense of *Yun Ching* even when their personal well-being was in jeopardy. However, ambivalence set in when these women were exposed to concepts of individuality and personal freedom as elements of happiness, and they realized that there were options other than what they used to imagine, so conflicts between the couples escalated. Because of the cultural beliefs that these Chinese immigrant families brought with them, men who embraced chauvinistic views were likely to assume authority over family matters and demand respect and service from their wives. The wives might have felt obliged to perform their "womanly" roles, even though their personalities might not lend themselves to these roles. However, when these women realized that they were no longer under the direct governance of the "old rules" in their new country, they would not put up with their husbands' behaviour.

Clearly, these women's struggles have been lengthy. Because family unity and face-saving are still prevalent in the Chinese culture, these women have tried their very best to be sympathetic, understanding, and supportive partners, so that they have spent quite some time tolerating their husbands' behaviour before they terminated the abusive relationships. For those who were sponsored by their husbands to come to Canada, they feel obliged to show their gratitude and give their husbands another chance rather than leaving them immediately or putting them in jail for the abuse. Subsequently, when the wives used external authorities to demand change from their husbands, ending the marriage is still not an ultimate goal. That is why some participants of this study reported feeling coerced into divorce. They thought they were just drawing the last card before they could win the game, meaning that their husbands would finally take their protests seriously.

Knowledge generated from this study has provided a better understanding of the challenges faced by abused Chinese immigrant women. First, when living in a new country and learning a new set of rules and standards, most Chinese immigrant women have to struggle continuously between independence and dependence; abused women juggle constantly to balance these two forces. On the one hand, they are emotionally, culturally, socially, and/or economically dependent on their husbands. On the other hand, they also try to be socially and economically independent by taking English courses, becoming familiarized with the new society, establishing new connections, and finding a job. All of these struggles overburden them, so it usually takes them longer to have their issues or ambivalent feelings resolved. Therefore, it is possible that, in some individual cases, leaving or ending the relationship is not the only viable option. After all, living in a foreign country where the only significant people available for them are their husbands, terminating the relationship would mean stripping away their identities and losing their recognition of being "someone" in a strange society. As such, many of the responses and behaviours of these abused women should be considered typical and be understood rather than judged.

Furthermore, instead of looking at limitations and weaknesses, our society needs to focus more on these women's strengths when examining how they deal with abuse in intimate relationships. From the accounts of the participants in this study, Chinese immigrant women demonstrate a high level of resilience and the ability to change even with limited resources. They strive in every way to improve themselves and to enrich their lives by studying a new language, making new friends, and connecting themselves to community resources, even though they have limited English. Thus, it is inappropriate to use Western measures, which often emphasize quick relief and instant results, to gauge these women's coping skills or strategies. These women take the chance to weigh their gains and losses and make their own decisions that fit their circumstances.

We must also recognize that sexism, racism, anti-immigrant discrimination, and all other -isms that exist in our social structure often shape these Chinese women's experiences. Current immigration policies are constructed around job categories and a points system that favours male applicants, and many immigrant women still have to rely on their husbands' sponsorship to enter this country. As such, their fear of losing financial support or immigrant status is very real, which often prevents them from radically responding to abuse. The fact is that as long as the social structure and system still convey to immigrant men that they are more worthy than immigrant women, these women will be easy targets of male violence. Additionally, as opposed to White immigrant women, Chinese immigrant women have to deal with racism in the system and in society. This will surely impact these women's chances of getting a job, thus hampering their powers of negotiation, or delaying the process of dealing effectively with woman abuse.

Currently, there is insufficient government funding available to help Chinese community organizations develop preventive programs and substantial services for abused women, and these organizations are limited in many ways in combating the issue or in educating the community. While there is a huge gap in the social service sector, providing only limited short-term and piecemeal services for abused Chinese immigrant women, we cannot expect the problem to go away or diminish. Moreover, because the Chinese culture often respects the elderly and values people's "self-sufficiency" (Tze Li Gung Xin), local interests are focused more on building retirement and nursing homes for the aged and providing resettlement services such as ESL classes and job-searching workshops for new immigrants. As a result, the larger Chinese community still does not take woman assault very seriously. Fewer resources are allocated to developing services relevant to this problem. In the end, women suffer.

Lastly, although this study has widened the narrow range of existing literature regarding wife abuse, identified some major predicaments that abused Chinese immigrant women encounter, and recognized some coping strategies that abused women use in dealing with male violence in their intimate relationships, more research needs to be done to thoroughly understand the phenomenon of woman abuse in the local Chinese community. For example, we need to gain knowledge of woman abuse from men's perspectives, to study what might be the most effective coping strategies for women, and what would be more effective intervention approaches from Chinese helping professionals' points of view. We also need to widen the scope in the examining woman abuse to include other power struggles and relations, not necessarily between genders or in a heterosexual context. We must appreciate and empower women's self-agency in every step while trying to reduce women's vulnerability and enable them to confront their abusers. Instead of victimizing women again in the system, or blaming them for their situations, we should identify and celebrate any small successes women have achieved. Human growth comes from taking actions through trial and error, no matter how small each step is. As clinicians or helping professionals, we should not expect abused women to take steps before they are ready or that go beyond their boundaries. Empowerment is achieved with our ability to recognize strengths, not shortcomings.

Chapter 10

Praying for Divorce: The Abuse of Jewish Women through Jewish Divorce Law

Lisa Rosenberg

What if your spouse has the power to deny you the divorce you desperately want unless you give in to his extortionate demands? Sometimes he says, "I will let you have a divorce if your family pays me money," and sometimes he demands the house, both cars, and full custody of the children. Sometimes he just threatens that he will never give you your freedom because he wants to punish you.

This scenario is not fictional. It is the real life story of women who are denied the fundamental right to divorce their husbands. Jewish law, called *halakhah*, adhered to by Orthodox and Conservative Jewish people with regard to divorce, dictates that only a husband has the right to end a marriage by granting a *get*, a divorce document, which is a contractual release. Without a *get*, a woman becomes an *agunah*, literally meaning one who is anchored or chained. This power imbalance means that some Jewish men either use the *get* as a bargaining tool to obtain better monetary, property, or custody settlements upon divorce, or they withhold a *get*, sometimes for years, to control, to punish, or just out of spite. Although an *agunah* may obtain a civil divorce, neither she nor her community will consider this a valid divorce. If a woman is religiously observant and abides by Jewish law, then only the religious divorce counts. She receives the *get* from her husband in front of a *bet din*, a Jewish court. Without it, she remains in limbo, chained to her recalcitrant husband, unable to remarry, and thus unable to have future children. If she does go ahead and have children without a *get*, these children have the status and stigma of *momzer*, which means that if they

215

are observant, and abide by Jewish law when they are adults, they can marry only other *momzers* or converts to Judaism.

While Jewish women can also become *agunot* (plural of *agunah*) if their husbands die or disappear without witness, or their husbands are declared not mentally competent to give the *get*, the vast majority of *agunot* today are victimized by recalcitrant husbands. Thus, this is a situation where a group of women, living in secular society, often choose to continue to abide by Jewish law even though their lives are so circumscribed by it. In Israel, all legal matters are adjudicated under civil law, except for matters of personal status, such as marriage and divorce, which are adjudicated by Jewish courts. This means that every Jewish Israeli woman, regardless of her level of observance, is bound by Jewish law when marrying or divorcing. Thus far, there is little remedy for *agunot* as the vast majority of Orthodox and Conservative rabbis today continue to interpret Jewish law as immutable; in addition, a coerced *get* is not legally valid, so men have to give *gittin* (plural of *get*) of their own free will. While a wife does have the right to refuse the *get*, her husband can remarry and have subsequent children (not *momzers*) and can override her refusal through Jewish legal means.

CHAPTER OVERVIEW

This chapter is designed to rectify a scholarly injustice. During the past 20 years, a limited group of scholars have mentioned *agunot*, although with brevity, in their books on various related topics. They have generally focused their discussions on the history and development of Jewish women's oppression within Jewish law or Jewish law's perceived inability to adapt to modern society. In most accounts, *agunot* are discussed either in an abstract manner as a whole community of women, or only on a case-by-case basis. None of these approaches is useful for discussing the lives of *agunot*. Rather, from a feminist perspective, this chapter addresses the needs and experiences of *agunot* themselves, not only by examining their individual life circumstances, but also by contextualizing and theorizing their collective experiences. By putting their lives at the centre of contemporary Jewish experience, and by giving them a voice, we examine the lives of these women whose husbands are preventing them from obtaining a divorce.

This chapter also contributes to feminist conceptualizations of male violence against women by broadening their definitions of abuse, for I propose that the denial of a *get* is a form of abuse, called *get* abuse. I have developed *get* abuse as a concept to underscore the husband's use of power and control during *get* denial, which is extremely abusive in its intent and consequence for *agunot*, causing the women emotional anguish and sometimes physical pain, as well as the marital constraint. *Get* abuse is also used as a concept to examine and explain the linkage I often uncovered in my research between a husband's physical and emotional abuse of his wife during the marriage and *get* denial upon marital breakdown.

This chapter also strongly emphasizes women's agency within oppressive structures. Although a Jewish woman who becomes an *agunah* is truly victimized by her husband, she is also an active agent as she navigates through her experience. Sometimes Jewish women even become survivors as they receive their *gittin* through traditional or even non-traditional means. While beyond the scope of this chapter, it should be noted that many Jewish women's groups have successfully supported and advocated on behalf of *agunot*.

JEWISH FEMINISM, JEWISH LAW, AND *AGUNOT*

This discussion will now begin to contextualize the plight of *agunot* by examining some important legal background. The story of *agunot* begins with a passage in the Old Testament, in Deuteronomy 24:1, which states: "A man takes a wife and possesses her. She fails to please him because he finds something obnoxious about her, and he writes her a bill of divorcement, hands it to her, and sends her away from his house."

From this passage rabbis devised an intricate system of regulations to deal with divorce. Historically, rabbis did not condone divorce; yet, however regretfully, they realized the need for a *get* when marriage dissolution did occur. Rabbis were torn between strictly interpreting the law and freeing *agunot*. They realized the consequences of being an *agunah* were tragic, and they were sometimes willing to use the tools available to them within *halakhah* to mitigate or alleviate men's control of the divorce process. For example, unless the rabbis deemed the woman rebellious, a *moredet*, when her husband divorced her he had to pay her the entire sum owed to her according to their *ketubah*, or marriage contract. In addition to enabling women to receive this early form of alimony, the rabbis felt that the prospect of having to pay this large sum would dissuade men from divorcing their wives in a rash manner. Moreover, women were also accorded the right to petition the *bet din* when they wanted to end their marriages and their husbands were unwilling. The rabbis recognized several grounds that would often lead them to compel husbands to divorce their wives and pay them the *ketubah* money owed them. These grounds included a husband developing a disease, denying his wife conjugal relations, denying her visits to her family, prohibiting her from attending a wedding or a house of mourning, forbidding her from wearing jewellery or using cosmetics, or forbidding her from eating certain foods. Even if she just declared, "He is loathsome to me," some rabbis felt it was incumbent upon them to compel a divorce. In addition, while some rabbis turned a blind eye to wife battery, others saw this as reason to compel a divorce.

How were the rabbis able to compel men to give their wives a *get*? Historically, in general, they often used leniency and creativity when interpreting the law, which rabbinical authorities today have been strongly criticized for not doing. More specifically, according to *halakhah*, when a husband denies his wife a *get* and she approaches the *bet din* for help, they must call him to appear before the court. If he refuses to come three times, the *bet din* can issue a *seruv*, basically holding him in contempt of court. Only then does the *bet din* have the authority to issue either a *yotzee* or a *kofin* order. A *yotzee* order, "We order him," allows the court to call for more minor measures against the husband, such as social ostracism. A *kofin* order is much stronger: "We compel him," or "We force him." Rabbinical authorities in the past interpreted this to mean that the use of physical force was legitimate.

Historically, the use of social ostracism was usually very effective since Jewish people lived in communities where every aspect of life was governed by religious law. Not speaking with a man, denying a man employment in the village or town where he lived, or denying him attendance at the synagogue was often enough of a deterrent. Today, in North America, for example, with civil and religious law being separate, a man cannot be forced to go before a *bet din*. If he fails to appear three times and the *bet din* issues a decree of social ostracism, it will not necessarily work. If he's denied synagogue membership, then he can go to another synagogue, move somewhere else, or stop going. If the decree is to stop employing him, he may find employment outside of the Jewish community; he may not have been working in the Jewish community at all. Moreover, in North America today, where it is illegal to use physical force against a recalcitrant husband, a *bet din* cannot use the *kofin* order; however, as will be discussed, this does not stop some *agunot* from trying to get *gittin* by having their husbands forced with violence.

How have Jewish feminist theorists responded to this situation, Jewish women's subordinate position within *halakhah* and as *agunot*? Analyzing the development of Jewish feminist thought in North America during the past 25 years, it seems that Jewish feminist scholars have, to a large degree, addressed multiple issues in a superficial manner rather than taking on a few core issues in a substantive way. This critique is in no way meant to diminish the radical nature of this scholarship, its vibrancy, its theoretical and practical challenge, or its profound effect on Jewish life. Rather, it is meant to highlight the massive undertaking that has been required to examine Jewish women's unequal status within Jewish law.

The scholars who have aimed their analytical lenses at Jewish women's inequality within *halakhah* have raised more questions than they have answered, but their questions are an important starting point for framing initial feminist insight into the plight of *agunot*. Regardless of their stance on the matter, the primary question these scholars pose is: In what manner of esteem do we hold *halakhah*? That is, they are asking the same question posed by feminist scholars who are working to change inequitable practices in secular systems such as government, law, education, and medicine. Do we work within a patriarchal system in order to change it, or do we forgo it in order to forge something else? Do we participate in a system that has subordinated women, or are efforts better channelled outside its boundaries? The question pondered by Jewish feminist scholars who are concerned with women's inequality in areas of *halakhah*, such as divorce law is: Should Jewish feminists attempt to mould *halakhah* and shape it in an image of justice, or should it be dismissed as ultimately inimical to Jewish feminist goals?

The scholars whose inclinations are to work within the system of *halakhah* in order to remedy the inequality rely predominantly on reasons related to their belief in the alleged dynamism of *halakhah*. They cite the historical ability of *halakhah* to change as proof that there is room for adaptability in the future. However, it is unclear from their analyses whether *halakhic* change will also include feminist ideals and practical solutions. Blu Greenberg, an Orthodox feminist who wrote *On Women and Judaism: A View from Tradition* (1981), states in an oft-quoted remark: "Where there was a rabbinic will, there was a *halakhic* way." She argues that rabbinical leaders should not "hide behind slogans of immutability that are dishonest caricatures of *halakhah*" (Greenberg, 1981, p. 43).

In 1981 Greenberg wrote that because of past *halakhic* dynamism, Jewish feminists have the right to cautiously, guardedly, change those specific areas of Jewish law that have engendered discrimination against women, such as divorce law, although the *halakhic* system as a whole must remain intact. Furthermore, although *halakhah* must adopt those feminist principles that support this process of redress, those aspects of feminist agitation that are dangerous to Jewish continuity must be relegated to the dustbin. The following remark sums up her opinion most appropriately: "I do not want to reject the basics. All I ask is that women have equal access to them" (Greenberg, 1981, p. 172). Thus, Greenberg is explicitly stating the desire for equal access to male privilege often implicit in the feminist decision to work within a system. Her analysis is bound by her legitimate need to safeguard *halakhah* and, by association, Jewish religious, social, and cultural continuity. Such an argument confines any feminist transformation of Judaism within a specific, strictly defined realm.

Perhaps an analysis such as Greenberg's should not be automatically faulted for not going far enough to remedy situations like that of *agunot*, but should be seen as a necessary first step. More than a decade after *On Women and Judaism: A View from Tradition* was published, Greenberg writes in "Jewish Women's Rights: For the Love of Law" that "Years ago when I first began to examine inequality in Jewish divorce, I believed the problem could and should be solved with as little change as possible to *halakhah*" (Greenberg, cited in Porter, 1995, p. 209). Because the *agunah* problem continued to worsen, she modified her earlier opinions: "Today I no longer believe that it is sufficient to address the symptom without addressing the root cause.... What is needed therefore is not a piecemeal approach to the problem ... but rather a fundamental *halakhic* reinterpretation of the basic principle upon which the law is based" (Greenberg in Porter, 1995, p. 210). In Greenberg's more contemporary analysis, *halakhah* is still untouchable as a system, but its foundations can be shaken. There is less concern with the resulting consequences and more emphasis on a solution. How to reinterpret *halakhah* fundamentally is still an unanswered question.

Another reason for working within the *halakhic* system, according to some scholars, is that if feminists decide it is too painful, too fruitless to even engage with *halakhah*, they are making a grave mistake in that they are leaving this contested terrain to their "enemies." As Leonard D. Gordon (1995) succinctly argues in his article, "Toward a Gender Inclusive Account of *Halakhah*," as much as women may have been excluded from positions of power in law historically, this historical exclusion has ironically led to a self-exclusion in our contemporary times. Jewish law, like American law, cannot be discarded. When feminism joins liberal Judaism in self-exclusion from *halakhah*, feminism risks reinforcing the characterization of women as "other" within Jewish systems (Gordon in Rudavsky, 1995, p. 10). There is undoubtedly some truth to this contention, and Jewish feminists should pay it some heed.

However, Susannah Heschel (1983), in *On Being a Jewish Feminist*, would disagree with the arguments above. She is critical of Greenberg's proposition that we can change the areas of *halakhah* that continue to subjugate women today, which is a proposition representative of the analyses of the majority of scholars who espouse the *halakhic* dynamism argument, such as Gordon. Heschel believes their contentions are theologically unsound. She raises a pivotal, immobilizing question when she asks: "Once we acknowledge the laws regarding women as the products of a particular historical period and outlook, what is to keep us from considering other Jewish practices—such as the synagogue service—as a comparable outgrowth that has outlived its meaning and relevance?" "In fact," she continues, "the entire system of *halakhah* might be similarly regarded as the religious expression of a particular community, living in Palestine and Babylonia nearly two thousand years ago" (Heschel, 1983, p. xxi). Thus, she believes that once you begin modifying certain laws, you place the entire system in jeopardy. Furthermore, using the plight of *agunot* as an example, she doubts whether the modification of *halakhah* is even an option available to us in our time as she maintains that "a living legal system never has the luxury to ignore a serious conflict; it must respond in one way or another. Only when a legal system dies can problems be ignored or passed over" (Heschel, 1983, p. xxvi). By implication, it seems that the only option left is to pursue a different path to non-*halakhic* redress.

Because of a strong concern for Jewish survival, which permeates much of Jewish feminist scholarship, only a few Jewish feminist scholars are willing to take their analyses beyond Heschel's statements about *halakhic* disrepair or even uselessness. They are clearer and more vehement about the need to envision other ways of organizing Jewish life. Rabbi Lynn Gottlieb, in *She Who Dwells within: A Feminist Vision of a Renewed Judaism* (1995), adamantly argues that "We cannot be expected to abide by norms we did not help create" (1995, p. 6). Rabbi Gottlieb practises what she envisions as she creates rituals that are meaningful to women by culling from sources from diverse contexts, including classical rabbinic texts, Jewish mystical writings, feminist notions of the Goddess, and Native American spirituality. To Gottlieb, and those who find spiritual sustenance in the same way as she does, *halakhah* can be accepted for the dictates that still have relevance, while those that no longer feel religiously comfortable can be rejected. In order to do this, the price they pay or the freedom they obtain, depending on how one views this, is that this practice removes them from the mainstream of organized Jewish religious life.

Perhaps one of the most important theorists to come out of the Jewish feminist movement is Judith Plaskow, author of *Standing Again at Sinai* (1990), primarily because she thoroughly applies her analysis of Jewish women's oppression to the core areas of Jewish theology, law, spirituality, and communal life. Throughout *Standing Again at Sinai*, Plaskow applies Simone de Beauvoir's (1952) concept of women as "other" in patriarchal society to the experience of women within Judaism. Plaskow believes that Jewish men have been, and continue to be, the "normative" Jews, and as such they have shaped Jewish practices in their own images, with profound consequences for Jewish women. As Plaskow states, "Women's Otherness is not just a matter of social and religious marginality, but of spiritual deprivation" (1990, p. 86).

In terms of *halakhah*, Plaskow believes that remedying specific laws, in keeping with the equal access focus of many Jewish feminists, will not only do little to further the fight against the underlying subordination women face within Judaism, but it could entrench it even further. She maintains that manipulating the system to change certain rules—even excising many of them—will not restore women's voices or women's power of naming. On the contrary, without the awareness of the broader context of women's silence, attempts to address concrete grievances may perpetuate the system of which they are part (Plaskow, 1990, p. 8). Thus, Plaskow's solution, like Gottlieb's, is to seek transformation, not limited to redefining areas within the law, but instead moving beyond it to ask "whether there are reasons why law as law should or should not be a central religious category in a feminist Judaism" (Plaskow, 1990, p. 61). However, while Plaskow's aim is to end Jewish women's subordination as a class, and in so doing find an alternative that is in keeping with feminist ideals of equality, unlike Gottlieb she still limits her analysis both by demarcating aspects of Judaism she will not reject, and by leaving open the question as to whether a transformed *halakhah* may indeed still have the ability to respond to feminist demands.

Other Jewish feminist scholars have approached the *halakhic* impasse from another direction. They believe that the reason the contemporary interpreters of *halakhah* are so hesitant to give in to change in matters such as divorce law is because Jewish men's control over Jewish women is being challenged. This helps to answer the question why Jewish feminists have been successful in arguing, in all areas of Judaism except for Orthodoxy, that women should have the right to become rabbis, but not successful in arguing that divorce law should be changed. Rachel Biale, in *Women and Jewish Law: An Exploration of Women's Issues in Halakhic Sources* (1984), explains this divergence by maintaining that the "public" face of Judaism has been much more amenable to change than the "private" realm of home and family, a contention that is supported by scholarship by Fishman (1990) and Baker (1993). Allowing small numbers of women to be successful in patriarchal institutions does not change the power imbalance in society. As Jewish feminists have learned, it just further obfuscates the impact of patriarchy. However, men's private privilege, ensconced in the family, is more difficult to fight.

It could be argued, then, within this analysis of public and private, that the reason *halakhic* authorities are so resistant to change is not only because of the stasis brought on by historical conditions, but also because the greater the perceived threat of feminism, the more entrenched those with male authority become. This relationship between the public and the private is exacerbated when the threat targets individual men's control of their wives, which is manifested today in the continued victimization of *agunot*. In "The Image and Status of Women in Classical Rabbinic Judaism," Judith Romney Wegner (1991) maintains that within *halakhah*, men's control of their wives stems from their historic right to "exclusive ownership of a wife's sexuality" (Romney Wegner, cited in Baskin, ed., 1991, p. 73). She uses Jewish men's control of Jewish women's social status to explain this contention.

According to Romney Wegner, a Jewish woman went from being a virgin daughter to a wife possessed in marriage by her husband. As we have noted, if he denied her a *get*, she was forbidden to any other man. The consequences of adultery were so severe that they kept most women in this situation confined in dead marriages. In contrast, men had the freedom to move on and marry another, without sanction or stigma placed upon them. Romney Wegner sees this historical control of women's sexuality as "a severe disadvantage that wreaks havoc for Jewish women to this day" (Romney Wegner, cited in Baskin, 1991, p. 72). Using her analysis to interpret today's reality, she also maintains that Judaism's current acceptance of "public" feminist demands and reluctance to deal with "private" challenges is also historically based in the *halakhic* system. Concurrent to women's sexual subordination and disabilities under divorce law were their other rights, amazing for their time, in the public realm of daily life. Women could still hold title to the property they brought into their marriages, and with their husbands' consent, women could also sell their property. Moreover, their husbands had no legal right to dispose of property owned by their wives if it was against the women's wishes (Romney Wegner, cited in Baskin, 1991, p. 72). Thus, it seems that Jewish men have always been more accepting of Jewish women's roles that take them outside of the family than those that keep them within.

LISTENING TO THE VOICES OF *AGUNOT* THEMSELVES

Most Jewish scholars, even many Jewish feminist scholars, regardless of their outstanding scholarly contributions, have thus written about the plight of *agunot* without understanding what individual *agunot* experience as a result of *get* abuse. Nor have they considered themes that might emerge from a study of many *agunot*. By contrast, I chose to use qualitative methodology in the form of interviews as my primary method of inquiry because it best fulfilled the goals I set out for my research. I wanted to understand how *agunot* conceptualize their lives, to understand *get* abuse, to examine how *agunot* pursue their freedom, and to explore potential solutions. Through interviewing *agunot* and former *agunot* living across Canada, I gathered a rich source of information about their experiences. I have used their recounting of *get* abuse as the basis of the description and analysis that follows. (All names and identifying characteristics have been changed.) To further add to my understanding, I also conducted interviews with the rabbis to whom *agunot* turn for help, and leaders of local, national, and international committees and coalitions advocating on behalf of, and trying to alleviate the plight of, *agunot*.

THE WEAPON OF DESPAIR: *AGUNOT'S* EXPERIENCES OF *GET* ABUSE

> Getting a *get* was an extension of our marriage, like the way he treated me in the marriage. And he was controlling in that and he wasn't going to give up control. This was his last stronghold, the *get*. He wasn't prepared to give up so fast." (Dena)

Women who divorce feel a whirlwind of emotions, such as sadness, hurt, anger, fear, and relief. Most palpable, perhaps, is fear: fear of the future, fear of supporting oneself financially, fear of not finding intimacy again. According to Patricia Diedrick, in "Gender Differences in Divorce Adjustment," during the initial post-divorce adjustment period, it is typical that women first grieve over their marriages, and then begin a process of psychological separation from their former spouses. During the second stage of adjustment, women usually gain back stronger feelings of self-esteem as they reconstruct and learn new ways of being in the world. Successful adjustment, in Diedrick's view, is "the development of a separate identity and the ability to function adequately in new roles" (Diedrick, cited in Volgy, 1991, p. 34).

However, for the Jewish woman who becomes an *agunah*, the divorce process is immeasurably compounded. She still experiences the usual range of emotions associated with marital dissolution, but she experiences them as a woman who is still religiously married. She is unable to go through Diedrick's adjustment periods and begin a new life because her husband is controlling her and trapping her in a dead marriage through *get* abuse, as Dena's story shows. While an *agunah* may grieve over her initial physical separation from her husband, she cannot psychologically separate from him as long as they are tied together in this manner. The identity that she constructs as a result of becoming an *agunah* is based on surviving *get* abuse and trying to free herself, and not on a growing sense of self-worth. Nor does her new way of being in the world conjure up for her positive images of future possibilities. Instead, she envisions future emotional distress until she is released. Thus, it can be persuasively argued that even though many *agunot* are divorced through civil law, in many respects their post-separation adjustment process is thwarted. In "Women and Divorce: Correlates of Women's Adjustment During the Separation and Divorce Process," Krisanne Bursik states: "The relationship between former spouses … appears to be a key predictor of divorce adjustment, especially when the former spouses continue to share child-rearing responsibilities. Several studies have found that a relationship with the ex-spouse which is hostile or strained is predictive of various types of maladjustment" (Bursik, cited in Volgy, 1991, p. 140). Unlike other divorcing women, their spouses' hostility directed toward *agunot* denies them their basic freedoms. If *agunot* are "maladjusted," it is because their husbands are controlling their futures and holding them in a form of captivity.

When describing this initial stage of *get* abuse, the women I interviewed spoke mostly of why their marriages ended, when they discovered their husbands had decided to use the *get* as a weapon, whether the *get* was being withheld until certain conditions were met, why it was important for them to receive the *get,* and how they felt about their situations. They did not speak much about how they were coping both emotionally and practically with being separated from their spouses. This was overshadowed by their feelings about being imprisoned within marriages they no longer desired. Furthermore, for most of these women, *agunot* and former *agunot* alike, memories of the initial period of coping with separation have faded as the years have passed. Residual for former *agunot* is the anger, and present for the *agunot* is the anger and despair.

When a married couple separates, and acrimony is a strong element of the divorce proceedings, it is usual for the husband and wife to complain to family, friends, and especially their lawyers, about who did what to whom. While pointing fingers is usually a futile exercise, understanding who initiated the marriage breakup, and why they did, is of utmost consequence for understanding how *get* abuse works, for in most cases it is the women who leave the marriage, often because they have suffered emotional and/or physical abuse. Examples of responses to the question, "Was there emotional and/or physical abuse present during your marriage?" are as follows:

> And when I tried to take the remote control away from him, to turn the TV off, and asked him to leave, he struck me. He just kept telling me that he was going to teach me, he said, that I was married to a real man. And when I put up my hand to block him from hitting me, he broke my hand from one of the blows. (Mira)

> I was very physically abused, and I was afraid for my life. My boys, they were my bodyguards.... The last time I saw Gilad, I was bruised all over my body. [The last time he was in Toronto] he told me that he wished the first week we were married he had killed me and dropped my body in the desert. (Dafna)

> He was very controlling, very emotionally abusive, verbally abusive, all those things. Everything up to actually laying a hand on me ... but I don't doubt that had I stayed, he would have. (Dena)

> He was fanatical when we were married. Part of the mental abuse was conforming to his standards of Orthodoxy. When I opposed him on this, there were physical consequences for me. (Moriah)

At first I was quite surprised repeatedly to hear the women I interviewed relate stories of marriages rife with emotional and physical abuse. Yet, upon closer scrutiny, viewed within the context of *get* abuse, it does not seem at all odd that abused wives would become *agunot*. While it is definitely the case that women who are not abused in any way still become *agunot*, and some abused women do receive their *gittin* without problems, it does seem that the number of *agunot* who were abused in their marriages is shocking. This is not only evidenced by my interviews, but is also reported by journalists, activists, and scholars who have mentioned individual cases of abused *agunot*.

Depending on their theoretical approach, feminist activists and scholars have differing theories about male violence against women and children, especially with regard to explaining how male violence interlinks with other systems of domination. However, for decades, most have agreed that the contemporary prevalence of male violence is rooted in how our patriarchal society is organized. That is, men's power, privilege, and control are enshrined in the institutions that govern our daily lives, and this is intrinsic to how women are socialized. In this way, men's perpetration of violence is normalized and socially regulated, and thus our society is riddled with assault, incest, and rape. As Michael Kaufman states in "The Construction of Masculinity and the Triad of Men's Violence," "men's violence against women is probably the clearest, most straightforward expression of relative male and female power" (1987, p. 15), hence the feminist belief that rapists commit rape not just for sexual gratification, but for the feelings of power and control that this act gives them. Those who physically assault their wives or partners are attempting to gain the same power and control through their acts of violence.

Jewish men who abuse their wives have learned well the lessons of our society, whose words condemn, but actions condone, male violence. For those who need to hold on to or reclaim the power that they lose when their marriage dissolves, the Jewish religion gives them a seemingly foolproof modus operandi, the perpetration of *get* abuse. Related to my supposition that a high percentage of battered Jewish wives become *agunot* is the conjecture that Jewish men who abuse their wives are more likely to use the *get* weapon because they have already used methods of violence to control their wives during their marriages. Once their marriage has dissolved, and a husband no longer has physical access to his wife, *get* abuse provides him with the opportunity and the means to continue his abuse. The need for control over one's wife after marital breakdown is also relevant to a man who did not abuse his wife during the marriage, but now wants to punish her. By vindictively withholding a *get*, thereby using it as a weapon, this man can use *get* abuse to make his wife suffer. The *get* weapon is also clearly appealing to some divorcing Jewish men not only because they can exert control over their wives, but also because they know the potential is present for them to be rewarded for their actions for *get* abuse can also mean extortion. If you can make your wife suffer and make money in the process, then why not? Thus, when *get* abuse is conceptualized as a form of violence against Jewish wives who become *agunot*, traditional conceptions of *get* denial can be broadened to include not only the use of male power sanctioned by Jewish law, but also the "coercive control tactics," which can be part of *get* abuse: using emotional abuse, using coercion and threats, using intimidation, using the children, and using economic abuse (Yllo, cited in Gelles & Loseke, 1993, pp. 54–55, 57).

Feminist research on male violence against women is also concerned with conceptualizing what happens when women either call the police for help, or eventually leave, or try to leave, their abusive partners. While the police's treatment of battered women is sometimes less than ideal when they are called to the scene of a "domestic dispute," we would hope that there would be harsh consequences for the abuser. What are the consequences for Jewish men who abuse their wives by withholding the *get*? No equivalent police force or judicial system exists to apprehend and punish these men for their abuse and make them stop. Rabbis who are asked for help can use moral suasion and employ certain sanctions, yet, nevertheless, the recalcitrant *get* abuser often ends up holding the key to his wife's jail cell instead. Often the key is dangled in front of her for years. How many Jewish women, observant to Jewish law, stay in abusive situations for years because they are threatened with *get* denial if they do not stay in the marriage and fulfill certain demands? Thus, for battered Jewish women, attempting to escape an abusive situation can be complicated in this manner.

It is important to state here that there is no religious reason whatsoever for withholding a *get*. Instead, it is used as a weapon, and can be used by any Jewish man who wants to hold his wife hostage. While it would seem that religiously observant men well versed in *halakhah* would be much more likely to use the *get* weapon, this is not necessarily the case. Some non-observant men have prior knowledge regarding the *get*, while others are told about *get* law after their marriage has broken up by family, friends, rabbis, or lawyers. It is an ironic feature of *get* abuse that some men use a tradition with which they are only nominally connected, or which they even disavow, to punish their wives. As well, some men learn about *get* law because of increasing awareness about the problem within the Jewish community due to the activities of Jewish women's activist groups. Some learn about the *get*'s power after they are made aware of just how badly their wives want it, as in Dena's case. Thus, the only prerequisite that exists is the wish to hurt their wives, via *halakhah*.

Although any Jewish man can use the *get* as a weapon, *get* abuse works as a control mechanism or bargaining chip only when obtaining a *get* holds great importance for his wife. *Agunot*, then, are a group of women who have defined the *get* as so intrinsic to their notion of being properly and fully divorced that they are willing to view themselves as still married regardless of whether or not they have obtained divorces under civil law. As confirmed in my interviews, it is mostly Orthodox and ultra-Orthodox women who consider themselves to be *agunot*. Orthodox and ultra-Orthodox women, by definition, abide by *halakhah*. However, the range of observance of women who consider themselves to be *agunot* is broader than one might initially expect, from Cheryl who is ultra-Orthodox, to Leah who is Reform. What is then apparent, and very interesting about *get* abuse, is that it can affect any Jewish woman who places practical or symbolic importance on obtaining a *get*, yet Orthodox and especially ultra-Orthodox women without *gittin* face an excruciating choice. If they decide to live in accordance with *halakhah* and ultra-Orthodox communal norms, they will sacrifice their personal freedom because their lives will be circumscribed by devastating prohibitions; that is, they can never marry again or have any future children. If they decide to embrace a future where they will be free to fulfill their own needs, to be in loving relationships with men, and to have children, then they will sacrifice their previous identities, religious observance, communal acceptance, and perhaps their families.

By contrast, even though non-observant women might want *gittin* to end their marriages, they do not face the same life choices. However, some non-observant women may become *agunot* because they are deciding to abide by *halakhah* with regard to divorce because they will not feel divorced without the *get*. Other non-observant women might choose to ignore the *get* requirement completely and go on with their lives without any desire for the *get*. Reform Judaism, for instance, does not require a *get* for remarriage. None of the non-observant women who wanted *gittin* whom I interviewed chose to ignore the *get* completely. Rather, most desperately wanted *gittin* in order to feel fully divorced and were willing to wait until they were *halakhically* released to remarry or have children. Only Leah remarried without a *get*. Over a long period of time, however, the other non-observant women made compromises they felt uneasy about, such as having relationships with new partners and even living with them in common-law situations. For these non-observant women, having *gittin* was important *halakhically*, spiritually, morally, and emotionally.

How does a Jewish woman first find out that she has become an *agunah*? What possible justifications for *get* denial would her husband give her? The following excerpts will reveal the perceptions my interviewees had as to why their husbands chose to withhold the *get*.

It was because he didn't want a divorce. He really believed, he honestly believed that I'd come to my senses and take him back.... I just thought it was one more way that he had to try to assert power, that he would try to use everything he could to get to me. (Mira)

I think it was just a way for him to hurt me, to punish me for leaving. He knew what it meant to me, and that was probably my biggest mistake, that I made it very clear how much I wanted it. (Dena)

It's a game because I'm the one who made the decision to separate and divorce.... I wanted a separation and he was not agreeable to it, and I had to force it by a court order that he leave the house.... This is a control factor.... It's part of everything else he has done, with child support, child custody, it's just an extension of that. (Debbie)

I got the child because the court realized what was the matter with [my husband]. So the only way he could get at me was not giving me the Jewish divorce.... He just took it as revenge. (Leah)

When my son talked with him he said, "Why don't you give her the *get*?" And he said, "I have to punish her." It's a punishment. I can't put it in another word.... This is the only way he can control me. He can't come into this house and tell me what to do, and he can't control his children's lives, so the only power he has over me is the *get*. (Dafna)

The voices of these *agunot* and former *agunot* clearly illustrate the theoretical analysis of why men choose to withhold the *get* by showing how these women's husbands rationalized *get* abuse. These women felt that their husbands were denying them a *get* because the husbands wanted to have power over them, control them, or punish them, often for making the decision to leave the marriage.

While power, control, and punishment are ambiguous terms, when tied to actions they become laden with meaning. This is powerfully exemplified in the husbands' attempts to blackmail or extort, offering a *get* in exchange for money, property, or custody rights. Because the consequences of being an *agunah* are severe, a husband has the perfect victim upon whom to make his demands, one who is vulnerable and desperate. The following excerpts from the comments of the *agunot* and former *agunot* show how this works in reality:

If I wanted the *get*, he told me I would have to give him the house. (Cheryl)

He wanted to take the existing court order and rewrite it so the kids would be with him more.... I won't use them [the children] as bargaining chips.... He won't give it unless it makes a difference in his life. (Moriah)

In my case, I don't have anything to bargain with Gilad, but he went to see my sister in Israel, and he told her that he wants my family to pay him for the 15 years he spent with me. He wants part of the will when my father passes away. (Dafna)

In 1991, he was demanding all the money from the other house and half from this. He started giving me a list of all of the furniture that he wants, and I said, "Well, what about a *get*?" He said, "Well, your parents are going to have to pay $50,000 for that." (Mira)

Of the four cases cited above, it is interesting to note that these women were physically abused by their husbands during their marriages. Are men who physically abuse their wives more likely to deny a *get* to blackmail and extort them? Perhaps this is so. What is certain are the frustration and outrage felt by *agunot* who must consider trading their money, their family's money, their possessions, or even their children in return for their freedom.

Cheryl was able, after years had passed, to receive her *get* without giving up her house. Moriah, whose husband attempted to use their children as pawns in his *get* battle, refused his demands, which were absolutely unacceptable to her. She is still an *agunah*. Even if Dafna wanted to give her husband money for the *get*, she does not have anything to offer him. She is still an *agunah*. Mira, who had the money needed to purchase her freedom, did effect her own ransom.

GET ABUSE: STRATEGIES FOR COPING AND GAINING FREEDOM

An *agunah* utilizes one or more of the following strategies in attempting to secure her *get*: attempting to use civil law in order to procure a religious divorce; asking rabbis or community organizations for assistance; allowing another person or group to use physical violence against her husband to coerce him to give the *get*; psychologically manipulating her husband, especially by shaming him into giving the *get*; giving in to her husband's extortionate demands; and, within limits, even accepting her situation. An *agunah* may choose one strategy over another depending on many variables. If her experience is the same as many *agunot*, she has already removed herself from an abusive situation when leaving her husband. Could this make her more inclined to choose one strategy over another? This is a question to consider as the following stories of survival are recounted.

CIVIL LAW

If an *agunah* retains a competent lawyer, well versed in religious and civil divorce law, and cognizant of any *get* legislation in her legal jurisdiction, then she may be more likely to pursue the *get* indirectly by going through the civil legal system. For example, in Canada, subsections of the Canadian Divorce Act and the Ontario Family Law Act state that a spouse must remove any barriers to his or her ex-spouse's subsequent religious remarriage, but loopholes in these laws have made them less effective than has been hoped. While delving into civil law is not the intention of this examination, it is both interesting and important to consider that civil law can potentially force a religious divorce.

RABBI OR COMMUNAL ASSOCIATION ASSISTANCE

An *agunah*'s response to her situation may be influenced by her physical location; if she lives in a city with a large Jewish community, she may have access to advocates such as sympathetic rabbis or members of Jewish women's organizations advocating on behalf of *agunot*. A very small numbers of rabbis, for example, are maintaining that the solution to the *agunah* problem is to retroactively annul marriages in the case of a recalcitrant spouse, but the vast majority do not see this as either plausible or desirable because the *halakhah* is upheld as unchangeable.

Turning to rabbis for help is a strategy almost all *agunot* use, at least at some point. While a rabbi has no authority to give the *get*, he can give an *agunah* support and try to intercede in her situation in indirect ways, such as talking privately with her husband and his family. As well, a rabbi can make sure that her husband is called to appear before a *bet din* or Jewish court. When the rabbis sitting on the *bet din* summon the husband, they can try to persuade him to give his wife the *get*. Although many women I interviewed felt that the rabbis they approached for assistance were sympathetic and helpful, most women reported that they were very frustrated and angered because rabbis kept telling them that their hands were tied because they had to work within the framework of *halakhah*.

VIOLENCE

Two popular Jewish authors have fictionalized the plight of *agunot* in mystery novels. In *Till Death Do Us Part* (1992) Rochelle Majer Krich tells the story of Dena, a young Orthodox woman, who has left her husband, Jake, because of his infidelity. She wants to be free of him *halakhically* so she can date and perhaps even marry Michael, the man with whom she has fallen in love. Jake knows how desperately Dena wants her *get*, so he decides to withhold it in order to alternately hold on to her, punish her, control her, and seek financial gain from her family. The novel is a frustrating account of Dena trying to free herself by using strategies such as seeking rabbinical help, reasoning with Jake, and finally planning to give in to his extortionate demands. Before this can happen, Jake is shot to death by another *agunah*, whose husband has gone insane and is therefore incapable of granting a *get*. After waiting years for her husband to have a lucid moment, this *agunah* has presumably gone insane herself.

Faye Kellerman has written a series of 13 murder mystery novels. In *Sanctuary* (1994), Honey has taken her children away from their ultra-Orthodox community in New York so she can visit her old friend in California, Rina, Kellerman's female protagonist. Soon after Honey arrives, she receives news that her husband has died. As the novel progresses, the reader learns that Honey's husband has been acting abnormally for a long time. She wanted to divorce him, but he had no intention of giving her a *get*. She left New York because she was aware that members of her community would try to use coercive measures to convince her husband to give her the *get*. He died, apparently accidentally, when the men who accosted him dunked his head repeatedly under water in a bathtub.

It is very interesting that the only "solution" these authors find to end the suffering of *agunot* is killing these women's husbands. Majer Krich's depiction of what life is like for an *agunah* is accurate until Jake is killed. Kellerman's premise—that a man who denies a *get* is accidentally drowned—is extreme without being totally unrealistic. Moreover, without excusing the violence in the least, extreme measures are more likely to be used in extreme circumstances.

Without any initial questioning or prompting on my part, three of the women I interviewed mentioned using violence or potentially using violence to obtain their *gittin*. The *agunot* who mentioned violence to me spoke about having their husbands held against their will. Janice is considering this action, Dena threatened it, and Rachel used it.

Janice no longer believes that she has any way to convince her adamantly recalcitrant husband to give her a *get*. Her feelings of frustration and hopelessness were evident when she said in an early part of the interview: "What do you do if the person just says no? What do you do? You use force." Later on in the interview, she again stated her intention to have her husband coerced if he does not change his mind soon: "And if I have to take matters into my own hands I will, ultimately, down the road. There are ways of getting it done, not pleasant ways. We try pleasant, and if somebody doesn't listen to the niceness then you got to do what you got to do, but you can't stay like this." If Janice does choose to have someone use violence against her husband, she knows a rabbi who will give her the number of someone to call to carry this out. She has heard that her husband would likely be confined in a room and not be given any food or water or be allowed to relieve himself until he agreed to give her the *get*.

Dena believes she finally received her *get* in part because, through other people, she let it be known to her husband that men who refuse their wives *gittin* are sometimes accosted and beaten. Dena had heard stories of this happening in other situations similar to hers: "[They] showed up at his bed in the middle of the night. They said, 'We're here to escort you to the *bet din*. Are you going to come willingly?' They basically threatened him. And in another case, they took the guy and they tied him to a tree and they held baseball bats. And they said, 'Now, either you walk with us and willingly go to the *bet din* or we'll break your kneecaps and you'll crawl to the *bet din*.'" Dena had the anger necessary to consider using violence. She said, "I'm not a violent person, but I wanted him beaten up. I wouldn't have any qualms about getting it done. If you think about it, what else am I going to do? And he was afraid." She also had people around her who were willing to do this for her. They told her, "We'll go and just teach him a lesson or two. We'll show him why it would be best to go." Dena never had to carry through with her threat, but perhaps if her situation had deteriorated and time passed with no other solution in sight, she would have followed through with it, especially since she is young and wants to remarry and have children.

Rachel admitted that her husband was coerced into giving her a *get*. As soon as her husband arrived from his home in another country to visit their children, a rabbi and several other observant men approached him. Then, as Rachel recounts it, "His arm was twisted, literally." When I clarified that she meant that actual force had been used, she replied, "Oh, definite coercion. And it was physical. And the *bet din* was contacted by [the rabbi involved] and it was told to them that if they don't do it immediately, then it won't happen." When pressed for further details, Rachel responded that "it was really, really mysterious and very like, you know, covert." Rachel believes that the use of physical force against recalcitrant husbands should not be openly spoken about within the Jewish community. Rather, she says, "Through word of mouth you take somebody quietly.... You don't start advertising because you risk them stopping their actions, and we need those types of actions."

Many interesting thoughts arise from these depictions of *agunot* considering, threatening, and using violence to obtain their *gittin* from their husbands. Although it is unclear how many *agunot* actually obtain their *gittin* through the use of force, precisely because of the covert nature of these events, perhaps this practice is more widespread than is commonly believed. It was surprising to find this information in three interviews. Regardless of its prevalence, though, the use or the threat of violence highlights the degree of desperation, anger, and fear that some *agunot* must feel to be able to turn their thoughts in this direction. Conversely, these depictions reveal the desperate nature of this problem—that physical violence is seriously considered to be a viable, albeit extreme, option by some.

The people who carry out these actions, as well as the *agunot* involved, are all culpable of knowing about or participating in illegal actions. This may not concern *agunot* because at this stage, the results are all-important. Of the *agunot* I interviewed, both Dena and Rachel obtained *gittin* faster than anyone else. They had been very fearful of becoming like other *agunot* and potentially having to wait for years for their freedom. An *agunah* might be more or less willing to view physical force as an option, depending on how long she has been an *agunah* and how observant she is. If she has been languishing in a state of marital limbo for a long time, a period that my interviewees subjectively defined as ranging from a couple of months to several years, and she has made the choice to continue to abide by Jewish law, meaning that she still considers herself married, then perhaps she would be more likely to perceive that the only way out of her seemingly hopeless situation would be to ask others to use physical coercion to force her husband to give her the *get*.

Halakhic precedent for using force to compel a *get* does exist. However, this should not be the solution chosen today as an *agunah*'s best chance for obtaining freedom, nor is it regarded as such by most rabbis. However, according to my interviewees, some of the rabbis they approached for help hid their inaction behind the *halakhic* fact that a *get* is not valid if it has been coerced. The rabbis who sanction the use of force coerce recalcitrant husbands to give the *get* "willingly." When I asked Rachel if she was worried that her *get* may be invalid because coercion was used to obtain it, she replied, "Well, he did say he was willing."

PSYCHOLOGICAL MANIPULATION: SHAMING

Dafna, Helen, and Dena decided to publicly shame their husbands into giving them *gittin*.

Dafna first went the traditional route of having a *bet din* ask Gilad three times to appear before them, to no avail. At that point, Dafna felt justified in turning to other measures. If Gilad would not listen to the rabbis, then maybe he would be embarrassed if his colleagues knew he was denying his wife a *get* and would then free her. To that end, with help from some local members of the Canadian Coalition of Jewish Women for the *Get* (CCJWG), Dafna held a demonstration outside Gilad's place of employment. The assembled women marched with signs and distributed flyers to shame Gilad and educate his co-workers. However, in Dafna's opinion, this only made Gilad angrier and more recalcitrant. As one of the organizers of the demonstration recounted to me in my interview with her: "It made us feel good to know that we could do something and embarrass him, but he told her flat out, 'You can have a hundred demonstrations and give out thousands of flyers. I'll never give you the *get*.' I think it just makes them angrier … so it didn't work." The *Canadian Jewish News* published an account of the demonstration and printed a copy of the flyer that had been distributed, so the educational value of this demonstration should not be overlooked. For Dafna, however, her failure to secure her freedom in this way just left her more demoralized. She concluded her description of the demonstration by saying: "Even if I have hundreds of support people around me, as long as the rabbis think I have to pay the price, nothing will change."

Helen's attempt to publicly embarrass her husband was more successful. She embarked on a high-profile campaign within the Jewish community in which she lives. She remained very active in the synagogue to which they had both belonged, and helped lobby synagogue board members to pass a bylaw stating that any member of the synagogue who was denying their spouse a *get* would lose their membership privileges. Because her husband was well known in the Jewish community, Helen surmised that publicly shaming him would help to extinguish his power over her life. She believed that because she had kept quiet and avoided scandal during their married life, he would probably continue to take it for granted that she would do the same after she left him. By doing the opposite and making people he knew aware of his behaviour, she took away his "trump card." Helen maintains that her husband finally gave her the *get* primarily because of the continual publicity and secondarily because of repeated pressure from the rabbi involved. Helen's case is a good example of how men like her ex-husband can be made to feel uncomfortable enough that they feel it is in their own best interest to give in and give the *get*. After receiving her *get*, Helen decided to publicize what she went through to educate others. Courageously, she agreed to talk about her situation in an article published in a large daily newspaper, and she was one of three women whose stories were shared in the film, *Untying the Bonds: Jewish Divorce*, produced by the CCJWG.

Dena devised her strategy of publicly shaming her husband after receiving little help from the rabbis from whom she sought counsel and assistance. She decided: "Well, I'll just do it myself. I'll embarrass him … he's going to feel the heat. And I started telling people that he wasn't going to give me the *get*. I knew who he respected in the community, so I decided to target these people and tell them that he hasn't given me the *get* … because maybe if it's coming from them or they lose respect for him…. Once I started telling people, and people at work knew, I think he realized that he had a problem." Although Dena's attempts to embarrass her husband at the Jewish store where he worked did not immediately cause him to change his mind, she feels it most likely contributed to his eventual capitulation several months later.

The use of this strategy is effective under certain circumstances. If the man has a high-profile job that places him in a vulnerable position if his image is tarnished, then an *agunah* might have a better chance of turning her situation around. This was the case with Helen's husband. What also helped in her case was the extent to which she publicized her situation. This might not be a viable option for many *agunot* who, like many Jewish women who are abused by their husbands, may not wish to divulge their circumstances to anyone other than a rabbi, family member, or close friend. The impact of this strategy, of shaming, also depends on the individual man being targeted. Some men, for various reasons, might be more or less resistant to being embarrassed. In Dafna's case, this strategy was not useful; in fact, it actually made matters worse. Gilad was operating from a position where he felt he had nothing to lose, and much to gain, by remaining recalcitrant. With Dena's husband, though, this strategy was more effective. Making her husband's behaviour known to those around him probably made him feel pressured and uneasy about future consequences at work if he continued to withhold the *get*.

Thus, an *agunah* has to decide to pursue this strategy based upon her own situation; that is, she needs to determine her own comfort level in publicizing the private details of her life. She also has to decide whether shaming her husband is likely to have a positive or a negative effect on her situation. It is also important to note that the *agunot* who attempted to use public shaming chose this method because other strategies they had tried had been ineffectual. While the strategy of public shaming is not nearly as radical a choice as resorting to violence to obtain the *get*, it is also a result of desperate circumstances.

GIVING IN TO DEMANDS

Moriah's husband wanted the children, and Cheryl's husband wanted the house. Janice has no doubt that her husband will eventually name his price; a rabbi has suggested to her that she use her house to buy her freedom. Someone also suggested to Dafna that she offer her husband money. But Moriah will not give up her children, and Cheryl and Janice need their homes to help ensure their financial security. Dafna does not have any money to offer.

Mira, on the other hand, who had the means to do so, decided to use money to her own advantage when her husband told her that her parents would have to pay him $50,000 for the *get*. While she was married, she and her husband owned both the home in which they lived and a townhouse. The townhouse was mortgage-free since it had been amalgamated onto the house mortgage. After they separated, Mira's husband did not want to live in the townhouse, so they sold it and put the money in trust, pending a divorce settlement. Later in the year, she came across an investment deal that appeared to be fraudulent, and she devised a plan to fool her husband, who was always looking for a deal so he could become rich. If she could get him to invest in this deal, she figured, then he would need the capital being held in trust in a hurry, and would sign the divorce settlement and give her a *get*. Even better, he would then lose his investment.

Mira enlisted the help of the man pushing this investment scheme. He befriended her husband and convinced him that if he invested $50,000, the same amount he tried to extort from Mira, then he could make $1 million in a year. Her husband quickly signed the settlement papers and gave Mira her *get*, whereupon the money was freed up. As planned, he invested and then lost this money. Due to her imaginative scheme, Mira obtained revenge and her civil and religious divorces. However, although her husband invested the $50,000 that was rightfully his from the sale of the townhouse, Mira did pay for her *get*: "It cost me, it actually cost me about $15,000 to set this up because this guy had to have seed money to show that he already had investors with hundreds of thousands of dollars.… Of course, I was supposed to get it back after they got his money, but I knew I'd never see it again because this was a con artist I was dealing with … but I figured $15,000 and all the rest of my legal costs was cheaper than it would have been."

The money was worth it for Mira, and Mira had the money available to indirectly pay for her *get*. Having access to money gives some *agunot* the means to buy their freedom if that is the option they choose. Her husband ultimately did not profit; however, it is morally repugnant that those men who are successful in reaping financial gain are rewarded for giving something they are rightfully obligated to give. For *agunot* who can afford it, enticing their husbands with money or property may be the only viable strategy available. How many unrecorded cases are there where the exchange of children, money, or property is settled quietly by the parties involved? If an *agunah* has nothing to bargain with, does this extend her time as an *agunah* or postpone her freedom indefinitely?

ACCEPTING THE SITUATION

Even though women who are *agunot* are living in limbo, this does not mean that they have not devised strategies to deal with their situations. Indeed, they have made personal choices regarding how to proceed with their lives. They have all determined for themselves how to deal with daily living, including whether or not to adhere to the strict dictates of the law. One of the most important examples of this is their choice about monogamy. Debbie, Dafna, and Leah have decided to enter into relationships with men, even though they are still married under Jewish law. They still want their *gittin*, but a religious divorce has become less relevant, especially for Dafna and Leah, who have become tired of waiting.

Debbie has become involved with a man who is a Reform Jew. She cannot foresee marriage in the future, however, even though she could marry him in a Reform ceremony because she still sees herself as legally, morally, and psychologically tied to her husband: "I mean, to me it's still, it breaks the rules of monogamy to have two husbands at one time. I have trouble handling that morally.... We're still married under Jewish law. There is still a tie. It's like the umbilical cord has been stretched as far as it can go, but still hasn't been cut. But no, it's not over. The whole society can view it as over. What do you need it for? It doesn't matter. It's a psychological thing." Although Debbie feels strongly about not marrying without the *get*, she does not want to be lonely. In the future, she can see herself living with the man she loves. Her decision is made easier because she has already had children, and she is past child-bearing years.

The same is true for Dafna and Leah. Dafna's situation is similar to Debbie's in that she is also in a relationship. She despairs that her husband will ever, in his lifetime, give her a *get*, and she does not want to put her personal happiness in a state of limbo as well. Nevertheless, she has ambivalent feelings regarding having another relationship without the marital and psychological freedom a *get* bestows: "… I want to move on with my life. I have a boyfriend. I don't want to get married, but I don't want anybody to say she's a married woman, and she's going out with another guy. Even for my children, I don't think it's right." Eventually, because she no longer considers herself to be observant, and because she has so little hope of ever receiving her *get*, she may reconsider not wanting to remarry.

When Leah's husband refused to give her a *get*, she was very upset, but not surprised. She had married him fully cognizant of the fact that he had not given his first wife a *get*. When it was her turn to end a marriage with this man, she was treated with consistent malice. They had initially married in a Reform ceremony, partly to circumvent the *get* issue, since Reform Judaism does not require a *get* to remarry, and because neither partner was observant. Even so, Leah felt it was very important to obtain her *get* to end her marriage, both to break the psychological bond and because she was concerned about any future ramifications that might arise from not having a *get*. Leah had married a man who had left his first wife, an observant woman, an *agunah*, but now she was concerned about her own future prospects for remarriage, wondering if eligible men would still consider her married.

When Leah determined that she had no chance of convincing her husband to give her the *get* because, as she said, "He wouldn't give it to me if I would stand on my head," she then began a new relationship. Yet, when they decided to get married and her husband-to-be wanted to be married in an Orthodox ceremony, she was in turmoil until she convinced him to marry in a Reform synagogue. Although he was not too happy with this turn of events, his strategy was to temporarily compromise his level of observance in order to marry. Leah's discomfort with remarrying without having a *get* was initially tempered by her wish to enter into this new relationship, and to feel justified in doing so: "If you don't get what you want, you find loopholes and alternatives, and an alternative is a Reform rabbi." She is happily married now, but uneasy feelings about not having a *get* still persist. On a deep emotional level, she still does not feel free from her first husband. As well, she often feels conflicted about turning to Reform Judaism in order to have relationships with men. Thus, although Leah's story shows one easy way around becoming an *agunah*, using Reform Judaism to accommodate her wish to marry, her decisions are not without serious reservations.

As has been discussed, this strategy is not a feasible one for those women who want to live observant lives. If an *agunah* is young and wants to have children, then the consequences for her are extremely severe and she may be more willing to become less observant. Is it more difficult in general for an ultra-Orthodox woman to fight the system? For observant women to even have to consider bargaining their degree of observance in order to have future relationships with men severely penalizes them, but, given the attendant constraints and as time passes, this strategy becomes more of an option for some women.

CONCLUSION: *GET* ABUSE REMAINS ENTRENCHED

Now, at the beginning of the 21st century, regardless of the past massive changes in Jewish observance and identity, and regardless of the Jewish women's movement, the women who endure and survive *get* abuse find themselves grappling with conditions that underline contemporary Jewish society's supremely unequal relations between women and men. Today, the dichotomous configurations of powerless and powerful, passive and active, while not completely absolute, do apply to many of the women and men who are engaged in *get* combat. The rules are such that the guise of neutrality in law, as critiqued by feminist legal theorists with regard to the secular legal system, is not even apparent in *get* law. Men have the power, and women must rely on the men's goodwill to be treated justly and respectfully when a marriage dissolves. Women's rights in relation to *halakhah* and Jewish divorce are still in their infancy.

Chapter 11

Violence against Women: Nigerian-Canadian Women's Experiences

Ngozi L. Nwosu

BACKGROUND TO THE STUDY

A woman unlocks her apartment door in downtown Toronto. She enters and sighs at the mess she sees everywhere. Dishes piled high in the sink from breakfast; her children's toys strewn all over the living room. In the middle of all this mess sits her husband, watching television. The woman sighs and calls her children to pick up their toys. Simple questions addressed to her husband—"How was your day? How did the job search go?"—unleash a torrent of verbal abuse. Mrs. Ogbona absorbs this abuse silently, knowing from experience that any remark would just enrage her husband further (Interviewee, 2005, Toronto). This woman's situation is hardly unique; more and more Nigerian-Canadian women are being abused by their partners. What was once a rarity is becoming all too common in the Nigerian community in Toronto.

I have always sought to understand why the issue of domestic violence has been (and still is) a major focus of research and policy over the years. In my quest, I have found that one reason is that domestic violence impacts negatively on the social and health status of individuals, women in particular. Domestic violence also threatens the security and fundamental human rights and liberty of women (United Nations, 1989), and this has implications for the well-being of members of the society as a whole. In Canada, a survey report on domestic abuse of women indicates that 29 percent of married women have been abused by their partners at least once (Statistics Canada, 2001).

"Domestic violence," a term that will be used interchangeably with the term "domestic abuse" in this chapter, refers to the pattern of controlling, subjugating, and dominating a woman against her will (Nwosu, 2005, p. 99). A woman may experience such violence at the hands of her husband, common-law partner, or other family members, especially in extended families. Domestic violence can take many forms: physical, psychological, emotional, financial, or spiritual.

To a large extent, the reasons why men abuse women are associated with social, cultural, and material factors, such as the low social status of women, early marriage, alcoholism, education, gender-role socialization, and income disparity (Agnew, 1996, 1998; Akpinar, 2003; Margulies, 1995; Isiugo-Abanihe & Onyediran, 2003; Nwokocha, 2004; Aderinto, 2003). Dobash and Dobash (1983) also point out that patriarchy and the high value placed on marriage are the major causes of (domestic) violence against women universally. Violence against women is generally committed by men who believe that patriarchy guarantees them the right to abuse women. As well, marriage unwittingly gives men unrestricted control over their wives, who may strive to retain their marital status even when they are abused (Dobash & Dobash, 1983, pp. 10–11).

Domestic violence cuts across cultures and socio-economic classes, but may be more common and severe in certain communities, ethnic groups, or classes. Studies in Canada indicate, for instance, that Black[1] immigrant women's experiences of domestic violence are far more complex than those of White Canadian women (Agnew, 1996; Smith, 1990; McDonald, 1999). The reason is that migration and immigration policies can create vulnerability, economic dependence, and isolation for Black women through non-recognition of their qualifications and experiences from their home countries (Idemudia, 1999; Agnew, 1996). Sheppard (2002, pp. 1–9) emphasizes that the nature and process of immigration policies add another layer of negative implication for abused Black immigrant women in Canada. Immigration policies seem gender-neutral at face value because both people are equally included, but the process—which guarantees recognition mainly to the principal applicant, often a man, while dependants are not recognized—clearly accentuates Black immigrant women's vulnerability to domestic violence. This is because many Black women migrated to Canada as members of the family class, their sponsorship borne by their husbands. Men have been known to use the threat of deportation or withdrawal of sponsorship to impose their authority upon women and to stop an abused wife from leaving an abusive relationship.

Roxanna Ng argues that Canadian immigration policies not only make Black immigrant women vulnerable to abuse, but systematically reinforce sexual inequality within the family by rendering one spouse, usually the wife, legally dependent on the other, the head of the family (cited in Sheppard, 2002, p. 9). In line with immigration regulations, once sponsoring partners withdraw their initial sponsorship consent, the only available option under which their partners could be considered for the grant of permanent residency is the option of applying for humanitarian and compassionate[2] consideration. However, certain stringent conditions are attached to permanent residency through such grounds. These conditions include stable employment, being well established in Canada, substantial financial means, and proper integration into the community through community involvement, volunteer work, or other activities.

Satisfying these conditions is a major problem for immigrant women who are in abusive relationships, given that often abusive men tend to limit their wives' social lives and impose strict financial restraints. The woman is thus almost entirely financially dependent on her husband. The implication is that such women are likely to submit to domestic victimization in order to not jeopardize regularization of their immigrant status. Sheppard (2002) advocates the state's recognition of the realities of domestic violence among immigrant and refugee women as a way of guaranteeing their rights and freedom from oppression and abuse. Bograd (1999) summarizes it this way:

> Domestic violence is not a monolithic phenomenon; intersectionalities color the meaning and nature of domestic violence within [Black] immigrant women of color. How it is experienced by self and responded to by others, how personal and social consequences are represented, and how and whether escape can be obtained. They exist in social contexts created by intersections of systems of power such as race, class, sexual orientation and oppression—prejudice, class stratification, gender inequality, [culture] and heterosexist bias. (p. 276)

Given these specific circumstances, it becomes necessary that women's voices and experiences be heard across different cultures in order to shape effective policy.

It is interesting to note that while great strides have been made in acknowledging and addressing the issue of domestic violence in some ethnic communities and helping women escape it, there is no research examining the dynamics of the issue among Nigerian women based in Canada. Many female Nigerian community workers in Toronto confirmed that male violence against women is a major concern within Nigerian families. This study was motivated by the desire to understand domestic violence in the Nigerian-Canadian context, from the women's perceptions and experiences; thus is possible the development of appropriate socio-cultural intervention programs to assist women to cope with abusive relationships. It was also my hope to use the findings of this study to urge social policymakers to work toward achieving a culturally inclusive society.

As traditions and cultures vary significantly and are known to have an effect on how women cope with domestic violence, there is a need to review the position of Nigerian women in their everyday experiences within Nigerian culture. Gender roles, patriarchal values, and beliefs related to marriage and family within the Nigerian society are highly embedded in their culture, which needs to be considered to see if there is a connection between the abuse of women and the women's responses. The contemporary Nigerian (Nigerian-Canadian) woman is abused as a result of many factors, yet she expresses or exhibits an inability and/or unwillingness to seek social and legal services when at risk. In conducting this study, I was hoping to find some answers to this phenomenon.

NIGERIAN CULTURE AND WOMEN'S EXPERIENCES

As Africa's most populous country, Nigeria has about 374 identifiable ethnic groups (Otite) with three of these predominant: Hausa, Yoruba, and Igbo. The Hausa are found mainly in the northern part of the country and are mostly Muslims, the Yoruba primarily occupy the southern part, and the Igbo are found in the eastern part of the country. A large percentage of Yorubas and Igbos are Christians, but the two groups differ culturally in terms of lineage and dialectic structures. There is no one Nigerian culture per se because of the multiethnic and multihistorical aspects of the country.

Although socio-cultural diversity among ethnic communities is evident in Nigeria, patriarchal values and heterosexual marriage values and ideas are common features that influence Nigerian women's experiences with domestic violence. The only aspect of culture that is common to all of the ethnic groups in Nigeria, with very few exceptions, is patriarchy, which impacts every aspect of society such as marriage, family, and socialization, among others.

Nigeria is a male-dominated society, with rigid gender norms and roles for men and women. Among all of the ethnic groups, women are regarded as men's "property," their duties being procreation and domestic work. Everything else in society is defined in relation to male interests, needs, and concerns, so women are assigned an inferior position in the family and in society as a whole. Many women have no control over their income, nor do they have legal rights over their children. In areas governed by Islamic law, women can inherit only half of what men do. In other parts of the country, women are not entitled to inherit immovable property or land even when they contribute to its acquisition. Men dominate and control all aspects of the society. In the northern (Hausa) part of Nigeria where, for instance, women are traditionally not seen, a man has the right to control and beat his wife at the slightest provocation (Imam, 1993, pp. 123–144). According to the Canadian Immigration and Refugee Board, Section 55 of the Nigerian Penal Code empowers a man to beat his Northern wife (Country of Origin Research Canada, 2002).

Gender inequality and patriarchal values become apparent from an early stage in a woman's life. Parents treat boys and girls differently, making different demands on them and introducing different sets of expectations. A girl is socialized and conditioned to believe that "a woman's place is in the kitchen"—cooking, taking care of all domestic chores, and child rearing. She is expected to assume a dependent, submissive, passive, and subservient stance in the world, while the man in her life makes decisions that often affect her life directly. Men, on the other hand, are encouraged to become strong and energetic. In later life and when they are working for economic survival, women are still expected to do housework and be obedient servants. With the input and involvement of family members, Nigerian women struggle to maintain societal gender expectations even when they work outside the home.

Nigerian women's participation in decision making and power relations within the household and community levels is restricted. A woman's attempt to challenge the status quo is greeted with remarks like "She is stepping out of line." Cultural values render women voiceless and often without rights before husbands in a society where rebelling against the status quo is culturally unacceptable.[3] Patriarchy explains the subordination of women, and any attempt to reject this subordination can lead to abuse. Mary Daly urges women to ignore the supposed securities offered by the patriarchal system, and instead create new spaces that would be women-centred (cited in hooks, 1994, p. 28). As Zahra notes, "It is within the home, from childhood, that the roles, prejudices, conditioning and exploitation of women in Nigeria begun, leading to its acceptance in the society" (1983, p. 8). For this reason, Nigerian women who attempt to challenge patriarchal ideologies and construct a safe place will suffer an incredible amount of social pressure. Members of the community vehemently rise against the "deviant" who wants to change an age-old tradition.

In Nigeria, as in other societies, male partners' domestic abuse of women is a serious and significant form of violence against women of all classes. In their study of Nigerian women's perception of domestic violence, Isiugo-Abanihe and Oyediran (2003) observed that domestic violence against Nigerian women is an expression of culturally unequal power relationships between men and women in society. The cultural values and ideas about patriarchy have much to do with the acceptance of wife-beating in Nigerian society as a sign of love—an acceptable way of correcting errant women. As a result, Nigerian women are socialized to believe that wife-beating is an integral component of marriage, even though they may disagree about the practice in principle. Dibie observed that Nigerian society does not see wife abuse "as a breakdown in social order, rather as an affirmation of a particular order. In this sense, abuse is being recognized as a norm and as such functional. Men use violence to control women" (Dibie, 2000, p. 39). In part, this is achieved through early childhood socialization, resulting in the subordination of married women later in life.

Domestic abuse affects women in a variety of ways, such as harming their mental and reproductive health; although the reality of domestic abuse against Nigerian women by their male partners is well known, there are few studies on this phenomenon in Nigerian society. Aderinto (2003) examined the social construction of domestic violence against women in post-colonial Nigeria and also observed the dearth of studies and attention directed at this phenomenon in Nigerian society, especially its socio-cultural context. Most attention has been on gender-based violence, such as female circumcision/genital mutilation and its consequences.[4]

Domestic abuse against Nigerian women is seen as a private issue that should be discussed only within the household even though the Nigerian government is a signatory to the December 1993 United Nations General Assembly's Declaration on the Elimination of All Forms of Discrimination and Violence against Women. The inability to address the issue of domestic abuse against Nigerian women in a public forum, it can be argued, is due to widely held patriarchal values.

Dobash and Dobash (1979), studying violence against wives within Caucasian societies, observed that a woman's struggle against domination and control (through a restrictive patriarchal system and gender roles) is constructed as wrong and immoral, and a violation of the respect and loyalty that a wife should accord her husband. In response, a husband may assert his authority by beating his wife into submission (p. 11). This situation can be explained by the fact that domestic violence against women in most male-dominated, ideology-driven societies is a manifestation of a patriarchal ideology and the subordination of women resulting from socially constructed gender roles. Barrett argues that "sex roles in … [patriarchal] societies [are] not simply 'difference' but a division, oppression, inequality, and inferiority for women" (1980, pp. 112–113). As such, cultural practices in patriarchal societies serve as weapons of male power used to abuse and dominate wives. Similarly, Collins maintains that "the objective of controlling images of womanhood as passive … reflects men's interest in maintaining women's subordination" (1991, p. 143). As well, hooks further argues that these controlling images also allow men to act as exploiters and oppressors of women (1984, p. 16). Ogundipe observed that women suffer maximum oppression and abuse within the institution of marriage in Nigeria (1994, p. 27). While marriage confers additional status for women, it also burdens them simultaneously because of the imposed gender constraints.

MARRIAGE AS INDISPENSABLE: UNDERSTANDING THE MYTH

The traditional sanctification of marriage in Nigerian society contributes to men's control and abuse of their wives. Marriage is regarded as an indispensable obligation that every woman has to fulfill. To call a woman married is to ascribe status and respect to her. Consequently, women protect their marriages at all costs, including remaining in abusive unions. Basden simply notes that "marriage looms upon the horizon of every maid and youth as an indispensable function to be fulfilled with as little delay as possible after reaching the age of puberty. The idea of a celibate life finds no favour whatsoever among most people. It is considered to be foolishness, as well as being utterly contrary to the laws of nature" (Basden, cited in Isiugo-Abanihe, 1987, p. 75).

This "idealization of heterosexual romance and marriage," as Rich (1980, p. 148) labels it, results in the perception that a single woman is unlucky and a disgrace for both the woman and her family. A single woman is viewed as "incomplete" and therefore is ridiculed and associated with evil (Isiugo-Abanihe, 1994). Such attitudes result in men exercising their control and authority regardless of their wives' wishes, given the recognition that every woman wants to be under a man's protection to avoid social stigmatization.

There are two types of marriages among Nigerians: monogamy and polygamy. In some communities a man's social status is measured by the number of wives and children he has. Ironically, women may enjoy the division of household responsibilities inherent in such a system. Presently, the perceived value of this practice has waned significantly due to the impact of education, modernization, and religion.[5] Both types of marriages involve the payment of dowry, bride price, or bride wealth. The bride price is a symbolic means of compensating parents for raising their daughters and for the impending loss of the daughter's services. It may be in the form of cash or material things such as clothing, wine, or yams.[6] Whatever medium it takes, the payment of bride wealth means that a woman is never completely free. She becomes the "possession" of a man (husband) and, as such, is voiceless and submissive to his authority. In the event of divorce, children born from the union belong to the man, while the woman has no right over the children she has laboured to bring forth and cared for.

As far as the bride's family is concerned, the marriage must be maintained and sustained by any means. The success of a marriage depends on the wife's obedience to her husband's authority and her ability to take care of domestic chores. She is constantly reminded, "If you leave, another woman will enjoy the fruits of your labour and your children will be deprived of their father's home" (Iweriebor, 1983, p. 152). A woman's family of origin would feel ashamed to see their daughter leave her matrimonial home, as such an act would be an admission of failure. The fear of facing this perceived shame makes women remain in abusive marriages (Isiugo-Abanihe, 1994). Consequently, there is a tendency toward further abuse as women rarely decide to defy the stigma of divorce.

METHODOLOGY/PRELIMINARY INFORMATION

The approach utilized for this study included in-depth interviews and key informant interviews. Given the sensitive nature of the thematic issues under investigation, in-depth interviews were adopted to capture the subjective experiences and meanings that people associate with events (O'Neil, 1995, p. 334). As other researchers have demonstrated, "In-depth interviews allow us to document women's subjective experiences of their social world and how it affects them" (Cousineau & Rondeau, 2004, p. 943). To a large extent, it is only by considering the person's own testimony that a deeper understanding of the issue is generated, and this also aids in social change for the victim whose voice is heard and documented (McDonald, 1999; Martz & Sarauer, 2002; Idemudia, 1999; Anderson & Jack, 1991; Nielsen, 1990; Maynard & Purvis, 1994). Thus, in-depth interviews provided the best opportunity for Nigerian-Canadian women's voices to be heard and their experiences to be articulated.

During the interview, questions were framed in a manner that allowed the respondents to narrate their experiences freely. In addition to the respondents' socio-demographic characteristics, questions explored the interviewees' histories and experiences of migration, family compositions and dynamics, experiences of violence in Nigeria and Canada, and views on the types of intervention that would effectively address such abuse. Data were analyzed by bringing together important components of respondents' views, information, stories, or concerns that emerged repeatedly or were seen as significant within or across interviews. I carried out the in-depth interviews in Toronto in July and August of 2005. The city was chosen for a number of reasons, most importantly because it is home to a very large number of Nigerians. According to a report from Statistics Canada (2001), almost 49 percent of Black women in Canada live in Toronto, while the rest live in Calgary, Montreal, Ottawa, Kingston, Vancouver, and Halifax. Of the total of 10,425 Nigerian immigrants and non-permanent residents who migrated to Canada from 1961–2001, 56.8 percent live in Toronto, while 4.6 percent live in Ottawa. The remainder live in cities such as Kingston and Montreal (Statistics Canada, 2001). Thus, the probability of the researcher having access to a sizable number of Nigerians in the selected location (Toronto) was very high.

The study sample consisted of 10 first-generation Nigerian-Canadian women, residing in Toronto, whose ages range between 35 and 55 years, as well as two key informants. The two key informants are from the Nigerian-Canadian community, and they are knowledgeable about the issues and concerns in the Nigerian community. According to one of the Nigerian-Canadian Association community leaders, the Nigerian community in Toronto comprises mainly of the three major ethnic groups of Nigeria: Hausa/Fulani, Igbo, and Yoruba. The Igbos and the Yorubas have the largest populations; the population of the Hausa, like that of most other ethnic groups in Nigeria, is small. Hence the study population was five Nigerian-Canadian women from the Igbo and five from the Yoruba ethnic groups, whose major native languages are Yoruba and Igbo. The respondents came from nuclear and polygamous families. Eleven out of the 12 respondents were Christians, while only one respondent was a Muslim. All of the women had formal education ranging from high school to tertiary education. Two of the respondents were divorced, while 10 were still living in their matrimonial homes. The respondents' duration of marital union ranged from 13–24 years. Their family composition showed that their children numbered between two and four per family.

All of the respondents were working for pay, and their annual incomes ranged between $10,000 and $100,000. They were engaged occupationally as cleaners, social workers, housewives, nurses, lawyers, caregivers, employment agents, and business executives. Interestingly, as will be discussed later, these Black Nigerian-Canadian immigrant women still experienced some form of abuse from their husbands or intimate partners regardless of their income and educational level. The length of their stay in Toronto ranged from three to 15 years. This research showed that the number of years in Canada had no correlation with the extent of abuse they experienced in Canada. For issue of confidentiality, pseudonyms are used throughout the chapter to protect respondents' identities.

DOMESTIC VIOLENCE AMONG NIGERIAN-CANADIAN WOMEN

Domestic violence is a common experience among Nigerian-Canadian women, but remains underreported principally because of the cultural belief that it is a "private issue" within the household, and also because of the stigma attached to it. Women are blamed for domestic abuse for reasons ranging from inability to satisfy their husbands sexually, to not being able to raise their children properly. Any of these reasons is seen as sufficient cause for a man to abuse his wife or partner. One of the respondents, Mrs. Philips, commented:

> There was a woman in our community who had been experiencing all kinds of abuse from her husband for 15 years. She was a teacher back home, but when she came to Canada, her husband did not allow her to upgrade her certificate. He kept her at home to raise children and abused her as it pleased him. The woman could not speak out due to fear of being blamed and ostracized from the community and families back home in Nigeria. Even among Nigerians here in [Toronto] Canada, it is a taboo to say my husband hit me so I will report him to the authorities; a woman has no right to do that. Some will even say you did something wrong [and] that is why your husband hit you. You are a bad woman (Interviewee, 2005, Toronto).

Men are not the only perpetrators of domestic abuse against Nigerian-Canadian women. In-laws and extended family members have much influence on the domestic abuse of a woman. Mrs. Olisah gave an account of her own experience with her sister-in-law. According to her:

> The influence of my sister-in-law changed my husband and my marriage. My husband hardly beat me; my problem started the moment my sister-in-law walked in. My loving husband and our marriage turned upside down. One day, my husband was cooking when his sister walked in; the moment she saw my husband assisting me in cooking, she reacted as if he was doing something abominable. She turned to him and asked: "How can you, the husband, be cooking? You have a wife. How can you do that? This is an abomination." She started calling me names and saying I'm a bad woman. She told her brother not to do that again. It is an atrocity unless he wants to be a woman's wrapper (which is to say he is a weakling—a man who cannot defend his status as the head of the house). From then on my husband stopped assisting me in cooking and becomes angry and scolds me whenever I ask him for help.

The consensus among the women interviewed was that most Nigerian men do not see physical abuse—such as slapping or using strong objects such as belts or *koboko* (unbreakable cane) to beat their wives and children—as abuse, but accept it as a normal part of growing up. In the Nigerian context, a man is the head of the household. He is seen not only as a king but also as a mini-god by family members, and whatever he says stands; women are not expected to challenge his authority. "If he is upset and thinks that the wife is not submissive to his authority or command, he has the right to hit her; it is perfectly fine" (Interviewee, 2005, Toronto).

What is understood as abuse from the Nigerian cultural perspective is if a man does not provide for his family's upkeep. However, Nigerian women living in Canada, due to their exposure to a new culture, are now beginning to break away from this kind of attitude and behaviour and are questioning the justification for their partners' verbal, physical, and sexual abuse.

CULTURAL PRACTICES AND DOMESTIC ABUSE

As mentioned earlier, Nigeria is a male-dominated society, and deference traditionally accorded to men at the expense of women is a problem, making Nigerian women resident in Canada vulnerable to domestic violence. Because men are valued more than women in Nigeria, they have unquestionable authority that women can never challenge. Authority and control are men's traditional rights and heritage; it's their innate superiority. It is quite disheartening that despite the belief that migration lessens male control over their wives because of the distance from home and the influence of a new culture (Menjivar & Salcido, 2002, p. 916), Nigerian men have migrated to Canada with a traditional mindset and could become violently angry at any perceived challenge to their superior authority socially constructed in their country of origin. It has disappointed their female partners that these men have migrated only geographically but not socially in a new context. The ideology is thus: "You are the woman, I am the man. I am the head; I am in charge. The woman is my slave, and she has to obey my commands as a goat tied on a rope. What I say goes. You correct 'her'—a woman—by beating or raining insults" (Nwosu, 2005, p. 100).

This becomes even more problematic given that these women want to exercise the freedom they have as Canadian residents, freedom greater than what they experienced in Nigeria. Most of the Nigerian men want to check and control any such perceived excesses the women might indulge in. According to the respondents, the conflict lies in the fact that when it comes to finances:

> na [sic] 50/50 [equal], oh! But when it comes to power, it shouldn't be 50/50. It should be 100/0 or 80/20. Any decision has to come from the man clearly because of the cultural belief that a woman is under the authority and control of her husband. The enlightened woman wants a 50/50 power-sharing relationship, while her controlling partner wants it 100 percent in his favour. As a result, men resort to physical violence in order to maintain the status quo, male-dominating attitude. (Interviewee, 2005, Toronto)

The sanctity of male domination and preference explains the unacceptability of childlessness and a lack of tolerance for female offspring. This makes women, especially those who have not been able to give birth to male children, vulnerable to domestic abuse. Many Nigerian men are impatient when it comes to childbirth because they believe that the purpose of marriage is exclusively child-bearing. As a result, a childless woman is exposed to much emotional and verbal abuse from family members and significant others. A woman with female children is like a "barren woman" and suffers abuse. For example, Mrs. Emmanuel describes her experiences of domestic abuse as a result of not having male progeny. She recounts:

I married young to a lawyer, but my marriage collapsed because of this cultural "girl, girl" thing. I had just two girls; there was no boy and, you know, having only female children in our culture is like a taboo. For that reason, my husband and his family were all over me, accusing me of witchcraft and lots of rubbish. Sometimes they would tell me that I personified bad luck and that I don't want a continuation of their lineage, which is why I purposely did not want to produce a male child. They believed that girls are other men's property.... It is only having at least a male child that can legitimize your marriage. The irony and agony of the whole thing is that it is not a woman that determines the sex of a baby. It is what a man releases inside the woman that determines the sex of the baby, but who cares in our society to listen? It is all the woman's fault. Our society needs to accept female offspring as human beings born to also succeed.

The emotional and verbal abuse experienced by these women as a result of a perceived lack of male offspring illustrates Brownridge's (2002) assertion that the various cultural forms of patriarchy expose women to different forms of violence. In an egalitarian society, where men and women possess equal opportunities, there is a lesser chance of domestic violence against women specific to the birth of either a boy or a girl.

A woman's popularity was another contributing factor to Nigerian-Canadian women's experiences of domestic abuse. As some traditional Nigerian men still hold on to the idea of social dominance over their wives, when there is a reversal of this idea and a woman becomes seen and heard, these men see it as an affront to them and may resort to violence to maintain their self-esteem. One of the study participants commented: "The higher a woman goes socially and not even financially, the hotter it becomes." In Canada, the abuse of Nigerian-Canadian women as a result of this experience is becoming a problem for some women.

The research findings also show that male partners' insistence on controlling family income is also a contributing factor in abuse. In Nigeria, men are the breadwinners in the family. They also control their partners' wages when both parties work. This is a widely accepted practice in the country to which women are forced to ascribe. The patriarchal environment empowers men to exert control over every aspect of their families. In Canada, the economic reality is such that both parties have to work. Working outside the home in a liberal country inevitably leads to a paradigm shift for Nigerian women, who come to realize that their wages can open the door to hitherto unknown freedom. This realization, however, is a threat to a Nigerian man raised in a patriarchal society, who believes in his traditional power over women. In order to maintain the status quo prevalent in Nigeria, Nigerian men demand access to their wives' wages. This is not so much for financial reasons, but stems from the man's need to remind the woman that he is powerful in the relationship. Women's refusal to comply will increase their risks of being yelled at, beaten, or abused through other forms of male violence.

Regarding the reasons why men desire to have total control over their families' affairs, including their spouses' earned income, the respondents noted that the payment of dowry appears to be strongly connected to the experiences of financial control, physical, emotional, and verbal abuse. Since some men pay so much to marry, a woman is seen as a man's property and not a person in and of herself. Nigerian men believe that they own a woman's body and soul and that women should be subservient to them. The men believe that they have a right to any income a woman makes. When they feel they are losing their power over women, they become abusive. It is very difficult for a woman to live with a man who is obsessed with power and control. Many married women are treated by such obsessive men as a possession, regardless of their level of education or income.

A Nigerian man's power is largely predicated on his ability to support and feed his wife and children. However, the Western economic situation has led women into the labour market to provide a second income for the family. Sometimes Nigerian-Canadian women make greater financial contributions to their households than their husbands. In this study, although some Nigerian women worked as factory workers and health care aides, many were nurses, doctors, teachers, and social workers; they earned more money than their husbands. This reality is a challenge to their husbands whose pride is wounded by their wives' greater earning power. To restore their traditional footing, the husbands resort to abusing their partner verbally, emotionally, or physically. Any little mistake or offending gesture by the woman becomes an excuse for the man to vent his frustration at not being the primary breadwinner for the family.

Differences in parenting approaches can also result in the abuse of women due to conflict between parents on how their children should be raised, especially when one parent wants to discipline the child in a way the Canadian government deems abusive. In Nigeria, spanking a child is an acceptable method of correction, but the same corrective method in Canada results in the child being taken away from the parent. When a wife prevents a husband from disciplining their children, she could be subjected to physical or verbal abuse. According to Mrs. Emmanuel:

Lack of mutual agreement on child rearing leads to constant arguments and beating of a woman. For instance, the man may be giving one instruction while the woman is giving another. The man may say to a child, "Shut up," and the woman tries to counter that by telling the child not to mind him, insinuating that he is verbally abusing the kid. Most times such attitude angers the man and could lead to him getting physical to bring mother and child to order, since in Nigerian culture the parents reserve the exclusive right to verbally or otherwise correct their children whenever they think she or he is doing something wrong.

SYSTEMIC FACTORS AS CAUSE OF ABUSE

Traditions and cultures are known to affect domestic violence against women; however, systemic factors in the new culture also play a major part in exposing Nigerian-Canadian women to domestic violence. A majority of the women who came to Canada with high hopes of survival were disappointed as a result of their inability to achieve this ambition for various reasons related to discrimination, unemployment, lack of social or immediate family support, racism, and economic pressures. These barriers and the accompanying disappointment have a big impact on their lives such as their state of mind, marital relationship, and family affairs. Maladjustment to the Canadian cash economy and its perceived economic consequences results in women's susceptibility to domestic abuse.

In Nigeria, women are not expected to pay taxes or other bills; these expenses are strictly borne by men. It is a man's honour to take care of his wife and children. It is rare to find households in Nigeria where family financial responsibilities are shared equally by husbands and wives. In Canada, however, these responsibilities are borne by both parties. Since most Nigerian women are not brought up to be equal economic contributors to household expenditures, they find it difficult to adjust to an entirely different approach in Canada.

Unfortunately, the situation of Nigerian women in Canada is worsened by the dual responsibility of domestic activities and paid work. In Nigeria, a woman's primary responsibility, irrespective of her level of education or social standing, is to carry out domestic duties and to have children. Male children in the family are exempted from household duties. Therefore, the Nigerian man does not want to be bothered with any domestic chores even when his wife is engaged in outside work. Hence, the woman is expected to be a "superwoman" much like other wives from other locations in the world, effectively combining these activities and gender roles, for which failure attracts some kind of abuse. Mrs. Adibe explains:

> No matter a woman's level of education or income, a woman's place is in the kitchen. Women are expected to serve men, and they are not expected to talk or challenge such gender roles and ideology. When it comes to child rearing, it takes a village to raise a child, not just the biological parents. And as such, there are usually no bills to pay to babysitters to take care of the children.... In Canada, we are faced with many challenges which force us to work and support our spouses. Can you imagine, working in the factory? After standing for eight hours working, sometimes you don't even have time for your lunch; you come home hoping to relax, only to find out he is sitting on a sofa doing nothing simply because in his culture, it is the women who do all the cooking and change the diapers. Yet, at night he still expects you to be "yours sincerely" and put a smile on your face for him. When I try to disagree or challenge him, he will strike me and call me unimaginable names.

Nigerian-Canadian women's experiences of domestic violence derive from complex factors that include racism, state policies on immigration, and institutional discrimination. Findings from the respondents show that Nigerian women suffer domestic abuse not just as a result of sexism in their own culture, but also as a result of the isolation and discrimination that they endure from the society at large because of their accent, colour, non-Canadian education, and immigration status. One respondent commented: "To tell you the truth, the non-recognition of my certificate [institutional discrimination] really affected my self-esteem more than the beating and degrading comments I encountered from my husband. Please, something has to be done." In this same way another woman, Mrs. Ezike, states:

> My experiences of abuse is not even an issue; the disregard and the kind of maltreatment I receive in the office because of my skin colour as a Black [immigrant] woman is frustrating and degrading to one's self-esteem. How can you go to the office and someone will tell you that you stink, you cannot speak well. They treat you as if you are not a human being. This verbal maltreatment translates into emotional abuse. It is really painful that after the pain one is enduring in the family ... the society also neither welcomes nor treats a class of people as human beings. To tell the truth, the effect of emotional and verbal abuse is more tormenting on a woman than a man hitting you

with any object. Hitting or slapping can only result in bruises, but emotional and verbal abuse is emotionally tormenting and can result in heart attacks or sudden death.

While identifying how racial and institutional discrimination, including the non-recognition of international education certificates, makes Nigerian women vulnerable to abuse, the women in this study maintained that most often their husbands were affected by such discrimination. The reality is that it is more difficult for Nigerian men to secure employment in Canada than Nigerian women, which makes the "domestic environment the center of explosive tension that leads to violence against women" (hooks, 1984, p. 122). Most male immigrants migrate with high hopes of a better life; when a man finds it hard to get a good job due to non-recognition of his certificate or discrimination against his skin colour, his wife becomes the victim of his discontent. This phenomenon is what bell hooks terms the "Control situation," a situation in which a man releases his anger and frustration without fear of retaliation or questioning (1984, p. 122).

Racial discrimination with regard to jobs is a common cause of frustration among Nigerian-Canadian women. One key informant summarizes it this way:

> I am talking to you from my experiences; racial and job discrimination are common causes of frustration among us and this further heightens abuse. For instance, you go for a job appointment and as soon as your surname is mentioned and you don't have an English surname like that of a Canadian, there is discrimination right there. What could be emotionally, psychologically, mentally, and physically disturbing like that? There are lots of abused women who hold PhDs and master's degrees who could have made it independently, but they are struggling and suffering double tragedy [social and cultural abuse] because they are not recognized in society. On the other hand, some Nigerian men who are graduates and came to Canada with high hopes of survival could not be gainfully employed due to non-recognition of their certificates. They instead have to take up low-paying jobs such as factory work, cleaning, babysitting, and cab driving. This situation makes women more vulnerable to abuse resulting from frustration among their partners. I know of a man who actually told his wife that as long as he is suffering all this discrimination, a romantic marriage is out of the question for them. We need policies that will be beneficial to both African immigrant men and women who have academic certificates. This will help prevent men from unleashing their anger and frustration on women.

ACCESS TO SOCIAL AND JUDICIAL SERVICES

Although more women are identifying their experiences as abusive, they are still reluctant to seek social services, such as going to a shelter or engaging the criminal justice system against their male partners. Nigerian women living in Toronto have various reasons why they have failed to report their abusers and/or seek relevant assistance. First, most Nigerian women are ignorant about the services available in Canada. However, lack of knowledge is not the main impediment to them accessing services. Social and cultural factors such as the value of children and marriage, reverence for family ties, fear of shame and ostracism, fear of documentation and misinterpretations of facts, and the view that domestic abuse is a family issue make it difficult for Nigerian-Canadian women to seek help or report their abusive experiences, even in situations that necessitate assistance. Because within the Nigerian culture domestic abuse is seen as a family matter, an abused Nigerian woman is faced with the dilemma of choosing between self-interest and community criticism and ostracism. Such a predicament most often results in women trying to conceal the abuses. Mrs. Adebayo explains:

> It is not in our culture. A woman calling the police on her husband is a taboo. How can I go to a shelter with my children or call the police? It is unacceptable. What will my community say? They will blame me and say I am not a good wife. How can I leave my husband and children because he hit me? Society normally believes that women are bad; men are good. Going to a shelter is not safe for a Nigerian woman. It is not in our culture for a woman to go to a shelter. We call it "running away"—to pack up from your husband's house and to go and live in a shelter. No, no, no, no. I personally will either prefer moving in with a friend, or renting my own apartment if I have enough money than seeking any other services. Besides, apart from cultural disapproval of the issue, most Nigerians are Christian—Catholics, Pentecostals, and Methodist—and, according to their religious beliefs, marriage is for better or for worse. A woman leaving her marital relationship is conceived as a violation of her religious faith and a sin against God. Given such beliefs, a woman finds it hard to ask for police assistance or seek for separation or divorce.

More so, fear of the consequences of documentation and social stigma cannot be overlooked. The consequences of reporting spousal abuse to the police or social services are inextricably bound up with Nigerian women's inability to seek social or legal services. Among the Nigerian-Canadian women, there is a general belief that once a man is reported to the police for spousal abuse, the record is indelible. This creates an unquantifiable barrier to such a man gaining employment. As such, once the husband cannot be gainfully employed, he ends up taking menial jobs with an income that hardly sustains the family. Consequently the whole family suffers economic hardship because of the report. Most abused women therefore decide to cover up such abuses because of the unforeseen financial consequences this might have on the entire family in the future. To buttress this point, Mrs. Olisa explains:

> Documentation of a case is sort of putting sand in your *garri* [food]—that is to say, adding more injury to one's pains. One of my friends reported her husband for abuse; this created a bad criminal record for the man, which tarnished his image in the society and has resulted in economic hardship for the whole family and emotional abuse of the wife from the husband. Because her husband could not secure a job appointment and when only she cannot pay all the bills, the family is suffering.

The issue of child custody also creates barriers for abused Nigerian-Canadian women in seeking services or leaving abusive relationships. According to Nigerian culture, a man has a right to the children, whereas the respondents believe that the woman has absolute right to her children in Canadian society.[7] When a woman decides to leave an abusive family, the family normally takes the children away from her. Many women are unwittingly bound to their marriages since no woman wants her children to be raised by another woman.

CONCLUSION

The recognition of the multifaceted factors that structure women's experiences of abuse is, on one hand, a positive move toward the elimination of domestic violence and, on the other, is significant in the establishment of meaningful social services for abused women. This study has shown that Nigerian-Canadian women's experiences of abuse cannot be separated from both cultural values and socio-environmental factors.

The fact that Nigerian men, irrespective of their socio-economic status, want to sustain their control over the affairs of the family, is a contributing factor to abuse. In Nigeria, male dominance is an integral part of custom within different communities in society. The patriarchal ethos, for instance, gives Nigerian men freedom to engage in behaviours that infringe on the rights of women. Furthermore, women's rights, prestige, and activities in Nigeria are defined in line with masculine ideology. Even in socialization, children are exposed to orientation embedded in gender dichotomy. As a result, most men are unable to discard some of those learned gender-skewed values, even as adults, in whatever society they find themselves. Any effort to challenge or alter these values is deemed unacceptable and consequently may lead to abuse.

The challenges posed by systemic factors also contribute to Nigerian-Canadian women's experience of abuse. Contrary to what prevails in Nigeria, where women are predominantly housewives and their husbands are bread-winners, the Canadian reality demands that women work in order to pay their bills. This makes it difficult for an abused Nigerian-Canadian woman to deal only with her culturally ascribed responsibilities, domestic chores, and child rearing. Also, as some respondents in this study pointed out, when they earned more money than their husbands, and when these men assumed that they had lost their financial leadership in the family, wife abuse occurred.

Nigerian-Canadian women are also faced with racial challenges. This includes non-acceptance of their professional training from outside Canada, and job discrimination owing to colour differences and accent. The pain and frustration of institutional and racial discrimination resulting from non-recognition of international certificates make Nigerian women in Toronto more vulnerable to domestic violence. This results in transferred aggression from men who may have been affected by such policies.

In support of earlier research, the respondents in this study reinforced the argument that the state immigration policy of sponsorship makes women vulnerable to verbal and emotional abuse. As well, this results in subjecting women to more male control, given that sponsored parties are required by law to live with their sponsors for a specified period of time. These women are forced to live and tolerate the abuses until they gain independence from their sponsors.

Findings of this study indicate that domestic violence among the Nigerian-Canadian women living in Toronto is a complex phenomenon that is influenced by socio-cultural, economic, and political factors.

THE WAY FORWARD

Sustained advocacy, through seminars and workshops to sensitize couples on their rights and responsibilities in marriage, has become paramount.

This will help improve their understanding about the essence of mutual respect and sensitivity. In addition, the establishment of vocational training centres where new immigrant Black women could be trained to be self-employed and thus become economically independent is suggested. This is necessary because most immigrant women remain in their matrimonial homes, irrespective of their marital plight, due to financial dependence. Women who are self-reliant are more likely to report abuse than those who depend wholly on their husbands. Equally, given that cultural ideals and values may invariably determine the kind of support or help an abused woman may seek, Nigerian women who seek professional assistance and social services will certainly put their cultural context into consideration. This calls for culturally sensitive services. As a sexual assault counsellor, I have often heard women seeking services emphasizing the significance of this.

There is also a need for the Canadian government to consider a policy that encourages or motivates employers to accept internationally educated professionals or workers who were trained outside the Canadian educational system. In this way, frustration arising from unemployment, which is a major source of domestic tension, would be diminished. Hence, aggression at the family level may be ameliorated. Finally, it is important to revamp our systems to ensure that all racial barriers against Black people can be eliminated so that women can have equal opportunity with other members of society and survive through healthy competition. This point was unequivocally recommended by the respondents as the surest way of allowing individuals to realize their inherent potentials. This could be achieved through educating other ethnicities about the benefits that individuals contribute to the nation regardless of race. Addressing this cultural need would go a long way toward increasing the level of assistance for abused Black immigrant women in Canada.

Chapter 12

Perceptions of Intimate Male Partner Violence and Determinants of Women's Responses to It: Findings from a Study in the Sri Lankan Tamil Community in Toronto

Sepali Guruge

INTRODUCTION

Violence against women is a major concern for women everywhere. Intimate male partner violence (IMPV), in particular, is the most pervasive form of violence against women. Intimate partner violence has been defined by the U.S. Centers for Disease Control as the threat of, or actual physical, sexual, and/or psychological/emotional abuse by a current or former spouse and/or non-marital partner (Saltzman, Fanslow, McMahon & Shelley, 1999). IMPV exists in most communities across the world, cutting across socio-economic, religious, cultural, and national boundaries (WHO, 1997, 2000, 2006). A recent World Health Organization (2006) study of IMPV in 10 countries in which little research on IMPV had existed indicated that rates of lifetime IMPV varied widely across the countries, as did women's perceptions of what was considered abuse, and responses to IMPV. These findings reinforce the need to develop context-specific knowledge about IMPV, including women's, families', and communities' perceptions of and responses to abuse, in order to ensure that health, social, and settlement services are appropriate and effective.

The overall focus of this chapter is on the perceptions of, and responses to, IMPV in one racialized immigrant community in Canada, the Sri Lankan Tamil community. This chapter is based on the findings of a doctoral study conducted in nursing.

LITERATURE REVIEW

Prevalence of IMPV

Very little information exists on the prevalence rates of IMPV among immigrant women in Canada. However, various community leaders and advocates have raised concerns regarding the prevalence of IMPV in their communities (Cohen & Ansara, 2002; MacLeod et al., 1993; Hyman, Guruge et al., 2004; McSpadden & Moussa, 1993; Morrison et al., 1999). Furthermore, MacLeod et al. (1993) has identified immigrant women, among other groups such as adolescent girls, pregnant women, women with disabilities, rural women, and Aboriginal women, as being at higher risk for IMPV. While some of the factors that contribute to a high risk of IMPV in these communities, such as isolation and poverty, may be common among some of these groups, additional factors such as language difficulties and fear of deportation may increase the vulnerability of immigrant women in abusive situations.

When Cohen and Ansara (2002) reanalyzed data from the recently conducted General Social Survey (2000) of 20,000 participants (14,269 women) from 10 provinces, they found that the rate of IMPV was lower among newcomer women than among long-term immigrants and Canadian-born women for both severe and non-severe forms of violence. Severe forms of abuse included being kicked, hit, hit with objects, beaten, choked, and sexually assaulted, as well as being threatened or assaulted with a gun or knife. Non-severe forms of violent behaviours that women's partners exhibited included threatening to hit, throwing objects, grabbing, shoving, pushing, and slapping. The authors noted that some of the disparity could be explained by the differences in the definitions and perceptions of IMPV.

Perception of IMPV

Despite attempts to develop common definitions of IMPV, differences exist in what constitutes IMPV. Most commonly perceived forms of IMPV include physical abuse, sexual abuse, verbal abuse, and emotional and psychological abuse, even though other forms, such as financial or economic abuse and spiritual abuse, are gaining interest and attention. The differences in definitions or perceptions of IMPV pose a significant problem in determining the numbers of women who experience it. When not all women acknowledge various forms of IMPV, or perceive abuse as abuse, it deters them from seeking help to deal with the abuse. In fact, correctly identifying and naming abuse is a significant step in being less controlled by an abusive husband or partner (Anderson, 2003).

The expression of IMPV is also shaped by the context, with certain forms taking on greater prominence in specific situations. For example, in the post-migration context, IMPV may be expressed in the following forms: not allowing women to access language training, taking away their immigration documents, and threatening deportation (Agnew, 1998; Raj & Silverman, 2002; McDonald, 1999). Women who live in rural settings might be kept in isolation by being denied access to transportation or a telephone (Bosch & Schumm, 2004; Hornosty & Doherty, 2002). "Mail-order brides" in the post-migration context may be subjected to forms of IMPV that incorporate racial, ethno-cultural, and religious domination of women at home (Glodava & Onizuko, 1994).

Over the past three decades, there has been an increase in health sciences researchers' interest in exploring the varied perceptions of IMPV in diverse communities. For example, in Greenblat's (1983) study of a group of men and women in the U.S., approximately a quarter of the participants indicated that there were circumstances in which it was appropriate or acceptable to hit one's partner. The participants' perception of the IMPV was dependent on the wife's behaviour and on the husband's motivation for hitting. In another U.S. study, Gentemann (1984) found that 18.8 percent of participants accepted certain situations in which IMPV was justified. Mugford, Mugford, and Easteal (1989) found that 20 percent of the respondents surveyed in Australia believed IMPV was justified under certain conditions. In a national survey in Singapore, Choi and Edleson (1996) reported that 5.5 percent of the participants strongly agreed with the statement that "sometimes it is alright for a husband to use physical force against his wife." Based on a study among engaged Arab men from Israel, Haj-Yahia (1991) reported that 44 percent of the participants expressed some level of agreement with the statement "there is no excuse for a man beating his wife." However, about 30 percent also noted some level of agreement with the statement "sometime it is OK for a man to beat his wife," and between 28 percent and 57 percent of the participants agreed that husbands have the right to beat their wives under certain conditions. These included women being unfaithful or disobedient, not respecting her husband's parents or siblings, insulting her husband in front of his friends, constantly refusing to have sex with her husband, not respecting her husband's relatives, and not living up to her husband's expectations. Based on a later study of a group of Arab husbands from Israel, Haj-Yahia

(1997) reported a general tendency to justify wife-beating. While approximately 58 percent of study participants strongly agreed or agreed that "there is no excuse for a man to beat his wife," 28 percent still strongly agreed or agreed that "sometimes it is OK for a man to beat his wife."

Recently, in a study with a group of Chinese American women (Senturia, Sullivan, Ciske & Shiu-Thornton, 2000), one third of participants defined IMPV more in terms of various types of physical abuse. In another study (Mehrotra, 1999), a group of Hindu-Indian immigrants to the U.S. identified IMPV as involving physical, mental, verbal, emotional, and economic abuse. Participants noted frequent comparison of wife against other women and purposeful isolation of a woman as other forms of abuse. In another study in the Asian American population, a group of researchers (Yoshioka, DiNoia, & Ullah, 2001) found that 24 to 36 percent of the study sample agreed that IMPV was justified in certain situations or contexts such as wife's infidelity, her "nagging" or her refusal to cook or clean. In Tang et. al.'s (2000) study in Hong Kong, women identified a range of behaviours as abusive including psychological and sexual aggression, and physical abuse, however, men perceived only physical abuse as abuse. More recently, a group of older Chinese participants in Shibusawa and Yick (2007) agreed that physical violence was not justified under any circumstance.

Responses to IMPV

Women's responses to IMPV are both individually and socially shaped, and depend on the perceptions of abuse as well as on the supports and services available to help them manage their lives within a particular community and society. Extended family members, neighbours, and co-workers can have a strong influence on the couple (Raj & Silverman, 2002; Abraham, 1999, 2000, 2002). In particular, in collectivist communities where values of family ties, harmony, and order prevail, women are taught to subordinate the self to the interests of the family (Agnew, 1998; Abraham, 2000; Bui & Morash, 1999), and therefore may feel that separation, divorce, and/or remarriage are not viable options. Women might also believe in the importance of keeping families together for the welfare of children (Morrison, Guruge & Snarr, 1999; Hyman et al., 2006; Varcoe & Irwin, 2004; Ford-Gilboe, Wuest & Merrit-Gray, 2005; Wuest, Ford-Filboe & Merrit-Gray, 2005). Many women are reluctant to seek help for IMPV due to shame, fear of being stigmatized, fear of having their children taken away, or fear of being pressured to leave their husbands (Hyman et al., 2006; Varcoe & Irwin, 2004; Ford-Gilboe, Wuest & Merrit-Gray, 2005; Wuest, Ford-Gilboe & Merrit-Gray, 2005). In addition, Western health care and social services based on paradigms that privilege the self and self-care may be dissonant with some immigrant women's values and beliefs. The director-general of the WHO (2006) highlighted the "need for a comprehensive health sector response to IMPV that addresses the reluctance of abused women to seek help." However, in order to accomplish this, research-based evidence on how IMPV is perceived, and what shapes the responses of women belonging to various ethno-cultural groups and/ or living in diverse geographical contexts is necessary.

THE STUDY

Study Purpose

Building on the findings of a previous ethnographic qualitative study conducted in the Sri Lankan Tamil community in Toronto (Morrison, Guruge & Snarr, 1999), the overall focus of this study was on understanding the production and perception of post-migration IMPV, and responses to it in the local Sri Lankan Tamil community.[1] Presented in this chapter are the findings related to the perception of IMPV and determinants of women's responses to it.

Community of Interest in the Study

Sri Lanka, formerly known as Ceylon, is a small island located off the southeast coast of the Indian subcontinent. The Sri Lankan population was 18.8 million in 1998 (United Nations, 1999), which included several different ethnic groups. According to the last census that was conducted in 1981, Sinhalese constituted 74 percent of the population, Tamils 18.2 percent, Muslims 7.4 percent, and others 0.4 percent (Government of Sri Lanka, cited in Cheran, 2000). A civil war has gone on for more than 20 years between the Sinhalese government and the Liberation Tigers of Tamil Eelam (LTTE), a Tamil militant/separatist group that has put forward an agenda for full independence and a separate homeland. As a result, approximately 60,000 civilians have died, and thousands of people have disappeared (Cheran, 2000). According to the U.N. Working Group on Disappearances (2001), Sri Lanka has the second largest unidentified disappearances in the world. In addition, close to 1 million people have been internally displaced and many others have sought refuge in other countries, including the U.K., the U.S., Norway, India, Germany, and Canada.

Sri Lankans are considered to be one of the fastest-growing immigrant communities in Canada. For example, in 1999, Sri Lanka was one of the three leading sources of refugees to Canada, representing 10.7 percent of the total population of refugees admitted to Canada. Recent census data also show that Sri Lanka is one of the top 10 sources of new immigrants to Canada (Citizenship and Immigration Canada, 2000a, 2000b, 2007). As is the case with most immigrant communities to Canada, the Sri Lankan Tamil community resettling in Canada has chosen to do so in major cities, including Montreal, Ottawa, Vancouver, Edmonton, and Toronto. According to community leaders, there are over 250,000 Tamils in the Greater Toronto Area (GTA).

Theoretical and Methodological Perspectives

A post-colonial feminist theoretical perspective was chosen to guide the study. "The field of postcolonial feminism arose in response to the gendered legacy of colonialism and to the limitations and the exclusions in Western forms of feminism" (Guruge, 2007, p. 60). In addition, an ecosystemic framework was also used in order to bridge the gap between the individual and (1) the microsystem (the family setting in which the IMPV takes place), (2) mesosystem (the social networks within which the family is located), and (3) macrosystem (the culture and society at large that reinforce various forms of domination to the advantage of some groups and not others).

A qualitative descriptive methodology was chosen for this study in order to come up with an in-depth description of the research topic, and to know the "who, what, and where of events or experiences, or their basic nature and shape" (Sandelowski, 2000, p. 339).

Data Generation and Analysis

Once approved by the University of Toronto Research Ethics Board, a combination of opportunity, snowball, as well as purposive sampling was used to recruit three sets of participants: community leaders (Set 1), women and men from the general community (Set 2), and women who have experienced IMPV (Set 3). The interviews and focus groups were about two hours long and were conducted at a time and place convenient for the participants. The audiotaped interviews and focus group discussions were transcribed verbatim. Each interview and focus group transcript was coded, and similar codes within and across interviews and focus groups were raised to the level of subcategories, which were then compared and contrasted to develop relevant categories (LeCompte & Schensul, 1999; Lofland & Lofland, 1995; Morse & Field, 1985). This research process has been described in detail elsewhere, along with the study's reliability as well as its limitations (see Guruge, 2007).

Study Sample

First, 16 community leaders employed in the health and settlement sectors in the GTA were interviewed (Set 1). This was a diverse group with regard to age (30s to 60s), education (Grade 10 to university), and length of stay in Canada (1.5 to 20 years). Approximately half the group was born in Jaffna, and a similar percentage had engaged in paid employment while in Sri Lanka. Next, focus groups were conducted in Tamil with women (n = 26) and men (n = 15) (Set 2). The number of male participants in focus groups varied from four to six and the number of female participants varied from six to 12. In total, eight sessions were conducted at three geographical locations in the GTA. The focus group participants were diverse with respect to age (24–70 years), education (grade 8 to university), length of marriage (three to 50 years), length of stay in Canada (one to 18 years), and location of residence in the GTA. Most women were in arranged marriages, whereas only approximately half of the male participants were in arranged marriages. Most men and approximately half of the women in focus groups had engaged in paid employment while in Sri Lanka. In addition, I also interviewed six women who had experienced IMPV since arriving in Canada were interviewed (Set 3). At the time of the interviews they were separated from their abusive husbands. This group was diverse in terms of age (20s to 50s), education (grade 8 to university), length of stay in Canada (three to 12 years), and number of children (0 to five children).

STUDY FINDINGS

Perceptions of IMPV

Various Forms of Abuse

During individual interviews and focus group discussions, both women and men spoke about various forms of threat, control, and abuse that some husbands inflicted on their wives. These commonly included physical, verbal, emotional, sexual, and financial abuse. Among these, physical abuse was considered by far the worst form of abuse. Specific examples of physically abusive acts that the participants noted included hitting or beating with fists, belts, or other items, and/or throwing objects at the woman. One of the female participants described her experience of physical abuse as follows:

> One time, I argue little, very little much, not more but he abused, abused many times, beat me in the face, everywhere bodies and everything and next day I had a lot of pain, everywhere it is blue. Everyday maybe, every, every, everyday, one week he abused me, okay. Next day, I can't turn, I can't see, my face is blue, blue. I don't know how to say, many bruise or something (Set 3, I #4).

Others spoke about their experiences or perceptions of verbal abuse. Verbal abuse was defined as swearing, using words that were degrading to women (such as "whore"), or using animal names. One woman said: "He calls me Nai [dog/bitch] and he calls me Vesai [slut] and he calls me these everywhere. I do not want to say these names because in Tamil it sounds worse. He says these things in front of children and my son has also begun to use some of the words" (Set 3, I #2). Some participants observed that women were called these names even in public when husbands were sure that no one present would understand Tamil.

Sexual abuse was also noted by the participants. As is often the case in most communities, sexual abuse was a more reserved topic of discussion. One community leader spoke about a woman who was experiencing sexual abuse:

> It is a big agony, you know, the sexual harassment. You don't want to have sex with somebody who is really harassing you sexually. He could be my husband, but I don't want to sleep with him. It is like sleeping with the enemy for the woman, which the relatives … she can't explain to them and they don't understand and … such cases are there. (Set 1, I #6)

Women often discussed sexual abuse with others only after the other forms of abuse were disclosed and their responses to other forms of IMPV were evaluated.

Several participants felt that the emotional abuse they endured was far worse than any physical abuse they experienced. The following excerpts indicate a number of examples of emotional abuse some participants described:

> Once in a while he wouldn't talk to me for one week. He would be very silent. I wouldn't know what I did wrong to make him mad … to not talk with me. I hope and pray that he would talk to me again soon. There were things like this. (Set 3, I #5)

> My husband after work would go to his mother's place. He would come home very late in the night to sleep. He was doing this for a while. So when I ask, [he would] say all these nasty things. He would say, "Oh, why you care if I go there and come? I went to see my mother, why are you getting mad? You cook, take care of your child, be home." And he wouldn't even help me to do the shopping and everything, even in the winter. I was kind of low and desperate for help. Mentally I couldn't go through this anymore. I was born as a Hindu. Through these experiences, then I thought where is God. 'Cause I was very honest, very honest. And I was thinking, you know, I didn't do any harm, why do I have to suffer? Where is God in all these things? (Set 3, I #6)

The emotional and psychological abuses that participants identified included: (1) preventing women from speaking with their family members; (2) giving the women the silent treatment; (3) destroying women's belongings and favourite items; (4) threatening to hurt the women or the children; (5) threatening to shame the women and their families with photos or letters; and (6) threatening to send the women back to Sri Lanka.

Financial abuse was also a concern for a number of women in the post-migration context. With this abuse, the husbands prevented their wives from spending any money for activities of which they disapproved. The impact of financial abuse was perceived to be more severe for those who had no family and friends in Canada, or for women who spoke no or limited English. The following excerpts capture the concerns a number of participants raised regarding financial abuse:

> I always take my kids to doctor. He gave to me only bus tickets, up and down, two tickets, no money. One time I ask to him, "Please give me $2 or $1 sometimes I

like ... not I like, sometimes I need to drink some juice or something." "No, no, no, you don't drink anything outside the home, you come back and drink juice. Why do you need for the money?" No. Sometimes [I ask for] 25¢ for urgent [situations], I want to phone ... okay, please. Nothing, only two bus tickets, only two, up and down. (Set 3, I #4)

I know a family ... the wife goes to work ... she brings the paycheque ... and the husband buys her 10 tickets every week and gives her the 10 tickets and that's all ... no pocket money ... once in a while one or two dollars ... and she earns about $1,800 a month. (Set 1, I #5)

Financial abuse was experienced by women in different circumstances: women who were unable or not allowed to engage in paid labour, those who received social assistance, and those who engaged in paid labour. Women who arrived in Canada hoping to support their own family members back in Sri Lanka were perceived to suffer even more when they were not allowed to do so (while the husband supported his own extended family back home).

In addition to the IMPV noted above, some participants discussed how husbands strategized to isolate women from others, and the impact of such isolation. The following quotes from two women who were in abusive relationships support this perception:

I didn't have any of my family, but he started isolating me from his family. Because whenever there is a function or things like that, he will bring up a fight, or he would just dress up and go and tell them that I am sick, or he will say something nasty about me. So they got nothing to do with me; that is his way of preventing me from them. (Set 3, I #5)

Five years I spent my time in home-jail, home-jail! Home was like a jail, I didn't go outside, always sitting in my home. Umh, sometimes he took the phone too at work. [He took the phone?] Yeah. The phone receiver, he took. (Set 3, I #3)

Some women were not allowed to gain further education or attend ESL classes. Others were placed under control and threatened even before the couples were married. For example, one woman (Set 3, I #6) spoke about how her future husband started threatening to inform her parents and neighbours in Sri Lanka about their love affair if she were to break up with him. To avoid shame to herself and her family, she remained in the relationship and eventually married him.

Often women experienced multiple forms of abuse. Some women experienced abuse from their husband as well as his family members. A number of participants spoke about women's experiences of abuse instigated or partaken in by their mothers-in-law because of dowry concerns. While abuse related to dowry also occurred in Sri Lanka, the post-migration financial situation is a major stress for many Tamils as a result of the pre-migration financial losses due to civil war and the cost of "illegal" travel they were forced to undertake,[2] as well as the employment situation in Canada (which is addressed later in this chapter).

Shame is often associated with being abused, and in the current study, Tamil women were concerned about the embarrassment, shame, and stigma attached to IMPV. Participants noted that a woman often considered leaving her husband only as the last resort for extreme forms of physical or sexual abuse, or if abuse occurred frequently or over a long period of time, or if there was a threat to her life or her children's lives. Furthermore, a "slap here and there" was not considered abuse. This perception is evident in the following quote from a woman participant in a focus group: "It is not like he is abusing her every day" (set 2). A number of women in the current study who had experienced IMPV initially felt that abuse was the result of a situation that had gotten out of hand and that it would stop after a particular crisis was over. The women were also hopeful that a change in their behaviour would stop or lessen their husbands' anger and frustration. The perception of abuse being temporary, as pointed out by many participants, was also related to the fact that in almost all cases they knew, IMPV began only after the couple immigrated to Canada.

The Conditions under Which IMPV Was Perceived as Justified

Both female and male participants in this study spoke about the general community belief in male dominance within the marital institution. They also spoke about a general perception in the community that sometimes it was necessary for the husband to discipline his wife if the woman deserved it or needed to be kept on track, or if it was used to prevent further and bigger family problems. A husband's disciplining his wife was perceived as acceptable when there is avoidance of household work, extramarital affairs are detected or suspected, the husband's "right to have sex" is refused, and the wife talks back or gives her husband a difficult time or asks for things at inappropriate times. Some of these ideas are captured in the following excerpts:

> When the husband comes back from work, he expects his wife to be very active and doing things and taking care of him. Whereas she sits in the corner and

mentally down, and maybe crying or watching TV or eating more … or staring at the wall or all sort of compensatory things she is doing when she must be doing things, and this leads to abuse. (Set 1, I #6)

For example, my father would say you can't beat your wife. He would put a stop to that, but for him, if a married woman is having an affair that is too much. In that case domestic violence would not be seen as that bad. Because then he [husband] has to, as a man, do something about it. (Set 1, I #8)

Ultimately the reasons and the conditions under which IMPV was perceived justified were very much shaped by the patriarchal notion of what constitutes a "good" woman/wife/mother, the unequal distribution of power at home, as well as the notion of a husband's authority. While both men and women subscribed to the ideas, overall these justifications were perceived to be held more strongly by men than women.

Determinants of Women's Responses to Abusive Situations in the Post-migration Context

Patriarchal Beliefs about a "Good Wife"
One of the factors that shaped women's responses to IMPV was related to patriarchal beliefs regarding the role of a good wife. Girls and young women are raised under the protection of their fathers and brothers, and are expected to be virgins at the time of marriage. While ideas about marriage and love are changing in the Tamil community, arranged marriage is still a common practice. These beliefs and practices place an enormous burden on the women to remain in and preserve their marriage at all costs. For example, one community leader spoke about the pressure for young women to remain virgins until they marry, which creates further pressure for them to get married if they have gone out with a man:

Her mother and father were pushing the girl to marry this boy because she was already going out with him. They were very upset because he was part of a gang or whatever … so the parents didn't want her to have anything to do with him, but she was adamant about going out with him, so they wanted her to marry him and at least register, you know. This is the problem in our community; they want the security. He started abusing her as soon as they got married. (Set 1, I #15)

Once married, the women felt pressured to remain in the marriage because of the general belief in the community about the ideal of one marriage for life. The impact of these pressures was felt more so by the women than the men since, as in many other communities, in the Tamil community, a married woman holds a higher social status than that accorded to a divorced, separated, widowed, or single woman. Leaving one's husband was also perceived to lead to both social isolation and gossip in the community about a woman's behaviour and her character.

Perceptions about a "Good Mother" and Children's Well-being

The ideal of a good mother meant that a woman's own needs were secondary to that of her children. Their children's safety and comfort were often the determining factors in many women's decision-making dilemmas. Supporting children on one person's income or the woman going on social assistance following separation was seen as depriving the children of comfort. Further, there appeared to be a perception that a husband was abusive only to the woman, the abuse was hidden from children, and that children did not experience any negative consequences of their father's violence toward their mother. The following quote supports this idea:

> She thinks if she decides to walk away from the relationship, then she is depriving the children. Maybe she doesn't know how to drive, maybe she does. Maybe she cannot provide enough for the children. Maybe the man is abusive only to her and not to the children, and he is very loving and concerned with them. So there is a difficulty in choices. (Set 1, I #9)

Women often agreed with the general community perception that it was important to have a strong presence and influence of the father in children's lives. Interestingly, four of the five woman participants with children noted that their children (all under the age of 10) were the strongest supporters of their decision to leave the abusive husbands. However, the adult children of a woman participant blamed her for leaving their father, and they and their father subjected her to ongoing harassment. It is possible that the latter response is related to the perception that a woman's decision to leave her husband can affect her children's future marriage opportunities within the community (which can be a more immediate concern for adult children).

Extended Family's Needs and Expectations of the Woman

The situation within which most Tamils leave Sri Lanka also influenced whether or not a woman would remain with her abusive husband. Because of the ongoing civil war, returning to Sri Lanka to one's parents was not readily considered an option. Further, as noted earlier, the Tamils who remained in Sri Lanka often were dependent on their family members in various diasporic communities for financial support and (family) sponsorship. In addition, because of the way the Canadian immigration system is set up, the women's actions—such as going on welfare, or being unemployed, or filing charges against the husband—could negatively affect the women's (and also the men's) chances of sponsoring relatives. One participant captured some of these concerns in the following manner:

> If she's sponsored by her husband and she walks away from him, and has to go on social assistance, as long as she's on social assistance, she cannot sponsor anyone from home. But if she—if she sponsored a man from outside, and he abuses her, and if he goes on social assistance, then there is no way she can sponsor anybody. (Set 1, I # 16)

Changes in the Husband's Professional and Socio-economic Status

The findings of this study indicated that many Tamils experienced a number of negative consequences as a result of migrating to a country in the West such as Canada. The problems with under-/unemployment, lack of credentials, deskilling, linguistic barriers, housing, and racism, in addition to the social and geographical adjustments they needed to make, created significant stress for them. In particular, some Tamil men who (owing to unemployment or underemployment they faced in Canada) lost their social status both at home and in the community had to deal with depression, anxiety, anger, and aggression, at times by turning to alcohol to cope with the situation. Some women were sympathetic to their husbands' underachievement in the "promised land" because of systemic barriers, and tended to rethink their responses to family conflicts and IMPV and remained in the relationship. Interestingly, none of the six woman participants who had left their abusive husbands considered the abuse to be the result of larger systemic issues; rather, the abuse was attributed to the husband's individual shortcomings or family issues.

The Women's Financial Situation

The women's economic positioning in Canada shaped their responses to IMPV in a number of ways. First, they were often able to acquire only low-status and low-paying jobs, with limited or no benefits or long-term employment security. Second, many women with limited education or lack of opportunity to learn English because of the ongoing civil war in Sri Lanka often engaged in paid employment within their community. These employers might not feel comfortable about continuing to employ the women (if they were to leave their husbands) for fear of offending their husbands. Third, the women who were responsible for financially supporting their family members still living in Sri Lanka could not do so with low income and minimal job security, or being on social assistance. Fourth, in some cases, women were told that in order to obtain government financial support, they must first obtain child support from their husbands. Fifth, as a number of participants noted, women were also concerned about the government's intrusions into the lives of those who go on social assistance. All the scenarios negatively affected women's responses to IMPV.

Isolation, Unfamiliarity, and Uncertainty That Women Experienced in the New Context

Canada was an unfamiliar space and place to many new immigrants, especially for women who did not speak English or French. Those who had their own family members and friends in the GTA found the process of getting to know the space and place much easier. Others were dependent on their husbands to become familiar with the city or to build social networks. Those who were purposely isolated by their husbands had no means to get around, become familiarized with the new city, or find the available services and supports. A community leader described the unfamiliarity some women experienced in Canada: "Maybe the woman has language issues, problems, because if she is a woman who has contacts outside, who's going outside, and being able to talk to someone … they will know about the services. Other women don't know. They have no way to know who does what and what helps" (Set 1, I #6).

It was difficult for women to deal with or to escape an abusive husband if they were not familiar with the public transportation system, unable to speak English fluently, did not have the ability to call someone without their husband's supervision, or were unaware of how to access various health and settlement support services. Some participants acknowledged that although in Sri Lanka some women did not receive social support, the women still knew where to go, who to contact, and what to do because they were familiar with the space and place. Because of the isolation, uncertainty, and unfamiliarity in the new context, women were, at times, hesitant to get away from the abuser.

Formal Supports and Services

One of the main factors that both positively and negatively affected women's responses to IMPV was the availability of and access to formal social supports. The participants believed that more formal social supports and services were available in Canada than in Sri Lanka, which included counsellors, agencies serving immigrants, shelters, and reduced-rent housing. The kinds of formal social supports women sought included the following: (1) advice about managing their immediate concerns regarding day-to-day living; (2) ideas about securing their safety at home; (3) advice regarding the impact of their decision on immigration-related matters; (4) emotional support; (5) information regarding potential sources of income and other support; and (6) information needed to access health care and shelters.

However, participants also noted that women were often unaware of the services because information was not readily available to them. Even if they were aware of such services, a number of limitations prevented women from using them. These limitations were described as pertaining to acceptability, appropriateness, portability, non-seamlessness, confidentiality, and racism and othering (which are addressed in detail elsewhere—see, for example, Guruge, 2007). Participants also spoke about the fear that women have in accessing certain services because of the criminalization of abuse, mandatory reporting, the potential for loss of their children because of racist assumptions of some service providers regarding immigrant women and their husbands, as well as the potential for deportation of themselves, their husbands, and their children back to Sri Lanka if the women sought help.

Despite the many barriers they encountered, the woman participants felt grateful for the kinds of services that are available in the post-migration and settlement context. One woman stated that she would have been dead if she was in an abusive relationship in Sri Lanka because there she would receive no support.

New Opportunities in the Post-migration Context

Regardless of the many health, social, and economic consequences of IMPV identified in the literature and the related difficulties women faced in dealing with IMPV and its aftermath, the women who participated in this study demonstrated remarkable resilience in coping with their situations in a manner that was suitable for them, their children, and, sometimes, their extended families. Women gained courage from the new possibilities in a new setting like Toronto. Several women spoke about having only non-Tamil friends and neighbours and avoiding geographical areas with more Tamils to avoid negative responses from the community toward themselves and their children. A woman stated: "Even if our community asks, I can say, 'I am in Canada and I live the way I want to live'" (Set 3, I #5). Yet at the same time, they also spoke very highly of the many female and male Tamil community leaders who actively addressed the issue of IMPV and supported women's decisions to leave their abusive husbands.

Regardless of the many health, social, and economic consequences of IMPV identified in the literature and the related difficulties women might face in dealing effectively with abusive situations, the women who participated in this study demonstrated remarkable resilience in coping with their situations in a manner that was suitable for them, their children, and, sometimes, their extended families.

DISCUSSION AND CONCLUSION

Participants of this study defined IMPV broadly and identified various forms of abuse including physical, psychological, sexual, and financial abuse, along with other forms of threats (such as threats to shame the woman's family) and control through social isolation. Similar findings were reported by Hyman et al. (2006), who examined the topic within the same ethnic community. In eight focus groups with single and married Tamil women of diverse ages, women spoke about various forms of abuse such as physical, sexual, emotional, psychological, and financial abuse. Hyman et al. (2006) further found minor differences between groups in the definitions of abuse. For example, while young women focused more on emotional abuse (such as control and insults about clothing, hair, and other aspects of appearance), middle-aged and older women frequently noted accusations of marital infidelity, jealousy, and mistrust as a form of IMPV. No other studies have examined the perception of IMPV within the Tamil community in the post-migration context in Canada. Available literature about IMPV in Sri Lanka (e.g., Gunaratne, 2002; Hussein, 1999; Samarasinghe, 1991; Wijayatilake, 2003) reports various forms of IMPV, even though in general the societal focus appears to be more on physical abuse. Although some research has reported cultural differences in the identification or recognition of IMPV (Mehrotra, 1999; Senturia et al., 2000), the current study's findings along with Hyman et al.'s (2006) showed that definitions of IMPV were not culturally specific.

Also, the reasons or the conditions under which IMPV is justified in the Sri Lankan Tamil community are not unique to the community. In a number of studies on IMPV in Sri Lanka (Samarasinghe, 1991; Gunaratne, 2002; Wijayatilake, 2003; Hussein, 1999), Tamil and Sinhalese participants identified a range explanations and/or justifications for the occurrence of IMPV, including infidelity, alleged misbehaviour by the women, a husband's suspicion of his wife having an extramarital relationship, and women's personality. These studies also suggest that in Sri Lanks women often lived with the abuse. However, Wijayatilake (2003) in particular has reported a number of other responses, including: seeking immediate safety, crying, hitting back, hiding, going to their mothers' houses, considering suicide, and informing the police. Women often obtained primary support from their mothers while other immediate and extended family members have also helped by giving advice, offering shelter, giving food, and assaulting the abuser.

In the post-migration context, deterrents to seeking help for and disclosing IMPV in the Tamil community were found in this study to pertain to a number of factors, including an initial belief that the abuse might stop, and the embarrassment, shame, and humiliation about the abusive experience as well as fear and stigma of separation and/or divorce. Morrison et al. (1999) also noted similar findings in their study in the Tamil community. However, a considerable amount of literature suggests that these reasons are common among women regardless of their ethno-cultural or socio-economic backgrounds. A group of American Muslim women in Hassouneh-Phillips's (2001) study reported their concerns about the stigma associated with divorce and abuse. Several other studies (such as Cohen & Savaya, 1997; Haj-Yahia, 2000) conducted in Arab and Muslim communities also identified the social stigma associated with divorce as a significant barrier to ending an abusive relationship.

Other determinants of women's responses to abuse included a number of meso- and macro-level factors, some of which included gender role socialization; family and community pressures to uphold the ideal notion of a good woman and wife; the belief in the institution of marriage; the ideal of one marriage for life; and the differences in social status between a married, divorced, or separated woman. The loss of or limited informal social support post-migration also affected negatively the decisions made by the women dealing with IMPV. Similar reasons for not leaving an abusive partner were noted in a number of other studies (Loring & Smith, 1994; Mazza, Dennerstein & Ryan, 1996; McCauley, Yurk, Jenckes & Ford, 1998; Rodriguez, Bauer, McLoughlin & Grumbach, 1999). Tamil women were also concerned about the rumours and false accusations about divorced or separated women. Similar concerns were noted in a number of other studies (see for example, Hassouneh-Phillips, 2001 and Haj-Yahia, 2000) with American Muslim women and Arab women, respectively. In these studies, participants reported fear of rumors and/or false accusations that significantly and negatively influenced family and community support for women.

One of the major determinants of women's responses to IMPV was related to their children's well-being, both immediate and long-term. The responses were shaped by the general community beliefs that children need both parents, that the man is abusive only toward his wife, that abuse is hidden from children, and that the woman's concerns were secondary to her children's comfort and their future marriage potential. The importance of children in shaping women's response to an abusive relationship was also observed in Hyman et al.'s (2006) study in the Tamil community. The role that children's welfare plays in women's responses to IMPV both in terms of remaining in the abusive relationship, as well as leaving the abuser, has been discussed extensively in the literature.

Another key determinant of Tamil women's decisions about whether to leave an abusive husband was their financial situation, and that of their children and extended families. Economic dependency has been noted in the literature as a major deterrent for women to leave an abusive husband (Browne, 1987; Websdale, 1998). However, how women's concerns regarding their husband's loss of professional and socioeconomic status shaped the women's responses to IMPV has not received attention.

The ongoing civil war was noted in the current study as a key concern and it is related to women's safety if they were to return to Sri Lanka, as well as to the sponsorship opportunities for, and financial welfare of, their extended families still in Sri Lanka. Concerns regarding how women's responses to IMPV are shaped by an ongoing war in their country of origin have not received much attention in the literature.

The findings of the current study highlighted a number of limitations in the formal social supports and services for Tamil women. Some of the limitations were related to the lack of information about the available services as well as their lack of culturally and linguistic appropriateness, and racism inherent in some of the services. Participants noted the negative impact of the criminalization of abuse on women's decisions. Similar concerns were identified in a number of other studies. Residency or immigration status was found to be a major concern for many women attempting to deal with IMPV in Canada (Fong, 2000; McDonald, 2000). Based on a number of studies (Abraham, 1999, 2000; Dasgupta, 1998), Dasgupta (2000) noted that "South Asian women's experiences of abuse are inextricably linked to their residency status in the U.S. [and that] the immigration policies of the U.S. have been universally biased against women and they have been playing a powerful, if unintended role in the battered immigrant women's lives" (p. 178). Concerns were also noted in other studies regarding women's fears about potential pressure to leave the relationship (Rodriguez, Craig, Mooney & Bauer, 1998), as well as the possibility of mandatory police reporting, which could harm their partner or lead to loss of custody of their children (Gerbert et al., 1996; Rodriguez et al., 1999). In the current study, the Tamil women's (or their friends') prior experiences of racism at the hands of various authorities, such as police and immigration officers, prevented them from calling the police. Richie's (2000) and Websdale's (1999) studies similarly indicated that women believed that, in general, those who are part of the criminal justice system have racist, stereotypical ideas about Blacks as being violent; therefore, the potential for extreme or unfair treatment of their husbands was a key concern for racialized women. Suspicions of people in authority in the context of the civil war in Sri Lanka has created even more heightened sensitivity for Tamil women regarding authorities, and a determinant to seeking help.

This chapter drew on data and findings from a doctoral study on the particular aspects within one immigrant community. The findings of this study demonstrated that contrary to the popular belief that immigrant women, in general, do not understand or accurately perceive different forms of IMPV, the participants identified and spoke about diverse forms of abuse they perceived as occurring in the community in the post-migration context. What is important is also the notion that men (and women, to a lesser degree) perceived that IMPV was justified under certain conditions. A woman's response was often based on the careful evaluation of benefits and risks, not only to herself and her children, but also to her other family members; of particular note is the vulnerability some women experienced because of the intersectionality of their gender, race, class, and ethnicity in the post-migration context in Canada as well as in the pre-migration context in Sri Lanka. Further studies exploring the topic are needed to understand to what extent these perceptions are prevalent, and the best ways to address these perceptions at the individual, community, and societal levels. Knowing more about the ways in which IMPV is expressed and perceived helps to enhance the capacity of communities and society at large to respond to IMPV, and to develop culturally, linguistically, and contextually appropriate interventions and programs.

Notes

CHAPTER 2

1. The coroner's report made recommendations in the areas of justice, social services, and education; training and prevention programs; coordination of services and shared information; and research, analysis, and reporting. Some of the key recommendations in these areas included audits of police services' responses to domestic violence; training for Crown attorneys in dealing with domestic violence cases; more extensive opening hours for courts to conduct bail hearings; more funding for both subsidized and second-stage housing; income support for women who leave abusive situations; more funding for community-based services for not only women and children, but men as well; money for education, training, and prevention programs, as well as public education campaigns; the coordination of shared services and information between community groups and the government; as well as research, analysis, and reporting of services and laws and their effectiveness (Chief Coroner, 2002).

2. To see more examples of Zero Tolerance Campaign materials, visit their website at http://www.zerotolerance.org.uk/

3. In August 2005, the website of the Ontario Women's Directorate stated that while the campaign's promotional materials are currently under development, the "campaign [will be] designed to reduce violence against women by promoting healthy, equal relationships between boys and girls at an early age" (see www.gov.on.ca/citizenship/owd/english/dvap/dvap_video.htm).

CHAPTER 8

1. This project was funded by the Canadian Institutes of Health Research—Institute of Gender and Health. We would also like to acknowledge the support of the Ethiopian Association in Toronto.

CHAPTER 11

1. The term "Black immigrant women" refers to all women who are born in Canada, but are of Caribbean, African, and Asian descent, as well as those who came to Canada from Caribbean, African, and Asian countries (Agnew, 1998).

2. For a full discussion of the humanitarian and compassionate grounds principles, see Sheppard (2002, pp. 13–20).

3. For a better understanding of women's roles in Nigeria, see Isiugo-Abanihe and Oyediran (2003) and Ogundipe (1994, p. 175).

4. Female circumcision/genital mutilation is a cultural practice performed on women in the belief that it prevents women from promiscuity. It is also a sign of initiation into womanhood. Parents socialize their young girls into accepting female genital mutilation as the norm so that the girl child will be able to get married. This practice is a term applied to the non-medical cutting away of part, or all, of a female's clitoris. The procedure not only involves removing the clitoris and external genitalia, but also sewing the raw edges of outer vaginal lips together with thread, leaving a tiny opening for menstruation. This practice is medically, psychologically, and emotionally harmful to women (Ibekwe, 2002).

5. These findings are derived from my personal experience of Nigerian culture and marriage system. There have been lots of changes in the cultural recognition of polygamy as a result of modernization.

6. See Okafor-Omali (1969), and Isiugo-Abanihe (1994) for a detailed discussion of the payment of bride wealth in Nigerian society.

7. Canadian laws provide for joint parental custody rights to children. If custody is disputed, the court is to decide custody based on the best interests of the children, taking into consideration such factors as the lifestyle and income level of each parent.

CHAPTER 12

1. There is no evidence to suggest that there is a higher prevalence of IMPV in this community than in any other immigrant community.

2. Tamils are unable to file a refugee claim in another country while still living in Sri Lanka and, because of the country's situation, it is not easy to obtain a visa to travel to other countries. Even when a family member is already living in a country like Canada, the backlogs delaying sponsorships, as well as difficulties obtaining required documents such as police clearances (when complete villages in Sri Lanka have been destroyed) delay family reunification. Therefore, many Tamils have sought the assistance of "agents," who have used means that involved breaking international travel regulations to take payees to another country. According to the study participants, the cost of such travel arrangements varied between $15,000 and $60,000 per person.

References

CHAPTER 1

Allard, S.A. (2005). Rethinking battered woman syndrome: A Black feminist perspective. In N.J. Sokoloff & C. Pratt (Eds.), *Domestic violence at the margins: Readings on race, class, gender, and culture* (pp. 194–205). New Brunswick, New Jersey: Rutgers University Press.

Allen, C.M. & Straus, M.A. (1980). Resources, power, and husband-wife violence. In M.A. Straus & G.T. Hotaling (Eds.), *The social causes of husband-wife violence* (pp. 188–208). Minneapolis: University of Minnesota Press.

Armstrong, L. (1983). *The home front: Notes from the family war zone.* New York: McGraw-Hall Book Company.

Avakame, E.F. (2001). Differential police treatment of male-on-female spousal violence. *Violence against Women, 7*(1), 22–46.

Backhouse, C. (1991). *Petticoats and prejudice: Women and law in nineteenth-century Canada.* Toronto: Women's Press.

Bandura, A. (1971). *Social learning theory.* New York: General Learning Press.

Bandura, A. (1973). *Aggression: A social learning analysis.* Englewood Cliffs, New Jersey: Prentice-Hall.

Basch, N. (1982). *In the eyes of the law: Women, marriage, and property in nineteenth-century New York.* Ithaca: Cornell University Press.

Bersani, C. & Chen, H.T. (1988). Sociological perspectives in family violence. In V. Van Hasselt, R. Morrison & A. Bellack (Eds.), *Handbook of family violence* (pp. 57–88). New York: Plenum Press.

Bloode, R.O. & Wolfe, D.M. (1960). *Husbands and wives: The dynamics of married living.* New York: Free Press.

Bograd, M. (1984). Family systems approaches to wife battering: A feminist critique. *American Journal of Orthopsychiatry, 54*(4), 558–568.

Bowker, L.H. (1993). A battered woman's problems are social, not psychological. In R.J. Gelles & D.R. Loseke (Eds.), *Current controversies on family violence.* Newbury Park: Sage Publications.

Browne, A. (1987). *Battered women who kill*. New York: Free Press.

Buckley, T. (1992). "Placed in the power of violence": The divorce petition of Evelina Gregory Roane, 1824. *The Virginia Magazine of History and Biography*, 100(1), 29–78.

Buckley, W. (1967). *Sociology and modern systems theory*. Englewood Cliffs: Prentice-Hall.

Buzawa, E.S. & Buzawa, C.G. (1990). *Domestic violence: The criminal justice response*. Newbury Park: Sage Publications.

Caplan, P.J. (1985). *The myth of women's masochism*. New York: New American Library.

Chapman, T. (1985). Women, sex, and marriage in Western Canada 1890–1920. *Alberta History*, 33(4), 1–12.

Chapman, T. (1988). Til death do us part: Wife beating in Alberta, 1905–1920. *Alberta History*, 36(4), 13–22.

Comack, E. (1993). *Feminist engagement with the law: The legal recognition of the battered woman syndrome*. Ottawa: CRIAW.

Cowan, L. (1982). *Masochism: A Jungian view*. Ann Arbor: Spring Publications Inc.

Dobash, E.R. & Dobash, R. (1978). Wives: The "appropriate" victims of marital violence. *Victimology*, 2(3–4), 426–442.

Dobash, E.R. & Dobash, R. (1979). *Violence against wives: A case against the patriarchy*. New York: The Free Press.

Dobash, E.R. & Dobash, R. (1992). *Women, violence, and social change*. London: Routledge.

Dutton, D. (1995). *The domestic assault of women: Psychological and criminal justice perspective*. Vancouver: UBC Press.

Dutton, D. (2007). *Rethinking domestic violence*. Vancouver: UBC Press.

Finkelhor, D. (1983). Common features of family abuse. In D. Finkelhor, R. Gelles, G. Hotaling & M. Straus (Eds.), *The dark side of families: Current family violence research* (pp. 17–28). Newbury Park: Sage Publications.

Gelles, R. (1979). *Family violence*. Beverly Hills: Sage Publications.

Gelles, R. (1996). Constraints against family violence: How well do they work? In E.S. Buzawa & C.G. Buzawa (Eds.), *Do arrests and restraining orders work?* (pp. 30–42). Thousand Oaks: Sage Publications.

Gelles, R. (1997). *Intimate violence in families*. Thousand Oaks: Sage Publications.

Gelles, R.J. (1974). *The violent home: A study of physical aggression between husbands and wives*. Beverly Hills: Sage Publications.

Gelles, R.J. (1985). *Intimate violence in families*. Beverly Hills: Sage Publications.

Gelles, R.J. (1993). Through a sociological lens: Social structure and family violence. In R.J. Loseke & D.R. Loseke (Eds.), *Current controversies on family violence* (pp. 31–46). Newbury Park: Sage Publications.

Gelles, R.J. & Straus, M. (1988). *Intimate violence: The causes and consequences of abuse in the American family.* New York: Simon & Schuster Publishing Company.

Giles-Sims, J. (1983). *Wife-battering: A systems theory approach.* New York: Guilford.

Glick, R.A. & Meyers, D.I. (1987). *Masochism: Current psychoanalytic perspectives.* Hillsdale: The Analytic Press.

Gondolf, E.W. & Fisher, E.R. (1988). *Battered women as survivors: An alternative to treating learned helplessness.* Lexington: Lexington Books.

Goode, W. (1971). Force and violence in the family. *Journal of Marriage and the Family, 33,* 624–636.

Goodman, L., Dutton, M.A., Vankos, N. & Weinfurt, K. (2005). Women's resources and use of strategies as risk and protective factor for reabuse over time. *Violence against Women, 11*(3), 311–336.

Gordon, L. (1988). *Heroes of their own times: The politics and history of family violence: Boston 1880–1960.* Boston: Penguin Books.

Greene, B. (1990). What has gone before: The legacy of racism and sexism in the lives of Black mothers and daughters. In L.S. Brown & M.P.P. Root (Eds.), *Diversity and complexity in feminist therapy* (pp. 207–230). New York: Haworth Press.

Hagg, P. (1991/92). The "ill-use of a wife:" Patterns of working-class violence in domestic and public New York City, 1860–1880. *Journal of Social History, 25,* 447–477.

Hammerton, A.J. (1992). *Cruelty and companionship: Conflict in nineteenth-century married life.* New York: Routledge.

Hartmann, H. (1981). The unhappy marriage of Marxism and feminism: Towards a more progressive union. In L. Sargent (Ed.), *Women and revolution: A debate of class and patriarchy* (pp. 1–4). London: Pluto Press.

Harvey, K. (1990). To love, honour, and obey: Wife-battering in working-class Montreal, 1869–79. *Urban History Review, 19*(2), 128–140.

Harvey, K. (1991). Amazons and victims: Revisiting wife-abuse in working-class Montreal, 1869–1879. *Journal of the Canadian Historical Association, 2,* 131–148.

Hines, D.A. & Malley, K. (2005). *Family violence in the United States: Defining, understanding, and combating abuse.* Thousand Oaks: Sage Publications.

Hoff, L.A. (1990). *Battered women as survivors.* London: Routledge.

hooks, b. (1984). *Feminist theory: From margin to center.* Boston: South End Press.

Hotaling, G. & Sugarman, D. (1986). An analysis of risk markers in husband to wife violence: The current state of knowledge. *Violence and Victims, 1*(2), 101–124.

Itzin, C. (2000). Gendering domestic violence: The influence of feminism on policy and practice. In J. Hanmer & C. Itzen (Eds.), *Home truths about domestic violence* (pp. 356–380). New York: Routledge.

Jasinski, J.L., Asdigian, N.L. & Kaufman-Kantor, G. (1997). Ethnic adaptations to occupational strain: Work-related stress, drinking, and wife assault among Anglo and Hispanic husbands. *Journal of Interpersonal Violence,* 12(6), 814–831.

Lamb, S. (1996). *The trouble with blame: Victims, perpetrators, and responsibility.* Cambridge: Harvard University Press.

MacKinnon, C. (1990). *Towards the feminist theory of the state.* Cambridge: Harvard University Press.

MacLeod, L. (1980). *Wife battering in Canada: The vicious circle.* Ottawa: CACSW.

MacLeod, L. & Shin, M. (1990). *Isolated, afraid, and forgotten: The service delivery needs and realities of immigrant and refugee women who are battered.* Ottawa: The National Clearinghouse on Family Violence.

Margolin, G., Sibner, L. & Gleberman, L. (1988). Wife battering. In V.V. Hasselt, R. Morrison & A. Bellack (Eds.), *Handbook of family violence* (pp. 89–177). New York: Plenum Press.

Martin, D. (1976). *Battered wives.* San Francisco: Glide Publications.

May, M. (1978). Violence in the family: An historical perspective. In J.P. Martin (Ed.), *Violence and the family* (pp. 135–168). Chichester: John Wiley & Sons.

Mihalic, S.W., & Elliott, D. (1997). A social learning theory model of marital violence. *Journal of Family Violence,* 12(1), 21–47.

Miller, N. & Dollard, J. (1941). *Social learning and imitation.* New Haven: Yale University Press.

Miller, S.L. (2001). The paradox of women arrested for domestic violence: Criminal justice professionals and service providers respond. *Violence against Women,* 7(12), 1339–1376.

Momsen, J.H. (2006). Women, men, and fieldwork: Gender relations and power struggles. In V. Desai & R. Potter (Eds.), *Doing development research* (pp. 44–51) London: Sage Publications.

Myers-Avis, J. (1988). Deepening awareness: A private study guide to feminism and family therapy. In L. Braverman (Ed.), *A guide to feminist family therapy* (pp. 15–46). New York: Harrington Park Press.

Neidig, P., Friedman, D. & Collins, B. (1986). Attitudinal characteristics of males who have engaged in spouse abuse. *Journal of Family Violence,* 1, 223–233.

Pagelow, M.D. (1981). *Woman-battering: Victims and their experiences.* Beverly Hills: Sage Publications.

Pagelow, M.D. (1984). *Family violence*. New York: Praeger Publishers.

Perkin, J. (1989). *Women and marriage in nineteenth-century England*. London: Routledge.

Peterson, D. (1992). Wife beating: An American tradition. *Journal of Interdisciplinary History*, 23(1), 97–118.

Pleck, E. (1987). *Domestic tyranny: The making of social policy against family violence from colonial times to the present*. New York: Oxford University Press.

Pressman, B., Cameron, G. & Rothery, M. (1989). *Intervening with assaulted women: Current theory, research, and practice*. Hillsdale, New Jersey: Lawrence Erlbaum Associations, Publishers.

Rajah, V., Frye, V. & Haviland, M. (2006). Aren't I a victim? *Violence against Women*, 12(10), 897–916.

Renzetti, C.M. (1992). *Violent betrayal: Partner abuse in lesbian relationships*. Newbury Park: Sage Publications.

Roy, M. (1977). *Battered women: A psychological study of domestic violence*. New York: Van Nostrand Reinhold Company.

Russell, D.E.H. (1990). *Rape in marriage*. Bloomington: Indiana University Press.

Russell, D.E.H. (1993). *Making violence sexy: Feminist views on pornography*. New York: Teachers College, Columbia University Press.

Schmidt, J.D. & Sherman, L.W. (1996). Does arrest deter domestic violence? In E.S. Buzawa & C.G. Buzawa (Eds.), *Do arrests and restraining orders work?* (pp. 43–53). Thousand Oaks: Sage Publications.

Seligman, M.P. (1975). *Helplessness: On depression, development, and death*. San Francisco: W.H. Freeman.

Shainess, N. (1977). Psychological aspects of wife-battering. In M. Roy (Ed.), *Battered women: A psychological study of domestic violence* (pp. 111–119). New York: Van Nostrand Reinhold Company.

Skafran, L.H. (1990). Overwhelming evidence: Report on gender bias in the courts. *Trial*, 26, 28–35.

Snell, J., Rosenwald, R. & Robey, A. (1964). The wifebeater's wife. *Archives of General Psychiatry*, 11(August), 107–112.

Snider, L. (1991). The potential of the criminal justice system to promote feminist concerns. In E. Comack & S. Brickey (Eds.), *The social basis of law: Critical readings in the sociology of law* (pp. 238–260). Halifax: Garamond Press.

Stanko, E.A. (1985). *Intimate intrusions: Women's experience of male violence*. New York: Routledge & Kegan Paul.

Stanko, E.A. (1993). Ordinary fear: Women, violence, and personal safety. In P.B. Bart & P.G. Moran (Eds.), *Violence against women: The bloody footprints* (pp. 155–164). Newbury Park: Sage Publications.

Straus, M., Gelles, R. & Steinmetz, S. (1980). *Behind closed doors: Violence in the American family.* Garden City: Doubleday.

Walker, G.A. (1990). *Family violence and the women's movement: The conceptual politics of struggle.* Toronto: University of Toronto Press.

Walker, L.E. (1984). *The battered woman syndrome.* New York: Springer Publishing Company.

Walker, L.E.A. (1995). Racism and violence against women. In J. Adleman & G. Enguidanos (Eds.), *Racism in the lives of women: Testimony, theory, and guides to antiracist practice* (pp. 239–250). New York: Harrington Park Press.

Yllo, K. & Bograd, M. (1988). *Feminist perspectives on wife abuse.* Beverly Hills: Sage Publications.

CHAPTER 2

Artuso, A. (2000). Tories expand anti-abuse bill. *Toronto Sun* (September 28, p.7).

Attorney General. (2000). More protection for victims of domestic violence. Retrieved November 20, 2002, from http://www.newswire.ca/government/ontario/english/releases/September2000/27/c7543.html

Attorney General. (2002a, July 11). Ontario government investment helps women build new lives. Retrieved October 18, 2002, from http://www.gov.on.ca/citizenship/english/about/n110702.htm

Attorney General. (2002b). Ontario government to review Hadley jury recommendations. Retrieved November 20, 2002, from http://www.newswire.ca/government/ontario/english/releases/February2002/08/c0199.html

Baker, L.E.A. (2001). *Understanding the effects of domestic violence: A handbook for early childhood educators.* London: Centre for Children and Families in the Justice System.

Blackwell, T. (2000). Ontario proposes to toughen restraining orders. *National Post* (September 28), p. A4.

Boyle, T. (2000). Tories get tough on domestic violence. *Toronto Star* (September 28), p.NE01.

Brodie, J. (1997). Meso-discourse, state forms and the gendering of liberal-democratic citizenship. *Citizenship Studies, 1*(2), 223–241.

CCSD. (2004). *Nowhere to turn? Responding to partner violence against immigrant and visible minority women.* Ottawa: Canadian Council on Social Development (CCSD).

Chief Coroner. (2002). Inquest touching the deaths of Gillian Mary Hadley and Ralph Alexander Hadley (verdict of Coroner's Jury). Toronto: Chief Coroner, Province of Ontario.

Cross, P. (2000). *Follow-up to emergency measures for women and children delegation at Queen's Park*. Toronto: Ontario Women's Justice Network.

Cross, P. (2001, March 27). The Domestic Violence Protection Act: Will it prevent domestic violence? Retrieved October 24, 2002, from http://www.owjn.org/issues/w-abuse/domact.htm

Cross, P. (2002a). *Open letter to Premier Harris*. Toronto: Cross-Sectoral Violence against Women Strategy Group.

Cross, P. (2002b). *What's happening with the Domestic Violence Protection Act?* Retrieved October 24, 2002, from http://www.owjn.org/issues/w-abuse/domup.htm

CSVAWSG. (2002a). *Emergency measures for women and children*. Toronto: Cross-Sectoral Violence against Women Strategy Group.

CSVAWSG. (2002b). *Women murdered since the release of the May-Iles recommendations*. Toronto: Cross-Sectoral Violence against Women Strategy Group.

Davis, R. & Taylor, B. (1997). A proactive response to family violence: The results of a randomized mixed experiment. *Criminology, 35*(2), 307–329.

Dobash, E. & Dobash, R. (2000). The politics and policies of responding to violence against women. In J. Hanmer (Ed.), *Home truths about domestic violence: Feminist influences on policy and practice* (pp. 187–205). London & New York: Routledge.

Duffy, A. & Momirov, J. (1997). *Family violence: A Canadian introduction*. Toronto: James Lorimer & Company.

Elman, A. (2001). Refuge in markets: Movements to end male violence in Britain and the U.S." Retrieved November 10, 2002, from http://pro.harvard.edu/papers/118/118001ElmanR0000.pdf

Ghez, M. (2001). Getting the message out: Using the media to change social norms on abuse. In C. Renzetti (Ed.), *Sourcebook on violence against women* (pp. 417–439). Thousand Oaks: Sage Publications.

Gillan, E. (1999). The zero tolerance approach to domestic violence. Prepared for the Foyle Interagency Forum on Domestic Violence: Londonderry, Northern Ireland. Previously available at http://www.domesticviolenceforum.org/DomesticViolence%20(1).pdf. Currently available through http://www.foyledvpartnership.org/files/aboutlimavady.php

Gillan, E., & Samson, E. (2000). The Zero Tolerance Campaigns. In J. Hanmer (Ed.), *Home Truths About Domestic Violence: feminist influences on policy and practice* (pp. 340-356). London & New York: Routledge.

Gordon, L. (1988). *Heroes in their own lives: The politics and history of family violence, Boston 1880–1960*. London: Virago.

Government of Ontario. (2000). Domestic Violence Protection Act.

Hester, M.E.A. (1996). *Women, violence, and male power.* Buckingham: Open University Press.

Jasinski, J. (2001). Theoretical explanations for violence against women. In C. Renzetti (Ed.), *Sourcebook on violence against women* (pp. 5–23). Thousand Oaks: Sage Publications.

Jiwani, Y., Janovicek, N. & Cameron, A. (2001). *Erased realities: The violence of racism in the lives of immigrant and refugee girls of colour.* Vancouver: FREDA Centre for Research on Violence against Women.

Klein, E.E.A. (1997). *Ending domestic violence.* Thousand Oaks: Sage Publications.

Landsberg, M. (2000). Tories ignore common sense on violence. *Toronto Star* (September 24), p. 2.

Levan, A. (1996). Violence against women. In J. Brodie (Ed.), *Women and Canadian public policy* (pp. 319–353). Toronto: Harcourt, Brace & Company.

Mackie, R. (2000). Ontario wife-abuse measures assailed. *Toronto Star* (September 28), p. A11.

Maslow Cohen, J. (1994). Private violence and public violence: The fulcrum of reason. In M. Fineman (Ed.), *The public nature of private violence* (pp. 349–383). London & New York: Routledge.

McCarten, J. (2002). Canada's largest urban police forces poised for pitched battle. *Toronto Star.* Retrieved December 4, 2002, from http://ca.news.yahoo.com/021105/6/q2at.html

METRAC. (2002). More about us: An overview of METRAC.

Mies, M. (1986). Patriarchy and accumulation on a world scale: Women in the international division of labour. London & Atlantic Highlands: Zed Books.

Minaker, J.C. (2001). Evaluating criminal justice responses to intimate abuse through the lense of women's needs. *Canadian Journal of Women and the Law,* 13, 74–106.

Ministry of Citizenship. (2002a, September 5). *Ernie Eves' government invests more than $21 million in campaign against domestic violence.* Retrieved October 18, 2002, from http://www.gov.on.ca/citizenship/english/about/n050902.htm

Ministry of Citizenship. (2002b, September 5). *Fact sheet: Domestic violence—new initiatives reflect Ontario's commitment to address domestic violence.* Retrieved October 10, 2002, from http://www.gov.on.ca/citizenship/english/about/f050902.htm

Ministry of Citizenship (Ed.). (2004). *A domestic violence action plan for Ontario.* Toronto: Ministry of Citizenship.

Moller Okin, S. (1989). Justice, gender, and the family. Toronto: Faculty of Law, University of Toronto.

Morgan, J. (1995). Feminist theory as legal theory. In F.E. Olsen (Ed.), *Feminist legal theory: Foundations and outlooks* (pp. 743–759). New York: New York University Press.

O'Brien, M. (2001). School-based education and prevention programs. In C. Renzetti (Ed.), *Sourcebook on violence against women* (pp. 387–417). Thousand Oaks: Sage Publications.

Pratt, A. (1995). New immigrant and refugee battered women: The intersection of immigration and criminal justice policy. In M. Valverde, L. MacLeod & K. Johnson (Eds.), *Wife assault and the Canadian criminal justice system* (pp. 84–103). Toronto: Centre of Criminology, University of Toronto.

Rebick, J. (2000). Harris ignores measures to end violence against women. *CBC Newsworld* (columns).

Rowland, R. & Klein, R. (1990). Radical feminism: Critique and construct. In S. Gunew (Ed.), *Feminist knowledge: Critique and construct* (pp. 271–304). London: Routledge.

Schneider, E. (1994). The violence of privacy. In M. Fineman (Ed.), *The public nature of private violence* (pp. 36–59). London & New York: Routledge.

Walker, G. (1990). *Family violence and the Canadian women's movement*. Toronto: University of Toronto Press.

CHAPTER 3

Avakame, E.F. (2001). Differential police treatment of male-on-female spousal violence. *Violence against Women, 7*(1), 22–46.

Basch, N. (1982). *In the eyes of the law: Women, marriage, and property in nineteenth-century New York*. Ithaca: Cornell University Press.

Busch, A.L. & Rosenberg, M.S. (2004). Comparing women and men arrested for domestic violence: A preliminary report. *Journal of Violence, 19*(1), 49–57.

Buzawa, E.S. & Buzawa, C.G. (1996). *Domestic violence: The criminal and justice response*. Thousand Oaks: Sage Publications.

Campbell, J.C., Webster, D., Koziol-McLain, J., Block, C.R., Campbell, D.W., Curry, M.A., Gary, F.A., Glass, N.E., Sachs, C.J., Sharps, P.W., Ulrich, Y., Wilt, S.A., Manganello, J., Xu, X., Schollenberger, J., Frye, V. & Laughon, K. (2003). Risk factors for femicide in abusive relationships: Results from a multisite case control study. *American Journal of Public Health, 93*, 1089–1097.

Canadian Council on Social Development. (2004). *Nowhere to turn? Responding to partner violence against immigrant and visible minority women*. Ottawa: CCSD.

Chapman, T. (1985). Women, sex, and marriage in Western Canada 1890–1920. *Alberta History, 33*(4), 1–12.

Chapman, T. (1988). Til death do us part: Wife beating in Alberta, 1905–1920. *Alberta History, 36*(4), 13–22.

Chesney-Lind, M. (2002). Criminalizing victimization: The unintended consequences of pro-arrest politics for girls and women. *Criminology & Public Policy, 2,* 81-90.

Comack, E. (1993). *Feminist engagement with the law: The legal recognition of the battered woman syndrome.* Ottawa: CRIAW.

DeLeon-Granados, W., Wells, W. & Binsbacher, R. (2006). Arresting developments: Trends in female arrests for domestic violence and proposed implications. *Violence against Women, 12*(4), 355–371.

Dutton, D.G. (2003). *The abusive personality: Violence and control in intimate relationships.* New York: Guildford Press.

Gelles, R. (1996). Constraints against family violence: How well do they work? In E. S. Buzawa & C. G. Buzawa (Eds.), *Do arrests and restraining orders work?* (pp. 30-42) Thousand Oaks, CA: Sage Publications.

Gillis, J.R., Diamond, S.L., Jebely, P., Orekhovsky, V., Ostovich, E.M., Macisaac, K., Sagrati, S. & Mandell, D. (2006). Systemic obstacles to battered women's participation in the judicial system: When will the status quo change? *Violence against Women, 12*(12), 1150–1168.

Hamberger, K. & Potente, T. (1994). Counseling heterosexual women arrested for domestic violence: Implications for theory and practice. *Violence Victim, 9*(2), 125–137.

Henning, K. & Feder, L. (2004). A comparison of men and women arrested for domestic violence: Who presents the greater threat? *Journal of Family Violence, 19*(2), 69–80.

Henning, K., Jones, A. & Holdford, R. (2003). Treatment needs of women arrested for domestic violence: A comparison with male offenders. *Journal of Interpersonal Violence, 18*(8), 839–856.

Henning, K., Jones, A. & Holdford, R. (2005). "I didn't do it, but if I did I had a good reason": Minimization, denial, and attributions of blame among male and female offenders. *Journal of Family Violence, 20*(3), 131–139.

Henning, K., Renauer, B. & Holdford, R. (2006). Victim or offender? Heterogeneity among women arrested for intimate partner violence. *Journal of Family Violence, 21*(6), 351–368.

hooks, b. (1984). *Feminist theory: From margin to center.* Boston: South End.

MacKinnon, C. (1990). *Towards the feminist theory of the state.* Cambridge: Harvard University Press.

Martin, M. (1997). Double your trouble: Dual arrest in family violence. *Journal of Family Violence, 12*(2), 139–157.

Mathes, D. (1991). Understanding wife assault. In F. Rafiq (Ed.), *Towards equal access* (pp. 31-44). Toronto: Immigrant & Visible Minority Women Against Abuse, Education Wife Assault.

Miller, S.L. (2001). The paradox of women arrested for domestic violence: Criminal justice professionals and service providers respond. *Violence against Women*, 7(12), 1339–1376.

Morris, M. (2006, November). New federal policies affecting women's equality: Reality check. *Fact Sheet*. Ottawa: Canadian Research Institute for the Advancement of Women.

Nicolaidis, C., Curry, M.A., Ulrich, Y., Sharps, P.W., McFarlane, J., Campbell, D.W., Gary, F.A., Laughon, K., Glass, N.E. & Campbell, J.C. (2003). Could we have known? A qualitative analysis of data from women who survived an attempted homicide by an intimate partner. *Journal of General Internal Medicine*, 18, 788–794.

Pagelow, M.D. (1984). *Family violence*. New York: Praeger Publishers.

Perkin, J. (1989). *Women and marriage in nineteenth-century England*. London: Routledge.

Pollack, S. & Mackay, L. (2003). *The women's safety project pilot study*. Unpublished paper.

Rajah, V., Frye, V. & Haviland, M. (2006). Aren't I a victim? *Violence against Women*, 12(10), 897–916.

Schmidt, J.D. & Sherman, L.W. (1996). Does arrest deter domestic violence? In E. S. Buzawa & C. G. Buzawa (Eds.), *Do arrests and restraining orders work?* (pp. 43-53) Thousand Oaks, CA: Sage Publications.

Stanko, E.A. (1985). *Intimate intrusions: Women's experience of male violence*. New York: Routledge & Kegan Paul.

Stanko, E.A. (1993). Ordinary fear: Women, violence, and personal safety. In P. B. Bart & P. G. Moran (Eds.), *Violence against women: The bloody footprints* (pp. 155-164). Newbury Park: Sage Publications.

Statistics Canada. (2005). *Family violence in Canada: A statistic profile 2005*. Ottawa: National Clearinghouse on Family Violence.

Stuart, G.L., Moore, T.M., Gordon, K.L., Hellmuth, T.C., Ramsey, S.E. & Kahler, C.W. (2006). Reasons for intimate partner violence perpetration among arrested women. *Violence against Women*, 12(7), 609–621.

Syers, M., & Edleson, J.L. (1992). The combined effects of coordinated criminal justice intervention in woman abuse. *Journal of Interpersonal Violence*, 7, 490-502.

Tolman, R.M. (2001). Domestic violence in the lives of women receiving welfare. *Violence against Women*, 7(2), 141–159.

Woman Abuse Council of Toronto. (2002). *Best practice guidelines and implementation checklist*. Retrieved December 1, 2006, from http://www.woman-abuse.ca/publications.html

Woman Abuse Council of Toronto. (2005). *Women charged with domestic violence in Toronto: The unintended consequences of mandatory charge policies.* Retrieved December 1, 2006, from http://www.womanabuse.ca/publications.html

Yoshioka, M.R., Dinoia, J. & Ullah, K. (2001). Attitudes toward marital violence: An examination of our Asian communities. *Violence against Women, 7*(8), 900–927.

CHAPTER 4

Adams, H. (1999). *Tortured people: The politics of colonization.* Pentiction: Theytus.

Agnew, V. (1998). *In search of a safer place: Abused women and culturally sensitive services.* Toronto: University of Toronto Press.

Baskin, C. (2005). *Mino-yaa-daa*: Healing together. In K. Brownlee & J.R. Graham (Eds.), *Social work readings and research from northern and rural Canada* (pp. 170-181). Toronto: Canadian Scholars' Press Inc.

Baskin, C. (2006). Systemic oppression, violence, and healing in Aboriginal families. In R. Alaggia & C. Vine (Eds.), *Cruel but not unusual: Violence in Canadian families: A sourcebook for educators and practitioners* (pp.15-48). Kitchener: Wilfrid Laurier University Press.

Baskin, C. (2003). From victims to leaders: Activism against violence towards women. In K. Anderson and B. Lawrence (Eds.). *Strong women stories: Native vision and community survival* (pp. 213-227). Toronto: Sumach Press.

Bruce, L. (1998). A culturally sensitive approach to working with Aboriginal women. *Manitoba Social Worker, 30*(2), 1, 8–10.

Cuthand, D. (2005). Homolka fuss reminder of Crawford's victims. *The Star Phoenix* (July 15).

Dean, R.G. (2001). The myth of cross-cultural competence. *Families in society: The Journal of Contemporary Human Services, 32*(6), 623–630.

Green, R.J. (1998). Race and the field of family therapy. In M. McGoldrick (Ed.), *Revisioning family therapy* (pp. 93–110). New York: Guilford Press.

Gunraj, A. (2005). Reaching out for safer communities. *Envisioning a safer society for all* (Spring). Biannual newsletter. Toronto: METRAC. Retrieved from http://www.metrac.org/about/newsspo5.htm

Jaaber, R.A. & Dasgupta, S.D. (2003). *Assessing social risks of battered women.* St. Paul: Minnesota Center against Violence and Abuse.

Jawani, Y. (2001). Intersecting inequalities: Immigrant women of colour, violence and health care. Retrieved on August 4, 2009 from http://www.vancouver.sfu.ca/freda/articles/hlth.htm

Laird, J. (1998). Theorizing culture: Narrative ideas and practice principles. In M. McGoldrick (Ed.), *Re-visioning family therapy* (pp. 20–36). New York: Guilford Press.

Macleod, L. & Shin, M. (1990). *Isolated, afraid, and forgotten: The service delivery needs and realities of immigrant and refugee women who are battered.* Ottawa: National Clearinghouse on Family Violence.

Miedema, B. (2000). Barriers and strategies: How to improve services for abused immigrant women in New Brunswick. Retrieved on October 7, 2007, from http://www.unb.ca/arts/CFVR/barriers.html

Pinedo, M.R. & Santinoli, A.M. (1991). Immigrant women and wife assault. In F. Rafiq (Ed.), *Toward equal access: A handbook for service providers working with immigrant women survivors of wife assault* (pp. 65-75). Ottawa: Immigrant and Visible Minority Women against Abuse.

Province of Nova Scotia. (2000). *Fact sheet 11: Abuse in ethno-cultural and new Canadian communities.* Halifax: Province of Nova Scotia.

Smith, E. (2004). *Nowhere to turn? Responding to partner violence against immigrant and visible minority women.* Ottawa: Canadian Council on Social Development.

Tjaden, P. & Thoennes, N. (1998). *Prevalence, incidence, and consequences of violence against women: Findings from the national violence against women survey.* Atlanta: Centers for Disease Control and Prevention.

West, C. (1997). *Partner violence in ethnic minority families.* Raleigh, North Carolina: USAF and National Network for Family Resiliency.

CHAPTER 5

Anderson, E.N. (1992), Chinese fisher families: Variations on Chinese themes. *Journal of Comparative Family Studies, 23,* 231–247.

Berry, J. (2001). A psychology of immigration. *Journal of Social Issues, 57*(3), 615–631.

Chambon, A. (1989). Refugee families' experiences: Three family themes—family disruption, violent trauma, and acculturation. *Journal of Strategic and Systemic Therapies, 8,* 3–13.

Dutton, D. (1995). *The domestic assault of women: Psychological and criminal justice perspective.* Vancouver: UBC Press.

Dutton, D. (2007). *The abusive personality: Violence and control in intimate relationships.* New York: Guilford Press.

Freedman, L. (1985). Wife assault. In C. Guberman & M. Walfe (Eds.), *No safe place* (pp.41-60). Toronto: Women's Press.

Gallin, R. (1992). Wife abuse in the context of development and change: A Chinese (Taiwanese) case. In D.A. Couunts, J.K. Brown & J.C. Campbell (Eds.), *Sanctions and sanctuary: Cultural perspectives on the beating of wives* (pp. 219-227). Boulder: Westview Press.

Gelles, R.J. & Straus, M. (1988). *Intimate violence: The causes and consequences of abuse in the American family.* New York: Simon & Schuster Publishing Company.

Glasser, B.G. (1992). *Emergence vs. forcing: Basics of grounded theory analysis.* Mill Valley: Sociology Press.

Goodwin, R. & Tang, C. (1996). Chinese personal relationships. In M.H. Bond (Ed.), *The handbook of Chinese psychology* (pp. 294-308). Hong Kong: Oxford University Press.

Gordon, L. (1988). The frustrations of family violence social work: An historical critique. *Journal of Sociology and Social Welfare, 15*(4), 139–169.

Hartmann, H. (1981). The unhappy marriage of Marxism and feminism: Towards a more progressive union. In L. Sargent (Ed.), *Women and revolution: A discussion of the unhappy marriage of Marxism and Feminism* (pp. 1-41). London: Pluto Press.

Leong, F.T.L. & Lau, A.S.L. (2001). Barriers to providing effective mental health services to Asian Americans. *Mental Health Services Research, 3,* 201–214.

Leong, F.T.L. & Ponterotto, J. (2003). Internationalizing counseling psychology: A proposal. *The Counseling Psychologist, 31*(4), 381–395.

MacKinnon, C. (1990). *Towards the feminist theory of the state.* Cambridge: Harvard University Press.

Patton, M.Q. (1990). *Qualitative evaluation methods.* Beverly Hills: Sage Publications.

Pedersen, P.B. (2003). Culturally biased assumptions in counseling psychology. *The Counseling Psychologist, 31*(4), 396–403.

Russell, D.E.H. (1990). *Rape in marriage.* Bloomington: Indiana University Press.

Russell, D.E.H. (2000). *The epidemic of rape and child sexual abuse in the United States.* Thousand Oaks: Sage Publications.

Shainess, N. (1977). Psychological aspects of wife-battering. In M. Roy (Ed.), *Battered women: A psychological study of domestic violence* (pp. 111-119). New York: Van Nostrand Reinhold Company.

Yllo, K. & Bograd, M. (1988). *Feminist perspectives on wife abuse.* Beverly Hills: Sage Publications.

CHAPTER 6

Access Alliance Multicultural Community Mental Health Centre. (2003). *Best practices for working with homeless immigrants and refugees.* Executive Summary. Toronto: Access Alliance Multicultural Community Mental Health Centre.

Acevedo, M.J. (2000). Battered immigrant Mexican women's perspectives regarding abuse and help-seeking. *Journal of Multicultural Social Work*, 8(3/4), 243–282.

Bonilla-Santiago, G. (1996). Latina battered women: Barriers to service delivery and cultural consideration. In A.R. Roberts (Ed.), *Helping battered women: New perspectives and remedies* (pp. 229-234). New York: Oxford University Press.

Campbell, D.W., Masaki, B. & Torres, S. (1997). "Water on rock": Changing domestic violence perceptions in the African American, Asian American, and Latino communities. In E. Klein, J. Campbell, E. Soler & M. Ghez, *Ending domestic violence: Changing public perceptions/halting the epidemic* (pp. 64-87). Thousand Oaks: Sage Publications.

Davis, N.J. (1988). Shelters for battered women: Social policy response to interpersonal violence. *The Social Science Journal*, 25(4), 49–66.

Donnelly, D.A., Cook, K.J. & Wilson, L.A. (1999). Provision and exclusion: The dual face of services to battered women in three Deep South states. *Violence against Women*, 5(7), 710–741.

Epstein, S.R., Russell, G. & Silvern, L. (1988). Structure and ideology of shelters for battered women. *American Community Psychology*, 16(3), 345-367.

Huisman, K.A. (1996). Wife battering in Asian American communities: Identifying the service needs of an overlooked segment of the U.S. population. *Violence against Women*, 2(3), 260–283.

Klein, E., Campbell, J., Soler, E. & Ghez, M. (1997). *Ending domestic violence: Changing public perceptions/halting the epidemic*. Thousand Oaks: Sage Publications.

Lee, M.Y. (2000). Understanding Chinese battered women in North America: A review of the literature and practice implications. *Journal of Multicultural Social Work*, 8(3/4), 215–241.

Legault, G. (1996). Social work practice in situations of intercultural misunderstandings. *Journal of Multicultural Social Work*, 4(4), 49–66.

Loseke, D.R. (1992). *The battered woman and shelters: The social construction of wife abuse*. New York: State University of New York Press.

MacLeod, L. & Shin, M.Y. (1990). *Isolated, afraid, and forgotten: The service delivery needs and realities of immigrant and refugee women who are battered*. Ottawa: National Clearinghouse on Family Violence, Health and Welfare Canada.

MacLeod, L. & Shin, M.Y. (1993). *"Like a wingless bird": A tribute to the survival and courage of women who are abused and who speak neither English nor French*. Ottawa: National Clearinghouse on Family Violence, Health Canada.

O'Keefe, M. (1994). Racial/ethnic differences among battered women and their children. *Journal of Child and Family Studies, 3*(3), 283–305.

Paredes, M.P. (1992). *Setting the precedent: Process as change in meeting the needs of immigrant and refugee women surviving abuse and sexual violence.* Toronto: Advisory Committee, Immigrant and Refugee Women's Project: Education Sexual Assault and Ontario Ministry of Health, Women's Health Bureau.

Preisser, A.B. (1999). Domestic violence in South Asian communities in America. *Violence against Women, 5*(6), 684–699.

Rafiq, F. (1991). *Toward equal access: A handbook for service providers working with survivors of wife assault.* Ottawa: Immigrant and Visible Minority Women against Abuse.

Raj, A. & Silverman, J. (2002). Violence against immigrant women: The roles of culture, context, and legal immigrant status on intimate partner violence. *Violence against Women, 8*(3), 367–398.

Sharma, A. (2001). Healing the wounds of domestic abuse: Improving the effectiveness of feminist therapeutic intervention with immigrant and racially visible women who have been abused. *Violence against Women, 7*(12), 1405–1428.

Srinivasan, M. & Davis, L.V. (1991). A shelter: An organization like any other? *Affilia, 6*(1), 38–57.

Supriya, K.E. (2002). *Shame and recovery: Mapping identity in an Asian women's shelter.* New York: Peter Lang Publishing, Inc.

Tutty, L.M., Weaver, G. & Rothery, M.A. (1999). Residents' views on the efficacy of shelter services for assaulted women. *Violence against Women, 5*(8), 898–925.

Wiebe, K. (1985). *Violence against women and children: An overview for community workers* (2nd ed.). Vancouver: Women against Violence against Women/Rape Crisis Centre.

Yick, A.G. (2001). Feminist theory and status inconsistency theory: Application to domestic violence in Chinese immigrant families. *Violence against Women, 7*(5), 545–562.

CHAPTER 7

Abouguendia, M. & Noels, K.A. (2001). General acculturation-related daily hassles and psychological adjustment in first- and second-generation South Asian immigrants to Canada. *International Journal of Psychology, 36*(3), 163–173.

Abraham, M. (2000). Isolation as a form of domestic violence: The South Asian immigrant experience. *Journal of Social Distress and the Homeless, 9*(3), 221–236.

Abraham, M. (2005). Fighting back: Abused South Asian women's strategies of resistance. In N.J. Sokoloff & C. Pratt (Eds.), *Domestic violence at the margins: Readings on race, class, gender, and culture* (pp. 272–293). Picataway: Rutgers University Press.

Agnew, V. (1996). *Resisting discrimination: Women from Asia, Africa, and the Caribbean and the women's movement in Canada.* Toronto: University of Toronto Press.

Agnew, V. (1997). Tensions in providing services to South Asian victims of wife abuse in Toronto. *Violence against Women, 4*(2), 153–179.

Agnew, V. (1998). *In search of a safe place: Abused women and culturally sensitive services.* Toronto: University of Toronto Press.

Ahmad, F., Riaz, S., Barata, P. & Stewart, D. (2004). Patriarchal beliefs and perceptions of abuse among South Asian immigrant women. *Violence against Women, 10*(3), 262–282.

Almeida, R.V. & Lockard, J. (2005). The cultural context model: A new paradigm for accountability, empowerment, and the development of critical consciousness against domestic violence. In N.J. Sokoloff & C. Pratt (Eds.), *Domestic violence at the margins: Readings on race, class, gender, and culture* (pp. 301–321). Picataway: Rutgers University Press.

B.C. shooting victim speaks out against domestic violence. (2007, April 4). *CBC News.* Retrieved April 4, 2007, from http://www.cbc.ca/canada/british-columbia/story/2007/04/04/woman-shot.html

Belanger, A. & Malenfant, C.R. (2005). *Ethno-cultural diversity in Canada: Prospects for 2017.* Canadian Social Trend, Catalogue no. 11-008. Ottawa: Statistics Canada.

Burman, E., Smailes, S.L. & Chantler, K. (2004). "Culture" as a barrier to service provision and delivery: Domestic violence services for minoritized women. *Critical Social Policy, 24*(3), 332–357.

Calliste, A., Dei, G., & Belkhir, J. (1995). Canadian perspective on anti-racism: Intersection of race, gender and class. *Race, Gender & Class, 2,* 5–10.

Choudhry, U.K. (2001). Uprooting and resettlement experiences of South Asian immigrant women. *Western Journal of Nursing Research, 23*(4), 376–393.

Das Dasgupta, S. (2000). Charting the course: An overview of domestic violence in the South Asian community in the United States. *Journal of Social Distress and the Homeless, 9*(3), 173–184.

Das Dasgupta, S. & Warrier, S. (1996). In the footsteps of "Arundhati": Asian Indian women's experience of domestic violence in United States. *Violence against Women*, 2(3), 238–259.

Declaration on Elimination of Violence against Women. (1993, December 20). *UN Issuing Body: Secretariat Centre for Human Rights*. Retrieved March 10, 2007, from http://www.hri.ca/uninfo/treaties/ViolWom.shtml

DeKeseredy, W.S. & Schwartz, M.D. (2003). Backlash and whiplash: A critique of Statistics Canada's 1999 General Social Survey on Victimization. *Online Journal of Justice Studies*. Retrieved March 09, 2007, from http://ojjs.icaap.org

Fact sheet on domestic violence in Asian communities. (2005, July). San Francisco: Asian & Pacific Islander Institute on Domestic Violence.

George, U. & Ramkissoon, S. (1998). Race, gender, and class: Interlocking oppressions in the lives of South Asian women in Canada. *Journal of Women and Social Work*, 13(1), 102–118.

Gill, A. (2004). Voicing the silent fear: South Asian women's experiences of domestic violence. *The Howard Journal*, 43(5), 465–483.

Gill, A. & Rehman, G. (2004). Empowerment through activism: Responding to domestic violence in the South Asian community in London. *Gender and Development*, 12(1), 75–82.

Jiwani, Y. (2005). Walking a tightrope: The many faces of violence in the lives of racialized immigrant girls and young women. *Violence against Women*, 11(7), 846–875.

Kim, M. (2002). *Innovative strategies to address domestic violence in Asian and Pacific Islander communities: Examining themes, models, and interventions.* Asian & Pacific Islander Institute on Domestic Violence. Retrieved June 12, 2007, from http://www.apiahf.org/apidvinstitute/ResearchAndPolicy/innovative.htm

Liao, M.S. (2006). Domestic violence among Asian Indian immigrant women: Risk factors, acculturation, and intervention. *Women and Therapy*, 29(1/2), 23–39.

Merchant, M. (2000). A comparative study of agencies assisting domestic violence victims: Does the South Asian community have special needs? *Journal of Social Distress and the Homeless*, 9(3), 249–259.

Preyra, C.M. (1998). *Experiences of South Asian women in a Canadian shelter for battered women.* MA thesis, University of Toronto, Toronto.

Rafiq, F. (1991). *Towards equal access: A handbook for service providers working with survivors of wife assault.* Toronto: Immigrant and Visible Minority Women Against Abuse.

Raj, A. & Silverman, J. (2002). Intimate partner violence against South Asian women in greater Boston. *Journal of American Medical Women's Association*, 57(2), 111–114.

Reavey, P., Ahmed, B. & Majumdar, A. (2006). "How can we help when she won't tell us what's wrong?" Professionals working with South Asian women who have experienced sexual abuse. *Journal of Community and Applied Social Psychology, 16,* 171–188.

Reitz, J. (1995). *A review of literature in aspects of ethno-racial access, utilization, and delivery of social services.* Toronto: Ontario Ministry of Community and Social Services.

Richardson, J., Coid, J., Petruchevitch, A., Chung, W.S., Moorey, S. & Feder, G. (2002). Identifying domestic violence: Cross sectional study in primary care. *British Medical Journal, 324,* 274–297.

Shriwadkar, S. (2004). Canadian domestic violence policy and Indian immigrant women. *Violence against Women, 10*(8), 860–879.

Tran, K., Kaddatz, J. & Allard, P. (2005). South Asians in Canada: Unity through diversity. *Canadian Social Trends* (pp. 20–25). Catalogue no. 11-008. Ottawa: Statistics Canada.

WHO. (2005). *Multi-country study on women's health and domestic violence against women: Summary report of initial results on prevalence, health outcomes, and women's responses.* Retrieved March 6, 2007, from http://www.who.int/gender/violence/who_multicountry_study/en/index.html

CHAPTER 8

Berry, J.W. (1995). Psychology of acculturation. In N.R. Goldberg & J.B. Veroff (Eds.), *The culture and psychology reader* (pp. 457–488). New York: New York University Press.

Bui, H.N. & Morash, M. (1999). Domestic violence in the Vietnamese immigrant community: An exploratory study. *Violence against Women, 5*(7), 769–795.

Campbell, J.C. (1992). Prevention of wife battering: Insights from cultural analysis. *Response, 14*(3), 18–24.

Canadian Council on Multicultural Health. (1989). *Canadian cultures and health: Bibliography.* Toronto: Canadian Council on Multicultural Health.

Canadian Task Force on Mental Health Issues Affecting Immigrants and Refugees. (1988). *After the door has been opened: Mental health issues affecting immigrants and refugees in Canada.* Ottawa: Ministry of Supply and Services.

Dobash, R.E. & Dobash, R.P. (1979). *Violence against wives: A case against the patriarchy.* New York: Free Press.

Dobash, R.E. & Dobash, R.P. (1997). Violence against women. In L.L. O'Toole & J.R. Schiffman (Eds.), *Gender violence: Interdisciplinary perspectives* (pp. 266–278). New York: New York University Press.

Goode, W.J. (1971). Force and violence in the family. *Journal of Marriage and the Family*, 33, 624–636.

Hyman, I., Guruge, S., Mason, R., Stuckless, N., Gould, J., Tang, T., et al. (2004). Post-migration changes in gender relations among Ethiopian immigrant couples in Toronto. *Canadian Journal of Nursing Research*, 36(4), 74–89.

Jewkes, R. (2002). Intimate partner violence: Causes and prevention. *Lancet*, 359(9315), 1423–1429.

Jewkes, R., Levin, J. & Penn-Kekana, L. (2002). Risk factors for domestic violence: Findings from a South African cross-sectional study. *Social Science and Medicine*, 55(9), 1603–1617.

Krulfeld, R.M. (1994). Changing concepts of gender roles and identities in refugee communities. In L. Camino & R.M. Krulfeld (Eds.), *Reconstructing lives, recapturing meaning: Refugee identity, gender, and culture change* (pp. 71–96). Washington: Gordon & Breach.

Kulig, J.C. (1994). Sexuality beliefs among Cambodians: Implications for health care professionals. *Health Care for Women International*, 15, 69–76.

Locke, L.M. & Richman, C.L. (1999). Attitudes toward domestic violence: Race and gender issues. *Sex Roles*, 40, 227–247.

McSpadden, L. & Moussa, H. (1993). I have a name: The gender dynamics in asylum and in resettlement of Ethiopian and Eritrean refugees in North America. *Journal of Refugee Studies*, 6, 203–225.

Morash, M., Bui, H.N. & Santiago, A.M. (2000). Cultural-specific gender ideology and wife abuse in Mexican-descent families. *International Review of Victimology*, 7, 67–91.

Morrison, L., Guruge, S. & Snarr, K. (1999). Sri Lankan Tamil immigrants in Toronto: Gender, marriage patterns, and sexuality. In G. Kelson & B. Delaureat (Eds.), *Gender, immigration, and policy* (pp. 144–160). New York: New York University Press.

Narayan, U. (1995). "Male-order" brides: Immigrant women, domestic violence, and immigration law. *Hypatia*, 10, 104–119.

Oxman-Martinez, J., Abdool, S.N. & Loiselle-Leonard, M. (2000). Immigration, women, and health in Canada. *Canadian Journal of Public Health*, 91, 394–395.

Raj, A. & Silverman, J. (2002). Violence against immigrant women: The roles of culture, context, and legal immigrant status on intimate partner violence. *Violence against Women*, 8, 367–398.

Sorenson, S.B. (1996). Violence against women: Examining ethnic differences and commonalities. *Evaluation Review*, 20(2), 123–145.

Sugarman, D.B. & Frankel, S.L. (1996). Patriarchal ideology and wife-assault: A meta-analytic review. *Journal of Family Violence*, 11(1), 13–40.

Tang, T.N. & Oatley, K. (2002, August 22). *Transition and engagement of life roles among Chinese immigrant women.* Paper presented at the American Psychological Association Annual Convention, Chicago.

West, C.M. (1998). Lifting the "political gag order." In J.L. Jasinski & L.M. Williams (Eds.), *Partner violence: A comprehensive review of 20 years of research* (pp. 184–209). Thousand Oaks: Sage Publications.

Yick, A.G. (2001). Feminist theory and status inconsistency theory: Application to domestic violence in Chinese immigrant families. *Violence against Women,* 7(5), 545–562.

Yick, A.G. & Agbayani-Siewert, P. (1997). Perceptions of domestic violence in a Chinese American community. *Journal of Interpersonal Violence,* 12(6), 832–846.

CHAPTER 9

Ahmed, F., Riaz, S., Barata, P. & Stewart, D. (2004). Patriarchal beliefs and perceptions of abuse among South Asian immigrant women. *Violence against Women,* 10(3), 262–282.

Bond, M.H. & Lee, P.W.H. (1981). Face saving in Chinese culture: A discussion and experimental study of Hong Kong students. In A.Y.C. King & R.P.C. Lee (Eds.), *Social life and development in Hong Kong* (pp. 288–305). Hong Kong: The Chinese University Press.

Canadian Mental Health Association. (1989). *Social action series: Immigrants and mental health.* Toronto: CMHA.

Chambon, A. (1989). Refugee families' experiences: Three family themes—family disruption, violent trauma, and acculturation. *Journal of Strategic and Systemic Therapies,* 8, 3–13.

Chan, S.L. (1989). *Wife assault: The Chinese Family Life Services experience.* Toronto: Chinese Family Life Services of Metro Toronto.

Chang, J. (1992). *Wild swans: Three daughters of China.* New York: Anchor Books, Doubleday.

Cheung, F.M.C. (1986). Psychopathology among Chinese people. In M.H. Bond (Ed.), *The psychology of the Chinese people* (pp. 179–185). New York: Oxford University Press.

Chin, K.L. (1994). Out-of-town brides: International marriage and wife abuse among Chinese immigrants. *Journal of Comparative Family Studies,* 25(1), 53–69.

Chinese Information and Community Services. (1998). *Needs assessment of Chinese immigrant women with multiple barriers.* Toronto: CICS.

Citizenship and Immigration Canada. (1998). *Citizenship and immigration statistics 1995*. Ottawa: Minister of Public Works and Government Services Canada.

Community Legal Education Ontario. (1994). *Immigration fact sheet: The point system*. Toronto: Community Legal Education Ontario.

Coutinho, T. (1991). Culture. In F. Rafiq (Ed.), *Towards equal access: A handbook for service providers working with immigrant woman survivors of wife assault* (pp. 49-64). Toronto: Immigrant and Visible Minority Women against Abuse.

Crichlow, H. (1993). There is racism here. In A. Mukherjee (Ed.), *Sharing our experience* (pp. 128-133). Ottawa: Canadian Advisory Council on the Status of Women.

Croll, E. (1983). *Chinese women since Mao*. London: Zed Books.

Dawson, J.B. (1991). *Moon cakes in gold mountain: From China to the Canadian plains*. Calgary: Detselig Enterprises Ltd.

Dion, K.K. & Dion, K.L. (2001). Gender and cultural adaptation in immigrant families. *Journal of Social Issues, 57*(3), 511–521.

Edwards, R.G. (1989). *The refugee filtering process and host country resettlement issues in Canada: A critical theoretical analysis*. Waterloo: Wilfrid Laurier University Press.

Embassy of the United States (2007, March 6). Country reports on human rights practices. Retrieved August 4, 2009, from http://beijing.usembassy-china.org.cn/hr_report2006.html

Fong, J. (1999). Where do they belong?: The "fate" of Chinese immigrant women. *Canadian Women's Studies,19*(3), 65–68.

Frye, B.A. & D'Avanzo, C.D. (1994). Cultural themes in family stress and violence among Cambodian refugee in the inner city. *Advances in Nursing Science, 16*(3), 64–77.

Gallin, R. (1992). Wife abuse in the context of development and change: A Chinese (Taiwanese) case. In D.A. Counts, J.K. Brown & J.C. Campbell (Eds.), *Sanctions and sanctuary: Cultural perspectives on the beating of wives* (pp. 219–227). Boulder: Westview.

Gilmartin, C. (1990). Violence against women in contemporary China. In J.N. Lipman & S. Harell (Eds.), *Violence in China: Essays in culture and counterculture* (pp. 203-226). Albany: State University of New York Press.

Goodwin, R. & Tang, C. (1996). Chinese personal relationships. In M.H. Bond (Ed.), *The handbook of Chinese psychology* (pp. 294–308). Hong Kong: Oxford University Press.

Health and Family Services Sub-committee. (1994). *A study of psychological distress of Chinese immigrant women in Metropolitan Toronto*. Toronto: Chinese Intra-agency Network.

Ho, C.K. (1990). An analysis of domestic violence in Asian American communities: A multicultural approach to counselling. *Women and Therapy, 9,* 129–150.

James, C.E. (1989). *Seeing ourselves: Exploring race, ethnicity, and culture.* Oakville: Sheridan College of Applied Arts and Technology.

Jang, D. Lee, D. & Morello-Frosch, R. (1990/91). Domestic violence in the immigrant and refugee community: Responding to the needs of immigrant women. *Response to the Victimization of Women and Children,* 13(4), 2–7.

Jiwani, Y. (2002). Race, gender, violence, and health care. In K. Mckenna & J. Lakin (Eds.), *Violence against women: New Canadian perspectives.* Toronto: Inanna Publications and Education Inc.

King, Y.C. (1993). *Chinese society and culture.* (Chinese version) Hong Kong: Oxford University Press.

Kinkead, G. (1992). *Chinatown: A portrait of a closed society.* New York: Harper Collins Publishers.

Lai, D.C. (1991). *The forbidden city within Victoria.* Victoria: Orca Book Publishers.

Lee Yao, E.S. (1983). *Chinese women: Past & present.* Mesquite: Ide House, Inc.

Leslie, A.L. (1993). Families fleeing war: The case of Central Americans. *Marriage and Family Review,* 19(1–2), 193–205.

Leung, J.C.B. (1991). *Family mediation with Chinese characteristics: A hybrid of formal and informal service in China.* Monograph Series on Social Welfare in China. Hong Kong: Department of Social Work and Social Administration, University of Hong Kong.

Li, P.S. (1988). *The Chinese in Canada.* Toronto: Oxford University Press.

Liang, S.Y. (1994). *The essence of Chinese culture.* (Chinese version) Hong Kong: Joint Publishing Company Ltd.

MacLeod, L. & Shin, M. (1990). *Isolated, afraid, and forgotten: The service delivery needs and realities of immigrant and refugee women who are battered.* Ottawa: The National Clearinghouse on Family Violence.

McLellan, W. (1992). New group seeks to help immigrant communities. *Vancouver Sun* (May 6), C1, C3.

Menjivar, C. (2002). Immigrant women and domestic violence: Common experiences in different countries. *Gender and Society,* 16(6), 898–920.

Milwertz, C. (2003). Activism against domestic violence in the People's Republic of China. *Violence against Women,* 9(6), 630–654.

Nah, K.H. (1993). Perceived problems and service delivery for Korean immigrants. *Social Work,* 38, 289–296.

Naidoo, J.C. (1990). Immigrant women in Canada: Toward a new decade. *Currents: Readings in Race Relations,* 6(2), 18–21.

Ng, R. (1996). *Politics of community services: Immigrant women, class, and the state*. Halifax: Fernwood Publishing.

Ong, A. (1995). Women out of China: Travelling tales and travelling theories in postcolonial feminism. In R. Behar & D.A. Gordon (Eds.), *Women writing culture* (pp. 350-372). Berkeley & Los Angeles: University of California Press.

Pilowsky, J.E. (1993). *The price of a wife is thirteen cents: An exploration of abused Spanish-speaking women*. Unpublished doctoral dissertation, Ontario Institute for Studies in Education, Toronto.

Sing Tao Daily. (1998). HKG2 (September 7).

Sing Tao Daily. (2008). National Census of 2006: Chinese in Canada (April 3), A1.

Statistics Canada. (1998). *Family violence in Canada: A statistical profile*. Ottawa: Ministry of Industry.

Statistics Canada. (2003). *Ethnic diversity survey: Portrait of a multicultural society*. Ottawa: Ministry of Industry.

Statistics Canada. (2006). *Measuring violence against women: Statistic trends 2006: Risk factors associated with violence against women*. Ottawa: Ministry of Industry.

Thakur, U. (1992). Combating family violence: The South Asian experience in Canada. *Canadian Women Studies*, 13(1), 30–32.

Tsai, S.H. (1986). *The Chinese experience in America*. Indianapolis: Indiana University Press.

Valiante, W. (1993). Domestic violence in the South Asian families: Treatment and research issues. *South Asian Symposium 1992: A reader in South Asian Studies* (pp. 111-121). Toronto: The Centre for South Asian Studies Graduate Union.

Wallis, M. (1988). *Racial minority immigrant women and race relations*. Toronto: Women Working with Immigrant Women.

Williams, P. & Rouette, J. (1993). *Changing the landscape: Ending violence-achieving equality*. Ottawa: Minister of Supply and Services Canada.

The Women's Book Committee, Chinese Canadian National Council. (1992). *Jin Guo: Voices of Chinese Canadian women*. Toronto: Women's Press.

Wong, F.M. (1981). Effects of the employment of mothers on marital role and power differentiation in Hong Kong. In A.Y.C. King & R.P.C. Lee (Eds.), *Social life and development in Hong Kong* (pp. 217-233). Hong Kong: The Chinese University Press.

Woon, Y.F. (1998). *The excluded wife*. Montreal & Kingston: McGill-Queen's University Press.

Wright, R.T. (1988). *In a strange land: A pictorial record of the Chinese in Canada 1788–1923*. Saskatoon: Western Producer Prairie Books.

Yip, C. (1995). *Searching for voice: Chinese immigrant women in the process of racialization and in abusive relationships*. Master Thesis. Halifax, Nova Scotia: Dalhousie University.

Zhang, A.Y., Snowden, L.R. & Stanley, S. (1998). Differences between Asian and White Americans' help seeking and utilization patterns in the Los Angeles area. *Journal of Community Psychology, 26*(4), 317–326.

CHAPTER 10

Baker, A. (1993). *The Jewish woman in contemporary society: Transitions and traditions*. New York: New York University Press.

Baskin, J.R. (Ed.). (1991). *Jewish women in historical perspective*. Detroit: Wayne State University Press.

Biale, R. (1984). *Women and Jewish law: An exploration of women's issues in halakhic sources*. New York: Schocken Books.

Breitowitz, I.A. (1993). *Between civil and religious law: The plight of the agunah in American society*. Westport: Greenwood Press.

Bursik, K. (1991). Women and divorce: Correlates of women's adjustment during the separation and divorce process. In Sandra Volgy (Ed.), *Women and divorce/men and divorce: Gender differences in separation, divorce, and remarriage* (pp. 137-162). New York: The Haworth Press.

Diedrick, P. (1991). Gender differences in divorce adjustment. In Sandra Volgy (Ed.), *Women and divorce/men and divorce: Gender differences in separation, divorce, and remarriage* (pp. 33-46). New York: The Haworth Press.

Dutton, D.G. (1995). *The batterer: A psychological profile*. New York: Basic Books.

Fairley, G. (1991). *Wife beating and its relationship to the control of wives and male adherence to familial patriarchal ideology*. Ottawa: National Library of Canada.

Fishman, S.B.. (1990). *A breath of life: Feminism in the American Jewish community*. New York: Free Press.

Fonow, M.M. & Cook, J.A. (Eds.). (1991). *Beyond methodology: Feminist scholarship as lived research*. Bloomington: Indiana University Press.

Gelles, R. & Loseke, D. (1993). *Current controversies on family violence*. Newbury Park, CA: Sage Publications.

Glazer, M. (1991). Exorcising the *get*: A ritual of healing. In E.R. Levine (Ed.), *A ceremonies sampler: New rites, celebrations, and observances of Jewish women* (pp. 61-65). San Diego: Woman's Institute for Continuing Jewish Education.

Goldstein, Rabbi E. (1998). *ReVisions: Seeing Torah through a feminist lens*. Toronto: Key Porter Books.

Gordis, R. (1990). *The dynamics of Judaism: A study in Jewish law.* Bloomington: Indiana University Press.

Gordon, L. D. (1995). Toward a Gender Inclusive Account of Halakhah. In T. Rudavsky (Ed.), *Gender and Judaism: The Transformation of Tradition* (pp. 3-12). New York: New York University Press.

Gottlieb, Rabbi L. (1995). *She who dwells within: A feminist vision of a renewed Judaism.* San Francisco: Harper Collins.

Greenberg, B. (1981). *On women and Judaism: A view from tradition.* Philadelphia: The Jewish Publication Society of America.

Grossman, S. & Haut, R. (Eds.). (1992). *Daughters of the king: Women and the synagogue: A survey of history, halakhah, and contemporary realities.* Philadelphia: The Jewish Publication Society of America.

Haut, I. (1983). *Divorce in Jewish law and life.* New York: Hermon Press.

Haut, I. (1993). The alter weeps: Divorce in Jewish law. In R.M. Geffen (Ed.), *Celebration and renewal: Rites of passage in Judaism* (pp. 151-166). Philadelphia: The Jewish Publication Society of America.

Heschel, S. (1983). Introduction. In E. Heschel (Ed.), *On being a Jewish feminist: A reader* (pp. xiii-xxxvi). New York: Schocken Books.

Horton, A.L. & Williamson, J.A. (Eds.). (1988). *Abuse and religion: When praying isn't enough.* Lexington: Lexington Books.

Joseph, N.B., Brook, E. & Bicher, M. (1997). *Untying the bonds: Jewish divorce.* Montreal: The Coalition of Jewish Women for the Get.

Kaufman, M. (1987). The construction of masculinity and the triad of men's violence. In M. Kaufman (Ed.), *Beyond patriarchy: Essays by men on pleasure, power, and change* (pp. 1-25). Toronto: Oxford University Press.

Kaufman, M. (1993). *The Jewish woman in Jewish law and tradition.* Northvale: Jason Aronson.

Kellerman, F. (1994). *Sanctuary.* New York: Avon Books.

Lewittes, M. (1994). *Jewish marriage: Rabbinic law, legend, and custom.* Northvale: Jason Aronson.

Majer Krich, R. (1992). *Till death do us part.* New York: Avon Books.

Plaskow, J. (1990). *Standing again at Sinai: Judaism from a feminist perspective.* San Francisco: Harper Collins.

Porter, J.N. (Ed.). (1995). *Women in chains: A sourcebook on the agunah.* Northvale: Jason Aronson.

Reinharz, S. (1992). *Feminist methods in social research.* New York: Oxford University Press.

Rudavsky, T. (Ed.). (1995). *Gender and Judaism: The transformation of tradition.* New York: New York University Press.

Sever, A. (1992). *Women and divorce in Canada: A sociological analysis*. Toronto: Canadian Scholars' Press Inc.

Smith, P. (Ed.). (1993). *Feminist jurisprudence*. New York: Oxford University Press.

Syrtash, J. (1992). *Religion and culture in Canadian family law*. Toronto: Butterworths Press.

Volgy, S. (1991). *Women and divorce/Men and divorce: Gender differences in separation, divorce, and remarriage*. New York: The Haworth Press.

Walker, G. (1990). *Family violence and the women's movement: The conceptual politics of struggle*. Toronto: University of Toronto Press.

Wegner, J.R. (1988). *Chattel or person? The status of women in the Mishnah*. New York: Oxford University Press.

West, G. & Blumberg, R.L. (Eds.). (1990). *Women and social protest*. New York: Oxford University Press.

Yllo, K. & Bogr, M. (Eds.). (1988). *Feminist perspectives on wife abuse*. Beverly Hills: Sage Publications.

Yllo, K. A. (1993). Through a feminist lens: Gender, power and violence. In R. Gelles & D. Loseke (Eds.), *Current controversies on family violence* (pp. 609-618). Newbury Park, CA: Sage Publications.

CHAPTER 11

Aderinto, A.A. (2003). Public concern or private affair: Social construction of domestic Violence against women in post-colonial Nigeria. Paper presented at the 2003 Congress of the South African Sociological Association. Retrieved February 14, 2005, from: http://www.interaction.nu.ac.za/sasa2003/new_page_9.htm

Agnew, V. (1996). *Resisting discrimination: Women from Asia, Africa, and the Caribbean and the women's movement in Canada*. Toronto: University of Toronto Press.

Agnew, V. (1998). *In search of a place: Abused women and cultural sensitive service*. Toronto: University of Toronto Press.

Akpinar, A. (2003). The honor/shame complex revisited: Violence against women in the migration context. *Women's Studies International Forum*, 26(5), 425–442.

Anderson, K. & Jack, D. (1991). Learning to listen: Interview techniques and analyses. In S. Berger Gluck & D. Patai (Eds.), *Women's words: The feminist practice of oral history* (pp. 11–26). New York: Routledge.

Barrett, M. (1980). *Women's oppression today: Problems in Marxist feminist analysis*. London: Villiers Publications.

Bledsoe, C. & Pison, G. (1994). *Nuptiality in Sub-Saharan Africa*. Oxford: Clarendon Press.

Bograd, M. (1999). Strengthening domestic violence theories: Intersection of race, class, sexual orientation, and gender. *Journal of Marital and Family Therapy*, 25, 275–289.

Brownridge, D.A. (2002). Cultural variation in male partner violence against women: A comparison of Québec with the rest of Canada. *Violence against Women*, 8(1), 87–115.

Collins, H. (1991). *Mammies, matriarchs, and other controlling images: Black feminist thought*. New York: Routledge, Chapman, and Hall.

Country of Origin Research Canada. (2002). *Immigration and Refugee Board*. Retrieved February 13, 2005, from http://www.irb- cisr.gc.ca/en/research/ndp/ref/? action=view&doc =nga40002e

Cousineau, M.M. & Rondeau, G. (2004). Toward a transnational and cross-cultural analysis of family violence: Issue and recommendations. *Violence against Women*, 10(8), 935–949.

Dibie, R. (2000). Feminism and family abuse in Nigeria. *New Global Development*, 16, 36–46.

Dobash, R. & Dobash, R. (1979). *Violence against wives: A case against patriarchy*. New York: Macmillan Press Inc.

Dobash, R. & Dobash, R. (1983). *Violence against wives: A case against patriarchy*. 2nd edition. New York: Macmillan Press Inc.

Heise, L.L. (1993). *Violence against women: The hidden health burden*. Washington: World Bank.

hooks, bell. (2002). *Feminist theory: From margin to center*. Boston: South End Press.

Ibekwe, J. (2002). *To live or to die?* Ibadan: Spectrum Books Limited.

Idemudia, E.P. (1999). The racialization of gender in the social construction of immigrant women in Canada: A case study of African women in a prairie province. *Canadian Woman Studies/Les cahiers de la femme: Immigrant and Refugee women*, 19(3), 38–44.

Imam, A. (1993). Politics, Islam, and women in Kano, Northern Nigeria. In V. Moghadam (Ed.), *Identity politics and women: Cultural reassertions and feminisms in international perspective* (pp. 123–144). Boulder: Westview Press.

Isiugo-Abanihe, U.C. (2003). *Male role and responsibility in fertility and reproductive health in Nigeria*. Lagos: Ababa Press.

Isiugo-Abanihe.U.C. (1994). *Consequences of bridewealth changes on nuptiality patterns among the Ibo of Nigeria*. In Blesdoe, C. and Pison, G. (Eds.) *Nuptiality in Sub-Sahara Africa; Contemporary Anthological Perspectives* (pp. 74-92). Oxford: Clarendon Press.

Isiugo-Abanihe, U.C. (1987) "High bridewealth and age at Marriage in Ibo land." In. E. Van de Walle, Etienne (Eds.), *The Cultural Roots of African Fertility Regimes*: Proceedings of the Ife Conference. Ile-Ife, Nigeria: Obafemi Awolowo University. 25 February to 1 march. 1987.

Isiugo-Abanihe, U.C. & Oyediran, K.A. (2003). *The perceptions of Nigerian women on domestic violence: Evidence from 2003 Nigerian Demographic and Health Survey.* Unpublished manuscript, University of Ibadan.

Iweriebor, I. (1983). Women in the family: Labour and management: What can be done? In A. Imam, R. Pittin & H. Omole (Eds.), *Women and family in Nigeria* (pp. 145–160). Dakar: Codesria.

Krane, J., Oxman-Martinez, J. & Ducey, K. (2000). Violence against women and ethno-racial minority women: Examining assumptions about ethnicity and "race." *Canadian Ethnic Studies*, 32(3), 1–14.

Margulies, P. (1995). Representation of domestic violence survivors as a new paradigm of poverty law. *Washington Law Review*, 63(1995), 1071–1104.

Martz D. J. F., & Sarauer D. B. (2002). Domestic violence and the experiences of rural women in East Central Saskatchewan. In McKenna, K.M.J and Larkin, J. (Eds.), *Violence against women: New Canadian perspectives* (pp. 163- 195). Toronto: Inanna Publications and Education Inc.

Maynard, M. & Purvis, J. (1994). Doing feminist research. In Maynard, M. & Purvis, J. (Eds.), *Researching women's lives from a feminist perspective* (1-9). London: Taylor and Francis.

Menjívar, C. & Salcido, O. (2002). Immigrant women and domestic violence: Common experiences in different countries. *Gender and Society*, 16, 898–920.

McDonald, S. (1999). Not in the numbers: Domestic violence and immigrant women. *Canadian Woman Studies/Les cahiers de la femme: Immigrant and Refugee Women*, 19(3), 163–177.

Nielsen, M.J. (Ed.). (1990). *Feminist research methods: Exemplary readings in the social sciences*. San Francisco: Westview Press.

Nwokocha, E.E. (2004). Gender inequality and contradictions in West African development: The need for centriarchy. *African Journal for the Psychological Study of Social Issues*, 7(1), 30–47.

Nwosu N.L. (2005). The experience of domestic violence among Nigerian-Canadian women in Toronto. *Canadian Woman Studies/Les cahiers de la femme: Ending Woman Abuse*, 25(1, 2), 99–106.

Ogundipe-L.O. (1994). *Recreating ourselves: African women & critical transformations*. Trenton: Africa World Press, Inc.

Okafor-Omali, D. (1969). *A Nigerian villager in two worlds*. London: Faber & Faber.

O'Neil, B. (1995). The gender gap: Re-evaluating theory and method. In S. Burt & L. Code (Eds.), *Changing Methods* (pp. 327–356). Peterborough: Broadview Press.

Otite, O. (1990). *Ethnic pluralism and ethnicity in Nigeria.* Ibadan: Shanessor Ltd.

Rich, A. (2002). Compulsory heterosexuality and lesbian existence. *Signs, 5,* 631–660.

Sheppard, C. (2002). Women as wives: Immigration law and domestic violence. *Queens Law Journal, 26,* 1–41

Smith, D. (1990). *The conceptual practices of power: A feminist sociology of knowledge.* Toronto: University Toronto Press.

Statistics Canada. (2001). *Census standard data products Statistics Canada.* Retrieved February 13, 2005, from http://www12.statcan.ca/English/census/on/products/standard/themes/retrieve/.

United Nations (1989). *Violence against women in the family.* New York: Centre for Social Development and Humanitarian Affairs, United Nations.

Zahra, I.N. (1983). Women in Nigeria: The way I see it. In A. Imam, R. Pittin & H. Omole (Eds.), *Women and family in Nigeria* (pp. 7–16). Dakar: Codesria.

CHAPTER 12

Abraham, M. (1999). Sexual abuse in South Asian immigrant marriages. *Violence against Women, 5*(6), 591–618.

Abraham, M. (2000). Isolation as a form of marital violence: The South Asian immigrant experience. *Journal of Social Distress and the Homeless, 9*(3), 221–236.

Abraham, M. (2002). *Speaking the unspeakable: Marital violence among South Asian immigrants in the United States.* New Brunswick: Rutgers University Press.

Agnew, V. (1998). *In search of a safe place: Abused women and culturally sensitive services.* Toronto: University of Toronto Press.

Anderson, D.J. (2003). The impact on subsequent violence of returning to an abusive partner. *Journal of Comparative Family Studies. Special Issue: Violence against Women in the Family, 34*(1), 93–112.

Bender, A., Clune, L., & Guruge, S. (2009). Considering place in community health nursing. *Canadian Journal of Nursing Research, 41*(1):128-143.

Bosch, K. & Schumm, W.R. (2004). Accessibility to resources: Helping rural women in abusive partner relationships become free from abuse. *Journal of Sex and Marital Therapy, 30*(5), 357–370.

Browne, A. (1987). *When battered women kill.* New York: Free Press.

Bui, H.N. & Morash, M. (1999). Domestic violence in the Vietnamese immigrant community: An exploratory study. *Violence against Women, 5*(7), 769–795.

Cheran, R. (2000). *Changing formations: Tamil nationalism and national liberation in Sri Lanka and the diaspora.* Unpublished doctoral dissertation, Centre for Refugee Studies, York University, Toronto.

Choi, A. & Edleson, J. L. (1996). Social disapproval of wife assaults: A national survey of Singapore. *Journal of Comparative Family Studies, 27*, 73–88.

Citizenship and Immigration Canada. (2007). *Facts and figures: Immigration overview.* Retrieved on July 9, 2007, from http://www.cic.gc.ca/english/pdf/pub/facts2007.pdf

Citizenship and Immigration Canada. (2000a). *Facts and figures 1999: Immigration overview.* Retrieved June 9, 2006, from http://www.cic.gc.ca/english/pdf/pub/ facts2001.pdf

Citizenship and Immigration Canada. (2000b). *Recent immigrants in the Toronto Metropolitan Area: A comparative portrait based on the 1996 census.* Ottawa: Ministry of Public Works and Government Services Canada.

Cohen, M. & Ansara, D. (2002). *Women's health status report.* Toronto: Women's Health Council.

Cohen, O. & Savaya, R. (1997). "Broken glass": The divorced woman in Moslem Arab society in Israel. *Family Process, 36*(3), 225–245.

Dasgupta, D. (2000). Charting the course: An overview of domestic violence in the South Asian community in the United States. *Journal of Social Distress and the Homeless, 9*(3), 173–185.

Dasgupta, S.D. (1998). Women's realities: Defining violence against women by immigration, race, and class. In R.K. Bergen (Ed.), *Issues in intimate violence* (pp. 209-219). Thousand Oaks, CA: Sage Publications.

Fong, J. (2000). *Silent no more: How women experienced wife abuse in the local Chinese community.* Unpublished doctoral dissertation, York University, Toronto.

Ford-Gilboe, M., Wuest, J. & Merrit-Gray, M. (2005). Strengthening capacity to limit intrusion: Theorizing family health promotion in the aftermath of woman abuse. *Qualitative Health Research, 15*(4), 477–501.

Gentemann, K. (1984). Wife beating: Attitudes of a non-clinical population. *Victimology, 9*, 109–119.

Gerbert, B., Johnston, K., Caspers, N., Bleecker, T., Woods, A. & Rosenbaum, A. (1996). Experiences of battered women in health care settings: A qualitative study. *Women and Health, 24*(3), 1–17.

Glodava, M. & Onizuko, R. (1994). *Mail-order brides: Women for sale.* Fort Collins: Alaken, Inc.

Greenblat, C.S. (1983). A hit is a hit is a hit ... Or is it? Approval and tolerance of the use of physical force by spouses. In D. Finkelhor, R.J. Gelles, G.T. Hotaling & M.A. Straus (Eds.), *The dark side of families: Current family violence research* (pp. 235–260). Beverly Hills: Sage Publications.

Gunaratne, S. (2002). State and community responses to domestic violence in Sri Lanka. Colombo: Center for Women's Research.

Guruge, S. (2007). *The influence of gender, racial, social, and economic inequalities on the production of and responses to intimate partner violence in the post-migration context.* Doctoral dissertation, University of Toronto, Toronto.

Haj-Yahia, M. (2000). Wife abuse and battering in the sociocultural context of Arab society. *Family Process, 39*(2), 237–255.

Haj-Yahia, M.M. (1991). Perceptions of wife beating and the use of different conflict tactics among Arab-Palestinian engaged males in Israel. Unpublished doctoral dissertation, University of Minnesota, Minneapolis.

Haj-Yahia, M.M. (1997). *Explaining beliefs about wife beating among Arab men from Israel through their patriarchal ideology.* Unpublished manuscript.

Haj-Yahia, M.M. (1998). Beliefs about wife beating among Palestinian women: The influence of their patriarchal ideology. *Violence against Women, 4*(5), 533–558.

Hassouneh-Phillips, D. (2001). American Muslim women's experiences of leaving abusive relationships. *Health Care for Women International, 22*(4), 415–432.

Hornosty, J. & Doherty, D. (2002). *Responding to wife abuse in farm and rural communities: Searching for solutions that work.* Saskatchewan Institute of Public Policy Paper no. 10. Regina: Saskatchewan Institute of Public Policy.

Hussein, A. (1999). *Sometimes there is no blood: Domestic violence and rape in rural Sri Lanka.* Colombo: International Center for Ethnic Studies.

Hyman, I., Guruge, S., Mason, R., Stuckless, N., Gould, J., Tang, T., et al. (2004). Post-migration changes in gender relations among Ethiopian immigrant couples in Toronto. *Canadian Journal of Nursing Research, 36*(4), 74–89.

Hyman, I., Mason, R., Berman, H., Guruge, S., Manuel, L., Kanagaratnam, P., et al. (2006). Perceptions of and responses to intimate partner violence among Tamil women in Toronto. *Canadian Woman Studies, 25*(1 & 2), 145–150.

LeCompte, M.D. & Schensul, J.J. (1999). *Analyzing and interpreting ethnographic data.* Walnut Creek: Altamira Press.

Lincoln, Y.S. & Guba, E. (1985). *Naturalistic inquiry.* Newbury Park: Sage Publications.

Lofland, J. & Lofland, L.H. (1995). *Analyzing social settings: A guide to qualitative observation and analysis* (3rd ed.). Belmont: Wadsworth.

Loring, M.T. & Smith, R.W. (1994). Health care barriers and interventions for battered women. *Public Health Reports, 109*(3), 328–338.

MacLeod, L., Shin, M.Y., Hum, Q., Samra-Jawanda, J. W., Minna, M. & Wasilewska, E. (1993). *Like a wingless bird: A tribute to the survival and courage of women who are abused and who speak neither English not French.* Ottawa: National Clearinghouse of Family Violence.

Mazza, D., Dennerstein, L. & Ryan, Y. (1996). Physical, sexual, and emotional violence against women. *Medical Journal of Australia, 164,* 14–17.

McCauley, J., Yurk, R.A., Jenckes, M.W. & Ford, D.E. (1998). Inside "Pandora's box": Abused women's experiences with clinicians and health services. *Journal of General and Internal Medicine, 13*(8), 549–555.

McDonald, S. (1999). Not in the numbers—domestic violence and immigrant women. *Canadian Woman Studies, 19*(3), 163–167.

McDonald, S. (2000). *The right to know: Women, ethnicity, violence, and learning about the law.* Unpublished doctoral dissertation, University of Toronto, Toronto.

McSpadden, L.A. & Moussa, H. (1993). I have a name: The gender dynamics in asylum and in resettlement of Ethiopian and Eritrean refugees in North America. *Journal of Refugee Studies, 6*(3), 203–225.

Mehrotra, M. (1999). The social construction of wife abuse: Experiences of Asian Indian women in the United States. *Violence Against Women, 5,* 619-640.

Moracco, K.E., Hilton, A., Hodges, K.G. & Fraser, P.Y. (2005). Knowledge and attitudes about intimate partner violence among immigrant Latinos in rural North Carolina. *Violence against Women, 11*(30), 337–352.

Morrison, L., Guruge, S. & Snarr, K.A. (1999). Sri Lankan Tamil immigrants in Toronto: Gender, marriage patterns, and sexuality. In G.A. Kelson & D.L. DeLaet (Eds.), *Gender and immigration* (pp. 144–161). New York: New York University Press.

Morse, J.M. & Field, P.A. (1995). *Qualitative research methods for health professionals* (2nd ed.). London: Sage Publications.

Mugford, J., Mugford, S. & Easteal, P. (1989). Social justice, public perceptions, and spouse assault in Australia. *Social Justice, 16,* 102–123.

Raj, A. & Silverman, J. (2002). Violence against immigrant women. *Violence against Women, 8*(3), 367–398.

Rianon, N.J. & Shelton, A.J. (2003). Perception of spousal abuse expressed by married Bangladeshi immigrant women in Houston, Texas, U.S.A. *Journal of Immigrant Health, 5*(1), 37–47.

Richie, B. (2000). A Black feminist reflection on the antiviolence movement. *Signs, 25*(4), 1133–1137.

Rodriguez, M.A., Bauer, H.M., McLoughlin, E. & Grumbach, K. (1999). Screening and intervention for IPV. *Journal of the American Medical Association, 282,* 468–474.

Rodriguez, M.A., Craig, A.M., Mooney, D.R. & Bauer, H.M. (1998). Patient attitudes about mandatory reporting of domestic violence. Implications for the health care professionals. *Western Journal of Medicine, 169*, 337–341.

Saltzman, L.E., Fanslow, J.L., McMahon, P.M. & Shelley, G.A. (1999). *Intimate partner violence surveillance: Uniform definitions and recommended data elements, Version 1.0*. Atlanta: National Center for Injury Prevention and Control, Centers for Disease Control and Prevention.

Samarasinghe, S. (1991). *Report on some observations of the incidence of domestic violence in 4 locations in Sri Lanka and the attitudes of the women towards the violence*. Colombo: Women in Need.

Sandelowski, M. (2000). Focus on research methods: Whatever happened to qualitative description? *Research in Nursing & Health, 23*, 334–340.

Senturia, K., Sullivan, M., Ciske, S., & Shiu-Thornton, S. (2000). *Cultural issues affecting domestic violence service utilization in ethnic and hard to reach populations: Executive summary* (No. 98-WTVX-0025). Seattle, WA: Public Health, Seattle & King County.

Shibusawa, T. & Yick, A. G. (2007). Experience and perceptions of domestic violence among older Chinese immigrants. *Journal of Elder Abuse & Neglect, 19*, 1-17.

Smith, M.D. (1990). Patriarchal ideology and wife beating: A test of a feminist hypothesis. *Violence and Victims, 2*, 39–57.

Tang, C. S. Wong, D., Cheung, F.M.C., & Lee, A. (2000). Exploring how Chinese define violence against women: A focus group study in Hong Kong. *Women's Studies International Forum, 23*(2): 197-209.

Torres, S. (1991). A comparison of wife abuse between two cultures: Perceptions, attitudes, nature, and extent. *Issues in Mental Health Nursing, 12*, 113–131.

United Nations. (1999). *Convention on the elimination of all forms of discrimination against women (CEDAW)*. Consideration of reports submitted by states parties under article 18 of the Convention on the elimination of all forms of discrimination against women: Third and fourth reports of states parties. Manhattan, New York City: United Nations.

United Nations. (2001). *Working group on disappearances*. Retrieved January 10, 2006, from http://www.ahrchk.net/hrsolid/mainfile.php/2000vol10n005/483/

Varcoe, C. & Irwin, L. (2004). "If I killed you, I'd get the kids": Women's survival and protection work with child custody and access in the context of woman abuse. *Qualitative Sociology, 27*(1), 77–99.

Websdale, N. (1998). *Rural women battering and the justice system: An ethnography*. Thousand Oaks: Sage Publications.

Websdale, N. (1999). *Understanding domestic homicide*. Boston: Northeastern University Press.

WHO. (1997). *Elimination of violence against women: In search of solutions.* Executive summary of the WHO/FIGO pre-congress workshop. Retrieved June 11, 2006, from http://whqlibdoc.who.int/hq/1999/ WHO_HSC_PVI_99.2.pdf

WHO. (2000). *Prevalence of violence against women by an intimate male partner.* Retrieved June 11, 2006, from http://www.who.int/violence_injury_prevention/ vaw/prevalence.htm

WHO. (2006). *Multi-country study on women's health and domestic violence against women. Summary report: Initial results on prevalence, health outcomes, and women's responses.* Geneva, Switzerland: WHO.

Wijayatilake, K. (2003). Harsh realities: A pilot study on gender-based violence in the plantation sector, UNFPA. Battaramulla, Sri Lanka: Plantation Human Development Trust.

Wuest, J., Ford-Gilboe, M. & Merrit-Gray, M. (2005). Regenerating family: Strengthening the emotional health of mothers and children in the context of intimate partner violence. *Advances in Nursing Sciences, 27*(2), 257–274.

Yoshioka, M. R., DiNoia, J., & Ullah, K. (2001). Attitudes toward marital violence: an examination of four Asian communities. *Violence Against Women, 7*(8), 900–926.

About the Contributors

Andalee Adamali is a community practice consultant for Toronto Community Housing.

Cyndy Baskin, PhD, is a professor in the Faculty of Social Work at Ryerson University in Toronto. She has many years of experience working with Aboriginal peoples in Canada in areas such as community organizing, culture-based program development, and healing from trauma. Her research interests include food security and Indigenous peoples, youth and homelessness, bringing Aboriginal world views into education, and structural determinants of health, with particular emphasis on the impacts of colonization.

Ritu Chokshi is a community engagement consultant. With a Masters in Immigration and Settlement Studies, she focuses on creating equitable access for immigrant communities in Toronto and is committed to violence prevention. Her current projects include working with the South Asian Legal Clinic of Ontario (SALCO) in creating informative and accessible resources around the issue of forced marriages.

Sabra Desai is a professor at Humber College with the school of social and community services. She is also one of the founders of the South Asian Women's Centre as well as Interim Place, the first shelter for women and children survivors of family violence in Peel.

Josephine Fong, PhD, is a Faculty Advisor/Adjunct Professor in the Faculty of Arts, Tyndale University College. In addition to teaching, she is also a mental health professional, a freelance research consultant, trainer and community activist. She has ample experience working with assaulted women, hospitals and health care organizations, ethnic minority communities, and local social service organizations. Her research interests focus on preventing male violence against women, promoting women's agency and strengthening people's mental health and coping strategies.

Judy Gould, PhD, is a research scientist at the Women's College Research Institute and an assistant professor in the Department of Public Health Sciences at the University of Toronto, Toronto.

Sepali Guruge, RN, PhD, is an associate professor in the School of Nursing at Ryerson University, Toronto.

Ilene Hyman, BSc, PhD, is a research scientist, Violence and Health Program, Centre for Research in Women's Health, and an assistant professor, Department of Public Health Sciences, University of Toronto, Toronto.

Samantha Majic is an assistant professor, Department of Government, City University of New York/John Jay College. Her research interests are in the field of gender and politics in North America, where she has examined how policies in the areas of domestic violence, disability, and welfare reform have impacted women. Her dissertation research at Cornell University examined how sex workers developed and run health outreach organizations in the San Francisco Bay area.

Robin Mason, PhD, is research scientist, Violence and Health Program, Centre for Research in Women's Health, and assistant professor, Department of Public Health Sciences, University of Toronto, Toronto.

Girma Mekonnen, MD, is research assistant, Centre for Research in Women's Health, Toronto.

Ngozi L. Nwosu, MA, is a researcher and advocate for the eradication of violence against women. She is currently working as an outreach and sexual assault counsellor at the Women's Resources of Simcoe County, Midland. Her research focus is on violence against Nigerian-Canadian women and their families, particularly its cultural, health and social impact, and social reforms.

Lisa F. Rosenberg, PhD, is adjunct professor, School of Women's Studies, York University, Toronto. She is a founder of United against Violence against Women, a non-profit organization based in Toronto that advocates on issues of woman abuse locally, nationally and internationally.

Angie Rupra, RSW, MSW, has worked in the violence against women sector for over six years. Her experience includes working in shelters for abused women and children, community-based agencies, government, and coordinating agencies. She is currently employed with Springtide Resources: Ending Violence against Women, as the community outreach and education coordinator. She also teaches at Humber College's Social Service Worker Program and is actively involved in addressing issues of pet loss and eating disorders.

Noreen Stuckless, PhD, is undergraduate director, Department of Psychology, York University, Toronto.

Taryn Tang, PhD, is research associate, Women's Mental Health and Addiction Research Section, Centre for Addiction and Mental Health, Toronto. Her research focuses on immigrant experiences and mental health through a gender-based analysis.

Hiwot Teffera, MA, is research assistant, Centre for Research in Women's Health, Toronto.